Advance praise for
The Hebrew Priestess

"This is an extraordinary and amazing work. On a foundation of intensive and broad scholarly research into the history of the female divinity once worshiped by Jews and the roles of Jewish women as spiritual leaders throughout the centuries, The Hebrew Priestess builds a vision for the present and the future. The authors do not only write about women's potential sacred power as prophetesses, artists, guardians, midwives, shamanic healers, seekers, mourners, and more. They have put their ideas into practice in the Kohenet Institute, founded in 2006, which trains women to become priestesses, using a wide variety of Jewish traditions. The personal experiences of the authors and their students and Kohenet graduates will speak to spiritual seekers of all sorts, and readers of this book will never see Judaism—past, present, future—the same way again."

— **Alicia Ostriker**, author of *The Nakedness of the Fathers: Biblical Visions and Revisions*, and of *For the Love of God: the Bible as an Open Book*

"The Hebrew Priestess recovers and discovers, transforms and transcends, the biblical Judaism of earth and body, weaving ancient threads of women's Body-Spirit with our own generation's threads of sacred feminism into a richly colored fabric for our day and for the future. A future for us all, those of all genders and mixtures."

—**Rabbi Arthur Waskow**, director, The Shalom Center; author of *Godwrestling — Round 2*; *Down-to-Earth Judaism: Food, Money, Sex, & the Rest of Life*; and (with Rabbi Phyllis Berman) *A Time for Every Purpose Under Heaven*

"Jill Hammer and Taya Shere have done something remarkable: They have gathered up all the strands and abandoned shreds relating to Jewish priestesses from biblical, talmudic, historical, and folk testimony, and woven them together. They reveal treasures to us: of wise-women and prophetesses, of shrines, festival dances and songs. This is a book to savor. For some it will be a beacon on their spiritual journey, while for others it will be an invaluable sourcebook to study, re-read, and to absorb its far-reaching implications."

—**Max Dashu**, creator of the *Woman Shaman: The Ancients* DVD series and of the on-line Suppressed Histories Archives

Advance praise for
The Hebrew Priestess

"When I felt myself called into Spiritual Leadership, I didn't know what to call myself. I decided to become a rabbi and then put my effort into redefining what it meant to be a rabbi. And now Jill Hammer and Taya Shere have given words to my calling. In The Hebrew Priestess I find the articulation of my dreams and longings. This is a book that allows me to reclaim a precious legacy, so that I might walk the once-hidden paths of the Hebrew Priestess with joy and honor."

—**Rabbi Shefa Gold**, author of *Torah Journeys*, *In the Fever of Love*, and *The Magic of Hebrew Chant*

"Don't be fooled by this book. It masquerades as a spiritual memoir, but it is pure liberating subversion. The Hebrew Priestess not only celebrates the spirituality of Jewish women, but reclaims the lost Divine Feminine without whom God the Father is a frightened and frightening bully. By all means read this book, but don't stop there—live it as well!"

—**Rabbi Rami Shapiro**, author of *Amazing Chesed: Living a Grace-filled Judaism*

"The Hebrew Priestess is a valuable contribution to the understanding of the historical role of women and female power in Judaism and its antecedents. Rabbi Hammer does a fine job of tracing the ancient Canaanite and Hebrew Goddesses and the contributions of women as judges, prophets, healers, shamans, and carriers of tradition. A very readable and much-needed book!"

—**Starhawk**, author of *The Spiral Dance: A Rebirth of the Ancient Religion of the Goddess*

The Hebrew Priestess

Ancient and New Visions of Jewish Women's Spiritual Leadership

Jill Hammer
and Taya Shere

Ben Yehuda Press
Teaneck, New Jersey

THE HEBREW PRIESTESS ©2015 Jill Hammer. All rights reserved. No part of this book may be used or reproduced in any manner whatsoever without written permission except in the case of brief quotations embodied in critical articles and reviews.

Published by Ben Yehuda Press
122 Ayers Court #1B
Teaneck, NJ 07666

http://www.BenYehudaPress.com

Ben Yehuda Press books may be purchased for educational, business or sales promotional use. For information, please contact:
Special Markets, Ben Yehuda Press,
122 Ayers Court #1B, Teaneck, NJ 07666
markets@BenYehudaPress.com

ISBN13 978-1-934730-46-1

Library of Congress Cataloging-in-Publication Data

Hammer, Jill, author.
 The Hebrew priestess : ancient and new visions of Jewish women's spiritual leadership / Jill Hammer and Taya Shere.
     pages cm
 Includes bibliographical references and index.
 ISBN 978-1-934730-46-1 (alk. paper)
 1. Women in Judaism. 2. Women in the Bible. 3. Women in Rabbinical literature. 4. Women--Religious aspects--Judaism. 5. Feminism--Religious aspects--Judaism. 6. Spiritual life--Judaism. 7. Jewish women--Religious life--United States. I. Shere, Taya, author. II. Title.
 BM729.W6H36 2015
 296.082--dc23
                                        2015016146

15 16 / 10 9 8 7 6 5 4 3 2   20150730

Note: Taya Shere is the author of all practice sections of *The Hebrew Priestess* (the final sections of each chapter) and the Personal Priestess Paths section in the Introduction. Other parts of the book, unless otherwise noted, were written by Jill Hammer. Jill Hammer and Taya Shere are the co-founders of the Kohenet Hebrew Priestess Institute and facilitate that community together.

God, Goddess, and God/dess are all used in this book to refer to the Source of Life, depending on the context. God is used to refer to traditional biblical/Jewish/masculine God forms, Goddess to feminine images of deity, and God/dess when both at once are meant.

Contents

Dedication	xi
Introduction	**1**
Chapter 1: A Brief History of The Hebrew Priestess	**17**
The Biblical Period	18
Holy Women	20
The Second Temple and the Post-Temple Period	21
The Egyptian Jewish Community	23
The Medieval Period and the Mystics	25
Contemporary Priestesses	28
Chapter 2: A Brief History of The Hebrew Goddess	**31**
The Biblical Period	32
The Goddess and the Temple	37
Sages and Mystics	39
The Contemporary Hebrew Goddess	41
The Priestess Paths	44
Chapter 3: Weaver-Priestesses	**47**
Biblical Women Weavers	47
The Second Temple and Post-Temple Period	49
The Middle Ages and the Modern Era	52
Weaver-Priestess Incarnations	53
Beginning a Spirit Journey Practice	55
Spirit Journey: The Weaver	57
She Who Weaves Worlds With Words:	
The Practice of Creating Personal Prayer	58
Resources for Creating Meaningful Personal Prayer	60
Chapter 4: Prophetess-Priestesses	**61**
The Biblical Period	61
Prophetesses in the Roman Period and the Talmud	65
The Mystic Prophetesses	68
Locating the Female Prophetic Voice in Modern Times	70
Prophetess-Priestess Incarnations	70
Spirit Journey The Prophetess	72
She Who Receives Visions *The Practice of* Dreamwork	73
Resources	75
Chapter 5: Shrinekeeper-Priestesses	**77**
The Biblical Period: Mirror-Priestesses	78
The Biblical Period: Shrine-Priestesses	80
The Talmud and How the Table Became an Altar	82

The Middle Ages and Beyond	82
Shrinekeeper-Priestess Incarnations	84
Spirit Journey The Shrinekeeper	86
She Who Creates Sacred Space *The Practice of* Altar-Craft	87
Resources	90
Chapter 6: Witch-Priestesses	**91**
The Witch in the Bible	92
Witches in the Book of Enoch	95
Witches in the Talmud	95
Witches in Mystical Text	97
The Middle Ages	98
Witch-Priestess Incarnations	100
Spirit Journey The Witch	102
She Who Receives Signs *The Practice of* Divination	102
Resources	104
Chapter 7: Maiden-Priestesses	**105**
The Biblical Period	105
The Rabbinic Period	107
The Maiden According to Philosophers and Mystics	108
The Maiden Priestess in Jewish Ritual	110
Maiden-Priestess Incarnations	111
Spirit Journey: The Maiden	114
She Who Becomes New: *The Practice of* Blood Wisdom	115
Resources	117
Chapter 8: Mother-Priestesses	**119**
The Biblical Period: Mother in Israel	120
The Mother as Nazirite	122
The Middle Ages: The Mother as Kindler of Souls	124
Into the Modern Era	126
Mother-Priestess Incarnations	127
Spirit Journey: The Mother	129
She Who Heals by Her Presence: *The Practice of* Motherline Healing	130
Resources	131
Chapter 9: Queen-Priestesses	**133**
Biblical Queen Mothers	133
The Maccabean Period	137
The Book of Judith: Queen as Defender	138
The Mystics and the Sabbath Queen	140

Spirit Journey: The Queen	143
She Who Embraces Her Power:	
The Practice of Shadow Integration	144
Resources	146
Chapter 10: Midwife-Priestesses	**147**
The Biblical Period: Midwife as Savior	147
The Rabbinic Period: Midwife as Wise Woman	150
Midwives as Healers and Ritualists	151
Midwife-Priestess Incarnations	153
Spirit Journey: The Midwife	155
She Who Supports Transformation:	
The Practice of Being With What Wants To Be Born	156
Resources	157
Chapter 11: Wise-Woman-Priestesses	**159**
The Biblical Period: At the Crossroads	159
The Talmudic Era: Keepers of Knowledge	163
The Middle Ages and the Modern Era	166
Wise-Woman-Priestess Incarnations	167
Spirit Journey: The Wise Woman	169
She Who Knows and Guides: *The Practice of* Initiation	170
Resources	172
Chapter 12: Mourning-Woman-Priestesses	**173**
The Biblical Period: Ritual Grief	174
The Mythic Mourning Woman in the Post-Temple Period	176
The Talmud, the Middle Ages, and the Modern Era	178
Mourning-Woman-Priestess Incarnations	180
Spirit Journey: The Mourning Woman	181
She Who Remembers and Releases:	
The Practice of Mourning as Transformation	182
Resources:	185
Chapter 13: Seeker-Priestesses	**187**
Inner Pilgrims: Jewish Women Monastics	
in Alexandria and Ethiopia	188
Women Pilgrims in the Biblical Period	190
Women Pilgrims in the Middle Ages and Beyond	193
Seeker-Priestess Incarnations	195
Spirit Journey: The Seeker	198
She Who Seeks: *The Practice of* Pilgrimage	199
Resources	202

Chapter 14: Lover-Priestesses — **203**
    The Biblical Period: On the Threshing Floor — 204
    The Song of Songs — 206
    Cherubim: The Second Temple Period and the Talmud — 208
    Sacred Marriage: The Mystics — 209
    Spirit Journey: The Lover — 215
    She Who Loves: *The Practice of* Erotic/Sexual Healing — 216
    Resources for Further Study — 217

Chapter 15: Fool-Priestesses — **219**
    The Biblical Period: Tricksters — 219
    The Talmudic Period: Breaking the Jars — 220
    The Middle Ages and Beyond: Jesters — 223
    Fool-Priestess Incarnations — 226
    Spirit Journey: The Fool — 228
    She Who Shatters: *The Practice of* Embracing Change — 229
    Resources — 231

Chapter 16: The Future of the Hebrew Priestess — **233**
    The Weaver-Priestess: Reverence for the Web of Life — 233
    The Prophetess-Priestess: Modes of Revelation — 235
    The Shrinekeeper-Priestess: Temple Consciousness — 236
    The Witch-Priestess: Taking Spirit Seriously — 238
    The Maiden-Priestess: Creating Safe Space — 239
    The Mother-Priestess: Speaking about Goddess — 241
    The Queen-Priestess: Sharing Power — 242
    The Midwife-Priestess: Holy Transformation — 243
    The Wise-Woman-Priestess: Creating Lineages — 244
    The Mourning-Woman-Priestess: Rethinking Death — 245
    The Seeker-Priestess: Becoming Spiritual Pilgrims — 246
    The Lover-Priestess: Intimate Priestessing — 247
    The Fool-Priestess: Not Knowing — 248

Chapter 17: Epilogue — **251**
Appendix: MotherLine Ritual Materials — 253
Appendix: Kohenet Biographical Statements — 259
Endnotes — 267
References — 285
Index — 297
Acknowledgments — 313
About the Authors — 317

Dedication

For Raya Leela, beloved little priestess:

Your small hands… in these hands
I could trust the world, or in many hands like these…
        Adrienne Rich, "Twenty-One Love Poems" (1977)

Introduction

Let me begin with a dream.

> *There is a vast temple divided in two: One half is occupied by priests, and the other by priestesses. There are high stone walls. The temple is under siege.*
>
> *The high priestess awakens at night, gathers her handmaidens, and goes to the priests' dwelling. She contacts the high priest. She is looking for a lost sacred object.*
>
> *The high priestess and other men and women enter the underground tunnels beneath the temple. The group arrives at an inner chamber. They wait. They are expecting a communication.*

This is my dream, and in a way, it is my story. I too am looking for something sacred that is lost: the lives of the Hebrew priestesses. The Bible hints at these lives, as do later texts and folk traditions. I am looking for an inner chamber: the shrine of the divine woman who persists through Israelite history, whose presence still erupts in rabbinic and kabbalistic lore. I am also looking for something sacred in my own day: a community to live this lost truth in new ways. I am waiting for a communication: a flash of insight or an artifact from the past, a tiny door that shows me a hidden world.

The story of the Jewish people, and all the peoples that story has come to affect, cannot be fully understood without a consciousness of the lives of priestesses and the Divine Presence they represented. The story of the biblical priestesses unfolds in Miriam with her frame drum, in Devorah under her palm tree, in Ruth on the threshing floor, in the dancing maidens of Shiloh and the queen mothers of Israel. The story of the Divine Mother emerges in Lady Wisdom of the Book of Proverbs, in the hidden spaces of the Temple, and in Eve, mother of all life.

We are not taught to know the priestesses of the Bible. Yet we can know them, if we are willing to go to subterranean places of myth, text and tradition and find them. As in the dream, this is not only a story for women. It is a story for priestesses and priests, shamans and mystics—anyone who wants to enter the underground tunnel.

A priestess, like a priest, is a facilitator of the connection between worlds. She tends the relationship between human and divine. She may do this through ritual, through the maintenance of a sanctuary, through trance and prophecy, through creation of sacred words and objects, or through music and dance. She is a medial person in the Jungian sense—through the mystery she offers, she allows others to open to the realms of spirit and the depths of human experience.

This book tells the story of the Hebrew priestesses of biblical times, the women of later generations who followed in their footsteps, and the contemporary women who have chosen to live out that story in their own lives. This book also contains a history of the Goddess as She appears in the Bible and later Jewish tradition, because the priestess and the Goddess cannot be separated—they are mirrors of one another, human and divine feminine. Finally, the book contains thirteen examples of how we can connect to the Hebrew priestess legacy in the present, with contemporary spirit journeys and practices for the modern seeker.

I am a rabbi ordained by a seminary that values both tradition and contemporary scholarship. I live, and teach, Jewish texts, beliefs, and practices. I have the conviction, born of years of Torah study, that if a truth is not lived in the present, it dies. So too, I have the conviction that the study of ancient priestesses is not sufficient to make them real to us. If we believe in them, it is not enough to research them. We must become them.

And that is why, before I tell the story of the Hebrew priestesses, I need to tell a little of my story. I want to share a series of bends in the underground tunnel: moments of revelation and transition that have led me to the work I do and the community I helped create. These moments have a logical flow to them, but they remain mysterious to me. I came here because I chose a certain path, but I could not have arrived here on my own.

Mother Moon

In my room in Fishkill, New York, surrounded by the hills and woods of the Hudson Valley, I kept a children's Bible next to my bed. I loved the stories in it. I had a sense of what "holy story" meant: a story that was more than real, that had characters and events in it but also something larger than people or places. These stories were journeys. I loved the Torah because it took me to Rebecca's well, Esther's palace, Jacob's ladder, and because it invited me to become part of something larger than myself. When our temple gave all the students copies of the Pentateuch, I read mine so frequently that the rabbi commented on its crumpled pages.

On the bookshelves all around me were books of myth: Norse, Hawaiian, Korean, Greek, German, Russian, African. My mother knew I loved myths and fairy tales and provided me with many. These stories too resonated with me. I did not think of them as conflicting with the Torah, but rather as other universes, other possible journeys.

I read constantly, but I read in nature. My parents grew vegetables, flowers, chestnut trees and pear trees, and loved the ocean, the sun, and the earth. Outside my window in the winter nights was the full moon, which I called Mother Moon, my caretaker while I slept. Orion, the hunter, was my friend and guardian. The pine trees outside were nests, castles, secret passages. The woods were a world. God was a cloud overhead: mysterious yet deeply involved in the landscape. To me, everything was alive. What I loved best were paths that turned in the trees or the tall grass, paths that were hidden, where one could not see the end. I was driven not by religious doctrine—I knew almost none—but by a sense of the numinous. Looking back, I would now say that I had a shamanic childhood, the childhood of a priestess.

I wanted to be a rabbi. I read about prayer, holidays, and mysticism. My bat mitzvah sermon was a discourse on free will and the Garden of Eden. I learned Hebrew, protested on behalf of Soviet Jews, cried about the Holocaust, discovered kabbalah through Adin Steinsaltz's book *The Thirteen-Petaled Rose*. I also read voraciously about nuns. I was fascinated by the possibility of women living together in a sacred way. I knew Jewish women couldn't be nuns, but something about convents spoke to me: They offered clues to who I was called to be.

I didn't yet know the word "countertext." I didn't yet know that sacred myths conflict, that the Bible could be in tension with other sacred truths. What I did know was that once, when I was fourteen or so, I saw a deck of tarot cards for the first time, and encountered the image known as the High Priestess. A woman sat within a temple, wearing a veil and a crescent crown like the moon, with a sacred scroll on her lap. Mother Moon come to life, with the Torah cradled in her arms. I had a shock of recognition, as if I knew who she was, as if she offered me an example I could live by. A year later, I discarded the tarot cards because I had been told divination was forbidden to Jews. I wanted to obey God's commandments, but I couldn't forget the image I had seen.

The conflict I was feeling is one that is best expressed by the title of Leonard Shlain's book: *The Alphabet vs. The Goddess*[1]. The cultural conflict between text and image is deeply underlined in Jewish culture because of the Jewish prohibition against images of the divine. The words of my culture, as I received it as a child, did not contain language for the sacred that included female sacred servants or deities (at least not that I knew of then), nor did it contain language that fit with my experience of God-in-nature (at least not that I knew of then). I knew of rabbis, a few of whom were female. I knew of sages, prophets, and priests, and they all had beards and prayed to a transcendent and hidden God. Priestesses I knew only from a few fantasy novels. Yet the second I saw an image of the priestess archetype, I recognized it, and knew it was part of my life as a Jewish girl. Truths can be plowed under, but they cannot be completely repressed.

Lady, By All Your Names

I discovered Talmud and feminist poetry at the same time. I attended Brandeis University, which had a legendary Judaic Studies department, specifically so that I could deepen my Jewish knowledge. Once out of my parents' non-observant home, I immediately set about observing Shabbat, learning to lead services, wearing tefillin, and leading the local Conservative egalitarian student minyan. I walked into the Jewish section of the campus library, pulled a volume of Talmud off the shelf, and never looked back. I loved the intricacy of Jewish story and law—the many-layered delving into each word, ideal, and thought. I appreciated the poetry of Jewish prayer. I began to develop my knowledge of ritual, which I saw as a doorway into the divine realm. I attended the Jewish women's group, learned how to lead creative new moon ceremonies, studied women's traditions, wrote my own liturgy. I wanted to devote myself to God.

I began reading Jewish women poets: Rachel Adler, Malka Heifetz Tussman, and Marge Piercy. To me, what these women were writing could not be defined solely as poetry. It was liturgy. God was mother, lover, bride, queen, even rebel lesbian, all kinds of images I hadn't imagined but found thrilling and a little disturbing, since inside me, God was mostly a cross between a cloud and a dad. I learned the word Shekhinah—divine presence, bride of God—and then heard a respected professor rail against Jewish feminists' use of the word. Many Jews seemed to believe that seeing God as female was a half-step away from idol worship. Why all the anger? I began to wonder. What is there to be afraid of in a female image of God?

In exploring these images, mother as well as father, queen as well as king, I wasn't just discovering women. I was discovering the body: my body, in its particularity. I was discovering the human spirit trying to understand and free itself. I was rejecting the notion that a fundamental human/divine archetype can be forbidden because it doesn't fit the orthodoxy of tradition.

One poem, by theologian Rachel Adler, has stayed with me all my life since then:

> lady, by all your names,
> the lost, the forgotten, the not yet born, I swear
> I'll never again
> pray against my own flesh…
>
> I am your daughter, Lady,
> and pregnant with you.

Holy wind whistle through me,
been a long time
since you had a pipe for this music.[2]

"The lost, the forgotten, the not yet born..." Something had been lost, something had survived in spite of being lost. I could sense it as I read relentlessly male-voiced Talmudic texts side by side with the feminist midrash of Judith Plaskow. There was a river under the biblical and Talmudic texts, a nameless underground presence that was already being born into the light. People were being called to birth it: midwives of a spiritual consciousness that included the bodies and experiences of women.

What compelled me about these poets was not only their sense of justice but their sense of calling. They weren't bound by what other people had told them about divinity. They were alive to the presence of God/dess speaking inside them. They were no longer listening to the voices that said God couldn't appear as a woman. Jews by education and commitment, they also felt called to unearth a new/old vision of God. Over the years, I came to understand that I heard the same calling, the same holy wind. I was becoming a pipe for music that had not yet been heard.

The Pregnant God

At that point in my life, I couldn't imagine becoming a rabbi. I applied and was accepted to graduate school in social psychology at the University of Connecticut. I quickly learned that I did not want to become a research psychologist. My classes did not resonate with me. My first marriage, though to a loving and intelligent man, was in trouble. The local synagogue did not speak to my spiritual needs, though I attended dutifully. I devoted myself to what I would now call priestess work. At the Wesleyan Jewish student union (I did not attend Wesleyan but spent much time there), I led creative feminist services, created rituals based on resurrected North African Jewish women's holidays, and enjoyed my role as theological rabble-rouser. I continued to lead a traditional yet egalitarian Jewish life: keeping kosher, observing the Sabbath, praying three times a day and laying tefillin.

Then I had a turning point: an encounter with a rabbi named Paula Reimers who came to speak at Wesleyan. She claimed it was forbidden to imagine God as a mother, because the mother-God would love and forgive us too much. We would have no morality, and we would all become pagans. I knew from my reading that goddesses around the world had severe as well as nurturing attributes. I knew it was wrong to claim that a female God couldn't make laws. I knew it was wrong to say God couldn't appear as a woman. And I knew her dismissive words about religious traditions that revered goddesses were simplistic and bigoted. I was especially angry about the way Paula Reimers waxed eloquent about her personal experience of having God as a male lover. Why couldn't I have God/dess as a female lover? After passionately debating the speaker during the question-and-answer session, I stormed off. I had had it with people who thought they could tell me what God looked like.

That winter, I went to a "Take Back the Night" march—a nighttime protest against rape. The march ended with a chant: "We all come from the Goddess, and to her we shall return, like a drop of rain, flowing to the ocean."[3] I stood transfixed, astonished by the power of women singing this song together. I began to understand what Goddess could mean for me: the divine-in-nature of my childhood, the Shekhinah of the kabbalists and the feminists, the High Priestess whose image I could not forget.

In the spring, I had a dream. In the dream, I was at a cocktail party. Everyone was abuzz because God was going to attend this cocktail party. When God arrived, She was an immense pregnant woman glowing with light, attended by angels. She sat down next to me. I shared some of my theological ideas. She thought they were very funny (and clearly not up to cosmic par). Then she summoned an angel and gave me a gift. It was an old-fashioned wrought iron lantern, unlit. There was something I was supposed to do with this lantern, but when I woke up, I could not remember what it was.

The day after the dream, I called the Jewish Theological Seminary, and asked for an application to rabbinical school. I couldn't put off my calling anymore. I was accepted, and deferred my acceptance to finish my doctorate. Then my husband and I moved, and I became a commuter to Manhattan.

The night before my first Talmud class, I had another dream. I dreamed I passed by the seminary gates and kept walking, and went to witch school. In the morning, I woke up, marveled at the weirdness of the dream, and went to Talmud class. But the dream was telling me something I wasn't yet ready to hear. The kind of spiritual leader I was becoming had a past, and it wasn't in the rabbinic academy.

Altars

I began rabbinical school with delight, yet soon found myself in the position of spirit warrior. I attended the Seminary in the days when women were still a relatively new presence. There were many issues: how to pray together when some still did not count women in a minyan; whether women could serve as witnesses under Jewish law; whether rewriting liturgy was permissible. I was deeply unsettled to see brilliant women and men spending huge amounts of time trying to prove legally and ethically that women were entitled to basic spiritual and communal rights. The onus seemed to be on women and their supporters to prove their point against the halakhic system, a system that had evolved almost entirely without women's participation. (The onus was similar for other marginalized groups.) Many teachers were sympathetic, but at other times, when students raised arguments about the way texts understood gender, we were regarded as overly modern, ungrounded in tradition, or worse, as pests who were putting our feelings ahead of our Torah study. Watching this drama unfold over and over again, I became more radical in my view of Judaism.

Meanwhile, I continued to read. There were brilliant contemporary midrashists—Yehuda Amichai, Alicia Ostriker, Rivkah Walton, Peter Pitzele—who wryly played with text and added their own voices. This, I saw at once, was a way of claiming the text. Characters like Leah, Vashti, Huldah, King David, and Solomon's daughters came alive for me. I began to write midrash, editing a journal of contemporary midrash for two years and publishing my first book of original midrash, *Sisters at Sinai: New Tales of Biblical Women*[4].

In my private prayers, my encounter with Shekhinah—the rabbinic and kabbalistic version of the Goddess—deepened. Shekhinah appears in a variety of classical Jewish texts as a weeping mother of Israel, as the Sabbath bride, as a personified girl version of the Torah. She frequently appears next to God, her husband, but she is also God, and she is also the people Israel. But where did She come from? How did a monotheistic Jewish culture evolve a semi-goddess figure of this kind?

Destiny, and rabbinical school requirements, brought me an answer. Accompanied by my husband, I went to study in Israel for a year. Mechon Schechter, the Conservative rabbinical school in Jerusalem, brought us on historical tours around the country. I would wander away the first chance I got. All I wanted to do was go into caves. My favorite place was Hezekiah's tunnel, which is an underground water channel made by the biblical king Hezekiah 2700 years ago, and feels like a primordial birth canal. I explored a cave in the Wadi Sorek with underground stalactite formations like breasts, and bathed a hot water spring in Tiberias that was like being in the womb of some immense being. My ancestors' land opened me up to the land-forms my ancestors saw and walked, and began to give me a new language for talking about the sacred in feminine terms. I began to find that the Goddess would not stay safely in contemporary feminist poetry. She was in the land and I saw Her everywhere. Inspired, I began to take spirit journeys: meditations that led me to new images for the divine and the world.

As I prayed with fervor in Jerusalem synagogues and studied with renowned scholars like Howard Schwartz and Avivah Zornberg, I began to discover ancient Hebrew inscriptions to goddesses, and appreciate the round female figurines found in ancient Israel. At the Israel Museum, I saw a four-cornered altar, not a grand one like in the Temple but a small village altar, and I began to see what my tradition had in common with other ancient Near Eastern traditions. I dived into goddess myths like the ancient Sumerian epic *The Descent of Inanna*, and found connections between the protective functions of goddesses and the qualities of the Shekhinah.

As I opened myself to ancient Israelite religion, I began to see that the Shekhinah hadn't come from nowhere. She was as native to my people as the stories in the Torah. And, I began to suspect, human women always had been a significant part of the spiritual picture too. The more I read and thought, the more I saw that priestesses weren't found only in "pagan" culture. There were Hebrew priestesses: women who acted as channels for the divine, women who prophesied and served at altars, women who wove or baked for Hebrew goddesses. Liberal Jewish seminaries hadn't invented women's religious leadership in 1972. Women had been priestesses, prophetesses, and poets long before the time of the Bible. Their existence had been erased for reasons that were not perfectly clear to me, but had something to do with the erasure of the female aspects of God.

Learning about these women made me more open to all the shamans, priests, diviners, and dreamers, those who were members of a national priestly cult and those who were village healers and oracles. I wondered what Jews had lost by abandoning a priestly, shamanic model for a model based in rabbinic law. I wondered what we had lost by separating the divine from the land. I began to identify with the indigenous Hebrews, and to see them, in all their diversity, in the biblical text. I began to understand that the mystics and dream interpreters of the kabbalah, and the miracle-workers and meditators of Chasidic tradition, had their roots in these early Hebrew spirit workers.

When I got back from Israel, I built a little altar in my room with sacred things: a shard of glass from the mystic city of Safed; a red string from Jerusalem; a stone from the tombs of the matriarchs and patriarchs; a shell that represented my receiving a divorce. That altar, even when I let it get dusty, was a statement of identity. I was beginning to identify not only with rabbis but with my other ancestors, the priestesses.

For me, this new identification was inseparable from realizing that I loved women. My husband and I separated while I was in Israel, after years of trying to overcome our difficulties. Within a few years of coming home, I was chasing after a beautiful, artistic, and brilliant percussionist and Jewish educator, whom I finally caught right after I was ordained. I had been questioning my sexual identity in rabbinical school, at a time when the Jewish Theological Seminary did not admit openly non-heterosexual students. Ordination was a huge relief because it allowed me to acknowledge a huge part of who I was. For me, recognizing myself as a woman who loved women meant honoring the erotic connection between me and Shekhinah, and honoring my desire to be in spiritual communion with other women.

I went to work for Ma'yan, a Jewish women's organization. The altar moved to my new apartment, and then to my new home with my soon-to-be wife, Shoshana Jedwab. I had been ordained as a rabbi—my lifelong dream. The irony was that I didn't feel exactly like a rabbi. Somewhere inside myself, I was waiting to be ordained as a priestess.

Cave Immersion

The years after rabbinical school were a sea of new, exciting experiences, calling me more and more deeply into a new spiritual life. I studied mystical texts, researched women's ceremonies from Jewish communities around the world, read feminist theology from Starhawk to Tikvah Frymer-Kensky. I learned spirit journeying with an Israeli trained as a shaman, and taught Jewish spirit journeying to a group of seekers on-line. I attended a festival where the prophetess Miriam was celebrated as a priestess, and went to conferences where I conversed with Goddess feminists. I began to lead Jewish seasonal rituals that combined Jewish stories and practices with a consciousness of Shekhinah and of the earth. This impromptu community was called Tel Shemesh, and we celebrated everything from the New Year of the Trees to the winter solstice and Chanukah. I wrote a book about the seasonal resonances and nature-based myths imbedded in the Jewish calendar. When Shoshana and I got married, there was a wedding canopy with a rabbi, and a wedding altar on the ground nearby. I began to see, slowly, that the synthesis I wanted was possible.

In 2004, with Jay Michaelson and Shoshana, I co-led a weekend retreat called the E-retreat: earth-based, embodied, ecstatic, energetic Judaism, the kind we wanted to practice. It was close to the Jewish new year. At the climax of the weekend, we traveled to a cave beneath a local stream to conduct a ritual for the month of Elul—a ritual of cleansing, transformation and letting go.

We waded through the streambed choosing stones, then wrote in water on them: things we wanted to cast away, give up, or release. We came to the cave's mouth: a hole in a dry part of the streambed. Jay went first. Shoshana went second, carefully lowering her djembe and then herself into the blackness of the opening. Then, one by one, the ritual participants disappeared into the darkness, each holding a stone. I was the last to enter.

The ladder was rickety and steep. I can see, as if it were a few minutes ago, the pattern of roots and earth behind the ladder's rungs. As I descended, I could hear the drumming rising up through the cave, an eerie sound, as if the ancestor spirits were greeting us with a drum circle. Shoshana was chanting simple words: *imma, abba, chesed, gevurah, teshuvah, selichah*. Divine mother-father, source of love and strength, grant us turning, grant us forgiveness. I stepped onto wet stone, in the candle-lit darkness of an underground chamber. Reflected light pooled in shallow waters. I remember thinking, feeling: this is the womb of the Goddess. All that happens here is holy.

We broke into pairs to speak about our mistakes, losses, and regrets. Then we went off into flickering corners of the cave to tell God/Goddess what we had just told one another. Without prompting, twenty individuals gave voice to the pain within. Cries echoed from the stone walls. It was the closest thing I have ever heard to Rebbe Nachman of Breslov's advice: "You must cry out to God from the very depths of your heart."

Then, knee-deep in the underground river, we gathered in a circle at the center of the cave. At Jay's prompting, I stepped into the center of the circle to preside over the ritual of casting away, blessing, and cleansing immersion in the river water. It was one of my first conscious moments of priestessing: escorting the larger forces of the universe into the realm of the human.

I asked each person who came into the center: "Are you ready to cast your stone?" Then I asked: "With what do you want to be blessed?" People asked for self-acceptance, for entry into the Jewish people, for healing, for love. We placed our hands on each person and murmured words of love and peace. The words overlapped so that they could not be heard in an ordinary way; they were like the cries of a flock of birds, like messages from the world beyond. Then each person immersed in the cold water.

All twenty of us went through this ritual. When it was finally my turn, another rabbi guided me through the ritual. I asked to know that I was not lost, not alone. The blessings that wafted toward me are still piercing, unforgettable. "We are with you." "You cannot ever be lost." One person blessed me simply with my own name. In my life, this blessing has come true: I am not lost. I have seen where the ancestors live. At least at times, I know my way through the underworld.

When the last person cast a stone and immersed, we sang a closing prayer for the new year, and emerged from the cave one by one. Shoshana sat near the narrow mouth of the cave, drumming everyone into the sunlight, crying: "It's a girl!" or "It's a boy!" A woman began to sing a chant: "Born of the Mother, we welcome you." When I climbed up the ladder and out, green was all around me, splashed with light.

After this experience, I knew what I wanted. I wanted to be part of a community that reclaimed the priestesses and priests—the dreamers, shamans, and bards of antiquity—as spiritual role models. I wanted to be with people who did not reject the Goddess but saw Her as a face of God.

The reality I wanted to live in turned out to be more abundant than I could have imagined. In the next years, I attended a celebration of the festival of Sukkot, led by Amichai Lau-Lavie and Storahtelling, a Jewish ritual theater company—a festival that re-enacted the ancient Temple water-drawing ceremony. I traveled to Germany to see the cave of a German birth goddess who had found her way into a Jewish baby naming ritual[5]. I learned of the work of Ohad Ezrahi and Dawn Cherie Ezrahi, who were discussing Hebrew priestessing with women in Israel. I found on-line communities of people devoted to the Hebrew Goddess. I discovered I was not alone.

I began to speak with the other Jewish women who called themselves priestesses, asking how one becomes a Jewish priestess. No one could answer me. "Just decide you are one," one woman said to me, but it didn't feel like enough. The Jewish women who had joined pagan or Goddess-focused or shamanic communities had places to study priestessing, but no Jewish institution could even imagine such a thing as a Jewish priestess. Without an institution or a tradition, how could the phrase "Jewish priestess" be anything but a fantasy?

Then Jay Michaelson introduced me to Taya Shere, who also felt the call of the priestesses. We confided to one another our dream of speaking aloud the word *kohenet*: the word for priestess in the ancient Hebrew language. We decided to make our dream real.

Altars, Revisited

In the summer of 2006, a circle of women gathered at the Elat Chayyim retreat center in Accord, New York, in a cottage we named Shekhinah House for the occasion. Taya Shere and I were convening the first-ever Kohenet Hebrew Priestess Institute. Women came from California, New York City, Washington D.C., Minnesota, from all around the country, to be part of our experiment. Some were formerly Orthodox. Some belonged to mainstream synagogues. Some were life-long feminists. Some considered themselves witches. Some of our participants told me that they cried when they heard of our program, because they had always wanted to be Jewish priestesses and never thought it was possible.

We asked everyone to bring a stone, as a reflection of the ancient Hebrew ritual of making pillars or cairns at holy sites. Each woman sang or spoke her name. Those in the circle reflected back her name three times. This is a practice borrowed from Goddess circles. Through this ritual, we invited each woman to understand herself as a priestess, a woman consciously embodying the Goddess. After she sang herself into the circle, each woman placed her stone on the altar. At the end, there was a crooked circle of stones at the center of the room: a cairn, a marker. Stones from the ocean, from Jerusalem, goddess-shaped stones, all pieces of Earth, reflected our diversity and our oneness.

Throughout the week, we studied ancient Israelite women's rituals and prophecies, and four priestess archetypes: the Prophetess, the Midwife, the Maiden, and the Fool. We prayed to Shekhinah. We learned peacemaking strategies, and also maskmaking and midrashic theater in which we wrote and performed the faces and voices of biblical women. We discussed God, created ritual, and spoke of the ways we wanted to heal the world.

The week had its stresses. Sometimes we all wanted to go home. One night I went out to a bonfire and drank a glass of bourbon—although I never drink—because everything felt so difficult, like moving through molasses. We were trying to find a language for something that had no words: a language of women encountering divinity, a language not based on things we must not say, but on things we saw, felt, and knew. We were reaching beyond an invisible wall we were not even taught was there.

On Shabbat, we appointed a group of welcomers to greet everyone who comes to prayer. They anointed us all with fragrant oil. We lit candles and sang songs to Shekhinah in the open air, on the porch of our cottage. I leaned over the railing and looked out at the dark shapes of the trees, the bright circle of the moon.

A participant later wrote: *As a Jewish woman, Kohenet has fulfilled the sacred birthright of knowing that I have a strong and meaningful place among Jewish women of ancient times, today, and the future.*

The Kohenet Institute now meets twice a year at the Isabella Freedman Jewish Retreat Center and in Northern California. The Institute teaches Hebrew priestesses their history and develops their ritual skills. This women's community has become a central part of my spiritual life. The sisters of the Kohenet community study Torah together, build shrines together, pray together, dance together, go on spirit journeys together, and create ritual together. We commit ourselves to an embodied, earth-based, and ecstatic practice, and to rediscovering Shekhinah in our lives in whatever way that makes sense to us. We try to remember, to re-invent, the ancient priestesses of our people.

The Temple Rebuilt

Let me end with a dream.

> *I am a priestess visiting a temple that looks like a white clapboard church. The temple suddenly catches on fire. The priest who is with me tries to grab up the holy things, but I tell him to drop them and run, or the fire will catch us. As we run across a field, we see the plume of smoke behind us.*

INTRODUCTION

With a group of priestesses, I am standing by a new temple. The high priestess shows us the center of the temple: a pit dug in the earth, with totem poles inside. Then she hands me a stained glass box. I recognize it as my daughter's box of treasures, a box she broke. The high priestess has pieced it together and rebuilt it. It looks a little different than I remember, but it is still beautiful. I am so glad to see the box that I begin to cry.

I look up and see the entrance to the inner shrine of the temple. Everyone is waiting to go inside.

For many of us, the old temple of Western religion is burning. We cannot keep its systems of thought intact. We are seeking a new temple, one that links our inherited traditions with our forgotten ancestors—symbolized in the dream by the totem poles. Within the new temple, we are piecing together treasures that were lost and broken—lives of the priestesses and stories of the sacred feminine. We will pass on these treasures to our children, not in exactly the same form as they existed in antiquity, but transformed by our experience. This is the secret of the stained glass box: We will take the shards of the old and make something new and beautiful for our children.

My priestess work, and my rabbinic work, has grown and changed over the seven years since the Kohenet Hebrew Priestess Institute was founded. I have gone on pilgrimages to Ireland, England, and Prague. I have continued to explore new faces of Shekhinah as she appears in mystical lore. I have re-approached the divine masculine and re-established a connection with a divine father/lover/friend. I've made many connections with female and male Hebrew shamans, priests, priestesses, and earth-based spiritual leaders.

I work with rabbinical and cantorial students at the Academy for Jewish Religion, teaching classes, leading meditation, creating rituals, and supervising spiritual direction. My title there is Director of Spiritual Education, but I like to think of myself as the priestess-in-residence. The Kohenet Institute ordained its first class of *kohanot*, Hebrew priestesses, in 2009 and graduates a new class every two years. A new branch of Kohenet, Kohenet West, now exists in Northern California. Many of the individuals whose words appear in this book are students and graduates of the Kohenet Institute. Taya and Shoshana also continue to teach at the Institute. Taya is a partner in visioning and creating the Institute with me and has written the contemporary spiritual exercises in this book. Shoshana and I now have a little girl, who uses the words God and Goddess interchangeably.

I wrote this book to help others encounter the Hebrew priestesses: past, present, and future. May those who read this volume venture into the underground tunnels. You too are here to find something that was lost. May you walk these once-hidden paths with joy.

—Jill Hammer

Personal Priestess Paths
—Taya Shere

Searching for God in graduate school, I immersed myself in an African-Brazilian spiritual tradition in which priestesses and initiates enter into trance-states and embody deity. I pilgrimaged to lush land in northeast Brazil, slept in a hammock under a mango tree, practiced yoga on the beach, and shared communal meals. I danced and drummed around a bonfire. I bled onto the earth. I gazed at the moon, feeling her pull on my body and spirit. I became present to primality, to the sacred power of the elements and the natural world, and to the transformative potential of tribe. In this wild, I found Goddess.

Returning to Philadelphia, I moved into a women's collective house that was a living laboratory of ecofeminist spirituality. We made ritual each new and full moon, dancing and chanting around altars, sometimes naked on our roof. Shelves were lined with amber jars of decocting herbal oils and the kitchen smelled of beeswax from crafting healing balms. We drew each other baths of lavender and lemongrass, rubbed warming salve on bellies, massaged temples and feet before sleep. We gathered with wider community in ceremony on solstices and equinoxes, and hosted spiritual-activist performances and skillshares. I experienced a 24/7 initiation into the art of priestessing. As my leadership capacities and opportunities expanded, I needed grounding in my own tradition, which I had so vehemently left behind. I sought to heal at the roots, to find a way to love Judaism.

The bridge between my reverence for Goddess, earth and Jewish spirituality was built in stages. My beloved challenged me to stop connecting with his (African) ancestors, and to begin connecting with my own. I railed in response, terrified at the truth in his words and what I might face in myself to get there. Witnessing destruction in clear-cut forests in the Pacific Northwest, I experienced my first visceral understanding of the Holocaust.

I studied the Jewish calendar's cycling with the moon and the seasons. I explored teachings on the elements of fire, water, and air in the most ancient kabbalistic text. Drawing on my menstrual sabbath practice, I found a window into Shabbat. My time in earth-based spiritual community gave me tools to access and translate the beauty and power in Jewish practices I had dismissed and misunderstood. I led my first Shabbat prayer service since my bat mitzvah, casting a circle with Hebrew chant, teaching a Torah of liminal spaces and blood wisdom.

Thirteen years later, my spirit-connection and passions remain rooted in body, earth and the sacred feminine. I bow to, am broken open and buoyed by the elements and nature. Initiation comes to me through fire, flood, tornado, and tree. I integrate in healing waters, dancing in the desert, cuddling with my cat, being silent, harvesting white sage. I engage erotically in the world. I choose conscious touch, sound, breath, and movement.

Primal priestessing is my path: Loving and leading into liminal space. Supporting experiences of sacred sensuality. Teaching body-awareness-based trauma-healing to transform tribal PTSD. Crafting contexts informed by indigenous initiatory wisdom for those becoming bar and bat mitzvah. Creating chant albums and experiences communing cosmic and immanent divine. For many, worship is about serving God. For me, worship is embodying Goddess.

At a recent Shabbat gathering for new members at the suburban shul I serve, a board member chastises me: "You forgot to put your title on your name tag." I respond sheepishly, "Really, you need me to put Rabbi in front of my name for the new members?" She replies, "No, I meant "Goddess-in-Chief!" I breathe deep, grateful, even inside of this somewhat normative Jewish context, to be seen and to have space to be myself. Grateful that I can serve as both a congregational rabbi and as co-founder of Kohenet. Grateful that for my goddess-daughters, singing to Shekhinah, dancing, drumming and circling around trees and bonfires is what they know of communal Jewish prayer. Grateful that my album covers can include images of words from Torah scribed along my spine.

I am awed to be alive here and now, in a world ripe for co-creating community and in which our individual and collective embodied, earth-honoring expressions of spiritual practice and leadership are sought, celebrated and cherished. I welcome you who have journeyed through space and time—thousands of turnings, tides and texts—to arrive at these words.

Welcome to a moment in which reclaiming and innovating the path of the priestess is possible. Which texts, stories, spirit-journeys or practice exercises in *The Hebrew Priestess* resonate most deeply with you? What priestess paths will move you to your core and call your attention to how you must live? What priestess possibilities terrify you or evoke emptiness inside? How do you feel about your lover-self, your shamaness, your mourning woman, your trickster-fool? How do you midwife, mother, or maiden? How do you seek and where will you pilgrimage? How do you weave and what is your loom? What is the priestessing—for self, family, community, or world—that is most vibrant and juicy for you? What guides, nurtures and inspires you? Why do you priestess, if you do? And how?

Know that you are not alone and that you are necessary. The world, Jewish and beyond, is gifted and transformed by your unique expression of spirit-connection and leadership. Your work and play and prayer are powerful. Your dancing and your loving are medicine. Your waking and sleeping dreams are sacred. Your laughter and your tears are holy. Your being is ancient and new and alchemical. We need your priestessing. We need you, priestessing. We need you, priestess.

Chapter 1: A Brief History of The Hebrew Priestess

> *Not only the priestly tribe but every single individual from among the world's inhabitants, whose spirit is moved and who has the understanding to stand before the Divine to serve and minister... behold, this person has been completely consecrated...*
> —Maimonides [1]

Four thousand years ago, in the ancient Near East, women were poets, drummers, scholars, dancers, healers, prophets, and keepers of sacred space. Even in societies where women had severe legal and cultural handicaps, they were an important part of ritual. From Enheduanna the poet-priestess of ancient Sumer to the oracle at Delphi, from the weavers of Athena in Greece to the prophetesses of Hathor in Egypt, from the vestal virgins of Rome to the drumming-priestesses of Crete, from the bee-priestesses who served Demeter to the warrior-priestesses of Scythia, women were facilitators of the connection between human and divine. This has been true all over the world in all times. There were (and in many cases, still are), Ifa (Yoruba) priestesses in Nigeria and the African diaspora, druidesses in Ireland and Germany, women shamans among the Lakota and the people of Siberia and Korea, Shinto priestesses in Japan, and women saint-poets in India.[2] Because the Bible tends to avoid and even repress the existence of priestesses, one might believe that no such archetypes or examples exist in the religions of the west. A closer examination of the text reveals that remnants of the priestesshood remain for those who seek them out.

In the cultures around ancient Israel, a priestess might have been called by any number of titles or honorifics. In Akkadian culture, we can find *entu* (high priestess), *naditu* (monastic woman), *qadishtu* (holy one), *harimtu* (forbidden one/sacred prostitute), *muhuttum* (prophetess), or *kulu'u* (singer, musician, and dramatic performer). The *tawananna* was a Hittite high priestess, sister of the king. An Egyptian priestess might be *wabet* (one who cares for the temple's purity), *dewat neter* (god–wife), *rekhet* (wise-woman who spoke with the dead), *imi-unut* (astronomer-priestess) or *hener* (temple musician and dancer). A Greek priestess might be *hiereia* (she who takes care of holy things), *melissa* (bee), *ergastinai* (weaver of sacred garments), *kanephoros* (basket-bearer), *pythia* (the oracle at Delphi), or even *maenad* (madwoman).[3] An intimate reading of the biblical texts related to women will show that there are also many Hebrew words for priestess.

The Biblical Period

The Bible uses the word *kohen* or priest to refer to an individual who engaged in sacred service of the Divine through ritual. A *kohen* may be an Israelite priest, or a priest of another temple or religion. For example, Aaron and his sons, ancestors of the Israelite priesthood, are *kohanim* (the Hebrew masculine plural for kohen). Jethro, father-in-law of Moses and priest of Midian, is called a *kohen*.[4] Joseph's wife Asnat is daughter of "*kohen on*," the Egyptian priest of On.[5] The word *kohen* may come from a word meaning "established, lasting," "to make prosperous," or "to bow before." Or, it may come from a word meaning "diviner."[6] The task of the *kohen* was to maintain the sanctuary and its rituals—initially, serving the portable sanctuary known as the *mishkan* or Tabernacle, and then, once it was constructed, the 'brick-and-mortar' Holy Temple. In other words, the priest maintained the sacred space that was a point of connection between the people and the Divine.

The word *kohenet* cannot be found in the Bible. The word *khnt*, priestess, appears in ancient Phoenician writings of approximately the same period as a parallel to *khn* or priest. The queen was a *khnt* of the city deity. Another woman is listed in an inscription as a *rb khnt*, a high priestess (literally, master-priestess).[7] The term for high priest was *rb khnm* (literally, master of priests). In Phoenicia, the term *khn* or *khnt* usually refers to a high-level administrator with cultic functions, rather than the many sacred functionaries such as sacrificer, scribe, singer, diviner, conductor of the new moon festival, keeper of the temple curtains, and so forth. An inscription at De'ir Alla, made in 800 BCE in a language close to Hebrew, describes many kinds of sacred service that were known to the Israelites, and uses the word priestess or *khnh*.[8]

Though the word *kohenet* does not appear in the Bible, there are several female relatives of priests (*kohanim*) who play prominent roles in the Bible: In the book of Exodus, Moses marries Zipporah, daughter of Jethro the priest, who then saves his life when he is attacked by God (or a spirit) on his way to Egypt. Zipporah, upon recognizing that her husband is under spiritual attack, circumcises her son and makes an offering of the foreskin.[9] Scholar Mark Leuchter has suggested that Zipporah's sacrificial action, as well as her lineage, marks her as a priestess.[10]

Other women of priestly lineage appear throughout the Bible. In Genesis 41, an Egyptian priest's daughter, Asnat daughter of Poti-phera priest of On, marries Joseph and becomes the mother of the tribes of Ephraim and Manasseh. In II Kings 11, Jehosheba is an Israelite princess, married to a high priest. She saves the life of a prince from a murderous usurper and helps him regain his throne. In an ancient context, these women might have been seen as priestesses because of their family connections.

CHAPTER I: A BRIEF HISTORY OF THE HEBREW PRIESTESS

Most prominently, Miriam, daughter of a Levite and a sister of Moses and Aaron, appears as a prophetess, a musical leader, and a participant in tribal power struggles. She leads a group of women in song and dance after their crossing of the Sea of Reeds, an activity with which priestesses in cultures all over the Mediterranean would have been familiar. She celebrates God's victory over Pharaoh. She is called by the title *neviah*, and claims to communicate with God.[11] These roles are not only similar to the duties those of other ancient Near Eastern priestesses but also to roles that the Levites played had within the Israelite cult: sacred musician, conduit for the Divine, warrior. The biblical figure of Miriam may well represent a patron or ancestor for women Levites who later served in priestly functions.[12] Prophecy is a common function among priestesses and priests—Ninsun, the priestess-queen who appears in the epic of Gilgamesh, is one example of a prophetess-priestess, and the high priest in the book of Exodus carries a divining device in his breastplate. The activities of women prophets and judges are very much in the traditions of the ancient priestesses (see chapter 4).

Deborah, a judge and tribal leader who appears in chapters 4 and 5 of the book of Judges, has a name that means "bee"—many Greek and Minoan priestesses were known as *melissae* or bees. Deborah is called a prophetess, and utters a true prophecy to her general Barak: that his victory will be achieved by the hand of a woman. After Barak is victorious, Deborah sings a victory chant, an activity which would have been accompanied by drums and dance—both of these were common priestess tools associated with trance and prophecy.

The term *tzovah*, or "ministering woman," appears in Exodus 38:8 and I Samuel 2:22-23. This word refers to women who worship or serve at the door of the sacred shrine. *Tzovot* may have been singers, diviners, or women who made offerings, or may even have had a sexual function (see chapter 5). The word *tzovah* comes from the same root as the word "army"—a similar word, *tzadi-vet-aleph*, is used to mean priestly service.

The witch—*mechashefa* or *baalat ov*—was also a likely member of the priestesshood (see chapter 6). Connecting to the dead was an important part of a community's religious life. Women who did this work appear in the Bible in the story of the Witch of Endor and elsewhere. Usually the Bible condemned them for communing with the dead. Individuals bringing harvest sacrifices to the Temple had to promise that the food had not been placed with the dead[12a], which may indicate that food offerings to departed spirits was a common custom. Scholars have speculated that women might have had a particular connection to this tribal spirit work.[13] Priests in the Temple were forbidden spiritual or physical contact with the dead, leaving a spiritual void that needed to be filled, officially or unofficially. And so, women's spirit work with the dead, though not sanctioned or sacralized by the cult, had a place and filled a need.

Holy Women

The Bible uses the term *kedeisha*, holy woman, to mean a woman who serves as a priestess, making offerings at shrines, or who offers herself for sex as a religious rite. The corresponding masculine term *kedeish* (pl. *kedeishim*), which appears a number of times in biblical texts, has been translated "male prostitute" but may also be a word for a priest. *Kedeishim* serve in the Temple and are expelled from there by the monotheistic reformer King Josiah. Deuteronomy instructs: "No daughter of Israel shall be a *kedeisha*."[14] In Hosea, Israelite men are chastised for going to prostitutes and for making offerings with the *kedeishot*.[15] (See chapters 5 and 14.)

The term *kedeisha* is related to *kadishtu*, a Sumerian/Babylonian term for a priestess.[16] Qodshu or Qodesh (the Holy One) was a name for Asherah, Canaanite mother of the gods, and a *kedeisha* may be a priestess of Asherah. A woman who engaged in sacred sexuality in Sumer was usually called not a *kadishtu* but a *harimtu*—"forbidden woman" or "woman under a sacred ban." In the epic of Gilgamesh, the *harimtu* Shamhat tames the wild man Enkidu by introducing him to lovemaking. It is a matter of controversy whether the word *kedeisha* meant ritual prostitute in its true context in ancient Israel—it could be that the Bible labels priestesses of Asherah prostitutes to denigrate them.[17]

In a memorable episode from Genesis[18], Tamar, the daughter-in-law of Judah, one of the sons of Jacob, is called a *kedeisha*. Tamar marries Judah's son Er, who dies not long after the wedding. Tamar has no child, so the rule of levirate marriage applies. In levirate marriage, the brother of a deceased man marries the deceased man's childless widow, in order to provide his brother with substitute offspring. Judah marries his second son, Onan, to Tamar, but Onan dies too. Judah sends Tamar home to her family until the third son, Shelah, is grown up. Shelah grows up but Tamar remains a childless widow, bound to Judah's family. In desperation, Tamar veils herself and goes out to sit by the city gate—a place where there would have been sacred shrines.[19] Judah takes her for a prostitute and hires her.

Judah sends his payment by his friend Hirah, but when Hirah asks for Tamar, he does not say "Where is the prostitute?" but rather "Where is the holy woman (*kedeisha*)?" The people answer him that there has been no holy woman, and so Judah's fee goes unpaid. Meanwhile, Tamar becomes pregnant. Judah wants to have Tamar burned—a punishment that may suggest she is a priestess, since only priestly women are burned for unchastity.[20] However, Tamar shows him the objects he gave her when he lay with her. Judah acknowledges his wrong, and Tamar gives birth to twins, Peretz and Zerach.

The story implies that by dressing in a veil and soliciting a man for sex, Tamar is acting like a shrine priestess, a woman dedicated to sacred sexuality. Judah, as well as the children Tamar produces, are ancestors of the kings of Israel. This suggests that a priestess/*kedeisha* may have been invested with the power to confirm sovereignty upon the king through intercourse, just as the *en*-priestess did in ancient Sumer. In this model, the priestess represents the goddess of the society, and her union with the king symbolizes his union with the land.[21] (See chapter 14.) Savina Teubal believes that the matriarch Sarah is fulfilling a similar mandate when, with Abraham's collusion, she briefly enters the harems of Pharaoh and King Avimelekh.[22]

In II Kings 23, which describes the purging of non-monotheistic practices from Jerusalem, women receive specific mention as weavers of cult objects for Asherah within the Temple compound. While this work could have been secular employment, it was more likely to be a priestess task—much as the *ergastinai*, weaving-priestesses of Athens, wove a robe for Athena. Dressing the gods and goddesses was an important task of priests in ancient Sumer, and the temple weavers of Jerusalem were doing similar work. (See chapter 3.)

The *gevirah* of the Judean royal court is the mother (or occasionally grandmother) of the reigning king.[23] Some scholars believe that the *gevirah* is an honorary title for the king's mother, without further significance.[24] Others are convinced that the queen mothers of Judah exercised political and religious leadership on a par with queen mothers of other Near Eastern regimes, serving as court officials and priestesses of the mother of the gods.[25] If so, the term *gevirah* may also refer to a biblical priestess, possibly related to Asherah, the Canaanite mother of the gods. The later Christian elevation of Mary, mother of Jesus, is only one example of the power of this archetype of the king's mother in the Near Eastern consciousness. (See Chapter 9.)

There are other biblical terms for women who perform priestess roles: *mekonenet* (wailing woman), *chachamah* (wise woman), *metofefet* (sacred drummer/dancer in Temple processions), and others. Each of these terms has a history that this book will trace through the biblical and post-biblical eras.

Official priestess roles already began to disappear prior to the First Exile of the Judeans in 586 BCE. Women were confined more and more to folk or lay ritual, while the official cult was restricted to men. The exile to Babylonia (which included most or all of the elite of Judean society) would have put a final end to these already attenuated priestess roles.[25a]

The Second Temple and the Post-Temple Period

During the Israelite exile in Babylonia, absent the centralizing influence of the Temple, the Israelite cult evolved into something resembling the Judaism we see today. Text-based monotheism—a belief in a single God revealed in the Torah—became the norm. Priests, prophets, court officials and scribes held religious power. Once Jews returned to the land of Israel and rebuilt the Temple, fewer women seem to have had access to prophecy, ritual leadership, or other priestess roles, though a few texts in the book of Nehemiah continue to mention women singers as part of the Temple cult[26]. This change may be connected to the shift away from worshipping goddesses, or to a societal discomfort with women's leadership. Yet we can still detect a few hints of an ongoing tradition of priestesses or quasi-priestesses in the Second Temple period and in the Mishnaic period that followed.

The Mishnah, the Jewish law code of the second century CE, records many Temple rituals and priestly rules. While we do not know how accurately the Mishnah is depicting the priesthood of the end of the Second Temple period (or the priesthood in the centuries immediately following the Temple's destruction), we do see that the Mishnah uses the word "priestess." In the Mishnah, *kohenet* means a wife or daughter of a *kohen* or priest.[27] (A *leviya* or female Levite similarly means the wife or daughter of a Levite.) Such women could eat *terumah*, food that had been donated in a sacred manner to the Temple, while ordinary Israelites could not. However, they were not allowed to engage in Temple ritual, any more than a layperson would be. A *kohenet* did not have to maintain strict ritual purity because she did not do Temple service, nor could she eat of the ritual sacrifices offered in the Temple. If she was a priest's daughter and married a layperson, or she was a priest's wife and he divorced her, she lost her status as *kohenet*. Unlike the law for priests, there were no restrictions on whom the daughter of a priest could marry.[28]

However, other Talmudic traditions show that sometimes *kohanot* were viewed as members of the priesthood for certain purposes. Rabbinic statements accord certain honors to a *kohenet*: for example, the Talmud states that only a *kohen* or Torah scholar should marry a *kohenet*.[29] In Tractate Chullin, the sage Ula argues that a *kohenet* is a female *kohen*, and therefore can be given *matanot*, or priestly gifts such as the first fruits of the harvest, even though she cannot perform Temple offerings.

> *The sage Ula used to give matanot (food gifts donated to the priesthood) to a kohenet… Rav Kahana ate [matanot/priestly gifts] due to his wife (who was a kohen's daughter), Rav Papa ate due to his wife, Rav Yeimar ate due to his wife, R. Idi bar Avin ate due to his wife. The law is according to Ula.*
> —Babylonian Talmud, Chullin 131b-132a

This text states that some people, including rabbinic sages, made personal offerings to God through women of priestly families, and that some men ate *matanot*—sacred food—because their wives were *kohanot*. This is the most direct Talmudic evidence that priestly women had priestly roles—that is, roles in ritual that facilitated a connection to the Divine.

A first century CE funerary inscription in Jerusalem reads: "Megiste, priestess" (*hierise*, a Greek translation of *kohenet*).[30] An inscription in Beit Shearim, a vast burial site from the second century CE, reads: "Sarah the daughter of Nehemiah, mother of the priestess, the lady Maria." In these cases, *hierisa* or *hiereia* appears to be a title in its own right, accompanied by the honorific "lady." It may mean "wife of a priest," but since Maria's husband's name is not listed, the title may have other meanings as well. The Talmud may be giving us a hint of how such women were regarded when it notes that sages used to give ritual gifts to *kohanot*.

A Roman Jewish woman of the same period is also identified as *hierisa* or priestess on her tombstone: "Here lies Gaudentia, priestess, age 24 years."[31] Another Roman tombstone refers to a woman named Maria as "daughter of a priest"[32] (possibly a different status than *hierisa*). Other tombstones of the period designate women as *archisynagoga* (head of synagogue) and *presbytera* (elder, a term that indicated honor within a synagogue community and was also used to mean priestess or priest's wife in early Christianity). Bernadette Brooten argues that these titles on tombstones had ritual meaning.[33] In Rome, the wives of priests were sometimes considered priestesses, and Roman matrons could be priestesses in their own right, so *hierisa* could well have had meaning in the Jewish community too.

In addition to the women of priestly families, the Talmud as well as other Jewish and Christian texts report the existence of sacred weavers as part of the Temple cult. These sources depict the Temple weavers as young unmarried girls, noting that their work on the curtains of the Holy of Holies was considered sacred (see chapter 3). The Temple weavers may have been a last vestige of a Jerusalem weaver-priestesshood.

The Egyptian Jewish Community

In addition to the central Temple in Jerusalem, we know of two Jewish temples in Egypt during the same time period. These temples, where there was ritual sacrifice as in Jerusalem, were part of garrison cities where Jews lived among other ethnic groups. They were staffed by priests of the Aaronide line. As the sources below will indicate, both of the Egyptian Jewish temples may have had female functionaries.

The Temple in the fortress of Elephantine (Yeb) existed in the fifth century BCE, and its practices are documented in numerous papyri found in that area. Inscriptions indicate that some worshippers at the Temple honored female deities like Anatyahu, Anat-Bethel, and Ashimyahu—all combinations of goddess-names with the god-name YHWH. This strongly suggests that, for some Jews, a female counterpart to YHWH was interwoven with the Temple cult.[34] Elephantine also had unusually emancipated Jewish women who could elect to divorce their husbands and who could be heirs of their fathers' holdings.[35]

Some of the Elephantine papyri deal with a woman named Tamet. Tamet was a freed Egyptian slave, a wife to Anani son of Azariah. Anani was an official or ritual servitor at the Temple in Elephantine: his title was "*lachan* of YHWH the god who dwells in Yeb the fortress." *Lachan* is a term borrowed from Akkadian that refers to a Temple functionary. It is unclear what the duties of this office were, but some have suggested that Anani might have supervised the musical parts of the ritual, as the Levites did in the Temple in Jerusalem.[36] Anani owned a house that shared a wall with the Elephantine Temple.

After Tamet became Anani's wife, the two sold their home. In the sale document, Tamet is called "*lachanah* of YHWH the god who dwells in Yeb the fortress."[37] *Lachanah* is the feminine of Anani's title. In Egypt, family units often shared ritual roles, so Tamet may have been a musician or other officiant at the temple. In the document of Tamet's manumission, it says she is "released to God," a phrase known from other documents to mean that she joined some sort of religious community.[38]

The Temple at Leontopolis stood in the year 300 BCE, two hundred years after the temple in Elephantine. Onias, a prominent priest during the Maccabean period, fled there during a period of political uncertainty and founded a temple. Bernadette Brooten notes that an inscription on a Jewish tombstone at Leontopolis (first century BCE) reads "O Marin, *hierisa*, good and a friend to all, causing pain to no one and friendly to your neighbors, farewell!"[39] Given that Leontopolis was a cultic center, *hierisa* may have indicated a spiritual function, rather than (or in addition to) the designation "wife or daughter of a priest." Marin may have had some role in the Temple at Leontopolis. At this same time, there was an order of Jewish female monastics known as the Therapeutrides, living outside Alexandria, in company with a parallel order of male monastics, in prayer, study, and contemplation (see chapter 13).

Even after the Temple in Jerusalem was destroyed, Jewish priests maintained some ritual roles in the Jewish diaspora, and led synagogues for some time afterward. Only slowly did ritual power pass to the rabbis and sages who wrote the Talmud and created rabbinic Judaism. Even in the absence of the Temple, local people would still have honored priests (and maybe priestesses) in addition to their commitment to study and synagogue life. However, as the rabbinic model of leadership took hold, the power of priests dwindled. Women's spiritual opportunities lessened as well—there were no more female heads of synagogues or monastic orders of women. Yet eventually, Jewish mysticism provided a new avenue for priestesses—women facilitating the connection between Divine and human—to continue their work.

The Medieval Period and the Mystics

Maimonides, the influential philosopher and legalist of the twelfth century, cautions: "For all positions of authority in Israel, we only appoint a man."[40]

In the Medieval period, few Jewish women could claim religious titles of any kind, though we hear of women such as Urania of thirteenth century Germany, who was "the chief of the synagogue singers", and Ceti of Zaragoza, a fifteenth century Spanish woman who held the title of rabbess.[41]

Starting in twelfth century Spain, the kabbalists began to speak of God in ways that were similar to the ancient ways of speaking about goddesses. For the kabbalists, the Divine was made up of multiple faces or aspects, some of which were male and some of which were female. In particular, the feminine face of God known as Shekhinah, Malkhut, or Bride had been separated from the male Godhead and needed to rejoin Her lover in order for redemption to occur. Everything in the worlds above had a counterpart in the world below; as there was a divine union of male and female, there should be a human union of male and female as well.

> *That night [the Sabbath] is the joy of the Queen with the King and their uniting... Therefore a person must prepare his table on the Sabbath night so that blessings from above will dwell on him... Scholars who know this secret mate only on Friday nights.*
> —Zohar II, 63b

In other words, the Jewish husband and wife are invested with the power to effect divine marriage—not that dissimilar from the union of king and priestess in ancient Sumer. We do not know how Jewish women experienced this ritualized sexuality, but the beliefs of the kabbalists must have made some impact on women's self-perception. Although the kabbalah maintained a relatively passive role for women and for the divine feminine, their imagery of the feminine was far more rich and diverse than their overarching theology suggests.

While the texts of kabbalah are written by and for men, women in kabbalistic circles performed functions that were similar to those of the ancient priestesses. There were many prophetesses among the kabbalists. For example, Francesca Sarah of sixteenth century Safed was a prophetess and dream interpreter for the kabbbalistic community.[42] Hayyim Vital, disciple of Isaac Luria, writes:

> *A woman was there, Francesca Sarah, a pious woman who saw visions in a waking dream and heard a voice speaking to her, and most of her words were true.*[43]

Similarly, the kabbalists who moved from Provence to North African freuquently passed down their meditative practices through the women of the family—Colette Aboulker-Moscat, a kabbalist and meditation teacher in Jerusalem in the late twentieth century, was a descendant of such a lineage. Her great-grandmother instructed kabbalists in esoteric meditative practice, showing them how to perfect their souls.[44]

Ordinary Jewish women also performed rituals to connect the worlds. In the seventeenth century, we find *tekhines*, prayers written for and sometimes by women in Yiddish, and influenced by mysticism. One prayer is for making candles during the High Holiday season. These candles are to remember particular souls and to invoke the protection of the dead (both biblical patriarchs and matriarchs, and the deceased of the family) on the living. Women unroll candlewick around graves and then use the wicks to make candles. When women make the candles, they recite Yiddish prayers like the one below:

> *Riboyne shel Olam (Master of the World), I ask you, merciful God, to accept my mitzve of making these candles for the sake of your Holy Name and for the sake of the holy souls… May we have the merit of donating candles to the holy temple as was done in ancient times… May… the candles that are made for the sake of the pure and holy souls cause them to awaken and inform each other until they reach the souls of the holy matriarchs and patriarchs…*
>
> *May the merit of our holy and pure patriarchs and matriarchs and the merit of our little children protect us so that the dead may arise speedily and soon and may they intercede for our future. May they awaken from their graves and pray for us that the coming year will be a good year and the attribute of justice will be united with the attribute of mercy. May all the pure and holy angels also pray that the dry bones will come to life speedily and soon.*[45]

In this prayer, women are engaging in ritual activity to awaken the dead and invite the intercession of the ancestors—patriarchs, matriarchs, the souls of children, etc.—to benefit and protect the community of the living. Through their actions, the women are hastening the time of redemption when the dead will arise from their graves. In concept, this is not so different from what mediums and oracle-priestesses might have done in ancient Israel. Notice that the women call this work a *mitzvah*, a divine commandment, even though technically there is no commandment to make soul candles. The women are defining their own work as sacred. The *tekhine* literature mentions priestly ritual frequently and invites the woman to see her prayers (not the community prayers of men but her own prayers) as reflections of priestly service:

> *Accept my prayer*
> *As you accepted the sacrificial offerings*
> *That the priest brought*
> *To the offering stool*
> *At the time when your House stood*
> *In great purity and holiness.*[46]

The more radical Jewish mystics became, the more prominent women were in their circles. Shabbetai Tzvi, the self-proclaimed Messiah of the seventeenth century, had a particular passion for the feminine, and his antinomian sect had many prophetesses. Women studied kabbalah alongside men in Sabbatean circles, and they spoke in trance during Sabbatean rituals. Jacob Emden, an opponent of Sabbateanism, writes of one of the Sabbatean prophetesses:

> *One reliable informant swore to me that he knew how this accursed woman made herself a prophet (like Sibylla to the Romans and Venus to the Aramaeans), by falling on the ground in a fit, like one possessed by a demon, and reciting passages from the Zohar by heart while in this trance.*[47]

Abraham Cardozo wrote to the rabbinic judges of Smyrna in 1669 regarding his family's Sabbatean visions:

> *My wife Judith… began to experience revelations of the light…*
> *And it appeared to her in the form of a man. He spoke to her many times while standing in the light, pure and gleaming…*[48]

Jacob Frank, who claimed to be Shabbetai Tzvi's successor and founded his own heretical sect, had his own wife and daughter honored as human embodiments of the Divine feminine. His wife Hannah was known by the title *gevirah*, lady—the same word as the ancient title for the queen mother. Interestingly, the Frankists also named the tarot card known as the High Priestess the *gevirah*, showing an understanding that the word meant "priestess." His daughter Eva was known as the Maiden, and considered an embodiment of the Divine Maiden.

The Chasidic movement, which began in the eighteenth century, was mystical in origin and focused on direct experience of God. Its leaders could be said to act as shamans, as part of their role was intervening with God to perform healings and exorcisms, and to journey to heavenly realms in prayer and meditation. Some Chasidic women served as channels of blessing and divine wisdom. Eydl the Baal Shem Tov's daughter and Rebbetzin Malka of Belz gave blessings and healings as did the rebbes of her era.[49] Hannah Rachel Werbermacher, the Maiden of Ludomir, was known as a miracle worker, and engaged in activities typically reserved for men, such as Torah study and the wearing of ritual fringes. These women were not called priestesses, but they were doing priestly work: meditating between the divine world and the human world.

Jewish women in the modern era have been sometimes named as priestesses of the home. Jenna Weissman Joselit quotes Nahida Remy, a Jewish writer on women's topics, as saying in 1916 that the Jewish woman is "Priestess of the Jewish Ideal, Prophetess of Purity and Refinement." The *Jewish Home Beautiful* wrote: "With woman as priestess to tend to its altars, each home is a Temple, each hearth is a shrine."[50] In a 1940s oral history, Sarah Cohen Berman writes: "The woman is not a mere housekeeper but the priestess of a *mikdash me'at*, a miniature sanctuary, when she conducts a truly Jewish home."[51] Ray Frank, a woman proto-rabbi of the nineteenth century, implored: "Every woman should aspire to make of her home a temple, of herself a high priestess."[52] This language is influenced by German bourgeois culture of the nineteenth century, which used similar priestess imagery, and reflects the romanticism of the age in which it was written. It bears witness to the durability of the priestess archetype even after thousands of years. There are modern practices which place Jewish women as priestesses of the home even today.[53]

Contemporary Priestesses

In the modern period, women have actively sought to take on religious leadership as equals to men, slowly gaining access to the rabbinate, the cantorate, and positions of Jewish authority. While these women are not called priestesses, they serve alongside their male counterparts as prayer leaders, interpreters of text, and spiritual counselors. Women have also taken on roles as educators and communal leaders: when educator and organizer Jeanette Miriam Goldberg died in 1935, she was eulogized as a "high priestess" of Judaism.[54]

It is still debated today in traditional Jewish circles whether daughters of modern Jewish *kohanim* are priests who are women (that is, they cannot take on the duties or taboos of a priest but still are priests theoretically), or are laypeople.[55] The Conservative movement has only recently ruled that the daughter of a *kohen* may offer the priestly blessing during holiday prayer, and may take on other honors given to priests. The Conservative movement uses the term *bat kohen* (daughter of a priest), not *kohenet*.[56] The Reform, Renewal, and Reconstructionist movements generally do not make distinctions based on priestly heritage for men or women. In at least one instance, the word *kohenet* has been used to call an Orthodox woman, daughter of a *kohen*, to the Torah at a women-only Torah service.

The Abayudaya Jews of Uganda, who converted to Judaism in the early twentieth century, understand themselves to all be priests. This belief comes from the biblical language in which Israelites are an *am kohanim*, a nation of priests. These Jews use the word *kohenet*, priestess, to refer to any female member of the community.[57]

Kohenet has also become a modern word for Jewish women who are reclaiming priestess traditions. This reclamation is partly inspired by historical inquiry into women's leadership models in ancient Israel, and partly inspired by the modern Goddess movement, which tends to name its female leaders as priestesses.[58] The Kohenet Hebrew Priestess Institute, founded by the authors of this book and housed at the Elat Chayyim Center for Jewish Spirituality, trains women in spiritual leadership and ordains them as *kohanot*, priestesses.[59] "Kohenet graduate Ashirah Marni Rothman writes: "The Kohenet program… is a program where I can live into my spiritual path of honoring the Divine feminine, the Earth, and the Jewish traditions of my ancestors."

This work is part of a larger conversation about re-integrating the role and history of priestesses into Jewish life. In 2004, Rabbi Ohad Ezrahi and Dawn Ezrahi gathered a group of women in Israel to discuss the possibility of a modern Hebrew priestesshood, and his event was titled "Kohanot."

In 2008, Deborah Grenn of the Lilith Institute wrote a thesis entitled "Claiming the Title Kohenet: Goddess Judaism and the Role of the Priestess through Conversations with Contemporary Spiritual Leaders," which was later published in *Women in Judaism: An Interdisciplinary Journal*.[60]

Women rabbis, and other Jewish women who serve as spiritual leaders, are also sometimes claiming the title *kohenet*. For the consecration of Rabbi Diane Eliot in San Diego in 2006, Rabbi Wayne Dosick wrote: "Let her be for us a *kohenet*; our pastor who creates sacred space, hallows our times and seasons, and brings sanctity to the tragedies and triumphs of our lives…"[61] Shulamit Wise Fairman has taken on the title of priestess along with her title of *hazzan/cantor*.[62] Rabbi Rayzel Raphael describes herself as a "priestess of Shekhinah."

A brochure describing the work of Jewish shaman Miriam Maron describes her as "a great priestess."[63] Israeli artist Dorit Bat-Shalom also calls herself a priestess. She writes: "How can there be peace in the Middle East without the Shekhinah? The Shekhinah has been driven away from the holy lands. We cannot heal without Her."[64] A sisterhood of women in the Jewish Renewal movement uses the term *eshet chazon* (woman of vision) in ways that are similar to the use of the word "priestess." This sisterhood honors women "whose life work [has] revealed her heart-connection to being a channel for Shekhinah."[65]

Modern Jewish priestesses are seeking a model of spiritual leadership that draws on the history of ancient priestesses, mystics, priests, and healers rather than merely seeking to emulate traditional male sages. Prayer in this mode may use ancient forms such as altars, drums, and divination, or may be conducted outside in natural settings. Topics of study may include shamanic practice within Judaism, Jewish dreamwork, Jewish eco-theology, or mystical multi-gendered views of the Godhead. Some male Jewish leaders are following a similar spiritual path, naming themselves Jewish shamans, mystics, nature rabbis, and so on.

This contemporary Jewish form of ritual work often arises from experiences of the Divine in which God/dess appears as embodied in a female form or in the form of the earth itself. This parallels ancient Israelite religion, where priestesses and goddesses might be connected to one another. To fully understand the historical context of this model of spiritual leadership, we need to explore not only the history of the Hebrew priestess but the history of the Hebrew Goddess.

Chapter 2:
A Brief History of The Hebrew Goddess

In Genesis 1, we hear: "Elohim created the humans in His image: in the image of Elohim created he him, male and female created he them." The humans, made in the divine image, are male and female. While the pronouns for the Divine are male, both male and female beings are made in that image. Further, the name used for the Divine is plural: Elohim, gods, not El, God. This leaves open at least the possibility of gender multiplicity in the Godhead.

This gender multiplicity is reflected in the archaeology and narrative of ancient Israel. While YHWH, the god of the Israelite people, was generally depicted as male, He could also have female traits (for example, in Isaiah 66:9 and Psalms 22:9, where He is described as a midwife). The Hebrew deity evolved with traits of male gods like El, but also with traits of goddesses. As we shall learn, for much of Israelite history, goddesses were still active divine entities in the lives of the Israelites. The history of Israelite and later Jewish monotheism includes a history of the attempt to either drive out, or assimilate, the goddess in the Israelite psyche.[1]

While not all priestesses worship goddesses, the ancient Hebrew priestesses may have been connected to goddesses in a variety of ways. Priestesses used ritual items like the frame drum, which was frequently associated with Near Eastern goddesses.[2] The Bible asserts that some priestesses engaged in rituals for the goddess Asherah or the goddess Anat. The Bible's ambivalence about priestesses—exposing them even as it tries to hide them—is related to the Bible's ambivalence about the archetype of the goddess. The Bible preserved goddess images in subterranean ways even as it sought to eliminate those images. Later, long after goddesses were removed from Israelite/Jewish life, Jewish mystics posited that human women could embody female faces of the divine—one of the sacred responsibilities of the priestess.

The worship of a feminine aspect or aspects of deity is virtually a universal phenomenon. The Virgin Mary, Kali Ma, Persephone, Kuan Yin, and Yemanja are all ways that different cultures have expressed devotion to some form of the sacred feminine. Frequently, they exist in dynamic tension with male aspects of the Divine: fathers, husbands, lovers, sons. In many cultures, the male aspect(s) of God and the female aspect(s) are deeply intertwined. These dynamic tensions and entwinements between masculine and feminine also occur in Israelite and Jewish statements about divinity.

It is important not to conflate the ancient role of goddesses with contemporary beliefs and practices concerning the divine feminine. The understanding of people who revere the Goddess in the modern world comes from contemporary ideas and needs. Yet, at least in the ancient Near East and the religions that grew out of that culture, it is surprising how consistent the imagery of goddesses has been across time. In the writings of the high priestess Enheduanna more than four thousand years ago, the goddess Inanna has many of the qualities many people associate with the Goddess today: creation, destruction, mercy, justice, stability, unpredictability, love, conflict, wisdom, holiness, and life itself. These often opposite qualities continue to appear in biblical texts and again in rabbinic and kabbalistic images of the divine feminine.

> *To destroy, to build, to lift up, to put down are yours...*
> *To hand out tender mercies is yours, Inanna.*
> *Prosperous business, abundance of money*
> *Indebtedness, ruinous loss are yours, Inanna*
> *To worship in lowly prostration,*
> *To worship in high heaven are yours, Inanna.*
> *To have a husband, to have a wife,*
> *To thrive in the goodness of love is yours, Inanna,*
> *to build a house, construct the women's rooms,*
> *to kiss a baby's lips are yours...*
> *to give the royal crown,*
> *the throne, the king's scepter,*
> *to grant cultic rites*
> *guide their execution, are yours, Inanna,*
> *to muster troops, raise the battle cry*
> *is yours, Inanna*
> *setting free is yours, Inanna.*
> —Enheduanna, trans. Betty deShong Meador[3]

The Biblical Period

Near Eastern myths often depict mother-figures as divine creators:

> *When on high the heaven had not been named,*
> *Firm ground below had not been called by name,*
> *When primordial Apsu, their begetter,*
> *And Mummu-Tiamat, she who bore them all,*
> *Their waters mingled as a single body...*
> —Enuma Elish[4]

CHAPTER 2: A BRIEF HISTORY OF THE HEBREW GODDESS

> *Marduk bound a structure of reeds upon the face of the waters,*
> *He formed dust, he poured it out beside the reed-structure.*
> *To cause the gods to dwell in the habitation of their heart's desire*
> *he formed mankind.*
> *The goddess Aruru with him created mankind...*
> —Creation myth from Asshur[5]

An earth-goddess does not appear in the Bible. The notion that the (masculine) god needs a partner in order to create life is at odds with the dominant world-view of the Bible, in which God is disembodied and singular. In the Bible, God does not have a body: "God spoke to you out of the fire; you heard the sound of words but you saw nothing, only a voice."[6] When God does appear in an embodied form, God appears as vaguely gendered masculine: "They saw the God of Israel, and under **his** feet there was the likeness of a pavement of sapphire..."[7]

In contrast to other ancient accounts of creation, in the book of Genesis, God creates by word, not by intercourse:

> *When God was beginning to make heaven and earth, the earth*
> *was formless and void, there was darkness on the face of the deep,*
> *and a wind of God was sweeping on the face of the waters. And*
> *God said: Let there be light..."*
> —Genesis 1:1-2

Though not explicit, we can still hear an intimation of Goddess-language in this passage: The word for deep, *tehom*, echoes the name Tiamat, the Babylonian goddess of the primordial ocean, whose body was torn apart to create the world. In the Bible, Tiamat's face is covered, literally: "darkness on the face of the deep." The Bible represses the image of God as mother giving Her body to make the world, but hints at it in the single word *tehom*.

This mother-image of a broken body holds within it all the ambivalence of the world toward mothers. Tiamat is a devouring monster: she and her male consort seek to wreck the world and its order. She represents the fear of the mother as one who erases boundaries and eats everything. One way to look at this is that human beings remember the all-powerful mother of their infancy and fear her. Another way to look at it is that in many societies, women are made to suffer social deprivation and degradation. This aggression is then projected back onto women, who are seen as sexual, lawless, chaotic—even as they are also seen as valuable mothers of the tribe.

Tiamat's repressed face appears in the first verses of Genesis because the Bible too has primal ambivalence about mothers. The Bible goes to a great deal of trouble to undo any hint of the necessity of the feminine, first by eliminating an explicit "Goddess birthing scene" at the beginning of creation, then by eliminating mothers from most genealogical lists, then by depicting the matriarchs as helpless to conceive without God, and then by banning rituals connected to goddesses. The earth as mother also becomes problematic in the biblical view: worship of features of the earth, trees, stones, etc. as embodiments of the divine is forbidden, and sacred trees and stones are to be destroyed.[8]

This process of de-iconization was mandated even as the local, indigenous ritual (such as the *asherot* or tree-goddess-figures) honoring feminine as well as masculine entities still remained in place. There are texts that imply that an Asherah tree or pole (object sacred to the goddess Asherah) stood in the Temple for most of its existence, and was only removed just before the first Exile.[9] Scholar and archaeologist William Dever analyses ancient figurines and inscriptions referring to "Yahweh and his Asherah" and writes: "We cannot avoid the conclusion that Yahweh could be closely identified with the cult of Asherah, and in some circles the goddess was actually personified as his consort."[10]

Biblical texts mention *terafim*, household spirits, which may have been gendered male and female. Archaeologists have discovered the offering-stands women used to perform ritual in their houses, probably to Asherah or Anat.[11] Excavations have revealed oil jars inscribed with the words "sanctified to Asherah."[12] Jeremiah and Hosea speak of women who worshipped the Queen of Heaven (most likely the goddess Anat) with cakes and fire rituals.[13] In fact, these women complain that attempts to stamp out the worship of Anat were responsible for the nation's troubles:

> *This word that you have spoken to us in YHWH's name, we will not listen to you! We will do everything that our mouths have vowed: to offer incense to the Queen of Heaven and pour libations to her, just as we and our ancestors have done, our kings and our princes, in the city of Judah. For then we were satisfied with bread, things were good with us, and we saw no evil. Since we stopped making incense offerings to the Queen of Heaven and pouring libations to her, we have lacked everything, and the sword and famine have consumed us... Is it without our men that we have made cakes of her likeness and poured her offerings?*
> —Jeremiah 44:16-18

This is reverse Deuteronomic theology: the belief that a goddess is responsible for all blessing, and turning away from her means famine and exile. Ultimately, public expressions of Goddess-faith lost ground to Jeremiah's monotheism, but his recording of this impassioned speech makes clear how many Israelite women and men felt strongly about their attachment to goddesses.

Some biblical texts sought to make a subterranean peace with the Goddess by evoking Her under the surface of the text. Consider the following trio, in which the Goddess is erased and made visible:

> *"You must not set up an Asherah beside the altar you build to the Lord your God."*
> —Deuteronomy 16:21

> *"And the man called his wife Eve, because she was the mother of all life [a title given to Asherah.]"*
> —Genesis 3:1

> *You neglected the Rock who gave birth to you.*
> —Deuteronomy 32:18

The Bible forbids explicit worship of the Goddess (in the first text) but allows aspects of Her to be projected onto Eve (in the second text) and even onto God (in the third text). Now consider these contradictory texts:

> *See that I am He,*
> *And there is no god with me…*
> *Deut. 32:39*

> *The Infinite made me at the beginning of his road,*
> *the most ancient of his works of old…*
> *I was with him as a nursling,*
> *I was the delight of the days,*
> *Playing before him always,*
> *Playing with the globe of his world*
> *And humankind was my joy.*
> *Now, children, listen to me,*
> *Happy are they who keep my ways.*
> —Proverbs 8:22, 27-32

In the book of Proverbs, Lady Wisdom (Chochmah), a mysterious female presence, speaks of her creation in the second passage. Clearly, she is God's creation, not God's creator. Yet if God is alone at the dawn of creation and has no partner and no children, who is playing before God in this passage? The key to this passage is actually the final phrase: "Happy are they who keep my ways."

Ashrei (happy) sounds like Asherah, and the word *ashrei* appears more times in this section of Proverbs than anywhere else in the Bible.

> *Wisdom has built her house.*
> *She has hewn her seven pillars.*
> *She has cooked the feast, mixed the wine,*
> *And set her table.*
> *She has sent her maidens to cry*
> *On the heights of the town:*
> *Whoever is simple, turn in here.*
> *Come feast on my food, and drink the wine I have mixed,*
> *Leave simpleness and live,*
> *walk in the way of understanding.*
> —Proverbs 9:1-6

The final phrase of the segment—"walk in the way of understanding"—uses an unusual verb for "to walk"—*ishru*. This word, which has the letters *aleph-shin-reish* just as Asherah does, again connects Wisdom to Asherah.

In ancient Israel, *bayit* or house refers to a shrine. The feast in Wisdom's house might refer to shrines and rituals dedicated to the Goddess. Women serve the feast of Wisdom, hinting at the former spiritual role of women as keepers of shrines. An Ugaritic text describing the goddess Asherah's feast parallels our Lady Wisdom and the meal she offers:[14]

> *Why has the Great Lady who Tramples Yamm come? Why has the Mother of the Gods arrived? Are you very hungry? Then eat! Are you very thirsty? Then drink! Eat food from the table, from goblets drink wine, from cups of gold the juice of grapes."*
> —KTU 1.4 IV 32-37[15]

Later on, Proverbs refers to Lady Wisdom as "a tree of life to all who cling to her," just as Asherah was once called Tree of Life, and ends the verse with "all who support her are happy"—*me'ushar*, containing the same letters as Asherah. The author of the Book of Proverbs appears to be weaving some of the old goddess religion into the new Israelite religion, by bringing the goddess Asherah along as Lady Wisdom.[16] The elimination of the Goddess from Israelite worship that the Torah presents as a *fait accompli* was not a fact of life at all for most of Israelite history, and some biblical writers aspired to include the divine feminine in their developing religion.

The Goddess and the Temple

The shrines described in the Bible—the portable Tabernacle (eleventh century BCE) and the Temple built in Jerusalem (953-586 BCE)—not only served as places to worship, but dynamically represented the whole of the earth. In the shrine, the world of humans and the world of the Divine came together and the worshipper could connect to the All. Rabbi Kaya Stern-Kaufman writes: "It is this experience of the unity of Creation that imbues one with the sacred."[17]

> *The mishkan was made to stand for His creation of the world... The heavens, the earth and the seas are homes for the all creatures therein. For the upper heavens, eleven curtains were made for the tent of meeting and for the firmament, ten curtains of the tabernacle were made. To represent earth, the pure Table was made and for the fruit of the earth they would arrange two loaves of bread in two columns of six apiece to represent the months of summer and winter. To represent the sea, a washbasin was made and for the heavenly lights (sun, moon and stars) a menorah was made."*
> —Midrash Tadshe 2

> *Every one of these objects [the Temple vessels] is intended to recall and represent the universe, as he will find if he will but consent to examine them without prejudice and with understanding.*
> —Josephus[18]

The Temple and its earlier form, the Tabernacle, contained objects connected to Eden. The Ark inside the Holy of Holies was sheltered under the wings of two cherubim, just as two cherubim guarded the entrance to Eden. The shrine also contained a menorah and a stylized tree, each of which would have referenced the Tree of Life. Even after the Asherah pole was removed from the Temple, the Tree of Life would have been a reminder of Asherah, and later of Lady Wisdom. Metaphorically, the shrine was an Eden, the place where Adam and Eve experienced an idyllic existence before being expelled into a harsh world, allowing the worshipper to imagine a place of peace and comfort reminiscent of the uterine life of the fetus; a place that provided spiritual nourishment and strength to face the cold realities outside the worship space.

As Bonna Haberman notes: "Enclosed space is often understood to indicate a female aspect of the material world...The holy spaces of the Jewish people are nested chambers that enclose holy objects.... The inner sanctuaries of the Jewish people are uterine."[19] Each year the high priest would enter the Holy of Holies, a sacred space that is usually vacant except for the Divine Presence. The high priest would cleanse the space by sprinkling blood on its curtain seven times. The number seven evoked the power of creation, and cleansing through blood is also something that occurs in the womb. In a sense, the priests and prophets of Israel hid a Goddess image in plain sight in their rituals and texts.

There were many ways that the Temple cult marginalized women. The Bible's Aaronide priestly cult was male-only (though, as we will see in later chapters, there are hints that women served at the entrance to the shrine and in sacred musical processions). According to the Bible, goddess-related objects were forbidden (though II Kings relates that the Asherah stood in the Temple for much of its history). Temple ritual treated the bodily fluids related to fertility, life, and death as impure and commanded that people undergoing birth, menstruation, and ejaculation separate from the sacred shrine. This was probably a departure from local ritual practices related to fertility and death, and would have had the effect of desacralizing those things and eroding the power of local clergy, particularly priestesses. Over time, women, who once represented the mysteries of fertility and death, were banned from the priesthood. Scholar Sarit Paz suggests that there was considerable resistance among the people to this exclusion of priestesses, as suggested by the many priestess figurines found in the biblical stratum of the archaeological record.[20]

When the Temple was destroyed in 586 BCE and Jews went into exile, the sacred space that connected divinity to the earth was lost. Jews compensated for this loss through the creation and canonization of a sacred text: the Bible. When they returned to their land, they built the Temple again. By this time, goddesses and priestesses were a distant memory, if they were even a memory. The loss of sacred space happened a second time with the destruction of the Second Temple in 70 CE.

Yet the priestly impulse to sanctify space and create channels of connection to the divine did not vanish. It went inward, into the mystical experience in which the world is God. To the mystic, the world becomes the Temple, and the world becomes God/dess too. Rachel Elior, in her book *The Three Temples*, details the process of how the Temple and its priestly class transformed over the generations into mystics who saw themselves as dedicants of an inner Temple.[21] This Temple is the hidden version of the once-physical Temple, and in it the cosmic processes of the world—which are fertile, sexual, and embodied—take place.

> *As long as the Temple stood, it served as the sacred bedchamber of God the King and His Bride, the Shekhinah. Every midnight she would enter through the place of the Holy of Holies, and She and God would celebrate their joyous union. The loving embrace of*

the King and His Queen assured the well-being not only of Israel, but also of the whole world.
—Howard Schwartz, *Tree of Souls*[22]

In fact, this sexualized cosmic space, with its divine inhabitants, echoes the ancient myths in which god and goddess, or king and priestess, came together to create the world. Kabbalists reclaimed the old myths, probably because they were having experiences that mirrored the myths—including erotic or filial relationship with the Divine as woman. Jewish mystics came to believe that embodied divinity, male and female, was the substance of the entire world. They interpreted all of Jewish practice as an attempt to bring the masculine God and the feminine Goddess together and re-unite them as one being. Those mystics innovated the custom, prior to the performance of many *mitzvot* (commandments), of reciting the formula "for the sake of the unification of the Holy Blessed One and the Shekhinah." This custom persists to this day. Thus every mitzvah becomes a symbolic enactment of the sacred marriage. This mystical understanding retains a role for the Goddess in mystical Jewish practice.

Sages and Mystics

Post-Temple Jewish ritual hints at the Goddess even as it erases Her. The Torah, dressed in finery and then undressed during the Torah service for a ritual of learning and knowing, is an image of a woman. Contemporary ritualist Amichai Lau-Lavie writes: "The ark, the Holy of Holies, is separated by a curtain, as it was in the Temple, and behind the curtain is the Torah, wearing a silver crown and velvet dress, always referred to in the feminine. Then we bring her out with great decorum, kiss her, undress her, open her up and commence the ritual of knowledge in the biblical sense."[23]

The sages of the talmudic era re-incorporated Goddess imagery into their stories about God. They spoke of Shekhinah, the indwelling presence of God, using a feminine-gendered noun. Sometimes She is a numinous, genderless cloud of glory hovering over communities of prayer, sickbeds, and the Temple; and sometimes She is the wife of God, the mother of the Israelites, weeping over their exile.[24] The term Shekhinah has its origin in the notion that God dwelt tangibly within the portable Tabernacle or *mishkan*. Rabbi Leah Novick notes: "Some argued that the Divine Presence... could live only in the land of Israel, and in fact could be felt only in the vicinity of the Holy Temple in Jerusalem. Others argued that the Shekhinah, as God's presence, was omnipresent... Slowly, Shekhinah develops into a figure semi-independent from God."[25]

In the Middle Ages, Jewish mystics re-mythicized the sacred feminine as bride, mother, bird, fierce warrior, holy apple orchard. The kabbalists' wives become stand-ins for the Shekhinah, so that the mystics can enact the sacred divine union through sex with their wives. "Rendered kosher by the Kabbalah, Shekhinah became immensely popular." [26] Kabbalah depicts Shekhinah as a receptacle and vessel for masculine divine energy, and learned men continue to be Her interpreters, yet many of the images the mystics draw on are consistent with goddess tales from the ancient world. [27]

She is Mother of male divinity:

> *As long as the people Israel is found with the Holy One Blessed be He, He too is in a state of completeness, and he nourishes himself to satiation by sucking the milk of Immah Ilaah, the supernal Mother.*
> —Zohar III, 88b

She is Mother of humans:

> *The Holy Shekhinah comes down and spreads Her wings over Israel like a mother embracing Her children.*
> —Zohar I, 148

She is Destroyer:

> *A thousand mountains before her are just one bite for her. A thousand great rivers she swallows in one gulp.*
> —Zohar I, 223a

She is Lover:

> *On the Sabbath, the Lady joins with the King and they become one body, and this is why blessings are found on that day.*
> —Zohar III, 296a

She is abundant Nature, the Holy Apple Orchard:

> *Every day dew trickles from the Holy Ancient One... and the Holy Apple Orchard is blessed.*
> —Zohar III, 296a

The loving, fierce, fertile, wandering Shekhinah captures what Raphael Patai calls the "mythic folk imagination." While kabbalistic doctrine defines Shekhinah as a passive entity, her folk presence is active. She calls people, summons them, teaches them wisdom. Personal visions of Shekhinah become common. The Shulchan Arukh, a law code written by Joseph Caro in the sixteenth century, contains statements such as: "A person who visits the sick should wrap up in a tallit and sit on the floor, for the Shekhinah hovers at the head of the bed."[28] Caro himself has mystical visions, and sometimes hears the Shekhinah speaking to him, saying: "I always embrace you and cling to you."[29] Hayyim Vital, kabbalist and student of Isaac Luria, envisioned a ladder to heaven and wrote:

> *Behold, a dignified woman, beautiful like the sun, standing on top of the ladder. And I thought in my heart that she was my mother.*[30]

The pietistic and mystical Chasidic movement also regards the Shekhinah as a feminine, intimate form of God. One Chasidic text attributed to the Baal Shem Tov teaches: "Prayer is a form of intercourse with the Shekhinah."[31] Among certain Chasidic sects, and among messianic sects like those of Shabbetai Tzvi, the Shekhinah had a prominent role in the drama of redemption.

A thousand years after the second Exile, Jewish mystics returned to the repressed bodies: the earth and women. They came to see the trees and stones as receptacles for God's energy, the woman as a symbol of God, the wife as a vehicle for Divine union. It is precisely because of the power and inevitability of these hidden bodies, lodged within Jewish tradition, that the mystics returned to them again and again.

The Contemporary Hebrew Goddess

Jews continued to need and to evoke the sacred feminine. In the late nineteenth century, the Hebrew poet Hayyim Nachman Bialik writes of the Shekhinah: "Take me in under your wing, and be to me mother and sister/let your lap be a shelter for my head..."[32]

The poet's sentiments found an echo in twentieth and twenty-first century feminism. Many contemporary Jews, from Anita Diamant (*The Red Tent*) to Savina Teubal (*Sarah the Priestess*) to Rami Shapiro (*The Divine Feminine in Biblical Wisdom Literature*) have tried to re-imagine how their ancestors might have seen the Goddess. The poet Alicia Ostriker writes of Shekhinah with a more doubled-edged understanding than Bialik:

> *womb compassionate pitiless*
> *eyes seeing to the ends of the universe*
> *in which life struggles and delights in life*[33]

Rabbi Julia Watts Belser writes of meeting Goddess in this way:

> *I met God the summer I turned fourteen... The sky was slowly turning purple, twilight shot through with darkening gold. The wind was crisp and bright against my face, and the rocks were humming against my hands, pulsing with a kind of kinship I'd never known. She was none of that and all of it: the Presence that flooded through me, the feel of my own body finding center, the press of the balcony rail against my skin, the strange, sudden wideness of the sky.*[34]

The modern feminist movement has transformed and reclaimed Shekhinah as a female experience of deity, a way that women may begin to see themselves in the Divine image, and a way that all people may begin to experience God as multigendered. Drawing on, but not limiting themselves to, traditional texts, contemporary Jewish mystics (male and female) have turned to Shekhinah as a way of accessing the sacred feminine and learning Her mysteries. The spiritual experience of meeting the Goddess is as powerful today as it was thousands of years ago.

> *I began to see Her everywhere. And worse, She started talking to me... She intruded on my meditation and prayer time, and just would not leave me alone... I shared what was happening to me with my friend and teacher Andrew Harvey, a devotee of the Mother in all her forms. "The Mother is chasing you," he said, "and you must surrender to Her."*
> —Rami Shapiro[35]

Some have revised Jewish liturgy to refer to God in the feminine as well as, or instead of, the masculine. The names in these liturgies include not only Shekhinah, but *Shaddai* (breasted God), *Rachamema* (Merciful Mother), *Ein haChayyim* (fountain of life), and other names. Strikingly, the contemporary versions of the Hebrew Goddess maintain many of the images associated with the ancient Hebrew Goddess: the earth, the tree, the well or ocean, the mother, wisdom, the birther and destroyer, the circle of life and death.

> *Let us bless the well*
> *Eternally giving*
> *The circle of life*
> *Ever dying, ever living.*
> —Marcia Falk, *The Book of Blessings*[36]

Modern Jewish feminism, like other types of spiritual feminism, has woven itself with the ecological movement. The ancient connection between goddess and earth has been reborn as a theory of the sacred interconnectedness of life. In this worldview, the biological and even astrophysical processes of growth and decay are revelations. Ecotheologian Rabbi David Seidenberg asserts that the Divine, through embodying each individual form of life, values and celebrates diversity of being.[37] Ariel Vegosen, an activist and a student of the Kohenet Institute, sees God/dess in the earth and in the connections among all people. She writes:

> *I find God in the rocks, in the trees, in the soil, in the dirt. I find God indigenous to this planet – in the bones of this circle. I find God when I am aware of all that is around me. I find God when I try something new, when I kiss someone for the first time, when I breathe with someone in rhythm, when I hug heart to heart, when I dance, when I smile... when I am brave enough to love big, wide, and present.*

The identification of Goddess with world can have the negative effect of identifying women with "primal" nature, while men become identified with civilization and power. This either has the effect of infantilizing women and giving men control of society, or of idealizing women and demonizing men. It is perhaps better for modern mystics to assert that all faces of God are embodied in the world, and all faces of the world are embodied in God. It isn't that Goddess (She) is nature, and God (He) is transcendent not-nature: the experience of immanence and the experience of transcendence are both unpredictable and personal, and both can appear as masculine or feminine, or both, or neither. Again, we return to Genesis 1, where Elohim, multiple-faced-deity, can be perceived in many ways. It is also important to acknowledge that gender categories extend beyond male and female, and God can be seen as transgender or without gender as well.

Many modern Jews are uncomfortable with the language of Goddess: For example, Ellen Umansky asserts that "to talk of God the Mother is not the same... as talking about the Mother Goddess."[38] In other words, the image of a Jewish God as female is qualitatively different from a Goddess image. Yet this is true only if we accept a psychological and spiritual split between God-She and the Goddess—one that does not really exist if we pay attention to how similar "God the Mother" and "the Mother Goddess" really are throughout history. Contemporary priestesses, and many others, are searching for creative ways to reframe and overcome the split between God and Goddess, and between modern religious tradition and its ancient priest/ess shadows. This is priestess work in its deepest sense: the bringing together of worlds.

> *The challenge is to embrace the diversity of images and the goddesses that have been hidden or excised from our past. People in my community are more threatened by the revival of the names of the ancient goddesses than the use of Shekhinah or feminized language. But this to me is where the struggle will be—to transform our prayers and rituals to be all-embracing and inclusive and more connected to our planet which we have been exploiting and abusing with abandon. I think that earth-based practices and the reclaiming of the feminine divine are integrally connected to a vision of the world redeemed.*
> —Shoshana Bricklin

> *As priestesses, we embody Goddess. Since the destruction of the Second Temple, we have carried the Spirit of the Divine One within us. Wherever we go, wherever we are, we are home; within us is Shekhinah, Divine Spirit. It is our duty to ourselves and to the Divine, to heal and love ourselves, that we may open fully to serve Her and others, as Her.*
> —Tiana Mirapae

The Priestess Paths

One way to see the priestess is that she is a microcosm of the Goddess. The roles that the Goddess assumes on a cosmic scale—creator, lover, guardian of ritual and societal order, oracle, wise woman, healer—the priestess emulates on a human scale. Whether or not she specifically serves a goddess, the existence of the priestess invites the possibility of seeing the divine in female form.

The next stage of this book is an exploration of thirteen specific priestesshoods documented in the Bible and/or later Jewish tradition. Each of the priestess paths is a form of divine service performed by real women in a variety of places and times, and each one embodies teachings and practices we can learn from today. In myth, thirteen is a significant number, representing the moons of the year and the months of a woman's cycle.

The word "priestess" is used here in three senses: 1) a woman who has the societal role of officiating at or leading a ritual as part of an organized religious structure; 2) a woman who temporarily assumes the role of officiant at a ritual; 3) a woman who embodies the human-divine connection in other important ways. Some of the priestesses in the chapters that follow are part of a priestly cult; some of them are temporarily entering a sacred state as part of a festival or because of a vow; and some are solitary practitioners of ritual, magic, healing, etc. Many of these women are not called priestess, but may have other titles. All of the priestess roles in the chapters to come, whether or not the practitioner carries the title "priestess," are consistent with priestess work from earliest times.

These priestess paths are also consistent with the wisdom of modern feminists and the life-paths of contemporary women. In their book *The Women's Wheel of Life*, Elizabeth Davis and Carol Leonard explore thirteen archetypes of women's spiritual development throughout life, including the Maiden, the Lover, the Mother, the Matriarch, the Priestess, the Sorceress, and the Crone. They discover these archetypes through interviews with contemporary women about their life-journeys. The priestess paths described in this book are partly inspired by the work of Davis and Leonard.[41]

Many of these priestesshoods have links to God-images that are female. Some of these chapters will contain not only a history of women on that priestess path, but mention of feminine God-images connected to that priestess path (such as Shekhinah as Mother in the kabbalah, or the Bat Kol/holy prophetic spirit in the Talmud). The human women and the divine images are interconnected, and influence one another.

Each chapter contains a history of a particular priestess path. At the end of the chapter, there are examples of contemporary Hebrew priestesses who embody that priestess path, a spirit journey (see the introduction "Beginning a Spirit Journey Practice" in chapter 3), and a practical priestess exercise. The purpose of this book is not only to bring to light the history of Hebrew priestesses, but to extend their work into the future. These priestess paths offer us ancient traditions of committing to spiritual service. Readers are invited to observe the ways these ancient practices resonate in their own lives.

Chapter 3:
Weaver-Priestesses

One of the books in my daughter's library is called *The Weaver*.[1] I can remember when she was one year old and I first read her the book. She could not yet speak, but managed to insist that I never turn the page, that I read the first page to her over and over. Maybe it was the words themselves, or maybe it was the tone in my voice as I read them. The first page reads:

> *Beyond the earth,*
> *near yet far,*
> *the weaver sits*
> *in the light of the rising sun,*
> *singing a song,*
> *watching the world,*
> *while her fingers are at work.*

I think of this quote when the retreats of the Kohenet Hebrew Priestess Institute begin. Hangings appear on the wall. The ceiling is draped in threads that join to form a single braided "umbilical cord" hanging at the center of the room. A cloth is spread on the floor. Then, as we sing to one another, each participant adds to this temporary altar something special of her own: a photograph, water from a sacred place, a sprinkle of soil from land she loves. This is a weaving: a bringing together of community in a single place and time, a reminder of the Weaver who brings us all together in a single world.

From the Fates of Greece and Rome to the Norns of the Norse peoples to Grandmother Spider of the Hopi to Iya Moopo of the Yoruba, divine women sit at the loom to guide creation. These images arise out of real cultural and biological experience: women weaving essential household goods, women sending life from their wombs with a red thread attached, women providing sustenance and nourishment. Over the course of history, in many cultures, including Jewish culture of Second Temple and Talmudic times, both women and men weave, yet it is usually women who have been associated with mythic weaving—weaving that makes the world.

Biblical Women Weavers

The Book of Psalms holds a hint of the mythology of the earth-goddess as weaver-creatrix:

> *My bones were not hidden from you*
> *When I was made in a secret place,*
> *When I was woven in the depths of the earth.*
> —Psalms 139:15

This fragment of text seems to refer to the making of human beings at the beginning of Genesis, when they were formed out of the earth, but it also invites comparison to the child formed in the womb.

Women play a significant role in bringing the materials for the Tabernacle and in working with the thread to make the tapestries for the Tabernacle walls. In Exodus 35:22, we learn that "they came, men and women, all who were generous of heart, bringing bracelets, earrings, rings, and pendants, gold objects of every kind." Later on, we hear:

> *All the wise-hearted women spun with their hands, and brought the spinning: blue, purple, scarlet, and fine linen. And all the women whose hearts lifted them up in wisdom spun the goats' hair.*
> —Exodus 35:25-26

The inclusion of women is notable given that biblical text does not often comment on women's participation in communal ritual life. This may be an indication that Israelites viewed the women's spinning and weaving work in particular to be an important contribution to the community's cultic centers. The shrine could not have been created without the female spinners and weavers.

In the Book of Kings, women are specified as the weavers of cult objects for Asherah. The Bible relates that during the Josianic reform, Asherah-objects were removed from the Temple and destroyed. *Batim*, houses, garments or shrines woven for Asherah within the Temple, were among the destroyed things.

> *He brought out the Asherah from the House of Adonai to the Wadi of Kidron outside Jerusalem, and burned her in the Wadi of Kidron, and ground her to dust, and scattered her dust over the burial ground of the people. He tore down the houses of the* kedeshim *[priests and priestesses] that were in the House of Adonai, for the women wove houses [batim] there for Asherah.*"
> —II Kings 23:6-7

Kedeishim would likely have referred to both priests and priestesses of Asherah, as a masculine verb could be applied to a mixed group.[2] *Batim* in this context would have been tents, canopies, garments, draperies, or shrines for Asherah worship. The scholar Ismar Peritz suggests that the word *batim* may once have read *ketonot*, garments.³ Savina Teubal, in her book *Sarah the Priestess*, notes that goddess figures were often enshrined in small houses or tents. Teubal suggests that this is what the holy weavers were weaving.⁴ So the use of '*Kedeishim*' may well have included the women who wove these holy dwellings

The scholar Susan Ackerman argues that Asherah is a goddess of weaving.⁵ We know for certain that Asherah is a goddess of creation because she is called *qaniyatu ilim* or *qnyt ilim*, creatrix of the gods, and also "mother of all."⁶ All of this suggests that the weaving that these women performed in the Temple served as a parallel for Asherah's creative power. The women themselves are creator-priestesses, weaving the holy fabric just as Asherah weaves the world.

In a Sumerian epic of creation, the goddess Ninmah and the god Enki have a contest to see who is the greater creator: Ninmah makes the shape of a person, but Enki decides a person's fate. Ninmah makes a variety of handicapped people to show her power over their destiny, but for each one Enki finds a special role. When Ninmah makes a barren woman, Enki makes her a "weaver for the queen."⁷ These women, since they had no families, might have been sacred weavers, and it is possible that the Israelite cult had a similar institution.

The Second Temple and Post-Temple Period

Temple weavers appear in the Tosefta, a contemporaneous supplement to the second century Mishnah containing material not recorded in the Mishnah. The Mishnah and Tosefta often record traditions (or memories) of what happened in the Temple. The Tosefta diligently notes which Temple workers were paid from the *trumat halishkah* (the census fund collected for the Temple from every citizen).

> *The women who wove the curtain,*
> *The house of Garmo who baked the showbread,*
> *The house of Avtinas who made the incense,*
> *Were all paid from the trumat halishkah.*
> —Tosefta Shekalim 2:6

The 'women who wove the curtain' for the Holy of Holies are named in the same list as those who bake the bread and make the incense, implying that they had an equal standing in the commerce of the Temple treasury. The house of Garmo and the house of Avtinas were houses of priests, priests who specialized in the production of holy bread and holy incense. Baking and incense-making was done on the Temple grounds, which suggests that the weaving might have been as well.⁸ Women weavers may have been daughters or wives of priestly families who specialized in this work, but there might have been other ways to become a Temple weaver.

Mishnah Shekalim 5:1 records the name of the priest who oversees the weaving of the curtain (Elazar) and the name of the priest who oversees the weaving and keeping of garments (Pinchas) but no women are mentioned.[9] Researcher Tal Ilan notes that the Mishnah may be hiding the tradition of women weavers deliberately, because of its embarrassment at finding a mention of women as part of the Temple cult.[10]

> *Rabban Shimon ben Gamliel said in the name of Rabbi Shimon ben haSegan: the curtain (parochet) was a handbreadth thick and was woven in seventy-two batches. Every batch consisted of twenty-four threads. It was made by eighty-two maidens/rivot. They made two every year, and three hundred priests would immerse it.*
> —Mishnah Shekalim 8:5

This text, in which eighty-two maidens make the curtain for the Holy of Holies, is from the Munich manuscript of the Jerusalem Talmud. The more common reading, which reads "eighty-two times ten thousand" (thousand=*ribo*, a word that sounds similar to *rivot*), makes no sense. The text was probably altered later by redactors who had forgotten the presence of women in the Temple cult.[11] Whether there were exactly eighty-two Temple weavers may not be as interesting to us as the fact that the text seems to verify the existence of the women weavers.

The weavers were unmarried girls, just as the weavers of Athena's robe were unmarried girls. If the weaving had to be done within the Temple or near it, a woman with a family could not take on the work. Also, the Temple cult had a tremendous concern for ritual and sexual purity, and it is possible that the *rivot* were pre-menstrual girls. This adds to the case for the weavers' quasi-priestly status, since their ability to live and work in the Temple would be an issue.

The Apocalypse of Baruch mentions the Temple weavers as part of its narration of the Temple's destruction. This is a Syriac text, probably originally composed in Hebrew in the late first or early second century. The text describes the holy weavers as "virgins."

> *You priests, take the keys of the sanctuary*
> *and cast them to the highest heaven*
> *and give them to the Lord*
> *and say: "Guard your house yourself,*
> *because, behold, we have been found to be false stewards,"*

> *and you virgins who spin fine linen*
> *and silk with gold of Ophir,*
> *make haste and take all things and cast them into the fire*
> *so that it may carry them to Him who made them*
> *and the flames send them to Him who created them.*

Like priests, the Temple weavers live in the Temple and are caught in the siege. Like priests, they protect the sacred things. The priests cast the keys back to heaven, and the young women who weave the curtains cast their tapestries into the fire—all so that the invader will not lay hands on the holy objects. The male priests and the female Temple weavers are placed opposite one another in a dual-gendered portrayal of priestly devotion.

A Christian text from the rabbinic period, the Protoevangelium of James, confirms some of the details of the Apocalypse of Baruch. The Protoevangelium of James depicts Mary as a Temple weaver, one of seven young girls of the house of David. Their duties were assigned by lot.

> *Then they brought them [the virgins] into the temple of the Lord, and the priest said: "Cast me lots, who shall weave the gold, the white, the linen, the silk, the hyacinth-blue, the scarlet and the pure purple." And to Mary fell the lot of the pure purple and scarlet. And she took them and worked them in her house.*
> —Protoevangelium of James 10:2

According to the Protoevangelium, Mary has been living in the Temple since the age of three as a devotee (much as Samuel is given to the Tabernacle at an early age). When Mary is twelve, she is given to Joseph as a ward, and the priests assign her sacred weaving to do in her home. It is powerful that Christian tradition saw Mary as a Temple weaver—the closest thing she could be to a priestess.

The Mishnah (Yoma 2:1-4) similarly records that priestly duties were assigned by lot at the beginning of each day. In ancient Greece and Rome, priesthood generally was assigned in one of two ways: by heredity or by lot.[12] The assignment of a task by lot seems to indicate its sacred nature and the need to "let God decide" who will serve and in what ways.

The apocryphal book of Enoch, written in the first century BCE and preserved by Ethiopian Jews and Christians, connects the *parochet* to the weaving of time and space (both Philo and Josephus say similar things about the curtain). The biblical personage Enoch receives a tour of heaven, and one of the things the angel Metatron shows him is the heavenly *parochet*:

> *Metatron said to me: come, I will show you the veil of the All Present One, which is spread before the Holy One Blessed Be He, and on which are printed all the generations of the world and all their deeds, whether done or yet to be done, until the last generation.*
> —3 Enoch 45

This text portrays the *parochet* as the weaving of history, just as the Fates and the Norns are said to have woven all the world's events into their tapestries. This depiction of the holy curtain names it as a metaphysical cloth, holding all of the past and future within its images. The sacred curtain spans life and death, and the birth of new generations. Jews of the Roman period sometimes buried their dead with spindle whorls, and this might be connected to the idea that spinning and weaving constituted creation and recreation.[13]

Jewish women who were sacred weavers, and who wove replacements for the temple curtains, may have had a deep intuition that they were, on some level, reweaving the fabric of the universe. The holy women weavers would have been the closest thing Jews had to human embodiments of a cosmic creatrix.

The Jerusalem Talmud reports that: "Women are accustomed not to prepare or attach warp threads to a weaving loom, from the new moon of Av until the ninth of Av (when the Temple fell), because during the month of Av the Weaving-stone was destroyed."[14] (The weaving-stone or foundation stone was a sacred stone said to exist within the Holy of Holies and to be the foundation "from which the world was woven."[15]) While the Talmud attributes the custom of not weaving to the destruction of the weaving-stone, a deeper interpretation might allow that this custom of not weaving during that special time arose in memory of the women who had woven the Temple curtains, as a statement that the Temple's destruction was spiritually akin to an unraveling of the world.

The Middle Ages and the Modern Era

Jewish women continued to do sacred weaving and to make curtains and adornments for sacred space. A Northern European Jewish blessing for the birth of a girl was: "May she sew, spin, weave, and be brought up to a life of good deeds."[16] The thirteenth-century Judah of Worms describes his daughter Bellette as "serving her maker and spinning and sewing and embroidering."[17]

Jewish women of past generations wove or embroidered a *parochet* for the Ark, or a Torah mantle, on the occasion of a birth or wedding, or in memory of a relative. In some countries, Jewish women embroidered a wimple (Torah binder) and donated it to the synagogue in gratitude for the birth of a healthy child.[18] The making of a wimple was a special part of the European baby naming ceremony known as Hollekreisch.[19] In Italy, a special blessing was chanted every Sabbath for the woman who had done weaving or other fabric work to benefit the synagogue.

It might be useful to parenthetically note that Jewish women did not only weave; they also did other kinds of sacred creative work. Asnat Barzani and the wife of Dunash bin Labrat wrote poems in Hebrew. Sarah bas Tovim (eighteenth century), Sarah Rebecca Rachel Leah Horowitz and other women wrote *tekhines*, devotional literature. Women were involved in book printing. Gittel of Prague wrote at the end of one book: "I also am engaged in noble work: Gittel bat Leib Zatshav, Prague."[20] Tcharnah Maizlish worked as a typesetter in Krakow and became the head printer: she was called "the lady who is involved in heavenly work."[21]

Jewish women today have re-discovered sacred fabric art, from wedding canopies to curtains for the Ark. Women such as Shonna Husbands-Hankin make *tallitot*, often specifically designed for women. Rabbi Geela Rayzel Raphael writes of her Husbands-Hankin tallit: "It's... part of the feminine tapestry of new traditions."[22]

Weaver-Priestess Incarnations

At the gatherings of the Kohenet Hebrew Priestess Institute, the Weaver is a central image of the Divine. One song we sing asserts: "The whole wide world is in the Weaver's hand/fire water air and land."[23] Another prayer calls: "Weaver and stoneworker/you spin the thread of life/and carve the channel through to death."[24] During one ritual for sharing dreams, we wove our community together by throwing a ball of yarn from one hand to another, until all of us were linked by a common thread.

Our community contains many modern-day sacred weavers. Ketzirah Lesser is an ordained *kohenet* and fabric artist. She has led a non-denominational earth-based magickal community in the Washington, DC area, and currently leads on-line earth-based Jewish services for OneShul. Ketzirah is a weaver in multiple ways: a sculptor of cloth, a weaver of sacred rituals, and a maker of community. During her time at the Kohenet Institute, she chose the title *m'agelet*, circle-maker, which is connected to the integrating role of the Weaver.[25] Ketzirah writes:

> *What does it mean to be a Weaver? It means you bring together different pieces into a distinct and new whole. It's different than creating a patchwork, where the original sources are pieced together. When you weave fabric or spin yarn, you draw on the best of the original source, but it is blended into a new, stronger creation. We*

> can do this literally with fiber, but we can also take this concept into the wider world.
>
> Jewish women weave wonders. We weave communities, and we weave dough to create challah. We weave cultures old and new to create modern Judaism. I weave worlds, and I am part of a long line of weavers whose stories have never been told. My way of life is not new. It's what our grandmothers did when they reached the shores of America and had to create new lives for their families while still retaining tradition.

Rachel Koppelman is a musician, healer, Kohenet Institute initiate, and devotee of the Goddess. She writes: "To me, everything is energy. When we do ritual work, that's an intentional heightening of energy. The role of the priestess is healer, medicine woman, and ritualist." Rachel sees her energetic work as a manifestation of the Weaver.

> The experience of the Weaver is an experience of fluidity: being able to channel whatever is appropriate or necessary or whatever can best serve the higher good. It's about letting something come through. There are different individual things that need to be focused on, but that's all in service to the bigger picture. The Weaver ties together different things in service to the whole.

Rachel imagines the Divine as a weaver of substances and events, an artist who pays attention to every element of the pattern. The Goddess is the one who ties together each individual reality with the cosmic reality.

> The Weaver is divine intelligence that takes the individual strands and disparate things and makes this synergistic new thing. The weaving is a process that happens infinitely across time and space.
>
> Think of the fractal. A fractal looks the same in microcosm and macrocosm. The pattern happens on the tiniest infinitesimal level, and what's happening at that level affects the big picture. Nothing is too small, nothing is insignificant to the larger perspective.

Sarah Shamira Chandler, a Kohenet graduate, has been the Director of Earth-Based Spiritual Practice at the Isabella Freedman Jewish Retreat Center. Sarah has innovated first fruits parades in celebration of the Shavuot harvest festival and has brought new connection to an ancient Jewish holiday: the new year of the animals. She is another kind of weaver, considering how to align and interweave the rhythms of humans with the rhythms of the earth. She writes:

> *For me, earth based Jewish spiritual practice allows individuals and community to connect with the divine, themselves and each other through aligning the Jewish calendar (holidays, Torah readings, anniversaries, etc) with the Jewish agricultural cycle (mainly based on the climate of the land of Israel) along with our local ecosystem. On Adamah farm at Isabella Freedman, we align one more dimension—the seasonality of our organic farm.*

The Weaver is essential to the community, sometimes in surprising ways. Rabbi Lynn Gottlieb tells the story of her visit to a synagogue, several decades ago when she was one of the first women rabbis. She was seated on the *bimah*. Although she was the rabbi's invited guest, two male synagogue leaders accosted her and demanded she leave the *bimah* because she was a woman. When she refused, they grabbed her arms and attempted to remove her from the *bimah*. The *shul* erupted in argument, and the service stopped. After extended conversation, one woman pointed to the curtain over the Ark and announced: "I embroidered that curtain myself, and if she goes, it goes!" This was the end of the argument: the service went on, and Rabbi Lynn stayed on the *bimah*. Such is the power of the Weaver.

Spirit Journey
Beginning a Spirit Journey Practice

Shamans and shamanesses all over the world engage in spirit journeys—inner visualizations that work with spirit. Spirit journeys are inner forays to the realm of myth and collective unconscious. Biblical figures such as Jacob and Joseph have dream visions, while Rebecca goes to inquire of the Divine through an oracle. Elijah and Elisha are fed by ravens, make requests of bears, and speak to whirlwinds. Rabbis of the Talmud frequently speak with Elijah or Abraham. The kabbalists imagine trysts with the Shekhinah as part of their prayer and meditation.

In the current generation, many of us are divorced from these visionary practices, with the result that many intuitive and imaginative gifts go unused and an ancient source of wisdom goes unpracticed. Yet the gifts of visualization, or spirit journey, are ours to discover.

Throughout this book are guided meditations, or spirit journeys. You can use these meditations to contact the faces of the Hebrew priestess as you experience them. You can also improvise journeys like these to open to your own sacred images. If you cannot remember the details of a particular journey while you are meditating, or your vision wants to go in a different direction, don't consider yourself bound by the words in this book. Go on your own spiritual adventure.

Preparing for a Journey

Find a quiet space that you can use regularly for the purpose of spirit journey. Sitting or lying down are both common postures. Choose a time when you are not distracted and not likely to fall asleep. If you wish, you can light a candle, say a prayer, or build an altar representing the theme of your journey. Some people wish to visualize a protective circle around them when they do work like this.

Begin by focusing on your breath. Allow the sensations of breathing in and out to fill your mind. If any part of you feels tense or uncomfortable, breathe deeply into that place to soothe it. If you become distracted, return your focus to the breath until you are able to regain a state of attention.

As you breathe in and out, notice the heaviness of your body. Gravity is holding you to the earth. This is the gift of body and presence. Also notice your spine and your ability to sit or stand upright. This gift connects you to the sky and to your aspirations. Finally, notice your heart: the center of your body. Now, close your eyes.

From this point, let your imagination carry you, guided by the parameters of the meditation, by whatever thoughts, feelings, and images you carry with you and/or by the unexpected turns your spiritual imagination will take. If you cannot remember all of the instructions written for a particular journey, focus on the instructions that you remember, or on those that seem important to you.

An Introductory Journey

Imagine that you are standing at a gateway. The gateway can be anything from a wrought iron artwork to a garden arch to an ordinary door. Step through the gateway. Remember as much about it as possible, because you can use this gateway to enter any of the journeys in this book.

You can be anywhere: a garden, a beach, a shrine, the subway, the Western Wall. Try to visualize fully where you are. Trust your instincts—if your choice of imagery seems strange, humorous, or unexpected, go with it anyway. Notice as much about your surroundings as possible.

Begin walking in any direction that compels you. Soon you will see a figure walking toward you. It may be a woman, a man, a child, a transgender or non-gendered being, an animal, an angel, or anything you imagine. Greet this being and ask if she/he/it is willing to be your guide to the realm of the Hebrew priestesses.

If you receive "yes," as an answer, ask why this particular guide has come to you. Ask anything you need to know about this realm, and ask about any gifts or dangers that lie ahead for you. You may also wish to ask your guide for a token that represents your connection—a stone, an amulet, an instrument, or another object. You can use this token in other spirit journeys if you need to call your guide. If the answer is "no," ask the being to direct you to another guide, and repeat the process as many times as necessary.

Thank your guide, and retrace your steps. Return to the gateway and step through. Become aware of your breath, notice the sensations of your body, and then open your eyes.

Returning from a Journey

A journey can take anywhere from five minutes to quite a bit longer. Don't stay longer than your body and psyche can manage. When you feel it is time to end your journey, make sure to return to your gateway and exit the same way you entered, before opening your eyes and leaving the meditation. This preserves the sacredness of the journey and avoids any difficulty in re-entering ordinary time and space.

Ground yourself by eating and drinking, saying your name aloud, or tasting salt. You can also put your hands on the ground or floor and imagine sending any excess energy back to the earth. Taking a bath is also a good grounding practice.

Journal about your experience. Spirit journeys are like dreams; one can forget them easily. Try to capture the imagery that feels important, and write a few lines about what it means to you. Give yourself a little time to recover before moving on.

Spirit Journey
The Weaver

You are standing before a temple: the Temple in Jerusalem, a temple you imagine, any temple in the world. See it as you imagine it. People are going in and out of the gate. You mingle with the crowds and slip inside. You meet a guide. This guide takes the form of someone who has been an important spiritual role model for you. The guide indicates to you that you have been given the honor of visiting the Weaver.

Your guide leads you to the ritual bath. When you are done with your immersion, you dress, and follow your guide until you come to a quiet courtyard. This courtyard has a table with twelve loaves of bread and a vessel of water, an incense altar, and a seven-branched lampstand that looks like a tree.

To the rear of this courtyard is a tent-like building. Walk around it. Each wall is a beautiful tapestry. When you look more closely, you discover to your surprise that each tapestry is a scene from your life.

You enter the tent and see a woman seated at a loom. The loom is an ancient one. The woman, without stopping her weaving, invites you to pull out a thread from the loom. This is your life-thread. The thread will tell you, in whatever way it will, what to do to help it heal, grow and serve life. The thread will also sing to you of the larger whole, the fabric of the galaxies. When you have heard all the thread has to say, let it go, and the Weaver will weave it back into the fabric of creation.

The Weaver will then pause from her work, place Her hands on your head and utter the priestly blessing: "May the One who Is bless you and keep you; May the One of Being shine the light of Her face on you and be gracious to you; May the One who is Becoming lift up Her many faces to you, and grant you peace."

Bow low before the Weaver and leave her chamber. Take your leave of the courtyard. Your guide leads you back toward the Temple's main court. You thank your guide and stay here awhile. There may be priests, priestesses, and sages here, dancers and sacred singers. Leave through the eastern gate and go out into the city, and back to your waking life.

She Who Weaves Worlds With Words
The Practice of Creating Personal Prayer
by Taya Shere

Prayer is communication with the sacred. As we pray, we come into connection with ourselves, our emotions, and our longings. While priestesses embody many kinds of communication with Spirit, words are the most common tools associated with prayer. Legend holds that angels place garlands woven of prayer at the feet of the divine. The weaving of personal prayer is a practice that can deepen our relationship to spirit.

Times of Prayer

Jewish tradition invites daily prayer practice. Choose a set time of day to pray: in the morning upon awakening, as you are traveling to work or play, as you prepare for sleep each evening. You can explore traditional options for prayer or offer spontaneous prayer from your heart. Or, drop into prayer in moments of need. When you are anxious or angry, elated or grateful, bored or confused or lonely, initiate a conversation with Spirit through prayer. Become aware of your body and your breath. Quiet your mind or enter into heart space. Find the words or images you most need to offer and share with Spirit.

Weaving a Prayer

Just as three strands weave together to make a braid, there are three core elements in Jewish liturgy: Praise (*hallel*), Gratitude (*hoda'ot*), and Petition (*bakashot*). Cultivate a practice of personal prayer using elements of praise, thanks and petition, or any prayer elements that are resonant with you. Offer your prayers aloud. Journal, collage, or paint your prayers. Dance and sing prayer. Allow your prayer to be spontaneous and heartfelt.

For the praise element of your prayer, use a divine name that is resonant and authentic for you in the moment. Reflect on the qualities of Spirit that are most present for you, or that connect you to an aspect or name of divinity that you want to invoke. Speak those qualities and names as the praise element of your prayer: *Gracious, giving Goddess. Shekhinah Who Sustains Us. Abundant Divine Mother.*

For the gratitude element of your prayer, give thanks. Prayers of thanks can be specific, global, or anywhere in between: *Thank you for your presence in my voice and my vision. Thank you for creative, conscious community. Thank you for love that is nurturing and profound.*

For the petition element of your prayer, request what you yearn for most deeply in that moment: *Please bless me with clarity in all that I communicate and all that I choose. Please support me as I dance my dreams into being. I am open to you, please allow me to encounter and embody you with grace.*

Build a full prayer by weaving these sections together:

> *Gracious, giving Goddess, thank you for your presence in my voice and my vision. Please bless me with clarity in all that I communicate and all that I choose; Shechina Who Sustains Us, thank you for creative, conscious community. Please support me as I dance my dreams into being. Abundant Divine Mother, thank you for love that is nurturing and profound. I am open to you, please allow me to encounter and embody you with grace.*

Making an Offering as Practice

Contemporary Jewish prayer does not usually involve making offerings, as priestesses did in ancient times—though you may want to consider the traditional practice of giving to those in need immediately after prayer as a sacred offering. If you are on a priestess path, you may also consider giving a gift to the Divine as part of your prayer. The weaver-priestesses made fabric as a gift. Create a wall hanging with words and designs that help you concentrate in prayer. This is known in Jewish tradition as a *shiviti* and frequently contains the words of Psalm 16:8: "I have placed the Divine before me always." Create spontaneous artwork that expresses the essence of your prayer, or the essence of Shekhinah as you understand Her. You can burn incense, write a poem, or bake bread and give it away. Or, in the tradition of the weavers, make a shrine out of cloth or other materials as a focus for your prayer practice.

Resources for Creating Meaningful Personal Prayer

She Who Dwells Within: A Feminist Vision of a Renewed Judaism by Lynn Gottlieb (Harper San Francisco, 1995), *The Path of Blessing: Experiencing the Energy and Abundance of the Divine* by Marcia Prager (Jewish Lights, 1993), *The Book of Blessings: New Jewish Prayers for Daily Life, the Sabbath, and the New Moon Festival* by Marcia Falk (Beacon Press, 1999), *Siddur HaKohanot: A Hebrew Priestess Prayerbook* by Jill Hammer and Taya Shere (Kohenet Hebrew Priestess Institute, 2008)

Chapter 4:
Prophetess-Priestesses

In the fall of 2011 I dreamed I was giving a lecture on the Bible—something I frequently do in waking life. In the dream, I was telling the participants in the class about the missing letters in the Bible, pointing to a chart of letters that did not exist but had once existed, and still did exist in their latent potential within the biblical stories. One of the letters had the sound *ng*, and I wanted to name myself after this letter. When I woke up, I had the sense that the dream was somehow real.

So, I searched the Internet and discovered that the Bible really does have a missing letter. The Hebrew letter *ayin* was originally two letters—the *ayin*, which looks like an eye, and the *ghayin*, which might once have looked like a twisted cord, and probably had the sound *ng*. Certain root words in biblical Hebrew can only be explained if you know that some of them once contained the letter *ghayin*. The Hebrew *ghayin* fell out of use in the early biblical period, though it still exists in Arabic.

For me, the *ghayin* is a symbol of what is missing from the spiritual traditions we have received. Its twisted cord shape is the umbilicus, the missing truths of our mothers—and it is the connection to the sacred which must be rediscovered in every time and place. The lost letter represents the voices of prophetesses, poetic and authoritative, which have been muffled by the din of history.

The role of the prophetess is to reveal hidden information. She may do this through a prediction about the future, a revelation about the past, or a declaration about the truth of the present. It may even come wordlessly, through drum and dance. The prophetess shows us the world in a way that compels us to understand it differently.

The Biblical Period

In Proverbs 31:3, the mother of King Lemuel sternly admonishes him:
> *Do not give your strength to women,*
> *Or your way to the* machot melachin.

This untranslated Hebrew phrase is often understood to mean "those who destroy kings," i.e. women. Melachin is readily understood as 'kings' or 'rulers.' However, *machot* is more troublesome—it is not, in fact, used anywhere else in the Bible. It appears to be a cognate of the Akkadian word *mahhutu*, an ecstatic prophetess (the male form was *mahhu*). Such prophetesses were part of the king's court and gave him oracular advice. In the epic Enuma Elish, an enraged goddess Tiamat goes into a frenzy and becomes "like a *mahhutu*." The phrase in Proverbs means "the king's prophetess," and shows ancient Israelite ambivalence about the power of prophetic women.[1]

The three prophetesses who have a significant presence in the Bible all receive messages from God. Two of the three are composers of poetic song. Miriam, called a prophetess in Exodus 15, is the sister of Aaron the high priest and of Moses. She is named specifically as sister of Aaron, and she engages in ritual music-making. She may be a mythic ancestor of a guild of female Levites who used music and prophecy, or she may be a representative figure standing in for the priestesses of ancient Israel.[2]

In Numbers 12, Miriam and Aaron confront Moses together, demanding: "Has YHWH spoken only through Moses? Has he not spoken through us as well?" Miriam and Aaron are making a bid to be viewed as prophets on an equal footing with Moses. If both are members of the priestly cult, they may be asking for more power for their own priesthoods. The Arabic word *kahin*, cognate to *kohen/kohenet*, means both priest and diviner—and in ancient Israel, prophecy was a very important aspect of the power of the priesthood. (The high priest of Israel carried the *urim* and *tummim*, divination tools, inside the sacred breastplate, and Moses and Samuel are depicted as serving in both prophetic and priestly roles.)

The brother-sister pair then goes on to criticize Moses' marriage to a Cushite woman, likely in an effort to undermine his absolute authority. The argument begins with "*vatidaber*"—and she spoke—suggesting that the critique is coming primarily from Miriam. God summons Miriam, Aaron, and Moses to the Tent of Meeting, the cultic center, and arrives in a pillar of cloud in order to reject the claim of Miriam and Aaron.

> *When a prophet of YHWH arises among you, I make myself known to him in a vision; I speak to him in a dream. Not so with my servant Moses, he is trusted in all my house. With him I speak mouth to mouth, through my image, not through riddles, and he beholds the likeness of YHWH. Why did you not fear to speak against my servant Moses?*
> —Numbers 12:6-8

This statement affirms that Miriam and Aaron, like Moses, are prophets as well as members of the priestly house. It also makes a categorical distinction between "ordinary" prophets and Moses, and thus puts the law of Moses above the pronouncement of priest-prophets like Aaron and Miriam. The conversation takes place in the community cultic center, which may serve to emphasize Moses' authority over the priestly ritual.

CHAPTER 4: PROPHETESS-PRIESTESSES

After God speaks, Miriam becomes covered with white scales—*tzara'at*—and becomes ritually impure. Aaron begs Moses to pray that Miriam be healed. Moses does so, but God replies: "If her father spat in her face, would she not bear her shame seven days? Let her be shut out of camp for seven days, and then let her be readmitted."[3] Miriam leaves the camp for seven days. Then she is readmitted and the camp moves on. She is not heard from again until her death.

This particular punishment of Miriam is singularly humiliating precisely because she is a priestess as well as a prophetess. *Tzara'at* is ritually defiling; it is the opposite of being a priest. Aaron refers to Miriam as being "like a dead person," and human death is anathema to the priestly sancta. To add to the irony, seven days is the length of a priestly ordination. Through this ordeal outside the camp, Miriam seems to lose whatever priestly status she has. This textual event may represent the humiliation and removal of priestesses from the priestly cult at some point in Israelite history.

Ironically, the ritual for bringing a person with *tzara'at* back into the community is an anointing of the ear, hand, and foot—very similar the anointing Aaron underwent for the priesthood.[4] In a way, this story confirms and rejects Miriam's status as priestess in one breath. The similarity between the ritual for "lepers" and the ritual for priests makes one think of Miriam as a kind of rejected priest—which, in our reading of the text, she is.

Yet the prophet Micah refers to Miriam as one of the three leaders of the Israelite nation in the wilderness.[5] Later, rabbinic legend depicts her as the source of a mysterious moving well of water that sustains the people in the wilderness.[6] Miriam is often connected to water, from the moment she watches over and preserves the life of her brother, Moses, through her demonstration of leadership in bringing the women's voices, instruments, and dancing to the song at the sea. Water can be seen as the inspiration for and primary instrument of Miriam's role as priestess.

The second biblical prophetess is also a wielder of tribal power. In Judges 4:4-5 we read:

> *Deborah, wife of Lappidot, was a prophetess; she judged Israel at that time. She used to sit under the palm tree of Deborah, between Ramah and Beth El in the hills of Ephraim, and the Israelites went up to her for judgment.*

Judges were charismatic military leaders and governors, inspired by God to preserve the Israelite tribes. Deborah is described as both judge and prophet. The palm tree of Deborah is probably a shrine or pilgrimage location—the people "went up" to her, and the verb is the same as "to go on pilgrimage."

Since the location of her tree is so carefully given, Deborah is probably a known and respected shrine priestess who gives oracles to those who come to request them of her. As noted in chapter 1, the word Deborah or bee may be related to Greek words for priestess that mean "bee," and the Delphic oracle was called "bee." The Hebrew word for "bee" is related to "shrine" (*devir*) and "word" (*davar*). The linguistic congruity strengthens the theory that Deborah is a shrine oracle—a dispenser of words (*devarim*) at the shrine (*devir*).[7]

It is likely that Rebecca, in distress in Genesis, seeks out a similar oracle when she goes to "seek God" to determine why her pregnancy has become so difficult.[8] Rebecca's nurse, who travels with Rebecca to Canaan when Rebecca marries, is also named Deborah. That Deborah is also associated with a sacred tree: Allon-Bakhut. This connection is too faint to fully interpret, but it could be that Deborah was a title for oracles in ancient Israel and that oracle-shrines centered on sacred trees.

The Deborah of Judges summons an Israelite general, Barak, and tells him that God has commanded him to strike Israel's enemies: the warriors of King Jabin of Canaan and the general Sisera. Barak replies: "If you will go with me, I will go, and if not, I will not go." Barak either sees Deborah as a holy woman who can guarantee his victory, or wants to make sure she believes in her own prophecy. In response to Barak's request, Deborah utters an oracle:

> *I will surely go with you, but it will not be to your glory, this road you are walking, for into a woman's hands YHWH will deliver Sisera.*
> —Judges 4:9

This seems like Deborah chastising Barak for his trepidation, but as the reader will soon learn, it is a prophecy. Barak will win the battle, the enemy general Sisera will flee, and a nomad woman named Yael will invite Sisera into her tent and kill him while he is sleeping. There is no way Deborah could know this except by divine inspiration. The Deborah story ends with a poem sung by Deborah and Barak, just as Moses and Miriam sing the Song at the Sea together; in it, Deborah refers multiple times to her leadership of the people and her pride in their victory, and also retells the story of Yael, the surprise heroine of the story.

In II Kings 22, we meet the prophetess Huldah. During the reign of King Josiah, a scribe named Shaphan finds an unknown scroll in the Temple, believed by many to be Deuteronomy, which demands strict monotheism from the Temple cult and threatens punishment if this discipline is not followed. The scribe reports the scroll's existence to the king. The king sends the scribe, the high priest Hilkiah, and the king's minister to the prophetess Huldah, to ask if the scroll is authentically God's word.

Huldah the prophetess is wife to Shallum son of Tikvah son of Harhas, *shomer habegadim* or keeper of the wardrobe. It is probable that Shallum takes care of priestly clothes, and may well be a priest himself, which would make Huldah a member of the priestly clan (a *kohenet*, in mishnaic terms). The couple lives in the Mishneh (second district) of Jerusalem. Huldah confirms that the scroll is accurate and that the punishments are real:

> *Thus says YHWH the God of Israel: I am going to bring disaster on this place and its inhabitants in accordance with the words of the scroll...because your heart was softened and you humbled yourself before YHWH... I will gather you to your fathers and you will be laid in your tomb in peace. Your eyes will not see all the evil I will bring upon this place.*
> —II Kings 22:19-20

Huldah goes beyond confirming the words of the scroll. Her pronouncement that because the king has listened to God, he will have a peaceful reign and will not see the exile that is to come has the character of ecstatic prophesy, and as a result King Josiah conducts a purge of all gods, goddesses, and religious practices not connected to YHWH. Josiah's soldiers burn the Asherah, and her devotees are expelled from the Temple. Huldah acts as the *mahhutu*, the king's prophetess—supporting the king's power over the people's religion.

It is interesting, to say the least, that a female oracle takes this role. This may be a co-opting of prophetesses—a way of saying that women too support the new monotheism, and that there is a role for them in that new religious model in spite of its restrictions on women's cultic participation. This text may have been written after the Exile to affirm the sacred status of the Deuteronomic code—and to encourage Israelite/Jewish women to adopt the new view of Judaism.

Like the prophets of ancient Israel, the prophetesses have a relationship not only to ritual but to ethics. Deborah counsels courage, Miriam decries the abuse of power, and Huldah affirms the Deuteronomic morality. All three women also have something of the warrior in them—each one celebrates victory or counsels the overthrow of an enemy.

Prophetesses in the Roman Period and the Talmud

The New Testament portrays several prophetesses. In Luke 2:36, Anna is a prophetess who prophesies the coming of Jesus as Messiah. She is portrayed as a woman who is constantly in the Temple: "She was a widow of about eighty-four years, who departed not from the Temple, but served God with fastings and prayers night and day." As with Miriam and Deborah, there is a connection between the prophetess and the priestly cult.

Between the first century BCE and the first century CE, in Thyatira in present-day Turkey, there was a shrine to a sibyl or prophetess named Sambathe (sometimes called Sabbe). She is said to have been Jewish, though this is disputed. A body of poetry called the Sibylline Oracle was believed to be her work, though scholars now believe it is a composite. Like many biblical prophets, the sibyl emphasizes the importance of piety and righteousness:

> *There is a city Chaldean Ur*
> *whence come the race of upright people who are right-minded,*
> *with good works...*
> *They do not, Chaldean fashion, astrologize, nor watch the stars,*
> *But they are concerned about righteousness and virtue.*
> *Their measures are just in field and city.*
> *They do not steal from each other by night,*
> *nor drive off herds of oxen and sheep and goats,*
> *nor does neighbor remove a neighbor's landmark,*
> *nor does the wealthy vex the poor one nor oppress widows,*
> *but rather assists them...*[9]

In the early second century CE, the Roman satirist Juvenal makes fun of a Jewish beggar-woman who interprets dreams for a fee, calling her "an interpreter of the laws of Jerusalem, high priestess with a tree as temple, a trusty go-between of high heaven."[10] This tells the reader that Jewish prophetesses existed in Roman times. Juvenal mocks the prophetess as a priestess with a very poor temple indeed, but he does see her as a priestess—and, like Deborah, she is associated with a tree. These textual fragments demonstrate an ongoing connection between prophecy and being a priestess of the shrine of a deity.

The Talmud pays lip service to prophetesses (and numbers among them biblical characters such as Sarah and Abigail who are not obviously prophetesses) but makes every effort to denigrate them and reduce their power. According to the Talmud, there are were seven prophetesses: Sarah, Miriam, Deborah, Hannah, Abigail, Huldah, and Esther.[11] The Talmud makes sure to mention that Miriam's only prophecy is that her brother Moses will be born and redeem the people.[12] Particularly harsh words are reserved for Huldah and Deborah:

> *Rabbi Nachman said: Haughtiness does not become women.*
> *There were two arrogant women, and their names are hateful:*
> *one is called hornet [Deborah, bee] and the other weasel [Huldah, weasel].*
>
> —Babylonian Talmud, Megillah 14b

The Talmud also indicates that Huldah was consulted about the scroll in the Temple only because her cousin Jeremiah was out of town.[13] The Talmud is uncomfortable with prophecy in general because spontaneous prophecy overturns the rabbis' ideas about law and interpretation. Women prophets are particularly troublesome, and so they become targets for particularly sharp barbs and criticism.

However, the Talmud does acknowledge one "female prophet"—a divine one. The sages of the Talmud (200-600 CE) believed that the age of prophecy had come to an end. Nevertheless, sometimes it was possible to hear a *bat kol*—literally, the daughter of a divine voice. This daughter-voice was an echo of the divine word, declaring God's wishes in times of uncertainty. The sages believed that the *bat kol* was the last remnant of the prophetic gift.[14]

There are numerous instances in Rabbinic literature in which people testify to the truth and the *bat kol* confirms what they say. In one of these stories, retold in several versions, the *bat kol* speaks in the court of King Solomon. Solomon is judging the famous case of two mothers. Two women come before Solomon, one with a living infant and one with a dead one. One woman tells Solomon that she is the mother of the living child and the other woman stole it. The second woman denies it, claiming the dead child is the first woman's true child.

Solomon orders a sword to be brought. He proclaims that his judgment is that both the dead child and the living one shall be divided, with half of each child given to each mother. One woman cries, "Give her the live child, and do not kill it!" The other woman callously insists, "The child shall be neither mine nor yours; divide it." Solomon declares that the live child shall be given to the woman who was willing to give it up, "for she is its mother."

As related in the Talmud, a *bat kol* whispers to Solomon that the caring mother is in fact the true mother:

> "*The king said: "Give her the living child, do not kill him, for she is his mother." How did he know? Maybe she was deceiving him! [Maybe she pretended to be compassionate in order to trick the king.] A* bat kol *went forth and said: "She is his mother."*
> —Babylonian Talmud, Makot 23b

The *bat kol* appears as the voice of personal intuition, of prophecy within embodied human experience. Solomon knows which woman is the child's mother, even if he cannot prove it. The *bat kol* inspires Solomon's own words ("She is his mother") as if the Divine Presence Herself, denied the power of speech, must speak through the mouths of humans to express prophetic truth. In this story, the *bat kol* is a kind of prophetess, providing a human voice with Her own words.

The Mystic Prophetesses

With the passage of time, prophetesses continued to inspire the people at moments of transition. Driven from Spain by the Inquisition, the Jews found themselves on the road with no possessions, not knowing where to go or where they might find sanctuary. A monk, Andres Bernaldez, who witnessed the scene wrote: "They left the country in which they were born. Great and small, young and old, on foot, donkeys or in carts, each followed the path to his or her chosen destination. Some stopped at the wayside, some collapsed from exhaustion, others were ill, yet others dying. No fellow creature could have failed to have pity on these unhappy people. All along the way there were constant appeals for them to accept baptism, but their rabbis instructed them to refuse and implored the women to sing, beat their drums, and to uplift their souls."[16]

In the Middle Ages, women who could not claim societal power sometimes were able to speak with divine force. This was true in the Christian community (consider Joan of Arc and Hildegarde of Bingen), and at a certain point we also begin to find this phenomenon among Jews. As mentioned in the introduction, there were a variety of women prophetesses in mystical communities such as Safed in Israel, and within the Sabbatean and Frankist sects. Hayyim Vital, student of the kabbalist Isaac Luria, documented many of these women. While they did not have shrines, these prophetesses continued the tradition of oracular speech that we see in the Bible.

Rachel Aberlin lived in Safed in the 1570s and 80s. Her husband had been close to Luria, and she herself was the sister of a prominent kabbalist. Aberlin saw visions—Vital reports that as he was preaching in Safed in 1578, Aberlin saw a pillar of fire above his head and the prophet Elijah supporting him as he spoke. Vital writes:

> *This woman is accustomed to seeing visions, demons, souls and angels, and most everything she says is correct, from her childhood and through her adulthood.*[17]

Vital and Aberlin became close friends, sharing and interpreting dreams. Aberlin became Vital's supporter and patron. She had a court in Safed where kabbalists could meet and work with one another. The mystics were far more comfortable with prophetesses than the earlier sages. This may have been because they recognized and valued spontaneous experiences of God. Additionally, their traditions already included aspects of the Divine feminine, which in some cases may have made them more aware of and open to women's spiritual experience.

While in Damascus, Vital met another prophetess: a young woman, daughter of Raphael Anav. He reported in his diary that the spirit of a sage possessed the girl and gave instructions to the community concerning repentance and the Messiah. The spirit departed the following week, but the young woman continued to see visions and dreams, by means of "souls and the departed, and angels, and also by means of that spirit on occasion."[18] She even spoke with Isaac Luria himself. These experiences are all congruent with kabbalists' beliefs about mystics channeling souls.

At one point, the daughter of Anav summoned a local kabbalist (one who had offended many local female ecstatics). She invited four deceased sages and an angel to enter the assembly through a mirror, and chastised the sage at length. She then went on to criticize the community at large for its moral failings, and concluded by denouncing Israel Najara, a prominent mystic poet, for sexual transgressions.[19] In her role as spirit channel and enforcer of ethics, the daughter of Anav carried on the tradition of the fiery voices of the prophets.

In the seventeenth century, women followers of Shabbetai Tzvi, the messianic figure, often had visions, trances, and dreams. For example, in Smyrna and Aleppo many women as well as men entered prophetic trance, prophesied that Shabbetai Tzvi was the Messiah, and saw Elijah in dreams or while awake. These trances spread throughout Europe along with the renown of Shabbetai Tzvi as Messiah. Critics were particularly incensed at the strong participation of women in these prophetic activities. A girl from Galata "had a mighty talent for supernal contemplation" and reported that "an angel had appeared to her, garbed in light, and holding a shining sword, and he had told her of the messiah for whom they had so hoped." Some of these women are named specifically: for example, Judith, the wife of Abraham Miguel Cardozo (a Sabbatean prophet), had prophetic visions, and even his little three-year-old daughter was said to experience visions and the sighting of angelic spirits. Jacob Sasportas, an observer, complained: "The spirit of prophecy has taken leave and gone far from the side of the male to the side of the female, nay, to the female of the lowest abyss."[20] The spiritual activities of women—mystical experiences, visions, prophecies, and dreams—in the mystical period show that women continued to engage in the prophetess work of their ancestors, even when others condemned or belittled this work. Women's interest in prophetic/ecstatic movements that had room for their leadership also suggests that some women needed avenues for their mystical experiences.

In the 19th and early 20th centuries, women in the early Chasidic movement were also considered prophetesses. Chasidic traditions relate that Udel (also called Eydl or Hodel), daughter of the Baal Shem Tov, took part in her father's journeys to other worlds, learned combinations of divine names, and received prophetic dreams. Udel's daughter Feiga, the mother of Rabbi Nachman of Breslov and the granddaughter of the Baal Shem Tov, was called a prophetess. Yentl, mother of Rabbi Isaac of Drohobycz, grandmother of Rabbi Michel

Zlochewer, was known as Yentl the prophetess and could sing with angels, according to the traditions about her.[21] In this case as well as in the case of the Sabbatean prophetesses, a young mystical movement with charismatic leadership and limited hierarchy could make room for women as prophetesses, even though they were not part of rabbinic leadership. Being related to powerful men could also put some women in a position to have their gifts recognized.

Locating the Female Prophetic Voice in Modern Times

Today, individuals with a strong sense of mission and justice are viewed by some as prophets. In that sense, activist Jewish women like abolitionist Ernestine Rose, anarchist Emma Goldman, and feminist Betty Friedan stand in the prophetic tradition. Visionaries, artists, and poets who uncover hidden truths and expose them to our sight may also be acting as prophets. And many modern Jews (including Sigmund Freud) have found value in paying attention to the visions we discover in dreams. Modern kabbalist Tamar Frankiel has written a book called *Entering the Temple of Dreams*, and scholar-ritualist Vanessa Ochs is the author of *The Jewish Dream Book*, which offers practices for Jewish dreaming.

Prophetess-Priestess Incarnations

Modern Hebrew priestesses continue to rely on dreams and visions as a source of intuitive wisdom and iconoclastic ideas. Sheva Melmed, a Kohenet Institute graduate, had a dream while in Turkey that speaks to the buried yet partially visible Goddess in the foundation of human history:

> *Traveling in Turkey, I had a powerful dream about a bearded father busying himself in the house, and I went down to the basement, in the rocks, underground to find my mother writing and working next to a goddess shrine. The symbols speak for themselves.*

This dream reflects the work of the priestess: recovering the traces and cords of connection to the face of female divinity that is buried in human history, and more specifically in our Jewish tradition. The mother in this dream is not one mother but all of our mothers who knew the Goddess. The basement is the underworld, the world of the earth and the Goddess, and the basement is also the repressed image of the mother at the core of civilization.

Kohenet Institute graduate Yocheved Landsman once dreamed of a dead turtle head with a seed in its mouth. The turtle traditionally symbolizes the sacred feminine, and in lore it has thirteen sections of its shell—the same number as the moons of the year, the same number as the priestess paths with which we work. As a community, we interpreted this dream to refer to the rebirth of the priestesshood. Yocheved later wrote:

> *As I was meditating this morning in a semi-dream state, I had a vision of the turtle coming up from great depths, swimming slowly upward. I thought of how, when we gathered in circle, I sensed a well in the middle of us: Miriam's well, deep, neverending, springing from the depths of the earth.*

Today, the women of the Kohenet Hebrew Priestess Institute participate in an on-line "dream basket" community, where dreamers can share, discuss, and interpret dreams. We see the dreams as messages both to the individuals who receive them and to the community as a whole. Our work affects the ways we dream: shrines, altars, labyrinths, and offerings frequently appear in our dreams. A number of our students and graduates work deeply with dream interpretation as a tool for healing and as a spiritual practice. We are following in the footsteps of the first dream-prophetesses.

Other Hebrew priestesses focus on the justice-seeking aspects of the prophetess role. Shoshana Bricklin creates *haftarot*, or "readings of the prophets," that "bring ancient and modern voices together to challenge the status quo and transform our world." A *haftarah* is a section of the books of the prophets (such as Isaiah and Jeremiah) that is read after the weekly Torah portion on the Sabbath and holidays. Shoshana chooses modern occasions like Martin Luther King Day and the anniversary of the bombing of Hiroshima and Nagasaki to craft modern prophetic readings.

Hebrew priestess Ellie Barbarash has been a community organizer, labor activist, mother, and musician. Her drum and flute grace many Kohenet Institute ceremonies, and she also engages the practice of speaking truth to power. She writes:

> *The prophetess fills in what is missing: what's not said but everyone feels, when you knows something's there but no one will talk about it. Talking about patterns that need to be understood. Disclosing and unpacking half-truths so everyone can witness them dissolving into clarity. Courage is a sacred language. Telling the truth is a form of prayer.*
>
> *Speaking my truth without enough community support around me burnt me out. I learned that to persist, and succeed in making change, I needed to not work alone. Not only to understand both sides of a story, understand the opposition, but to get others to join with me.*

Spirit Journey
The Prophetess

You are standing at the entrance to a cave in the desert. You hear a drumbeat within the cave. You enter. At the center of the cave is a well, spring, or pond. Drink the water. Feel its healing power flow and grow within you.

As you drink from the well, a woman appears beside you. She may be young or old, willowy or earthy, loving or stern. She guides you to each of the four walls of the cave.

On or near the eastern wall, you see the young Miriam waiting by the Nile. The basket with the baby Moses floats near her. Your guide urges you: "Reach out and pluck a reed from the Nile." You bring the reed to your lips and blow. Notice the qualities of the sound: high or low, sweet or sad, mellow or sharp. "Your song," the guide says. You blow and listen carefully, honoring this song.

You turn to the north. On or near the northern wall, you see Miriam dancing by the sea. Many women with drums accompany her. A drum is at your feet. "Your heart," the guide says to you. Strike the drum and listen to its sound. This is the strength of your heart. Give this strength an honored place inside you.

You turn to the west. On or near the western wall, you see Miriam alone in the desert. Her skin is white, scaly, diseased. Sand blows around her. She is writing in a scroll. "Your truth," your guide tells you. Read the scroll, which contains your story. Take as much time as you need.

You turn to the south. On or near the southern wall, you see Miriam as an old woman resting inside a tent. Her eyes are closed. Around her are many loved ones. At the foot of her bed are many pebbles. "Your dream," says the guide. You close your eyes, and Miriam shares with you an image from her final dream.

Your guide brings you back to the well at the center of the room. Thank her. She places her hands on your head and utters a blessing, giving you the gift of inspiration. As you reach the cave's entrance, turn back and look. The well is gone. A wind lifts you over the desert sands and carries you back to yourself.

She Who Receives Visions
The Practice of Dreamwork
by Taya Shere

We read in the Talmud, "A dream uninterpreted is a letter unread."[23] According to the Zohar, the interpretation of a dream is more important than the dream itself. We offer here core practices of a *Ba'alat Chalom*, a Dream Priestess. May your exploration of dreams and their power bring healing and transformation.

Sacred Sleep

The Hebrew word *chalam* means both to dream and to be in good health. Receiving consistent dream sleep supports physical, emotional and spiritual thriving. Practice a regular sleep routine. Wake and retire each day at roughly the same time. Create ritual to connect you with the sacred immediately before you sleep and immediately upon waking. Be aware of what thoughts are on your mind just before sleep and upon awakening. You might offer traditional Jewish prayers right before sleep (such as the Shema and surrounding evening prayers) and first thing upon awakening (Modah Ani). Or, you might craft your own prayers. When possible, allow yourself space to rejuvenate in reverie, the liminal space between sleeping and waking, before emerging from bed.

Keeping a Dream Journal

Keep your dream journal by your bed, with pen and flashlight, or a simple voice-recording device, from which you might transcribe when you are more fully awake. It is best to make a record of your dreams as soon as possible upon awakening, even before getting out of bed in order to preserve as much detail as possible. If you are not able to record your dream immediately upon awakening, try to do so before leaving the house that day.

While the most common way to record dreams is in writing, you can make use of whatever medium is most resonant for you when you are recording your dreams. Sketch, paint, sculpt in a way that captures the story of your dream.

Dream Incubation/*She'elat Chalom*/Asking a Dream Question

Basic dream incubation (asking for insight through dream) includes clearing your mind before sleep, and grounding and centering yourself. As you are beginning to drift asleep, call to mind your dream question, along with a prayerful request for guidance. You might bring your tallit or Bible or other sacred text with you to bed to support you in your dreaming journey.

The practice of mystical weeping is a dream incubation technique discussed by Isaac Luria, Hayyim Vital, and later Hasidic teachers. Falling asleep weeping is said to clear the soul and to open one to receiving a dream message.

Dreaming in Community

Eve Ilsen, in the tradition of kabbalist Colette Aboulker-Muscat, leads a group dream incubation in which participants sleep in the same space, heads all pointing to the center. They are guided in a day-review practice and also an incubation prayer before sleep. Native American medicine woman LaKota One-Heart guides her students and community in similar group incubation practices, inviting participants to all sleep in the prayer lodge together on nights before ceremonial dances and important rituals.

Dream circles are groups of friends who gather regularly or semi-regularly to meet and state an intention to support each other in dreaming. Dream circle practices and rituals may include prayer, space for dream sharing, and interpretation or dialogue. Gather a dream circle with folks in your community. Or, try a dream chevruta: having a friend with whom you share and interpret your dreams. At Kohenet retreats, we gather circle to share and reflect on our dreams in ritual space, and invite participants to check in with a dream chevruta each morning.

Dream Interpretation

In Kohenet Institute dream circles, in accordance with the kabbalistic teachings of the contemporary mystic Colette, we receive and respond to a dream as if it were our own. When we hear a dream, we listen to it imaging that we had dreamed it. When we respond, we begin, "In my dream of this dream..." We share what we notice or are moved by, or what we feel is important symbology.

The Talmud records the practice of convening a Dream Court, invoking the support of three trusted friends to transform a disturbing dream for good by proclaiming it so.

Another dream ritual is to ask a trusted spiritual teacher or companion to provide a positive interpretation of a frightening dream. For a text of a simple Dream Court Ritual, see *The Jewish Book of Dreaming* by Vanessa Ochs and Elizabeth Ochs. When a Dream Court is not feasible, it is traditional to pray for the transformation of one's dream in a prayer service during the priestly blessing.

Healing and Medicine Dreams

At times, we are gifted with healing or medicine dreams. These dreams have a unique quality, a sacred energy, and a physicality to them. When we awaken, we are aware that simply by the act of dreaming something has transformed. Medicine dreams are gifts from Spirit. Upon receiving them, it is appropriate to give prayers or make offerings of gratitude.

Resources

The Jewish Dream Book by Vanessa Ochs and Elizabeth Ochs (Jewish Lights, 2003). Catherine Shainberg's book *Kabbalah and the Power of Dreaming: Awakening the Visionary Life* (Inner Traditions, 2005) reflects the tradition of French-Algerian kabbalist Colette Aboulker-Muscat.

Chapter 5:
Shrinekeeper-Priestesses

On Yom Kippur in 2007, at the Isabella Freedman Jewish Retreat Center, I served as the leader of the Avodah service, the recitation of the priestly rite of purification for the day. This ancient liturgy describes how, on this most holy day of the year, the high priest would enter the innermost chamber of the Temple, the Holy of Holies, alone. He would perform the prescribed purification ritual, sprinkling blood seven times upon the altar, to cleanse the innermost shrine. The seven-fold sprinkling of blood, corresponding to the seven days in which the world was first created, represented the cleansing of creation itself, as if the high priest were spiritually returning the world to the pure state of its birth. In most Jewish congregations, this recitation is chanted without much explanation, if it is included at all. That year, assisted by women from the Kohenet Hebrew Priestess Institute, I decided to do something different.

I asked someone to make a wooden frame, about the height of a person. This frame was placed about three feet in front of the Ark of the Torah. The frame had white curtains, which were tied back for most of the service. When it came time for the Avodah recitation, I untied the curtains, allowing them to hang freely so that the Ark could not be seen.

One woman read the text of the priestly ritual: the bathing and the putting on of sacred clothes; the prayers for personal and communal forgiveness; the selection by lot of which goat would be sacrificed and which would meet an uncertain fate; the sending away of the scapegoat. Another woman alternated with the first, reading an anthropological text that described rituals of initiation. The juxtaposition of these would make the point that the high priest's ritual was an initiation and transition for the whole community. I stood between the two women, miming the high priest's actions.

There was a basket of red rose petals near the Ark. We invited each member of the community to come up, take a handful of petals, go into the curtained space in front of the ark, and cast them, as if casting the blood of the sacrifice. We began to chant and drum, and a long line formed in front of the ark. As each person passed me, I sprinkled rose petals on them to represent the bathing (and bloodiness) of the high priest. People went into the "holy of holies" one by one, stayed a moment alone in that small space, and came out again. Later, a number of people told me how profoundly affected they had been inside the sacred space we had created; a few told me they had experienced an initiation.

The shrinekeeper-priestess is a guardian of the temple to which people come on pilgrimage. She tends the divine presence through attention to ritual. By preparing the space and guarding the threshold, she creates the separateness and holiness that make a shrine sacred. In creating the impromptu holy of holies, the leaders of this ritual served as shrinekeepers, allowing seekers to experience entry into the sanctum. Ancient shrinekeepers had this same function.

The Biblical Period: Mirror-Priestesses

In reading the description in Exodus of the building of the portable shrine that will accompany the Israelites in the wilderness, we encounter a mysterious verse:

> *He made the laver out of copper, and its base out of copper, from the mirrors of the hosts* (tzovot) *of women who served* (tzavu) *at the entrance of the tabernacle.*
> —Exodus 38:8

The word *tzovot* (sing. *tzovah*) appears only twice in the Bible. In Numbers 4:23, 4:30, and other places, the same *tzadi-bet-alef* root refers to priestly service. It is also related to the hosts of angels (*tzva'ot*) who serve the Holy One. *Tzovot* can mean "hosts of women" or "women who serve as one of many," or "ministering women."[1] The Torah does not explain the term or provide any context.

Nachmanides, a medieval Jewish exegete,[2] sees the mirrors as an indication that these are women like nuns, dedicated to prayer, who have given up vanity:

> *Among the Israelites were certain women dedicated to God's service, who distanced themselves from worldly desire. They donated their mirrors to the Tabernacle, for they had no further use for beauty. These women would come each day to the entrance of the Tent of Meeting to pray and learn the mitzvot.*
> —Nachmanides on Exodus 38:8

However, the mirrors may suggest other readings of the *tzovot*. Kazakh priestesses were buried with bronze mirrors, and priestesses of the Cycladic islands were buried with obsidian mirrors. Hathor's priestesses in Egypt used mirrors to create a trance state during sacred dance, as well as for prophecy. The copper mirror is a symbol for the aspect of beauty and/or prophecy attributed to a number of ancient goddesses: Hathor (Egypt), Oshun (Yoruba), and Aphrodite (Greece). The life-sign of Egypt, the ankh, symbolized both sexual union and a hand-mirror. In India, the Great Goddess, counterpart of Shiva, was called "Mirror of the Abyss."

Mirrors symbolize women not only because women use them but because women create human "reflections" or "doubles" known as babies. Yet mirrors do not merely represent reproduction. In the ancient world, mirrors were considered doorways to the world of spirit. Mirrors function as passageways in and out of spirit-space, just as children emerge from the mysterious soul-world of the womb and into ordinary space.

As a door between the worlds, the mirror is used for divination. The association of *tzovot* with mirrors seems to imply that the mirrors were used for prophetic work, shamanic divination, or priestly ritual.[3] That the women are associated with the entrance to the Tabernacle gives us an idea that their work was sacred and probably had to do with communicating with God. Moses, Aaron, Joshua, and Miriam all speak to God at the door of the tent of meeting. The chieftains gather at the door of the tent of meeting to receive important messages from the Divine.

Gatekeepers had an important role in Near Eastern myth. The gatekeeper of the underworld, Neti, supervised the rituals of entering the world of the dead. The Egyptian god Anubis and goddess Ma'at served a similar role. Priestly gatekeepers existed in Akkadian and Sumerian culture. There are gatekeeping priests recorded later in the Bible, called *shomrei hasaf* (keepers of the threshold).[4] The gatekeeping function of the *tzovot* is part of their sacred status. The door, like the mirror, can be a symbol for a woman, probably due to the "entrance" of a woman's body, the vagina. The role of the women at the door may have to do with the liminality of doorways.

We might imagine these *tzovot* as "priestesses of the door"—diviners, musicians, or ritual gatekeepers who once served the people just outside the Tabernacle or Temple. If so, they may have been kept out of (or eventually excluded from) the inner chambers, which were reserved for priests. The priests who use the washbasins before officiating are using the power of these women's mirrors to enter the spirit world of the Temple. The story of the mirrors being made into the washbasin hints at the conversion of priestess symbols for use by an all-male priesthood.

In the second *tzovot* text, the *mishkan* now dwells permanently in the town of Shiloh, in the tribal lands of Judah. Eli's sons, the priests Hofni and Pinchas, are corrupt. They extort offerings from the people who come to the shrine at Shiloh.

> *Eli was very old. He heard all that his sons were doing to all of Israel, and how they were lying with the women who were tzovot at the door of the tent of meeting. He said to them: "Why do you do these things? I hear evil things about you from everyone."*
> —I Samuel 2:22-23

As in Exodus, the women who are *tzovot* serve at the entrance to the Tent of Meeting—now located the shrine in Shiloh. The priests, Eli's sons, lie with these women. It is possible the priests are harassing and coercing the *tzovot* as they go about their ritual business. Perhaps the priests are having ritual sex with the *tzovot* as part of the shrine's ceremonies. Or perhaps this story was cooked up to discredit the *tzovot* and paint them as sexually loose. In Chapter 7, we will learn that there were women's ritual dances in Shiloh, which gives a further indication that women had a place in the Shiloh cultic rituals. It appears that the *tzovot* were an institution—not random worshippers or even lay prophetesses, but priestesses of some kind. They may even be connected to Miriam, who is also a levitical woman associated with prophecy.

The Biblical Period: Shrine-Priestesses

Shiloh itself is one example of a larger Israelite institution that had priestesses. The Bible refers many times to sacred spaces outside the Temple, known as *bamot* or high places. These were hilltop shrines at which priests, priestesses, and individuals worshipped; some of them were located in cities and were cultic centers. Related places were *matzevot*, or sacred stones, and *asherot*, or sacred trees/pillars. These places could be dedicated to YHWH or to Asherah or other deities. Many texts in the Bible report that these were popular places of worship.

> *The people offered at the shrines, because no house for God's name had been built in those days.*
> —I Kings 3:2

> *They set up for themselves bamot, matzevot, and asherot on every high hill and under every spreading tree. And also kadesh [Asherah-worship] was in the land.*
> —I Kings 14:23-24

Later Deuteronomist theology condemned these shrines and those who worshipped at them, and spoke of repeated purges of the hilltop shrines:

> *You shall utterly destroy the places where the nations you shall dispossess worshipped their gods, on the high mountains, on the hills, and under every green tree.*
> —Deuteronomy 12:2

> *Hezekiah did rightly in the eyes of YHWH… he removed the bamot, he cut down the matzevot, he cut down the asherot.*
> —II Kings 18:4

> *And they will know that I am YHWH, when their people lie slain among their idols around their bamot, on every high hill and on all the mountaintops, under every spreading tree and every leafy oak.*
> —Ezekiel 6:13

However, *bamot* existed alongside the temple for much of its existence. Some rabbinic texts implicitly claim that before the Temple was built, *bamot* were permissible, and anyone could officiate at them. A rabbinic text, Sifra to Lev. 7:6, sanctions the officiation of women at *bamot* prior to the building of the Temple.[5] A text in Hosea tells us that women were priestesses at the *bamot*:

> *They sacrifice on the mountaintops and burn offerings on the hills, under oak, poplar, and terebinth where the shade is pleasant. Therefore your daughters turn to whoredom and your daughters-in-law to adultery... for they go aside with whores, and make offerings with the holy women [kedeishot].*
> —Hosea 4:13

In the Bible, "whoredom" often refers to the worship of other gods. The whores and *kedeishot* here may be shrine-prostitutes, but they may equally well be priestesses who officiated at the shrines through sacrifice. The ritual of cakes for the Queen of Heaven probably occurred at *bamah*-shrines. There were *bamot* in Jerusalem at the gates of the city,[6] and King Solomon was reported to have built shrines for all of his royal wives' gods and goddesses.[7] There is a great deal of archaeological evidence to support the existence of *bamot* at Hazor, Megiddo, Mt. Ebal, Tel el-Mazar, and Shiloh. Altars, offering-urns, enclosed sacred spaces, and other realia, such as Asherah-figurines found at these sites, point clearly to the conclusion that they were holy spaces, shrines.

Women also served as shrinekeepers within the home. Offering-stands have been found within ancient Israelite houses, and maintaining these was likely to have been the work of women. William Dever asserts, based on archeological evidence of home altars, that the women of an Israelite household had a ritual role within the local cult, making offerings in the home and at meals honoring the dead.[8] The moment in Genesis in which Rachel steals her father's household *terafim*,[9] (ancestor-spirits or clan gods), and the scene in the Book of Samuel where Michal daughter of Saul uses *terafim* as a ruse to allow David to escape her father, may reflect that women were keepers of ancestral spirits of the home.[10]

In the Second Temple period, we do not hear of women serving in the Temple. Sacred weavers do still exist (as we discovered in Chapter 3), and there may have been women still serving in the Jewish garrison temples in Egypt (as we learned in Chapter 1). During the Second Temple period, it appears that only male descendants of the Aaronide line tended the central shrine of the Jewish people.

The Talmud and How the Table Became an Altar

> *When the Temple was standing, the altar atoned for sin. Now that the Temple no longer stands, a person's table atones for sin.*
> —Babylonian Talmud, Menachot 97a

> *Those who host Torah scholars in their homes, the Torah considers them as if they offered a tamid-offering in the Temple.*
> —Babylonian Talmud, Berachot 10b

By the time of the Talmud, the primary locus of holy activity among the Jewish people was Torah, but the study of Torah was not accessible to most women. Priesthood was devalued—Aaronide priests were bought off with a few honorary rituals and deprived of spiritual power—and priestesshood had been erased. The synagogue was the gathering place for prayer. While priests may have been leaders in synagogues in the first and second centuries, over time this shifted and rabbis (as well as cantors and poets) became the primary clergy.

In the theology of the sages, prayer became a replacement for sacrifice after the demolition of the Temple. The home table, on which food was served, served as a replacement for the Temple altar if words of Torah were shared there. The Talmud doesn't specifically name women as officiants at the dinner table, but the implication is that if Temple equals home, the family are the priests of the home, and this includes women.

We have already noted the Greek titles sometimes given to Jewish women: *hiereia* (priestess), *mater synagogae* (mother of the synagogue), *archisynagoga* (head of synagogue), and *presbytera* (eldress; also *presbyterissa* or *presbytis*). These women may have been keepers of shrines in ways that were not rabinically documented, but are reflected in these titles of respect.

The Middle Ages and Beyond

The primary Jewish sacred spaces in the Middle Ages were the synagogue and the home. Both the synagogue and the home had elements that once existed in the Temple—an ark and an eternal light, in the synagogue, and a table on which ritual meals were eaten, at home. There were female shrinekeepers in both places.

CHAPTER 5: SHRINEKEEPER-PRIESTESSES

For hundreds of years, from the twelfth century until the twentieth, there were female cantors who led the women's section of the synagogue in prayer. These women received the title *firzogerin* or foresayer, or sometimes *zogerke* (sayer or reciter). Eleazar ben Judah of Worms, in the late twelfth century, eulogized his wife Dulcie as "chief of the synagogue singers" and noted that she knew "the order of the morning and evening prayers. In all the cities she taught women, enabling their pleasant intoning of songs."[11] A *firzogerin* had to be educated in Jewish liturgy as well as spiritually gifted. She was often from a rabbinic or cantorial family. Sometimes mothers passed down their office to daughters for several generations.

In the thirteenth century, Richenza of Nurenberg is named as a leader in the women's synagogue in a martyrology book. Urania of Worms, the daughter of a cantor, "officiated before the women to whom she sang the hymnal portions."[12] In the fourteenth century, Guta bat Nathan was "the important young woman who prayed for the women in her gentle prayers." In Rome in the sixteenth century, Anna d'Arpino led synagogue services in the women's section and was paid to do so.[13] The fourteenth century "rabbessa" Ceti of Zaragoza probably held a similar office.[14] Despite the religious limitations placed on European women in this period, the prayer needs of women were such that they had ritual prayer leaders—essentially, their own clergy. Some Sephardic communities had a similar custom. In 1715 in Suriname, Rachel Mendes Meza is identified on her tombstone as a *chazzan*, a cantor—even though normally this was not a title available to women. Presumably Mendes Meza was the equivalent of a *firzogerin*.[15]

A study of the shtetl, *Life is with People*,[16] states that the *firzogerin* "is able to read and understand Hebrew. She reads the prayers and they repeat it after her, following each syllable and intonation." This repetition by illiterate women often became a source of humor. Roiza Baila Charnachapka Jedwab, a *firzogerin* in the town of Drobnin, Poland, in the first half of the twentieth century, recalled telling her young son, "The key is under the doormat" so that he could go home from shul alone, and hearing the whole women's section drone in response: "The key is under the doormat."[17] Jewish women also were shrinekeepers of the home. Chapter 8, "Mother-Priestess," details how Jewish women light candles in the home just as the high priest did in the Temple. Ashkenazi Jewish women prayed over household tasks as if they were tasks performed in the Temple. Jewish women were exhorted to keep their homes pure and their children's environment sacred. The Talmud texts about the table as altar (and therefore the home as Temple) were reinterpreted to describe Jewish women as priestesses of the home.

In 1925, Rebekah Bettelheim Kohut, leader of the New York Council of Jewish Women, noted as an important development "the emergence of the Jewess not only as high priestess of the home but in the larger position, as high priestess of the higher life." The twentieth century saw the beginnings of a rabbinate for women: Ray Frank's impromptu rabbinate in the United States and the ordination of Regina Jonas in Germany (Jonas later died in the Holocaust).[18]

In 1972, after a lengthy debate about Jewish law and society, the Reform movement ordained its first woman rabbi, Sally Priesand, followed by the Reconstructionist movement in 1974 with Sandy Eisenberg Sasso and the Conservative movement in 1985 with Amy Eilberg. Women were also admitted to the cantorate. Several Orthodox women have also received ordination: In 2010 in New York, Rabbi Avi Weiss ordained Sara Hurwitz a *rabbah* (female rabbi), sparking widespread controversy. In the American Jewish liberal community, the number of women who preside over synagogue ritual continues to grow.

Shrinekeeper-Priestess Incarnations

Sarah Bracha Gershuny, a rabbi and Kohenet Hebrew Priestess Institute graduate,[19] carries a pouch of priestess tools: a knife, a firestarter, a bundle of incense. These are practical tools for creating sacred space. She writes:

> *Many experiences and roles inform my work as a tzovah: these include facilitating ritual and prayer experiences as a rabbinic figure; but also my experiences as a teacher of groups of children, teens and adults, my experiences as a witness, conscious listener, counselor and guide, and also my own experience of living in a shrine of my own making.*

Sarah Bracha once dreamed of a white tree with fiery leaves:

> *I dreamt of a place where there stood a beautiful white-barked tree alone in the middle of a field or glade, with leaves all of red and orange and gold. Very still and hushed and magical. Nothing was moving there, but the place was humming with a sense of expectation.*

The white tree with fiery leaves perhaps represent the menorah, the lamp shaped like a tree of fire. The tree is orange-leaved as if it is autumn, and there is a feeling of waiting, almost as if the sacred tree is about to be reborn. This lamp is a symbol of the heart of the Temple—woman as Shrinekeeper. The silence around the tree is the peace of the shrine, the inner humming of a place of power.

CHAPTER 5: SHRINEKEEPER-PRIESTESSES

When doing ritual, Ketzirah Lesser, a graduate of the Kohenet Institute, pays special attention to ways of creating a doorway into sacred space and time:

> *For me, sacred space is a matter of a shift of mindsets. Even land or places that become sacred are sacred because something happened there. The Western Wall isn't inherently sacred, but the centuries of people praying there have imbued it with sacredness. The cycles of the moon, the cycles of the seasons—they exist, whether we pay attention to them or not. The sacredness comes out of how we perceive them. The cycles matter because of the effect that they have on people.*
>
> *Repeated ritual unifies. A ritual done over time gains power because it is a repeated action. The first time you do something, it can be powerful, but there's no history to it and nothing to build on. Each time the ritual is done, it collects collective memory around it that helps to fuel it as it goes forward.*

When she works as a priestess, Ketzirah takes on the role of the spiritual gatekeeper—not only in the sense of one who lets someone in or out, but one who understands the workings of the door itself.

> *The* tzovah *is the guardian of gateways. This may not be about making someone comfortable, but rather about knowing how to open the right doorways and also how to close those doorways. If you're doing a ritual as priestess, your job is to know how to open that gate, and also how to close down whatever you open up.*

Annie Matan is a Kohenet ordinee, prayer leader, and musical performer. She says: "I see myself as a *tzovah*, a keeper of sacred space. People come to me to talk through things, to reflect. I feel that's priestess work." Like the Levites of old, Annie composes songs and poems, passionate in her intense expression of God/dess's love. As part of her graduation requirements at the Kohenet Institute, Annie wrote about the *tzovah* in the following way:

> *I can dip my hand into a well*
> *Stir my reflection*
> *And open the way…*
>
> *I am the guardian of the entrance*
> *I see into the hearts and souls of all who pass through my gates*
> *I am a sentinel at my post*

Refusing entry to the foolhardy and the unready
I hold the key to the lock on the door to forbidden worlds
I am a signpost pointing you on your way

My Temple is a holy place
To be entered with intention
When you are ready to be born again
I will prepare the way for you
You will awake as from a dream
I am your mirror
I am your water-bearer
I will bring you home.

At a number of rituals of the Kohenet Hebrew Priestess Institute, some of the ritual participants are assigned as gatekeepers. These ceremonial greeters wash guests' hands, anoint them with fragrant oil, or otherwise mark the entry into sacred space as a significant moment worthy of witness. In this way, we honor the ancient function of the *tzovot*, the women who stood at the door to the shrine, and at the door between the worlds.

Spirit Journey
The Shrinekeeper

Visualize a sacred place before you. It may be a temple, a holy tree or well, a lonely altar on a mountaintop, or anything else you imagine. This is the shrine you have been called to serve. Notice the time of day, the season, and the surroundings of the shrine.

Approach the shrine. A washing basin is before you. You bend down to wash your face, hands, and feet. The washing basin is lined with mirrors. You see yourself reflected as you wash. What do you see? How do you feel about what you see?

A priestess comes to greet you. She has brought you the garments of the high priestess of this place. There are a number of garments, each one very holy. She brings you to a place where you can dress. Visualize each priestly garment as you receive it and put it on. As you do this, discover whom you are here to serve, and what your offering must be.

Now enter the sacred place to perform your worship. The priestess may lead you to the shrine, you may be part of a grand procession, or you may come to the innermost holy space on your own. Bow low if that seems right to you, or take some other posture that indicates your reverence. Perform the ritual actions that you have come here to perform. Make your offering. What happens? Does something/someone appear? Does fire consume your offering? Is there a peaceful silence? See what comes. What you see and hear will tell you something about how your spiritual practice can unfold and grow.

Perform your rituals of farewell. Return past the laver to the place where you dressed in the priestly garments. Take off the priestly garments and return them to the priestess, thanking her. Keep one for yourself that means something special to you. Leave the area of the shrine and return to your waking self.

She Who Creates Sacred Space
The Practice of Altar-Craft
by Taya Shere

The shrinekeeper-priestess tends sacred space. An altar is a dedicated sacred space for connecting with, honoring, or being in communication with spirit realms. Altars are a tool for encountering and being in dialogue with divinity. An altar may be a vast collection of ritual objects, or as simple as a single item placed in a special way to symbolize or magnetize a particular energy. To experience the power and possibility of this practice, make an altar inside your home or in a dedicated outdoor or indoor space.

Intention

Altars often emerge where intuitive knowing and intentional crafting meet. You might choose to discern the purpose of your altar before you begin creating it, or its intention may emerge as it evolves.

Reflect on the purpose of altar you are creating or that is already in your space. Is it an altar to connect with or welcome a particular aspect of Spirit? Is it an altar celebrating your ancestors or loved ones? Or are you creating your altar to celebrate a particular elemental energy, season or holy day? Allow yourself to be guided to shapes and elements and objects without questioning yourself about why they are there.

Elements

At Kohenet retreats, we dedicate each retreat to an element. During our water week, we have a bowl to which each woman brings water that is sacred to her. During our air week, women bring feathers, vials of sacred scent oils, and aromatic incenses. During our fire week, women light candles and bring dragon, lizard, and snake figurines; creative projects in process; and Shabbat candlesticks. During our earth week, we craft our central altar with stones and any natural items that are connected to soil, grounding, and the element of earth.

If you are called to craft an elemental altar, decide on a location and bring together representations of earth, water, air, and fire. How does the process of crafting your altar support you regarding your relationship with elemental energies in your life? What elements are you particularly drawn to? What do you find yourself resisting or pushing away?

"Objects" from the Natural World

Many altars include items from the natural world. While it is easy to refer to these as objects, a recognition of the sacredness in the natural world is intrinsic to the altar-craft process itself. So while we might speak about a pinecone or a turtle shell as an object on an altar, it is an important part of altar-making to remember the living connections of these things, and to engage them in a way that honors the ways they are an essential and sacred aspect of creation.

Directions

Many communities work with four directions: North, East, South, and West. Others include Earth, Sky, and Center as directions as well. Jewish tradition also honors the elements and directions. Within Jewish tradition, the elemental materials and location in space are sacred: "Fire, air, earth, and water are the sources and roots of all things above and below, and on them are all things grounded."[20]

Become conscious of the directions in relation to your altar. What do you feel happening North, East, South, or West of you? While the east might traditionally bring an energy of air, if you are creating an altar in a place that has an ocean immediately to the east, you might decide to work with place-based directional associations instead.

Seasonal or Holy Day Altars

Altars can be created to bring additional meaning and power into Jewish holidays and to the seasons, equinoxes, and solstices. Crafting altars for Jewish and other holidays often begins with attention to the energies of that holiday—whether it is sap rising on *Tu Bishvat* (The New Year of the Trees), liberation during Passover, or revelation on Shavuot. Working with altars for these holidays can add depth to your practice, and allow you to tap into the sacred yearly cycles.

Priestess Path / Archetype Altars

If you feel called to working deeply with a particular priestess path offered in this book, create a shrine to this energy. For example, how would you create a shrine to the Lover energy—in the universe or in you? How might you envision your entire home space, or one area of it, as an altar to the Lover? If you choose to engage your bedroom as a Lover altar, you might think about how your sheets, pillows, and blankets connect you to your inner lover. Are there textures and colors pleasing to you and in resonance with lover energy?

Keeping Altars

You may decide to keep an altar in a fixed position for a set period of time and return to it again and again as part of a commitment to cultivating a particular experience. You may decide to transform your altar on a regular basis: daily, weekly, or monthly.

When first building altars, I created elemental altars (one in each of the four directions) every night before bed. I dismantled them each morning, and created them anew, different, again each night. This practice of altar creation and release became a profound tool for creative and spiritual expression, and for tracking, deepening, and expanding my journey. At this writing, altar-practice is more integrated into the landscape of my life. I tend home as altar–bed, bookshelf and counters kept as sacred. I refresh the altar of my space with care, revisioning at moments of seasonal shift or to support transition. I experience body as temple and adorn accordingly.

Tend your altar(s) with care. Keep the space clean and clear. Refresh bowls of water. Keeping candles regularly lighted and surfaces free of dust is essential. Pay attention when it is time to change the energy of an altar. Don't let altars stagnate. If something needs to shift, play with possibilities and see what emerges. If it is time to let the whole altar go, be willing to dismantle it gently, or with gusto, depending on what is called for. Give ritual water to the earth, recycle or burn papers, bury rocks or toss feathers to the wind. Compost and create anew.

Resources

For information on Jewish understandings on the energetics of sacred space, read *Between Heaven and Earth: Re-envisioning Synagogue Space* by Kaya Stern-Kaufman (rabbinic thesis, Academy for Jewish Religion, 2010). For inspiring images toward creating home as an altar, read *Altar Your Space: A Guide to the Restorative Home* by Jagatjoti Singh Khalsa (Mandala Publishing, 2007. For ways to work with elements in creating home altars, read *Feng Shui for the Soul* by Denise Linn (Hay House, 2000).

Chapter 6:
Witch-Priestesses

My wife Shoshana lost her mother the year we got married. At the burial, Shoshana felt a sudden urge to put a feather in the grave—specifically, a white feather a friend had given her at the funeral ceremony. I searched for it frantically but could not find it. A couple, friends of ours, asked me what I was looking for. "A white feather," I explained. "We have a white feather in our car," they exclaimed, and went and got it. The beautiful, soft feather went into the grave. Shoshana and I decided we would put white feathers in every grave we witnessed, to represent the soul sheltered beneath Shekhinah's wings.

Several years later the Kohenet Hebrew Priestess Institute was three years old, and we were about to ordain our first group of Hebrew priestesses. All the women who were to be involved in the ceremony went to the local lake for our ritual bath—a traditional Jewish cleansing ritual. Shoshana realized she needed to invite her mother's spirit to the ceremony, just as Jewish brides had once invited the souls of their deceased parents to a wedding. She went to one of the women who was to be ordained, already a skilled shamaness, and asked how to invite her mother to the ritual. She was told that she should invite the spirit by name and offer chocolate.

Shoshana spoke to her mother's spirit, but she didn't have any chocolate. She went to immerse in the lake. As she began to swim back to shore, she saw a single white feather floating toward her, one exactly like the feather that she had placed in her mother's grave. When she looked around, there was not a bird to be found on the pond. As she climbed out of the water, she saw an empty chocolate wrapper lying on the dock. She felt certain her mother had accepted the invitation to the ceremony.

Three years later, Shoshana went back to the same lake, with a friend and former student, to ritually immerse prior to the second Kohenet Institute ordination. A flock of geese landed right next to the two women, coming unusually close, while they were immersing. When Shoshana came up from the water, hundreds of white feathers were floating toward her.

A shamaness (sometimes known as a witch) is also a kind of priestess: one who mediates between the spirit world and the human community. She is a channel to the ancestors and the forces of nature. She is a diviner and an interpreter of signs. She is a healer and a spirit voyager. She knows the ways of the universe: how it unfolds, how it speaks.

The Witch in the Bible

The Bible bans "witchcraft" and specific magical practices including: divination, even though high priests divine using the breastplate; interpreting of signs, even though the prophets interpret signs; and communication with spirits, although numerous biblical characters communicate with angels. Exodus 22:18 famously declares: "You shall not allow a witch to live." In the Exodus verse, the witch is specifically female (*mechashefa*), but Deuteronomy broadens the prohibition to include men. It is unclear when or if these prohibitions were enforced.

> *There shall not be among you one who passes his son or daughter over the fire, one who performs magic, a medium, a diviner, or a sorcerer, a spell-caster, one who inquires of ancestor spirits, a wizard (lit. knowing one), or one who seeks out the dead.*
> —Deuteronomy 18:10-11

Other biblical texts concur. Ezekiel condemns women for doing witchcraft together with one another to kill people or save their lives.[1] The Book of Kings refers to Jezebel as a witch[2], and the book of Jeremiah describes a city as full of witchcraft[3].

Shaman and scholar Alexei Kondratiev believes that the Bible condemns magic and divination because it involves contact with the deceased[4]. Adonai/Yahweh is a transcendent sky-god. The cycles of life and death are chthonic (related to the underworld) and polluting for Him. This is an explanation for why priests of the line of Aaron may not approach dead bodies. Deuteronomy prescribes a particular formula to be recited by pilgrims over the harvest offering. Part of it reads: "I have not eaten of it while in mourning, I have not cleared any of it out while impure, I have not offered it to the dead."[5] Women were particularly involved in local death rites, and their status as religious officiants may have been affected by such pronouncements[6].

Women's ritual around the world tends to be less liturgy-based and more centered in what anthropologist Carol Meyers calls "religious culture"—feasts, sacred crafts, sacred objects, and gestures. "The religious lives of women in particular are characterized by non-verbal or non-textual activities."[7] Often these activities, such as ritual objects like amulets or placing a red ribbon on a crib, are called "magic." Women's magic is particularly likely to go unrespected and unrecorded. The Bible's prohibition on witchcraft may have meant that many spiritual activities of women would have been forbidden or ignored, while prophets and priests, who performed similar functions in more "orthodox" ways, would have been honored.

CHAPTER 6: WITCH-PRIESTESSES

However, local shamanic activity went on despite the prohibitions. There is one biblical scene where we can watch a witch in action. She is called the Witch of Endor. Endor is the name of her town, and it also means "well of generations." This is a clue to the nature of the Hebrew shamaness: She is keeper of the well of the ancestors. She has access to the wisdom of She'ol: the place deep within the earth where the dead sleep.

In I Samuel 28:3-25, the prophet Samuel has turned against King Saul, saying that God has rejected him. Saul consults dreams, divining tools, and prophets, all to no avail. Saul has passed a law forbidding mediums and witches, but in his distress, he ignores his own law and goes to a witch or shamaness, an *eishet ba'alat ov*, to ask for help. The word *ov* comes from the same word for *av*, father, and probably means an ancestor. This woman is a *baalat ov*, a keeper of an ancestor spirit.

> Saul disguised himself and put on different clothes. He and two men went to the woman at night, and Saul said: "Divine for me (kasami na) *and bring up for me the one I shall tell you.*" The woman said to him: "Don't you know what King Saul has done, how he has banned women-who-divine-by-the ancestors (ovot), *and the knowing-ones* (yidonim) *from the land? Why are you trying to get me killed?* Saul swore to her by Adonai and said: "As Adonai lives, you won't be considered a criminal for doing this."

The witch of Endor is afraid for her life if she practices her craft, because of Saul's law. She fears her visitor is trying to entrap her. Saul reassures the woman that she will not be punished, and she agrees to go forward.

> *The woman asked:* "Whom should I bring up for you?" *and Saul answered:* "Bring up Samuel for me."
>
> *The woman saw Samuel, and cried in a loud voice, and said to Saul:* 'Why have you deceived me? You are Saul!" *The king said to her:* 'Don't be afraid. What do you see?" *The woman said to Saul:* "I see a god/gods arising from the earth." *He said to her:* "What does he look like?" *She answered:* "An old man arises, and he is wrapped in a robe." *Saul knew that it was Samuel, and he bowed low with his face to the ground.*

When the witch sees Samuel, she realizes her visitor is Saul, perhaps because she knows the prophet Samuel would not arise from the land of the dead for anyone but the king. The witch's mention of "gods" may indicate that she usually works through a particular deity or deities, which might make her a priestess of that deity. She sees Samuel as an old man wrapped in a *me'il* or robe.

The *me'il* is significant and poignant. When the prophet Samuel was a little boy, his mother Hannah (from whom he was separated when he was a few years old) brings him a little *me'il* or coat every year when she comes on pilgrimage to the Temple. It is, perhaps, this *me'il* that Samuel wears in death. The witch accurately perceives Samuel's true nature: the little child who longs for his mother's love.

But Samuel has no good news for Saul. "Why have you disturbed me by raising me?" the dead prophet demands. Samuel goes on to deliver the grim prophecy that Saul will die the next day in battle with his enemies, and Saul's sons will die as well. "Tomorrow," Samuel cries, "you and your sons will be with me!" Terrified, Saul falls on his face.

> *The woman went to Saul and saw that he was terrified. She said to him: "Look, your handmaid listened to you—I took my life in my hands by listening to you! So now, you listen to your handmaid. Let me put before you a loaf of bread, and you eat. Then you will have strength for your journey."*
>
> *Saul refused and said: "I will not eat." But his servants and the woman urged him, and he listened, and got up from the ground, and sat on the bed. The woman had a calf in the house, and she slaughtered it and took flour and kneaded bread, and made matzah. She set [the meal] before Saul and his servants, and they ate, and arose, and departed [journeyed] that night.*

The witch of Endor is kind to Saul even when his prophet and his deity have rejected him. Like Sarah, she offers hospitality to strangers and feeds them her best food. She is engaging in good shamanic practice: after a spirit journey, eating is necessary to reground the body. She is also honoring the spirits by preparing a ritual meal following the spirit journey.

In her words to him, the witch gives Saul a teaching about his death: *yihiyeh becha koach ki telekh baderekh*—"there will be strength in you as you go out on your journey." The witch's words can apply equally to Saul's journey away from her house, and to his journey away from the world. She reminds Saul to spiritually prepare for the journey he must make.

It is possible to depict what the witch of Endor does as charlatanry. However, encounters with the dead are a real experience for many people: intimations of the presence of a dead parent; the intercession of rebbes and saints; the sudden, inexplicable, accurate knowledge of the death of a loved one. Science and theology may explain these experiences away, but they are common and powerful. The gifted shaman/ess is equipped with a language to deal with these experiences and give them meaning.

Witches in the Book of Enoch

In the third century BCE, the apocryphal Book of Enoch describes the journey of the biblical character Enoch through many levels of heaven. In Enoch 1:6-8, the book describes the biblical story early in Genesis in which "sons of God" (probably angels) take human women as wives. The Book of Enoch expands the story by saying that these divine-human marriages were how women learned about witchcraft.

> *They took for themselves, they and all the others with them, took themselves wives, and each chose for himself one. They began to come upon them and cleaved to them and taught them magic and witchcraft and they taught them to cut roots and plants.*[8]

This story provides an origin for the ritual and magical knowledge of women that is unorthodox, sinful, yet powerful and even divine. The women's knowledge is healing knowledge—roots and plants. The story suggests that women's magic was taken seriously and also feared.

In the Testament of Reuben, another work from the same period, the story is reversed—it is women who lead angels astray through witchcraft:

> *...For every woman who carries out these schemes will suffer eternal punishment, for it was thus that they led astray with their witchcraft the Nefilim before the flood.*
> —Testament of Reuben 5:5-6

These tales suggest that Jewish women of the Second Temple period were practitioners of ritual that was called magic or witchcraft. Writers felt a need to explain this phenomenon using a Torah text. The story lets us know that witches were also healers with a knowledge of plant medicine.

Witches in the Talmud

The Talmud condemns witchcraft as vociferously as the Bible does, even though the rabbis of the Talmud often perform miracles, discuss amulets and charms against demons, and do many things that witches do. The sage Abaye describes the difference between permitted and forbidden magic as follows:

> *Abaye said: The laws of sorcerers are like those of the Sabbath: certain actions are punished by stoning, some are exempt from punishment, yet forbidden, while others are entirely permitted. Thus, if one actually performs magic, one is stoned, if one creates an illusion, one is exempt, while what is entirely permitted? That*

> which was done by Rabbi Chanina and Rabbi Oshaya, who spent every Sabbath eve in studying the laws of Creation, and through it they would create a third-year calf and eat it...
> —Babylonian Talmud, Sanhedrin 67b

When the sages actually go about creating an animal through study and incantation, this is considered permissible because their power is God's power. The magical power of witches is considered demonic. One talmudic story tells of a rabbi named Shimon ben Shetach who burned eighty witches[9].

The Talmud speaks of many duels between rabbis and witches. In these duels, rabbis and witches both know the ins and outs of sorcery even if only rabbis are "sanctioned" to practice. Here is one such story:

> Yannai came to an inn. He said to them: give me some water to drink... Seeing the lips of the woman move, he spilled a little and it turned to snakes... He gave her to drink, and she was turned into a donkey, and he rode on her into the market. But then her friend came and broke the charm, and he was seen riding on a woman in public.
> —Babylonian Talmud, Sanhedrin 67b

A woman attempts to harm a sage by magic. The sage turns out to be a magician too, and he changes her into a donkey—a work animal, perhaps indicating what he thinks of women. Yet her friend and partner in witchcraft (*chaverta*; the same word that is used for a rabbi's study companion!) is able to intervene and change her back into a woman—thus embarrassing the rabbi and perhaps reminding him of the ways in which he desires and needs women. Yannai's ride on a woman is a funny image, but it also reminds us of the power of sexuality, as well as all the ways we "ride" on our mothers and other women, physically and emotionally.

> Abaye said: My mother told me all incantations that are repeated should mention the mother, and all ties [of an amulet] must be tied on the left arm. All incantations should be said the proper number of times, and if the number has not been specified, repeat it forty-one times.
> —Babylonian Talmud, Shabbat 66b

Abaye's mother is never called a witch, but her son Abaye, a great Talmud scholar, seems to know an awful lot about magic. He gives instructions for amulet-making. Including the mother's name connects the amulet to the power of birth. Forty-one is the numerical value of *eim*, the Hebrew word for "mother." Abaye's mother is the closest thing the Talmud has to a sanctioned witch.

> *The Sages learned: "If a person was walking outside a town and smelled a good smell; if the majority are heathens, he does not recite a blessing (on the good smell). If the majority are Jews, he does recite the blessing." R. Yose says, "Even if the majority are Jews he still does not recite the blessing, because Jewish women offer incense to witchcraft."*
> —Babylonian Talmud, Berakhot 53a

In other words, so many Jewish women were involved in witchcraft that in a Jewish city the smell of incense was assumed to be part of their rituals. The lighting of incense, once a common ritual in the Temple, had become a part of women's illicit priestesshood.

Witches in Mystical Text

Kabbalists were consummate magicians, using names of God, magical formulae, and amulets in their work. They continued to depict women who used magic as evil—there are no "good witches" in the kabbalah. In the Zohar, demonesses are often described as witches. A medieval mystic, Nachmanides, names the four main demoness-witches: Lilith, Naamah, Igrat, and Mahalat[10]. These four witch-queens rule over the equinoxes and solstices. They are all concubines of Samael, or Satan.

Igrat bat Mahalat is said to prowl the world on Wednesday and Friday nights with 180,000 demons.[11] She became the mother of Ashmedai, the king of demons, after lying with King David in his sleep. She is also said to have provided secret wisdom to the sage Amemar. Mahalat (a daughter of Ishmael in the biblical text) is also a witch—she lives in the desert and performs sorceries.

The mightiest mythic witch is Lilith, who becomes pregnant through nocturnal emissions and gives birth to many demons. Lilith is also responsible for the death of infants. In the Zohar, Lilith is not only a witch but also she seduces God—when Shekhinah is in exile, God copulates with Lilith.[12] Righteous actions are said to pull the Holy One away from Lilith and bring Him back to his proper wife, Shekhinah.

Many charms used by pregnant and birthing women guard against Lilith. A magical bowl from the first century CE, written in Hebrew, reads: "Designated is this bowl for the sealing of the house of this Geyonai bar Mamai, that there flee from him the evil Lilith…" The Babylonian Talmud (Shabbat 151a) says: "It is forbidden for a man to sleep alone in a house, lest Lilith get hold of him."

The Middle Ages

A few texts from the Middle Ages may give us an idea of the place of human witches in Jewish society. Sefer Hasidim, a pietistic German Jewish text from the twelfth century, accuses ritual bath attendants, and also women who attend childbirths (not midwives but something more like doulas or spiritual companions) of performing witchcraft to make labor difficult:

> *In one place where there were many women only few of them were pregnant, whereas in another place almost all are pregnant. They asked a wise man, and the wise man said: "I have investigated, and learned that in the place where they are pregnant, it is because the midwives go with the women to the ritual bath and are happy that they conceive, but in a place where few women conceive it is because those who go with the women to the mikveh are not midwives and they bewitch the women so that they do not become pregnant—so the women will be ritually impure and need to immerse often and pay the mikveh attendants a salary.*
> —Sefer Hasidim

The eleventh century scholar Rashi comments on a story about a gadabout widow named Yohani bat Retavi by saying:

> *She was a widow witch, and when the time came for a woman to give birth she would close her womb with magic, and afterward she would suffer much, and Yochani would say—I will go and beg mercy, perhaps my prayer will be heard, and she would go and reverse her magic, and the baby would come out. Once she had a day laborer in her home when she went to the home of the woman giving birth and her hired help heard the noise of magic rattling in a dish like an infant making noise in its mother's womb, and he came and removed the covers of the dish and the magic escaped and the infant was born. So everyone knew she was a witch.*
> —Rashi to Sotah 22a

Rashi portrays witches as venal and cruel, motivated by greed, enemies to other women. Most women's magic was intended to aid women in childbirth and to prevent illness, but in depictions like this, witches were the source of pain and illness. While there are no indications that the Jewish community executed any Jewish witches, these stories show fear of women who did magic.

Nevertheless, in the Middle Ages and beyond, women were experts at amulets, incantations, and other forms of spiritual protection, particularly around childbirth and children. Women would not have thought of these things as witchcraft—rather they all would have been considered forms of prayer. On the other end of life, Jewish women routinely prayed for and communed with the dead (as in the candlemaking ritual mentioned in chapter 1). Ansky's *The Dybbuk* records the Eastern European custom in which a bride would visit a graveyard to invite a deceased parent to her wedding.

In Sephardic homes, *las buenas madres* (the good women) were elderly women who knew *kozas de mujeres*, women's things: healing, household ritual, and spells[13]. Susan Sered writes about the ways Yemenite and Kurdish Jewish women in Jerusalem continue to do ancestor-work of the kind that has been practiced by Jewish women throughout the centuries. Their spiritual relationship to the ancestors is very similar to shamanic work around the world.

> *Guarding over, petitioning, visiting, and negotiating with ancestors is an important part of their lives... In a variety of rituals, the women "remember their ancestors." These rituals range from lighting candles on the festival of the new moon to visiting cemeteries and holy tombs. The women primarily seek from their ancestors help in caring for both their living and their as yet unborn descendants... The women can communicate with the dead by standing close to the tomb and talking. The dead can communicate by appearing in dreams.*[14]

Turkish Jewish women have a long tradition of magical cures to fix the sick. "These women knew about everything. They used to do it [a cure] for the evil eye, for [illnesses]. They were always respected... They were called *mujeres santas* (saintly women), *mujeres bendichas* (blessed women), and *almas dil Dio* (souls from God, saintly people)."[15] Their families continue these traditions even in America. One descendant of Turkish Jewish healers reports that the women of her family used dried powdered bones, or dried pulverized foreskin from a circumcision, as a medicinal/magical cure[16].

In the United States, contemporary women are recreating Jewish shamanic traditions. Rabbi Geela Rayzel Raphael teaches amulet-making; she is also creating a Jewish tarot deck based on the kabbalah. Miriam Maron and others (women and men) work as Jewish shamans, investigating Judaism as an indigenous shamanic tradition. Some women identify as "Jewitches" and are attempting to blend Judaism with modern American witchcraft traditions[17]. Other Jewish women, like the Wiccan theologian Starhawk, have left their ancestral tradition to pursue Goddess religion and/or witchcraft.

Witch-Priestess Incarnations

Leah Chava Reiner, a Kohenet graduate and earth-based practitioner, sees communion with the spirit world as part of her calling. She tells of an experience while lighting the Shabbat candles:

> *As I began to chant and light the candles, I found myself standing with my mother lighting the candles and then found myself surrounded by all the women in my bloodline, reaching back thousands of years, as they, we lit candles and chanted our faith in the Divine Spirit, our communities and tribes and ourselves. I found myself chanting and crying at the same time, feeling the presence of my ancestors supporting me, knowing that I stand on the foundation of faith they built over many years.*

This experience of being in contact with the ancestors, of having a foot in the spirit world, is an important part of shamanic work. Leah Chava considers her ancestors to be a daily part of her life. A trained shaman, she has recently focused her teaching on inviting Jews to learn about the shamanic qualities of ancient Judaism.

Tiana Mirapae, a shamanic practitioner, herbal healer, and Kohenet graduate, works with Jews to heal their ancestral lineages and deal with generational and Holocaust trauma. She describes her work in terms of indigenous practices found around the world.

> *A Guatemalan shaman told me to look at my own family culture for our shamanic traditions and medicine ways and he was right. As a Hebrew people, we go back thousands of years, tracing our ancestry back to our biblical family and beyond. All the indigenous cultures have a shaman, spirit healer, medicine wo/man. I work with my plant and animal spirit guides; with angels and archangels of various cultures.*

Juna Madrone (also called Tamar) is a healer, body worker, master of the tarot, and environmental/health activist. She acts as a priestess for a group of Jewish women in a remote area on the West Coast. Divination using the tarot (a fifteenth century European card deck with kabbalistic resonance) is part of her daily practice[18].

> *My practice typically consists of beginning the day with ritual hand-washing and blessing. I work with some verses from a prayerbook. I read the day's Torah portion. Throughout the day, I cultivate a spiritual approach to my life, paying attention to*

what opportunities present. I recite the Sh'ma before going to bed. Creating sacred space and ritual is part of my daily work.

Before I work with the cards, I have a ritual I go through inviting the spiritual world to be present. I chant and use my rattle, continuing until I have gotten rid of my rational mind. Then I begin to shuffle, until I can shuffle the deck three times without intrusion of the rational mind. The rattle sound is a spiritual shaft that allows you to penetrate the divine. It's like the shofar—it just cuts through.

There's so much truth in the tarot. Rabbi Nachman of Breslav, who moved away from traditional teaching methods, began using stories. The tarot is similar. We often have rigid precepts in our brains. Truth bumps up against us and we don't recognize it. Tarot cards, like stories, can circumvent the rational mind and give us a blast of truth, a direct soul connection. Tarot allows you to relax the rational mind, and it tricks you, going past your mind into your soul.

Juna, a Kohenet Institute graduate, is not alone in her dedication to divination as a way of communicating with deity. Some Kohenet Institute participants have daily divination practices. Like their earliest ancestors, they are interpreting signs and symbols, using divinatory practice as a way to be in touch with spirit. In many ways, this is like interpreting Torah; it is a creative process that begins with a dialogue between a "text" and the situation of the individual who reads it.

> *Divination is conversation, and therefore two-way, with the divine. It is daily, ordinary, and the ground of my being.*
> —Mei Mei Miriyam Sanford

> *When I divine, I am listening. More importantly, I am channeling, opening myself up and getting my monkey mind out of the way. I'm listening for what is beyond me. I'm listening for the extension of divinity that is willing to talk to people. Listening, seeing what's there, listening to myself.*
> —Carly (Ketzirah) Lesser

Spirit Journey
The Witch

It is night. You are walking in a place known to your ancestors: a shtetl, a nomad's tent, an ancient synagogue, a priestess temple, or your grandmother's house: whatever arises for you. You may see spirits walking here: people you know, people you don't know. The presences you perceive are shadowy, as if they exist in this place and other places at the same time.

You come to a place where there is a fire: a bonfire, fireplace, hearth, lamp, or lit candle. Sit down in this place. Soon someone will come to join you. She wears a veil. She reaches out to hold your hand. Notice what her touch is like: warm or cold, gentle or strong. Then she touches your forehead. Without being told, you know that now you are open to many worlds.

Someone else comes to sit by the fire. This person is someone in the spirit world who needs to speak with you; a loved one, an ancestor of yours, a guardian spirit, a biblical character. Open your heart to what she, he, or it, has to tell you. When the message is finished, thank your visitor. Your visitor will now depart.

Now the witch or shamaness returns. She carries a divination tool: a deck of cards, a pile of stones, whatever you imagine. She lays out a reading in front of you. Do not worry too much about what you see; listen to her voice and watch her face as she tells you what she sees. If you have a question, ask her, and listen to the answer. Thank her as she leaves.

Look into the fire one more time. Then rise and retrace your steps until you come to the place of your waking self.

She Who Receives Signs
The Practice of Divination
by Taya Shere

The Witch-Priestess discovers truths and possibilities through divining: merging sacred tools and symbols with her own intuitive vision. Divination tools—stones, shells, pendulums, cards—are her trusted allies and friends. She finds oracles everywhere, reading messages from birds in the sky, foxes who cross her path, a book falling open to a particular page, and synchronicities and serendipities emerging in the world around her at any given moment.

Prepare Yourself to Divine

Clear space. Put stray items in their place. Reshelve books, file papers, sponge the table, sweep the rug. Smudge with white sage or cedar. As you clean dirt or pockets of chaos from physical spaces, you invite similar clearing internally.

Define Sacred Space

If you are divining at a table, drape it in a fabric that calls to you. Light a candle or incense. If you are outdoors, draw a circle around you with a stick, or delineate sacred space by placing stones as markers around you in the directions of north, east, south, and west.

Turn to the Tools

Choose your tools. Allow yourself to be drawn to the deck, sacred book, or tool that feels most resonant right now. Cards, stones, runes, scrying bowl, dowsing rod or pendulum in hand, center yourself. Feel energy flowing between your hands and the tool inhabiting them.

Intend

Ask a question. State your intention. Call into your mind or heart, silently or aloud, what you are wondering, or what troubles you.

Get Out of the Way

If you are using cards, shuffle your cards and see which cards fall on their own, without needing to be spread or pulled. If you are practicing bibliomancy, allow the book to fall open, and let your fingers rest where they will. If you are divining in nature, allow yourself to be drawn to whatever in nature is speaking most to you, without needing to immediately understand the gift it brings.

Read the Signs

Be curious about what emerges. Words or images or colors on a card, symbols on a rune, textures or shapes of a stone, all carry layers of possible meaning. Interpret according to what jumps out at you. Suspend your analytic mind and open to what intrigues, attracts or repels. The same card or rune can carry vastly different meanings for different people, or for the same person, depending on the time, circumstance and intention of the reading.

Integrate

Journal about what you have received. Share with a friend. Reflect. Give the wisdom born from the uniting of your tools, intention and awareness time to affect you, to integrate and to settle.

Try It Now

If you have never divined before, you may imagine that you have no tools available. Take a moment to divine now. Practice the steps described above, and use this book your tool. Gather yourself and an intention or question, or simply clear your mind to receive whatever message is resonant. Close the book, and then allow it to fall open to any page. Let your finger fall to a passage, phrase or word that has guidance for you now. Welcome to the world of deciphering mystery and of merging messages from beyond with your own intuition.

Resources:

The Encyclopedia of Jewish Myth, Magic and Mysticism by Rabbi Geoffrey W. Dennis (Llewelyn Publications, 2007), *Jewish Magic and Superstition: A Study in Jewish Folk Religion* by Joshua Trachtenberg (recent edition by CreateSpace, 2012), and references to Jewish divination customs in *Divination, Magic and Healing: The Book of Jewish Folklore* by Ronald Isaacs (Jason Aaronson, 1998).

The books *Kabbalistic Tarot: Hebraic Wisdom in the Major and Minor Arcana* by Dovid Krafchow (Inner Traditions, 2005), and *The Oracle of Kabbalah: Mystical Teachings of the Hebrew Letters* by Richard Seidman (Thomas Dunne Books, 2001) offer practical paths of Jewish divination.

Circular, feminist divination decks include the *Motherpeace Tarot* by Vicki Noble and Karen Vogel and *Daughters of the Moon* by Fiona Morgan.

Chapter 7:
Maiden-Priestesses

When I was in my twenties, I dreamed that I climbed to the cave-entrance of an underground palace, situated inside a high mountain. The windows of the palace looked across valleys far below. I was a prince, sent for an unknown reason to this place. In the cavernous throne room, a king with a long beard sat brooding upon his throne. Not far from the throne was a large stone jar with a lid, of the kind you might see in a Roman or Chinese excavation. I went over to the jar and took off the lid. To my surprise, there was a little girl curled up inside the jar, a spindly little girl with wings. I knew I had come to that place to let her out of the jar.

In the next part of the dream, I was a statue. Then I became a princess in embroidered robes, standing in a luxuriant, blossoming garden carved out of the mountainside, looking out at the far valleys. All around me, people gathered in the garden and began to dance, shouting their joy that I had come home.

This dream has meaning for my life, but it is not a dream for me alone. The princess in the garden is the Maiden, teaching the joy of being alive and new in an alive, new world. The little girl in the jar is the trapped soul-spark, the imprisoned child within. In freeing her, we free ourselves. Maiden-priestesses are channels for the life-force in its fragility and its blooming.

The Biblical Period

While we don't think of a biblical priest as a young girl, there is evidence that, like young girls of ancient Greece, young girls of ancient Israel had a ritual role to fill. The Book of Psalms, which records some Temple ritual unmentioned elsewhere in the Bible, mentions the role of drummer-girls in a Temple procession:

> "They see your procession, O God,
> your procession into the sanctuary, my God and King:
> First come singers, then musicians,
> Then girls playing drums [alamot metofefot]."
> —Psalms 68:24-25

The term *alamot* specifically refers to young women or girls. Elsewhere, the same psalm speaks of *mevasrot*, "welcomers," or female musicians spreading the news of a military victory These could in fact be the same girls, since women used drums to announce victory.[1] If Temple processions contained female drummers, this might have implied that at one point Israelite women could enter the sanctuary in something like the role of Levites. Every temple in the ancient Near East had women musicians; it may be that at one time the Temple in Jerusalem did too.

The prophet Jeremiah uses the same image, the drummer-girl, to speak of a newborn Israelite nation returned from exile. Maiden Israel dances and drums in celebration of this renewal:

> *I will build you, and you will be built,*
> *Maiden Israel.*
> *Again you shall adorn yourself with drums*
> *and go out in joyful dances.*
> *Again you shall plant vineyards*
> *on Samaria's hills.*
> —Jeremiah 31:14

Here, the drumming and dancing maiden becomes a symbol of the people's restoration. Yet why would we suppose this young woman has a ritual role, as opposed to a cultural one? The vineyard Jeremiah mentions is important, because it appears that maidens had a special role in blessing the vineyards. Several biblical texts connect maidens to rituals of the grape-harvesting season.

We know from Judges 21:19 that young girls held a dance festival in the vineyards in Shiloh, a holy city. We hear about this festival in a terrible context. During a civil war, the men of the tribe of Benjamin have been prohibited from marrying women of other tribes. With the collusion of the other tribes, the Benjaminites plan to lie in wait for these girls, then rape and forcibly marry them.[2]

> *They said: the festival of God is at Shiloh, one that has happened for many years, north of Bethel and east of Beit Shemesh, on the road that goes up from Bethel to Shechem, south of Levonah.*
>
> *They instructed the Benjaminites: Go and hide in the vineyards. As soon as the girls of Shiloh come out to dance in the dances, go out into the vineyards; each of you seize a wife from the daughters of Shiloh and go to the land of Benjamin.*
> —Judges 21:19-21

Shiloh is a city of pilgrimage because the Tabernacle is there. The girls of Shiloh are performing ritual dances, for we are told this is a "festival of YHWH." Grapes are red like blood. There is a certain poetry in having young girls who have just come to menstruation treading the grapes—reminding the people of the fertility of bodies as well as land.

The story describes violence against these dancers—possibly this tale is a way of controlling and threatening women's ritual. Or, it might be that the story comes as a way of explaining the ritual: At some point, there might have been men going out to meet the dancers for a fertility rite, and this story may record that part of the ritual. Some believe that Greek storytellers altered the story of Persephone from a tale in which the Maiden went to the underworld and returned, to a story where Hades kidnapped and raped the young goddess.[3] It is possible that the biblical story was changed in a similar way, from a women's fertility rite to a story of rape.

In the book of Lamentations, as the poet-singer laments the destroyed Jerusalem, we see a possible confirmation of women's ritual role in the grape harvest.

> *Zion's roads are mourning*
> *For lack of pilgrims*
> *All her gates are desolate*
> *Her priests are sighing,*
> *Her maidens moaning...*
> *The Lord has rejected all the heroes in my midst;*
> *God has proclaimed a festival for breaking my young men.*
> *In the winepress God has trodden*
> *The virgin maiden Judah.*
> —Lamentations 1:15

In biblical poetry, one half of a poetic line often echoes the second half, sometimes adding details or clarifying. In the first part of the quote above, Zion is devoid of pilgrims—the image is one of a reverse pilgrimage festival, with no celebrants, only sufferers. The priests and maidens are paralleled with one another: both are miserable at the desecration of the holy city. Something about the priests and the maidens is similar—perhaps that both priests and maidens are involved in the celebration of harvest ritual.

In the second part of the quote, in words dripping with irony and rage, the poet claims that God has declared a pilgrimage festival for the purpose of killing Israel's warriors. God has invited the enemy to come from far away to destroy the youths of Jerusalem. Meanwhile, God is treading Maiden Judah in the winepress. This is an ironic reference to the maidens treading the grapes during the grape harvest festival. Again, the pilgrimage festivals are a parallel to the maidens and the grape harvest. We can discover why by turning to texts of the Mishnah in the rabbinic period.

The Rabbinic Period

The Talmud, recalling this custom of girls dancing in the vineyards, calls the grape-harvest festival Tu b'Av (the full moon of the summer month of Av) and tells us it was a love holiday. The maidens would also go out to dance, surprisingly enough, on Yom Kippur.

> R. Shimon ben Gamliel said: *The Israelites had no greater holidays than the fifteenth of Av and the Day of Atonement, on which occasions the maidens of Israel used to go out in white garments, borrowed so as not to put to shame one who didn't have a white garment. These garments were dipped in a ritual bath to purify them, and in them the maidens of Israel would go out and dance in the vineyards. The men would go there, and the maidens would say: 'Young man, lift up your eyes and see what you will select...'"*
> —Babylonian Talmud, Taanit 31a

By wearing borrowed garments, the women become equal, part of a sisterhood. The garments are immersed in a ritual bath, as if they are sacred (the curtain of the Holy of Holies, for example, is immersed in a ritual bath).[4] Wearing sacred white garments makes the women resemble priests—or priestesses.

The women dance to awaken the earth, and the relationships on which the women embark represent the fertility of the land itself. It may even be that the romantic meetings were not the original focus of the ritual—the ceremony may have been the sacred ritual of grape-crushing that poured out the red juice of life onto the land.

This ritual seems to have died out before the Talmud was written, since the sages speak of it in the past tense. It reappears in the Middle Ages in mystical text, but not in practice. Recently, modern Israelis have resurrected Tu b'Av as a kind of summertime Valentine's Day.

The Maiden According to Philosophers and Mystics

Until the modern era, most girls in Jewish society have received less education and spiritual attention than boys. The image of the daughter, though, is sometimes an exalted one—if the daughter is God's daughter.

Philo, the Jewish philosopher of first century Alexandria, writes about the Sabbath as Maiden:

> *Some have given to [the Sabbath] the name of the virgin, having before their eyes its surpassing chastity. They also call her the motherless, begotten by the Father of the universe alone...*
> —Philo[5]

In Philo's imagination, the Sabbath is the daughter of God. In Philo's mind, the female is inferior to the male, but the Sabbath is superior to the female because she is "motherless"– the male God is her only parent. The Sabbath—like

Athena who sprang forth from the head of Zeus—is a girl born from the Father God.

The Ethiopian Jews, the Beta Yisrael, have a distinct tradition stretching back to antiquity. They too imagine the Sabbath as divine daughter. The regal and beautiful Sabbath intercedes for mercy on behalf of those who love Her, while condemning those who violate Her. God accedes to all her requests, acting as a doting father. In the book Teezaza Sambat (Commandments of the Sabbath), we learn:

> *God sanctified the Sabbath, glorified Her and blessed Her with the Holy Spirit. The Sabbath will rise from Her seat on Friday at dawn... the archangels will crown the Sabbath of God, and the priests of Heaven will leap for joy...*"[6]
>
> *God said to Her: 'They who honor You are as if they honored Me, they who dismiss You are as if they dismissed Me, they who serve you are as if they served Me, they who receive You are as if they received Me, they who make the Sabbath a delight are considered as if they made a loan to Me...*"[7]

There are other Near Eastern legends where a father deity indulges his daughter—grandfather and magician-god Enki makes a drunken bequest of all the gifts of civilization to the maiden Inanna; besotted father Zeus gives Artemis all the mountains and forests of the world.[8] The Daughter charms her father and begins to exercise power in her own right. The image of Lady Wisdom playing at God's feet in the book of Proverbs is similar.

In later kabbalah, Shekhinah or Divine Presence is the most immanent face of the Divine. She, too, is often described as Maiden or Daughter. Often in patriarchal stories, the Daughter has an absent mother, or no mother at all. In the kabbalah, the Daughter-Sabbath has a supernal Mother, a hidden sacred feminine that is the source of all souls and of all creation. Like Demeter and Persephone meeting after a long winter, Binah and Shekhinah meet on Yom Kippur. Mother joins with Daughter inside the Holy of Holies so that they become one substance:

> *R. Elazar opened the verse: "Who (mi) is this (zot) that comes up from the wilderness?" (Song of Songs 3:6). The words mi and zot denote the two holinesses of the two worlds that is,* binah *and* malkhut *(the upper mother and the lower mother), in a single union and a single bond. This union is the true* olah *(burnt offering) that [on Yom Kippur] becomes the holy of holies.*
>
> —Zohar I, 10a

The Mother has joined the Daughter and the two are become as one.
—Zohar I, 183b

The Maiden Priestess in Jewish Ritual

The custom of rituals for the Maiden continued in the North African Jewish community. In North African Sephardic countries, the seventh night of Chanukah was set aside as *Chag haBanot*, the Festival of the Daughters. *Chag haBanot* falls on the new moon of the Hebrew month of Tevet. In Algeria, Libya, Tunisia, and Morocco, *Chag haBanot* celebrated women and particularly girls. Mothers gave their daughters gifts, and bridegrooms gave gifts to their brides. Girls who were fighting were expected to reconcile on *Chag haBanot*. Rabbis gave sermons about the heroism of women. Another tradition was for women to go to the synagogue, touch the Torah, and pray for the health of their daughters. There might also be a feast in honor of the Chanukah heroine Judith, who saved her town from attackers.[9] This holiday, probably a very old one, acknowledged Jewish girls and blessed them as Maidens.

Among Kurdish Jews, young women went out to the country together on a spring Sabbath called *Shabbat Banot* (Sabbath of the daughters). They would sing, be rowdy with one another, gather wood to heat a bath and bathe all together, and bake "bride cakes." The bath, said to make them beautiful like Queen Esther, must also have been a communal bonding, similar to the dances of Tu b'Av.[10]

The eighteenth-century Frankists, followers of the antinomian sect leader Jacob Frank, regarded the Maiden as a face of the Divine, and as the messianic redeemer. Influenced by the Catholic cult of Our Lady of Czestochowa, Frank asserted to his followers that the Maiden held the reins of spiritual power in the world.

> *Finally, he [Frank] spoke of the Maiden... saying that she is a shepherdess, and that she is the messiah, which has never occurred to anyone before—that the Maiden, who is the Lady, is the redeemer. The main thing is that first of all, the Virgin must be the redeemer, and one must hold fast to her.*[11]

> *You yourselves see that everyone calls her Eternal Maiden. They say of her that she is the Queen of Heaven. All kneel and bow before her.*

This theology affected not only the treatment of Eva Frank, Jacob Frank's daughter—revered by the Frankist community as the Maiden—but also girls in general. The Frankists had the custom of parading a young girl around the synagogue along with the Torah scroll, because the girl represented the presence of the Shekhinah.[12] This treatment of girls, similar to the worship of girls as goddesses in Nepal and India, invokes the girl as a channel for the sacred feminine and the forces of redemption—the role of a priestess.

In contemporary North America, in liberal and some Orthodox communities, the ceremony of bat mitzvah celebration honors the young Jewish girl as she begins to enter adulthood. The girl may read Torah, give a sermon, and lead prayers. This is a rite of passage in which a girl takes on leadership of the community, demonstrating her ability to be a conduit to the divine.

Some have attempted to sculpt this bat mitzvah experience, and other young Jewish adult rituals such as confirmation, into something more like an indigenous rite of passage. Sarai Shapiro has proposed a program called Bat Briyah, "daughter of creation."

> *Bat Briya provides initiatory earth-based experiences for Bat Mitzvah and 17-20 yr. old Jewish girls and young women. Participants are immersed in an inter-generational Jewish culture that models female collaboration and leadership and ecological communities. Through skills in wilderness, self-awareness, and creative arts, and drawing from ancient and contemporary teachings, students learn to be caretakers of the earth, to be authentically themselves and create positive change in the world.*[13]

Hebrew priestess and scholar Deborah Grenn studied *khomba*, the girls' initiation rite of the Lemba, an African tribe that shares practices with Jews and may have Hebrew roots. She compared the rite to bat mitzvah in order to better understand Jewish girls' initiation experiences. Grenn writes: "The importance of such rites to young girls, in having a public cultural acknowledgement of the changes they go through at puberty, cannot be overstated."[14]

Cantorial student Liz Sternlieb has created a ceremony for Jewish girls' coming of age (envisioned for high school) in which a young woman dons three veils representing her past, present, and future. She reflects on her past, makes amends for things she regrets, and receives blessings. A different adult woman guides her through each stage, and the removal of the veil associated with that stage. Contemporary rituals like this one continue to honor the sacredness of becoming a Maiden.[15]

Maiden-Priestess Incarnations

Chavah (a pseudonym) is a Kohenet graduate and performance artist. Chavah is also a believer in the power of ritual to heal and transform. When she created a ceremony to mourn her recent hysterectomy, she identified the ceremony as one where she was reborn as Maiden.[16]

During the ritual, Chavah told of the frightening experience of surgery to remove her womb. She also described the abuse both she and her mother had survived at the hands of the same family member, her maternal grandfather. She spoke of decades of silence and repression. At the end of her story, Chavah proclaimed to us: "I am my mother's redeemer." She claimed her role as one who remembers and one who transcends trauma. Two women wrapped Chavah in a prayer shawl, a ritual garment signifying holiness and protection. As part of her transformation, Chavah fell backward into their arms.

> *I still think about that moment. I had absolutely no concern about falling backward. I had absolute trust. That was the experience of the hysterectomy, having to surrender.*

Shoshana, a friend and co-participant, had knitted Chavah a womb out of red yarn to use in the ceremony. We sprinkled rose petals into this womb and offered Chavah words of blessing, encouragement and healing. She danced holding the womb, radiating joy.

> *Something real happens in ritual. There is a liminal space that you go through; then you are transformed. What was the transformation? I was reborn as Maiden.*

Later, Chavah shared that as a child, her initiation into maidenhood never occurred. It was taken from her. The hysterectomy ritual, which let her feel her injury and move beyond it, was a belated initiation into womanhood. It gave her the eerie ability to create a new self, a new life. This creative possibility arose out of her bringing her wound to consciousness and transforming it through ritual.

> *Early in Kohenet training, we did a class ritual on the Maiden, and I was angry. We had to draw with crayons and paper about the coming to maidenhood. I drew in red lines, everything was red lines. I realized that this was real anger. It was the beginning of consciousness for me.*

Ahava Lilith is also a graduate of the Kohenet program. She is often our community gatherer of information, maintaining contact information files and lists of ill people who need prayers. Like Chavah, Ahava Lilith has experienced childhood sexual abuse. Within the sacred space of her home, Ahava Lilith created ritual to overcome the abuse. She wore a silk "umbilical cord" in three colors: blue (signifying her connection with her mother), purple (signifying her connection with the spiritual aspect of the Goddess), and green (signifying her connection with the earthly aspect of the Goddess)." She slept in a darkened room for the whole month, allowing no natural light into the room. On the anniversary of her birth, she curled up in a fetal position and re-enacted her birth experience. She then took the spiritual name of Persephone Lilith.

Ahava Lilith and four other women who were also healing from sexual abuse created a healing group called the Courage Circle. This group gave Ahava Lilith a place to encounter her inner Maiden:

> *The women of the Courage Circle and I designed weekly rituals to facilitate our healing process. During these rituals and my weekly support group meetings, I nurtured my inner Maiden and helped her to feel safe. I brought my favorite stuffed animal to hold onto at the Courage Circle and during my support group sessions. I also did things to honor my inner Maiden's creative and playful needs. I did a lot of arts and crafts, colored in coloring books, and even played with stickers. I tried to bring an aspect of play into almost everything I did.*

The Maiden is not only about wound, however. She is about living the present moment with girlish abandon. Terri Alumah Schuster, a Kohenet graduate, yogini, and mystic, describes a moment of dancing during prayer that encapsulates the unselfconscious presence of the Maiden. This image of a woman moving in trance echoes the prophet Isaiah, who describes the reborn soul of the people as a girl dancing with joy.

> *As I sat in prayer, a stirring ran through my body, flowing to its limbs and organs, its bones, its very being. These stirrings awoke in me something long ago forgotten, long ago quelled by a culture refusing to see spirituality, sensuality, embodiment as a force to bring us closer to Divinity. I let those stirrings move within until they could no longer be held, until a voice from the very depths of my being said, "Dance, dance with me."*
>
> *I am not a trained dancer yet something took me over. It was no longer me dancing; I was being danced. The whole of me and all my surroundings were one. My body felt light, full, expanded, glowing, infused with energy. Ripples of joy came through me in waves. I felt I was being gifted and at the same bestowing a gift. Time and space merged, all merged, with awe and wonder, grace and gratitude.*

That voice that said "Dance!" opened for me doorways within doorways, doorways that opened my body and soul to receive what is our Divine Right and one of the greatest of gifts.

The maiden-priestesses of the Bible bring to their society an image of the human-divine Maiden complex: vitality, fertility, vulnerability, and joy. They are whole within themselves. Yet when girls are mentioned in the Bible, it is often because they are about to be married—as in Rebecca traveling on her camel to meet Isaac; or because something awful is about to happen to them—as in Dinah, who was raped. Our own contemporary society still struggles to welcome girls' strength, openness, and freedom. Naming the Maiden as priestess invites girls and all women, and all people, to move beyond fear and discover divine presence within themselves.

Spirit Journey The Maiden

You enter a vineyard. The sun is hot. The grapes are full and their scent fills the air. Hearing laughter, you walk among the trellises of vines and rough branches. Young women, gathered around a pool bordered with stones, are dipping and stirring white clothes in the water. White clothing is drying on the flat stones.

Choose dry white clothes for yourself from among those on the stones. You reach into the pocket of your chosen robe and find a note there. The note is from the owner of the dress: a blessing for you as you go out to dance.

You follow the women to an open field. Drummers, musicians, and spectators are gathered on the sides of the field. The music begins. The breeze is warm. The dance begins. Feel the Child within enjoying the melody and rhythm, the camaraderie and play.

Now a partner comes to join you. It may be the Maiden Herself who has chosen you; it may be an Israelite man or woman, or a relationship partner past or present; it may be a spirit guide or a friend or a stranger. Pay attention as you dance with this partner. What do you discover?

Everyone around you is bending down to touch the ground, blessing the soil, caressing the green plants, drawing warmth into the world. Some of the women are using grapevines dipped in fresh juice to draw or write on the earth. Look at what they are doing. You can add if you wish.

Darkness has fallen. The dance ends. You remove your borrowed white clothes and leave them on the rocks near the pool. The light of the full moon strikes your face. Around you there is a murmur: "Shekhinah's light embraces you." You dress in your own clothes. As you depart, someone presses a gift into your hands. Carry it with you as you begin to arise from your meditation.

She Who Becomes New:
The Practice of Blood Wisdom
by Taya Shere

A pivotal moment of maidenhood is menarche, which marks the beginning of becoming a bleeding being and a woman who has the power to create life from her body. The power of the birthing woman is sometimes recognized, but the powerful moments of not-pregnant, or menstruating, are often glossed over or subverted. For most women, there are many more cycles of menstruation than cycles of giving birth, many more moments of being a body that bleeds than of being a body that is nurturing life in the womb or with breast-milk. When we explore menstruation through the power in our bleeding bodies, we engage Maiden wisdom of celebrating the possibility of beginning again and again, each month, anew.

Not all women menstruate, or bleed regularly. Many of us are peri- or postmenopausal, breastfeeding, have had hysterectomies or experience health situations which disrupt our menstruation. Transgender women and some born women do not have the biology to menstruate. Women who are not menstruating can embrace practices of attuning to the moon, and to our own bodily, emotional and spiritual cycles. If you don't currently menstruate, pay attention to the cycles in your life that are significant to you.

Connect With the Moon

When women live surrounded by only natural light, with no electricity brightening the night, we cycle with the moon. In most indigenous cultures it is understood that women bleed with the new moon and ovulate with the full moon. Rosh Hodesh, the new moon celebration at the beginning of each month, is understood, in Susan Berrin's words, "as a symbol of renewal, as a women's covenant, as a marking of time, and as a reminder of cyclical development and focus." The Talmud records that "Whoever blesses the new moon in her time welcomes the Shekhinah."[17]

Today, while it may not be possible for each of us to live fully in accord with the moon, there are many ways to connect with the moon throughout our monthly cycle. You might go outside at night and gaze at the moon, paying attention to her cycles, and knowing where she is in her waxing and waning when your own bleeding time begins. You can use a moon calendar, coloring in the days of your moon blood and making notes about your experiences so you can trace patterns across lunar months. There is no right or wrong time for your moon blood to arrive. Trust the wisdom of your body. You may also to wish to gather in a circle of women to celebrate and mark Rosh Chodesh. Experience the renewal you are opening to in your own life, as the moon is renewed.

Shabbat: Keep a Bleeding Sabbath

Take the first day of your moon time as a bleeding sabbath. As soon as your moon blood begins, cancel whatever you can. Make time to give your bleeding body the space she needs. Whether you take the whole day or just two hours to yourself, be clear about allotting some amount of time and space to honor your bleeding body, and stick with what you decide. Once your body is absolutely clear that you are not going to try to force her to do things she doesn't want to do, or interact with people when she is not ready, your cramps will likely dissipate.

Experiment. Be creative. Give yourself a moontime uniform—dress only in flowing maroon clothes or wear your favorite red sweater. Eat reddish-purple foods—-beets, blood oranges, and pomegranates. Drink red juices. Only read books or listen to music created by women. Use burgundy sheets. Transform your space into a womb sanctuary. Make menstrual art with your blood. Anoint yourself.

During menstruation you are shedding your uterine lining, letting go of whatever you have been holding on to from the past month, as well as releasing the potential life in that particular egg that made the journey to your womb. Letting go is a process that necessitates going with the flow. Stopping up your body with tampons not only impedes blood flow (and generates risk of toxic-shock syndrome), it creates an energetic compression that is stressful and counterintuitive for a physical and energetic body that is in a mode to shed, release, and transform. Many women who have extremely difficult moon times, with cramping, nausea, and digestive discomfort, experience significant healing and release when they transition from tampons to pads.

At the beginning of each moon time, offer a blessing of gratitude for your bleeding body, for the process of releasing, renewing, and cycling with the moon: *B'rucha at shechina, she'astani isha, m'chadeshet et-haneshama im halevana*—A fountain of blessing are you, Shekhinah, who has made me a woman and who renews the spirit with the moon.

Resources

Resources for further exploration and wisdom include: *Blood, Bread, and Roses: How Menstruation Created the World* by Judy Grahn (Beacon Press, 1994), *Her Blood is Gold: Awakening to the Wisdom of Menstruation* by Lara Owen (Archive Publishing, 2009), *Celebrating the New Moon* edited by Susan Berrin (Jason Aronson, 1996).

Chapter 8:
Mother-Priestesses

I had already been in labor for two and a half days when I arrived at the hospital. It was the fifth night of Chanukah, and Christmas Day. I had been sick through almost the entire pregnancy and the delivery was almost two weeks late. My midwives spent fourteen hours with me, trying every method they knew to get me fully dilated. My wife and I paced the halls and even the local streets. I took a hot bath (which stopped my labor). My doula suggested I stand on my head to try and shift the baby's position. I kept seeing in my mind the vision I had a few days before: an adventurous girl together with me in a boat on the sea, the boat moving fast, racing toward dawn.

During the pushing stage, we discovered my daughter was a very large baby indeed. Her heart-rate dropped. The midwives were concerned. Shoshana and the doula were white-faced. Exhausted and in agony, I felt isolated and lost. The physician who had arrived to evaluate the situation turned to me and said: "We have to get this baby out now."

The midwives told me to push. More than anything, I wanted to tell them that I needed help, that I couldn't possibly keep pushing when I was so tired and in so much pain. A moment of clarity came amid all of the pain, fear and confusion, and my whole being understood that no one else could do this for me. Everyone was trying to assist, but ultimately, I was the only one who could give birth to this baby, and if I didn't do it, it was possible that one of us would die. It was not a spiritual moment as one usually thinks of that term. It was a split-second of focusing the will, like someone who acts without conscious thought to save a life. I pushed, and pushed, and pushed again. Suddenly, the pain lessened, and I heard a cry. Exactly at dawn, my daughter was born. I was a mother. They put her on my chest, and within seconds she was nursing at my breast.

Mother-priestesses embody the courage it takes to love and nurture others. They are vessels for the forces of life. Mothers can be biological, adoptive, or societal—caretakers and teachers as well as birthers. Mother-priestesses contain all of these possibilities: the womb, the home, the temple as uterine sanctuary.

In the Kohenet community, we have a ritual for those seeking to become mothers (biological or adoptive): we make them an amulet out of beads each member of the community has blessed. This amulet is passed on after the birth to others who may need it. The amulet reminds us that motherhood—of all kinds—happens in community and needs the support of community. The amulet also reminds us that the road to motherhood, and through motherhood, is not easy. Mother-priestesses give, but they also need others to give to them.

To be mother is to be nurturer but also to need nurturing in order to find the strength to go on mothering.

The Biblical Period: Mother in Israel

In ancient Israel, the term "mother in Israel" is a title. Deborah the prophetess calls herself "mother in Israel," and in the book of Samuel, the city of Avel is also called "mother in Israel."[1] Given the name, both the city and the prophetess are recognized as sustainers and protectors of the people.

The Asherah-pillar, and later the tree-shaped menorah in the Temple, were also symbols of the creative and nourishing power of the Mother. (It is not an accident that a branching shape like a tree appears on the placenta.) One of the biblical names for God is El Shaddai, which can be translated to mean, "God of breasts." God/dess as nursing mother would have been a well-known image in ancient Israel. The following Psalm reflects this:

> *I have centered and quieted my soul;*
> *like a child at its mother's breast,*
> *so my soul is within me."*
> —Psalms 131:3

Many goddess figurines from ancient Israel/Canaan have prominent breasts. These "pillar figurines" are from the eighth and seventh centuries BCE, which would have been the height of the Israelite monarchy—the culture that produced the Genesis stories. The figurines are so numerous that they must have been a common expression of devotion to the Divine Mother. Scholars link these figurines to Asherah, the divine mother of the Canaanite pantheon. The goddesses Asherah and Anat are both called "wetnurses of the gods."[2] An Akkadian text reads:

> *I call upon the gracious gods…*
> *Who suck the tip of Asherah's breast.*[3]

The first breastfeeding scene in Genesis may involve a priestess. Sarah, the wife of Abraham, has no child. Frustrated, she asks her husband to take her Egyptian slave woman, Hagar, as concubine. Savina Teubal argues, based on Sarah's multiple sexual encounters with kings—which may be sacred marriage rituals—and her epithet as Abraham's sister, that Sarah is an ancient Mesopotamian *naditu* priestess. In this reading, Sarah remains childless because of her priestess vows. Just as Babylonian noblewomen/priestesses could engage a concubine, a *sugetu*, to bear children for the family, so does Sarah use Hagar for that purpose.⁴ After significant conflict, Hagar bears a son, Ishmael. The tension in the family is almost unbearable, but Abraham considers Ishmael his heir.

Then, when Sarah is ninety, three mysterious men arrive at the tent of Abraham and Sarah. The couple rushes to feed these wandering strangers. Sarah eavesdrops on the men's conversation, and hears the prophecy that she will bear a child. Sarah thinks this is funny and laughs: "Am I to have pleasure, with my husband so old?" God asks: "Why did Sarah laugh? Is anything too wonderful for God?' We don't know if this is chastisement or playful teasing, but Sarah conceives as promised.

Months later, when Sarah gives birth to Isaac, she recites a birth poem:

> *Who would have said to Abraham*
> *that Sarah would suckle children!*
> *Yet I have borne a son in his old age.*
> —Genesis 21:7

Sarah is an impossibly aged nursing mother—a kind of fertile crone figure. As the mother of the Israelite nation, she is full of life even in old age: the renewed tree of life. Her words show us her amazement at the gift of fertility and the power of the mother to feed a child. Years later, at Isaac's weaning-feast, Sarah rejects Hagar and Ishmael and demands that they be expelled—perhaps her actions could be seen as sorrow at the loss of intimacy with her newly weaned son, and the visceral need to inflict the same loss on her long-time (unacknowledged) rival.

Much later in history, Jewish legends imagine Sarah's breastfeeding as a public miracle, in which Sarah convinces the world that Isaac is really her child by baring her full breasts. Rashi, the medieval commentator, writes:

> *Why does the verse say 'children' and not 'child'? On the day of the feast at Isaac's weaning, the princesses from surrounding nations brought their children, and Sarah nursed them. This happened because people were saying: 'Sarah did not give birth, but brought home a foundling from the market.'*⁵

An interesting fact: scholars believe the *kadishtu*, the holy woman/priestess of Akkadian culture, was a sacred wetnurse, suckling many children in a temple built for that purpose.⁶ The midrash intuits a similar image: Sarah sits suckling the royal children of the world, a human image of the Mother Goddess who feeds all. A later legend adds that all future converts to the Jewish people descend from those who nursed at Sarah's breasts.⁷ The later iconic Christian image of the Virgin Mary nursing the infant Jesus seems to reflect the same tradition.

"Mother" continues to be a term of respect in Jewish culture. In ancient Rome, in the third century CE, a Jewish woman named Beturia Paulina received the title *mater synagogae*, mother of the synagogue, from two separate communities. (Beturia Paulina was a convert to Judaism and took on the additional name of Sarah.) Another woman in Rome named Marcella received the same title. The title may have referred to a respected elder, a donor and patroness, or a woman with an established ritual role. Here, "mother" meant something similar to what it meant when Deborah called herself "mother in Israel"—a societal leader and caretaker.

Throughout Jewish history, motherhood in its traditional sense was a huge focus of ritual for Jewish women. In addition to the practice of going to the ritual bath after menstruating as well as after giving birth, there were amulets, prayers, and rituals for safe pregnancy and delivery, and for the protection of newborn children.

The Mother as Nazirite

> *YHWH spoke to Moses saying: Speak to the children of Israel and say to them: A man or a woman when he explicitly utters a nazirite vow, to set himself apart for YHWH, he shall abstain from wine and any other intoxicant....Throughout the term of his vow as nazirite no razor shall touch his head.... Until the period of his dedication to the LORD is over, he shall be sacred, and shall let the hair of his head grow freely. Throughout the term that he is consecrated to YHWH he shall not go near a dead person...*
> —Numbers 6:1-6

In the Bible, a *nazir* or *nezirah* means "a consecrated person." Such a person abstained from intoxicants and grew their hair long, and stayed away from the dead as priests do. At the end of a period of being a nazirite, special offerings were brought, including the cut hair of the consecratred individual. In a sense, becoming a nazirite was a kind of personal priesthood. The philosopher Philo equated the holiness of a nazirite with the holiness of a priest.[8]

Women as well as men could be nazirites. Elaborate laws governed when a man could annul the nazirite vows of his wife and daughters. This suggests that a nazirite vow was viewed suspiciously because it created a holiness in laypeople that rivaled the priesthood—and because it was an independent act, giving a woman a sacred status that distanced her from family life. The later rabbinic suspicion of vows as a spiritual practice may stem from the discomfort with the vows of nazirites. In fact, rabbinic tradition strongly discouraged taking a nazirite vow.[9]

CHAPTER 8: MOTHER-PRIESTESSES

In the book of Judges, chapter 13, a woman is meditating in a field when an angel appears to her. She is childless, but the angel informs her that she is about to bear a child, one who will achieve military victories for Israel when he is grown. This child must be dedicated as a nazirite. His hair must never be cut. His mother must drink no wine during her pregnancy. In a sense, she becomes a nazirite for the duration of her pregnancy.

The woman runs to tell her husband what has happened. Her husband, who seems to think her instructions are not good enough, prays to the angel to appear again and "tell what we shall do for the boy that is to be born." The angel does appear again, but only to the woman. The woman runs to get her husband, but when Manoah huffs and puffs into the angel's presence, the angel tells him: "The woman must take care about all that I told her." When the angel disappears, Manoah is afraid that he will die, but his wife tells him: "Had God desired to kill us... he would not have shown us all these things." The child she bears is Samson.

This nameless woman has received an angelic vision, as well as instructions about the way the child is to be raised. She, not her husband, is the guardian of the child's purity. She has also been instructed—three times!—to engage in abstinence herself during the course of the pregnancy. Samson's mother, portrayed as *nezirah* and prophetess, may represent many women who took sacred vows while pregnant, or perhaps while praying to become pregnant.

A similar event occurs in the life of Hannah, the mother of Samuel. She is a barren woman who comes to the shrine of Shiloh on pilgrimage. While there, she vows that if she has a son, he will abstain from alcohol and will be dedicated to the Temple (though he is not a hereditary priest). The high priest sees her praying and scolds her, but when she explains, he blesses her. The child is born, and Hannah brings him to the Temple when he is weaned. In this story, a woman creates priesthood for her son through her sacred vow.[10]

The insitution of self-consecration through a vow continues into the rabbinic period. One of the reasons given for such vows is the birth of a hoped-for child.[11] The Talmud and Josephus report aristocratic women becoming nazirites, including the Jewish king Agrippa's sister Berenice and Helena, queen of Adiabene.[12] A rabbinic text mentions the girl's name Nazirah as a sign of a daughter being dedicated in this way.[13] In fact, most of the specific individuals mentioned as nazirites in the Talmudic era are women:

> *Helene the Queen (of Adiabene)—her son went off to war, and she said: "If my son comes home whole and in one piece, I shall be a nezirah for seven years. Indeed her son did come home from war, and she was a nezirah for seven years.*
> —Mishnah Nazir 3:6

The Middle Ages: The Mother as Kindler of Souls

Midrash Tanhuma, a ninth century midrash collection, describes creation as a process of fetal development:

> When the Holy One began to create the world, the Holy One made it as a child grows within its mother. Just as the fetus in its mother's womb starts at the navel and spreads out this way and that way to the four sides, so too the Holy One made the world…
> —Midrash Tanhuma, Pekudei 3

In the Zohar, one of the ten divine spheres is called Binah, understanding, or Immah Ilaah, the Celestial Mother. With the help of Chochmah/Wisdom (also called Abba or Father), Binah produces all that is.[14] She gives birth to the souls of humankind:

> We ask the sukkah to spread itself over us and rest upon us and protect us as a mother protects her children, so that we will feel safe on every side. When Israel welcomes this sukkah of peace to their homes as a holy guest, the holy Divine presence comes down and spreads Her wings over Israel like a mother embracing her children. This sukkah of peace grants new souls to Her children, for all souls have their home in her."[15]

The Zohar comments on the Genesis creation story by saying:

> When the Holy One of Blessing created Adam's body, it was created from the earth of the earthly Temple [Shekhinah], but Adam's soul was given to him from the earth of the celestial Temple [Binah].[16]

That is, the human body is made of the substance of Shekhinah, but the soul is made of the substance of Binah, womb of souls. The God-name Elohim, according to the Zohar, refers to Binah. Souls return to Her after death. The following text from the Zohar explains that women light Shabbat candles because they are human representatives of the Divine Mother:

> Shabbat candles were given to the women of the holy people to light. The friends have said: because she [Eve] extinguished the candle of the world, and so forth, and that is a fine explanation. But there is a secret to these words. The sukkat shalom, the shelter of peace [that spreads over us on Shabbat] is the Lady [the Shekhinah].

> *The souls, that are the candles on high, dwell in her. In the role of the Lady, the women light, and because they do this, the Mother gives Sabbath souls to her children.*
> —Zohar I, 48a

In other words, the Talmud claims that women light Shabbat candles because they "put out the light of the world"—because Eve brought death into the world. In contrast, the Zohar imagines women as kindlers of life, emissaries of the Divine Mother. Interestingly, in the fifteenth century, in Ashkenazi Germany in the region of Furth, women would go to the house of a woman who had given birth to make candles for the circumcision ceremony—lights that represented the making of a new soul.[17]

In a number of Yiddish candlelighting prayers, we find the unusual metaphor of women as priests. Women serve God through the kindling of light, just as the *kohanim* served God by keeping the eternal flame. Chava Weissler has noted how unusual and powerful this association is, and how it elevates the status of woman from helpmeet to participant in the mystical secrets of the universe. The following prayer is part of a candlelighting *tkhine* for the Sabbath:

> *We must kindle lights for the holy day, to brighten it and to rejoice in it; so may we be worthy of the light and the joy of eternal life.... And may the lights be, in your eyes, like the lights the priest kindled in the Temple. And let our light not be extinguished, and let your light shine upon us.*
> —Tkhine Imrei Shifre, circa 1770[18]

Another *tkhine* from a different collection offers a prayer for candlemaking at the season of the High Holidays. This prayer imagines women as high priests, lighting the holy lamp in the Temple:

> *May the merit of my mitzvah of candles be accepted as equivalent to the flame that the high priest lit in the Temple, so that it may illumine the eyes of our children in the study of the holy Torah.*
> —Amsterdam, 1648[19]

Yet another tkhine, the *Tkhine Shloyshe She'orim* by Sarah bas Tovim, imagines the woman as high priest, kindling the eternal light.

> *Lord of the world, may my mitzvah of kindling the lights be accepted like the mitzvah of the high priest who kindled the lights*

in the dear Temple.... May the feet of my children walk on God's path and may the mitzvah of my candle lighting be acceptable, so that my children's eyes may be enlightened in the dear Torah...
  —Tkhine Shloyshe She'orim, Sarah bas Tovim, Ukraine, eighteenth century[20]

These Yiddish prayers, recited throughout Europe, gave women the role of priestesses of light. Through the act of lighting candles, the women brought light to themselves, their children and their community. Their homes became temples. Implicitly, they became vehicles for the Divine Mother to send souls into the world. In a similar vein in North Africa, Jewish women lit candles during all-female new moon rituals, reflecting their role as makers of souls.[21]

Into the Modern Era

In the Middle Ages and early modernity, many Jewish birthing customs treated the mother as connected to the holy Ark, just as the divine mother Binah was connected to the Temple. A birthing custom in Eastern Europe and the Holy Land has a pregnant woman hold onto a string, the other end of which is tied to the holy ark of the Torah. Some Ashkenazi Jews had birthing women hold or lie on top of the keys to the synagogue. Yemenite and some Sephardic Jews used to cover the birthing woman's head with the *parochet*, the sacred curtain of the ark.[22] The connection of the Ark/shrine with the womb is not just metaphorical, it is literal.

Also in the Middle Ages and through the modern era, there is the custom of inviting honored women to act as symbolic mothers in spiritual contexts. These women are called *kvaterin*, *komari*, *ba'alat brit*, or *sandakit*, the godmother of Ashkenazi lands. "Godmother" was a ritual role, and did not necessarily confer the task of spiritual mentor or foster-parent. The *kvaterin* (from German *gott-vaterin*) or *komari* (from Italian *comare*) or *sandekes* brought a newborn boy from his mother in the women's section to the circumcision ceremony in the men's section. It was an honor given to a family member or esteemed person.[23]

Sometimes a woman called the *sandekes* or *sandakit* (masc. *sandek*, from Greek *syndikos* or delegate) actually held the child during the circumcision. This was a great honor usually reserved for a man. In the early Middle Ages, sometimes a woman received the honor. The thirteenth-century legal scholar Samson ben Tzadok complains: "I am not at all in favor of the technically permissible custom one finds in most places: namely, that a woman sits in the synagogue among the men and they circumcise the baby in her lap...It is not appropriate to allow a beautifully-dressed-up woman to be among the men."[24]

Moses Isserles, a sixteenth-century decisor from Krakow, compared the role of the *sandek* to that of the *kohen*, the priest, who brings incense. In the same breath, Isserles forbade this role being given to women because of "licentiousness." Apparently he was concerned about women taking on this "priesthood." However, in modern times the role is given to women in many liberal circles.

Jewish tradition continues to value motherhood as an important part of community life. Jewish women have reclaimed the sacredness of motherhood by creating rituals to mark conception, pregnancy, birth, adoption, and other important events. In pace with medical and technological advances that make motherhood possible in new and miraculous ways, rituals have been created for modern fertility events such as insemination, meeting a prospective bio-parent, or making a decision to conceive. Rituals have also been invented to honor the relationships between mothers and daughters. Still other modern Jews, like scholar Tikvah Frymer-Kensky who wrote the book *Motherprayer*, have explored how the divine-human relationship connects to the concept of "mother."

Mother-Priestess Incarnations

At a Kohenet Institute retreat, a participant named Sarah Esther created an "umbilical cord" that she installed in our yurt. The cord hung down from the center of spokes about seven feet off the floor that were attached to the yurt's support cables. It was suspended just above the center of the room, at the middle of our altar. (We use an altar cloth on the floor, with sacred objects such as candles, stones, kiddush cups and spiceboxes, as part of our worship.)

Each woman took turns putting the umbilical cord to her navel, receiving sustenance from the Goddess through the long red cord that seemed to come from the sky. The web holding up the cord was a sacred placenta, a Tree of Life structure connecting us to the Goddess. Sarah, now an ordinee, reflects:

I was in the earlier stages of pregnancy so it was meaningful to artistically reflect something that was going on in my body.

The Mother is an image of Goddess for me. For me, the most powerful and meaningful metaphor for the divine has been parent.

Thea was adopted, so I didn't have the experience of being a physical mother to her the way I did for Zevi. I consider having both types of experiences, one of receiving a child as a gift and another as a "grow your own," as a tremendous gift in its own right. I have the gift of a perspective that allows me to separate the two "types" of mother, physical and practical. I value the experience of pregnancy and birth beyond measure, but I value it as a separate gift in many ways from the gift of my children.

I have been paying a lot of attention to how my body feels after the birth, which of course I had no reason to do after Thea

> was born. I am now often aware of my uterus as an empty space, and also as an emotional/spiritual space. I feel like a duplex with one vacant apartment. I feel that it actually takes a significant chunk of my spiritual and emotional energies to maintain this "empty apartment" in my body, this sacred vessel. This connects to how I view the earth itself as the wombspace for life, and how God/dess might experience the earth as part of Her own body.

The Kohenet Institute community continues to use the ritual umbilical cord at all of our retreats. Sometimes we tie it to the Torah. Sometimes we hold it at moments of devotion, stress or transition. It has become a communal link to the sacred.

The umbilical cord is a powerful image of the Mother, but it is important to remember that the Mother is not only a creatrix mother. She can also be a societal mother. Rabbi and Kohenet graduate Margie Klein tells a little of how she came to explore her inner matriarch:

> My role models are women activists in my family who are mothers and who extended their caring beyond the nuclear family. My grandmother was a first wave feminist and she worked her whole life on Planned Parenthood, which she saw as an effort to make women matter beyond the realm of the womb and to make sure everyone who enters the world enters with a welcome and a place.
>
> When I traveled in India in college, I had the opportunity to travel through central India on the Rally for the Valley, organized by author/activist Arundhati Roy to stop building of the harmful Narmada Dam. I got to sit on the bus with Devaki Jain, a major leader/writer of the Indian feminist movement, then in her late 60s. Devaki said to me that the Indian feminist movement wasn't primarily only about equality for women, but about cultivating women's concern, compassion, and untapped power to work for a better society as a whole. Amma, another Hindu woman spiritual leader, works out of a sense of compassion and caring. She identifies with motherhood even though she is not biologically a mother. She expands motherhood to a universal sense of concern for all creatures in our care.
>
> My grandmother died when I was twenty-one. I started saying that my goal in life is to be the matriarch of a large Jewish family of activists who can dance. At Moishe Kavod House [a Jewish activist community], we had a goal workshop, and I shared my

goal—with many caveats about how the family didn't have to be biological but could be a community. People said to me: "You are that here already."

Spirit Journey
The Mother

You find yourself walking through a wood. Eventually, you find yourself standing before an enormous tree. The tree may be lush with flowers and fruit, or it may be a magnificent redwood, or some other kind of grand tree.

At the foot of the tree is a very old woman who is pregnant. She sits on a throne of roots, her white hair spread around her. Perhaps this is Sarah the matriarch, or she may be someone else. She welcomes you and tells you that any fears or disabilities you may have will not prevent you from climbing the tree. You ascend through the branches, meeting birds, lizards, and other creatures. All of these creatures represent ancestors and guardians of yours, and each one has support and advice to offer you. Stop and talk to as many of these beings as you wish.

At some point you come to a hole in the trunk of the tree. It is big enough for you to enter. You find a flight of stairs that descends down through the tree-trunk and into the ground. Notice how these stairs appear. Are they spiral stairs or more like a ladder? Walk in the passageways along the roots, meeting insects and worms, until you come to a round earthen chamber just big enough for you to be comfortable.

Feel the life in the soil around you. Have a conversation with the earth. She may speak to you through a mother-figure who appears to you. She may appear through a root, an ant, the soil, a Divine voice, anything you imagine. If you wish, you will find a teat in the earth from which to drink and take in the Mother's abundance.

When you are ready, thank the Earth-mother and climb back up through the trunk into the branches of the tree. There will be a fruit dangling before you on a fragile stem. Bite into the fruit and see what it tastes like. The Earth-mother has granted you new knowledge with this gift from Her body. Only you know what this knowledge is. Use it wisely. Climb down and greet the old mother at the foot of the tree, and thank her. Thank the tree itself, knowing that it is the Tree of Life. Walk back through the wood toward your waking self.

She Who Heals by Her Presence:
The Practice of **Motherline Healing**
by Taya Shere

The mother-priestess nurtures and creates. Women drawn to priestessing are often committed to honoring the Divine Mother and to connecting with and protecting Mother Earth. Yet our relationships with our own mothers can be deeply fraught. Our mothers are not wholly perfect or imperfect—the Goddess is neither, our mothers are neither, we are neither. What does it mean to recognize your mother as an aspect and manifestation of the Mother divine? What does it mean about the Goddess if we allow her to have the qualities of our own mother?

Spend a focused hour in Motherline Healing ritual. For the ritual you'll need: a candle and matches, a photo or object symbolizing your mother, a pencil or pen, and a journal. Photocopy the pages in the appendix labeled "Motherline Divining Quotes" and "Motherscroll". Cut them into eighteen separate quotes. Spread the Divining Quotes face down around the candle in the center of your space. This candle will be your ritual altar/centerpiece.

Light the candle. Place a photo or object symbolizing your mother near the candle. Out loud, say your name and your motherline, in English, Hebrew, or any combination of languages that speak most to your heart and to the name and energies of the women in your motherline. Speak your own name and who you are daughter of. I am ____, daughter of _____, daughter of _____, daughter of _____. Name one or two generations back, or go as far back as you like. Bat (pronounced baht), is the Hebrew word meaning daughter of.

Choose (while still face down) three or four quotes from around the altar. Read one of your chosen quotes out loud, then journal on it for five minutes or so. Your journaling could include what emerges for you when reading this quote, what this quote triggers for you, what the quote makes you think of, or whatever else feels present, relevant or meaningful. Read out loud, and then journal on, each of your chosen quotes.

Take out your Mother Scroll (found in the Appendix) and a pencil. The Mother Scroll can be thought of as a Mother Mad Libs, one that you fill out with a description of your own mother as an aspect of the Divine Mother. Filling this out may not be easy the first time, so do stick with it for fifteen to twenty minutes, even if you spend the first ten minutes staring at a blank page.

It does not have to be all positive, and can include anger, rage, frustration. In your writing, it would be ideal to be open to both the accurate and the poetic. When your Mother Scroll is complete, read it aloud and then journal for a few minutes about what the experience was like for you. When you feel ready, extinguish the candle.

You can do this same ritual in a group, inviting each participant to bring a photo or object symbolizing her mother(s), light a candle, introduce her motherline, and choose a quote. Women can dialogue with partners about the quote they have chosen instead of or in addition to journaling. Then, have each woman fill out a Mother Scroll. Suggest that they fill out only one scroll per person per ritual. Some women with multiple mothers may want to fill out more, but it is better to focus on one at a time.

Offer the opportunity for people to break into dyads again and to share about what the experience of filling out the mother scroll was like for them. What was surprising? What was challenging? After they have shared their experiences, the dyad partners can read their scrolls aloud, (all or in part), to each other if they choose.

Close the circle with a collective Mother Scroll share. Read aloud the printed words of the blank mother scroll, allowing space for women to call out what is written on their scroll for some of the lines. This sharing is popcorn-style, with people speaking out if they feel called. Close the circle with a chant, and extinguish the candle. Pass around food/snacks or invite women to get up from their space to nosh. Take leisurely time leaving the space, giving everyone an easy transition to whatever is next.

Resources

Resources for further exploration and wisdom on healing the motherline include *Mother-Daughter Wisdom* by Cristiane Northrup (Bantam, 2006), *Stories from the Motherline* by Naomi Lowinsky (Jeremy P. Tarcher, Inc., 1999), *The Woman Who Gave Birth to Her Mother* by Kim Chernin (Penguin Books, 1999), and *In Search of Our Mother's Gardens* by Alice Walker (Mariner Books, 2003). Healing the Motherline Divining Quotes came from these books, and from *The Water of Life* by Michael Meade (Greenfire Press, 2006).

Chapter 9:
Queen-Priestesses

A Kohenet graduate, Mei Mei Sanford, once made me a staff, a tall branch of wood cut from an apple tree that had been growing in two different directions and needed to be pruned. When she gave it to me, it still had a few living leaves at its top. A vine wound around half of its length. Holding it, I felt the strength of its multiple meanings: staff, tree of life, power, protection, wand, weapon, support, scepter. The staff now stands in the corner of my house, reminding me of the power of my multiple strengths: a reality with which women are often so uncomfortable. It is also a reminder of my vulnerability and my dependence on the Tree of Life and its many branches: the Divine, and the other people in my world. I bring it out only rarely, when I most feel that I need a reminder that the Tree of Life is my shield.

In ancient times, ritual guardians—a role located somewhere between priest and warrior—stood at the gates of the Temple sanctuary. In modern Jewish life, ritual guardians called *shomrim* or *shomrot* watch over the bodies of the dead, and also protect a just-married couple who is in their first moment of marital privacy. These individuals serve as spiritual protectors and companions. In the Kohenet community, some women serve in the role of ritual guardian, standing at the door or in the corner of the room and offering their watchfulness as a spiritual protection for the participants. Sometimes we call such a guardian a *sho'eret* or gatekeeper, and sometimes we call her *gevirah*, a term that can mean "woman of strength," "mistress," "queen," or "warrior woman."

When I contemplate the word "queen," I think of Queen Esther and Queen Vashti in the Book of Esther, and I also think of the devotional Catholic image known as *sedes sapientiae*, the Throne of Wisdom. In these images, Mary sits regally on a throne with the infant Jesus on her lap, manifesting divine fecundity, power, and knowledge. To me, the infant sheltered in Mary's lap represents the Queen's mandate to guide and protect. Queen-priestesses are women who exercise power from the place of spirit—they are guardians of heaven and of earth.

Biblical Queen Mothers

In 800 BCE, the Judean royal court is the southernmost of the two Israelite kingdoms. The king sits on a throne in Jerusalem, where the Temple is a major site of pilgrimage. Next to him, on a throne of her own, sits the *Gevirah*, the Lady. She is not the wife of the king but rather his mother. Every time she enters the room, the king rises and bows to her.

This is not our usual picture of the biblical monarchy, but it is an accurate one. The *gevirah* (Lady) of the Judean (and sometimes, the Israelite) royal courts is the mother (or occasionally grandmother) of the reigning king.[1] The *gevirah* appears in the Song of Songs as the one who crowns the king:

> *Go out and see, daughters of Zion, Solomon the king*
> *in the crown with which his mother crowned him*
> *on the day of his wedding, the day of the joy of his heart.*
> —Song of Songs 3:11

Scholar Susan Ackerman theorizes that the *gevirah* may have served as a priestess of Asherah during a period when Asherah received worship in the Temple. Legends of Asherah depict her as providing heirs to the throne. In one myth, Baal says: "Lady Asherah, give me one of your sons, and I shall make him king."[2]

> *The political power of the Ugaritic queen mothers was vast, as is especially indicated by the fact that the Ugaritic king is repeatedly seen as acknowledging the authority of his queen mother... The Ugaritic kings describe themselves as paying homage to the authority of the queen mother by bowing at her feet... Israelite queen mothers take on many of the responsibilities elsewhere assigned to their Canaanite counterparts. For example, as the Ugaritic queen mother Akhat-milki began her tenure by asserting herself in matters concerning the royal succession, so too do Israel's queen mothers seem to be able to play a role in naming their husbands' heir.*[3]

A kingmaking scene like this happens at the beginning of the Book of Kings. As King David lies dying, Batsheva, his wife and once his illicit mistress, goes to meet with him to ask that her son be made king. The prophet Nathan supports her in her cause. As Batsheva enters the throne room, she bows to David:

> *Batsheva came to speak to the king, into the throne room, and the king was very old... Batsheva bowed and knelt to the king, and the king said: "What troubles you?"*

David promises to make Solomon king. A short time later, David dies. When Batsheva next goes to the throne room, to meet with her son King Solomon, he bows to her and has a throne set for her at his right hand:

CHAPTER 9: QUEEN-PRIESTESSES

> *Batsheva came to speak to King Solomon about Adonijah. The king rose to greet her and bowed down to her. He sat on his throne, and had a throne placed for the queen mother, and she sat at his right.*
> —I Kings 2:19

Most kings of Judah, the southern kingdom of Israel, are listed in the Bible along with the names of their queen mothers.[4] The prophet Ezekiel describes Hamutal, a queen mother who lived many generations after Batsheva, by saying: "What a lioness was your mother among the lions!"[5] The lioness is a frequent symbol on the throne of Asherah, mother of the gods. (Israelite women also worshipped a queen—the goddess Anat, the Queen of Heaven, as reported in the book of Jeremiah.)

Three named biblical women are given the specific title of *gevirah*: Maacah, Jezebel, and Nechushta. All of these women are associated with cults of the Divine feminine. Maacah (sometimes called Michayah), daughter of Avshalom, is the mother of Asa, king of Judah. According to the book of Kings, King Asa is a strict monotheist who expels the *kedeshim*, probably priests and priestesses of Asherah, from the Temple. Asa also deposes his mother from her role as *gevirah*, because his mother is a supporter of the cult of Asherah:

> *Also, he removed his mother Maacah from the office of gevirah, for she had made a miflatztah for Asherah. He cut down her miflatztah and burned it in the valley of Kidron.*
> —I Kings 15:13-14

The root of the word *miflatztah* implies something outrageous or disgusting. Probably Maacah had arranged for an image of Asherah, or a tree or pillar representing the goddess, to be set up in Jerusalem. The story implies that Maacah was a patroness of Asherah and perhaps a royal priestess.

Jezebel is a Phoenician princess, queen of the northern kingdom of Israel. Phoenicia was known to have royal high priestesses. Jezebel is a patroness of the cult of Baal and Asherah and an enemy of the prophet Elijah.[6] Her name (*iz-baal* in her own language) means "exalted Baal" or "where is the prince?" a phrase from Syro-Babylonian liturgy that refers to the return of Baal from the underworld. The Bible accuses her of corruption and murder. After a man called Jehu deposes and kills her son, Jezebel flees to Jezreel. Jehu encourages her servants to turn against her and push her from the window. Jezebel dies and a mob desecrates her corpse.[7]

Nechushta, daughter of Elnatan of Jerusalem and mother of King Yehoyachin, is the last of the queen mothers of Judah. In Jeremiah 29:2 we hear that

Nechushta goes into exile in Babylon along with most of her family. She is the only woman to whom a national prophecy is directed. Jeremiah relays Adonai's message to her and her son:

> *Say to the king and the queen mother,*
> *Sit low, for your tiaras are removed,*
> *Your crowns of glory.*
> —Jeremiah 13:18

Nechushta's name means "bronze serpent" or "divination." The male form of this name, Nechushtan, is the name of the bronze serpent Moses made to heal the people of snakebite.[8] Although Nechushta goes into exile, she carries within her name the symbol of renewal.

In Ezekiel 19:2, the queen mother appears. Ezekiel proclaims: "What a lioness was your mother among the lions! She brought up one of her cubs, and he became a strong lion." (Ezekiel 19:2) This queen mother has a staff, a ruler's scepter. She is a fruitful vine, a source of strength and leadership. Bowed by exile, she nevertheless remains a proud figure.

The Book of Esther: Queen as Intercessor

The Book of Esther shows us a Jewish queen in exile, and the story resonates with echoes of the priestess/goddess roles. In the ancient Persian religion, Spring was a time to draw lots to determine the king's new advisors. Ishtar, (goddess of love and war), and Marduk (god, of war and justice), would have been prominent characters in the new year ritual drama. The Book of Esther transforms the tradition into a saga of Jewish survival, appropriating the role of preserver of life (Ishtar) for Esther and the position of protector of the people (Marduk) for Mordechai. The Book of Esther allows Jews to be part of the larger culture's mythic tale of Spring and to remain true to their Jewish identity at the same time.

Esther's story is a twist on the descent of the goddess Ishtar into the underworld. In Babylonian myth, the goddess Ishtar strips herself of her clothing and royal garb to enter the underworld. Ishtar's sister, Ereshkigal queen of the underworld, afflicts Ishtar with disease and death. After the other gods plead with Ereshkigal to let Ishtar go, Ishtar's royal robes are returned to her.

Esther, a young Jewish girl, finds herself in a Persian harem. Esther must strip herself of her identity and pretend she is not a Jew, just as Ishtar must strip herself of her goddesshood in the underworld. Later, under the influence of the evil vizier Haman, the king makes a decree that all Jews be assassinated.

Esther's uncle Mordechai begs Esther to go to the king, even though it is forbidden, risking her life to save her people. Before doing so, Esther fasts for three days. Her three days of fasting may be an allegory for Ishtar's trials in the underworld.

> *On the third day, Esther garbed herself in royalty, and stood in the inner court of the king's palace, and the king sat on his royal throne in the palace opposite the doorway. When the king saw Esther standing in the courtyard, she found favor in his eyes, and the king extended to her the golden scepter in his hand, and Esther drew near and touched the scepter's head.*
> —Esther 5:1-2

One cannot miss the strong parallel between Esther's robing herself in royalty and Ishtar's queenly robing as she leaves the underworld. When Esther enters the king's throne room and touches the tip of his royal scepter, she is enacting the sacred marriage between Ishtar and the king. Although in a Jewish story this image is probably meant to be ironic, it can also be seen as Esther serving as a priestess, channeling the power of the divine feminine in the human realm.

Jewish mystics identify Esther with Shekhinah Herself. The Zohar notes that *malchut*, "sovereignty," the word for Esther's royal robes, is also a mystical term for the Divine She:

> "Esther put on royalty/malchut." What is the meaning of malchut? If you think it is glorious and purple garments, these are not called malchut. 'Esther put on malchut,' for she was clothed in the supernal Holy Malchut (Shekhinah). She was enveloped in the Holy Spirit.[9]

The Maccabean Period

The Hasmonean dynasty (first to second century BCE) came to power during the war with the Seleucid empire. The Hasmoneans were both members of the priestly house—*kohanim*—and reigning kings. The dynasty had one ruling queen, Salome Alexandra (in Hebrew, Shlomtzion). Her husband was Alexander Yannai, a king and high priest. On his deathbed, he granted power to his wife.

Salome Alexandra was a *kohenet*—the wife of a priest.[10] During her reign, she installed her eldest son, Hyrcanus II, as high priest in the Temple, reorganized the Sanhedrin (high court), supported the Pharisaic sect, and established an education system. She had considerable power over spiritual as well as temporal matters. According to one Bible scholar, the Hasmonean dynasty also granted political power to queen mothers.[11]

The Book of Judith: Queen as Defender

During the same time period, the Book of Judith, an apocryphal book, depicts a pious widow as both ascetic servant of God and leader/defender of her city. The events cannot be dated (a fact that leads many to think that the book is fictional) but the book takes place during a time of war with Nebuchadnezzar, king of Babylon. The king's general, Holofernes, is seeking to conquer Jerusalem. On his way, he lays siege to a walled mountain town called Bethulia (virgin of God). The inhabitants of the town are dying of hunger and thirst, and the town elders decide that if no one comes to their aid in five days, they will open the gates to the enemy.

> *Now in those days Judith heard about these things: she was the daughter of Merari… Her husband Manasseh, who belonged to her tribe and family, had died during the barley harvest… Judith remained as a widow for three years and four months at home where she set up a tent for herself on the roof of her house. She put sackcloth around her waist and dressed in widow's clothing. She fasted all the days of her widowhood, except the day before the sabbath and the sabbath itself, the day before the new moon and the day of the new moon, and the festivals and days of rejoicing of the house of Israel. She was beautiful in appearance, and was very lovely to behold. Her husband Manasseh had left her gold and silver, men and women slaves, livestock, and fields; and she maintained this estate. No one spoke ill of her, for she feared God with great devotion.*
> —Judith 8:1-8

Judith is known for her piety and simple lifestyle, as well as for her wisdom and beauty. When she comes to the town council to express her dismay at the council's decision, the mayor, Uzziah, says to her: "From the beginning of your life all the people have known your understanding." Judith sees that if Bethulia falls, the army of Holofernes will cross the mountains and take Jerusalem. She steps forward to save the town, and gives orders to the elders and the people of the city.

CHAPTER 9: QUEEN-PRIESTESSES

> *Then Judith said to them, 'Listen to me. I am about to do something that will go down through all generations of our descendants. Stand at the town gate tonight so that I may go out with my maid; and within the days after which you have promised to surrender the town to our enemies, the Lord will deliver Israel by my hand.'*
> —Judith 9:32-35

Judith puts away her widow's garb and dresses in finery, jewelry and perfume. She goes to the enemy camp, with her maid, and pretends to be a traitor to her city. She takes her own kosher food with her so she won't have to eat the Greek food. She tells Holofernes that her people are sinning by eating food intended for Temple tithes, and God is angry with them. She offers to give him information that will lead to his victory. Each morning, she will go and pray in the valley for God to tell her when the right time comes for Holofernes to attack.

Holofernes believes her promises, and he also wishes to seduce her. He commands that Judith be allowed to leave the camp every morning to ritually bathe in the river. After four days, he invites her to a banquet, intending to seduce her. Delighted by her, he drinks and becomes drunk. After he falls asleep, she takes a sword and beheads him.

> *Soon afterward she went out and gave Holofernes' head to her maid, who placed it in her food bag. Then the two of them went out together, as they were accustomed to do for prayer. They passed through the camp, circled around the valley, and went up the mountain to Bethulia, and came to its gates. From a distance Judith called out to the sentries at the gates, "Open, open the gate! God, our God, is with us, still showing his power in Israel and his strength against our enemies, as he has done today!"*
> —Judith 12:6-11

Judith hangs Holofernes' head on the town wall. In the morning the Assyrians are so terrified by the sight of Holofernes' headless body that they flee in panic, and the Israelites drive them off easily. Like Miriam before her, Judith celebrates her victory with dance:

> *All the women of Israel gathered to see her, and blessed her, and some of them performed a dance in her honor. She took ivy-wreathed wands in her hands and distributed them to the women*

who were with her; and she and those who were with her crowned themselves with olive wreaths. She went before all the people in the dance, leading all the women, while all the men of Israel followed, bearing their arms and wearing garlands and singing hymns.
—Judith 15:12-13

Judith presides over the procession with ivy wands, as if she is a maenad, a priestess of Dionysos, (who was also celebrated with ivy). Like the warrior goddess Anat, known as the Queen of Heaven, Judith has taken revenge on her enemies by cutting them in pieces. Judith leads the people to the Temple, reciting a psalm of victory. She dedicates the bed of Holofernes to the Temple. She never remarries—her life continues to be centered around her people and God.

Judith is an extraordinary depiction of a Jewish warrior-queen-priestess. Her life is dedicated to prayer and meditation, she advises and governs her city, she is a defender of her people and of Jerusalem, and she leads the victory procession to the Temple. Scholars have suggested that Judith's story was pattered after the prophetess Deborah and even after the goddess Anat—and that it may have been written in the Egyptian Jewish community, where Anat was revered.[12] If so, the procession of women with ivy wands may represent the celebratory roles of women in the Temple at Elephantine. Judith's story may reflect that certain powerful women, devoted to God, became spiritual and temporal leaders of the Jewish people.

The Mystics and the Sabbath Queen

The notion of giving women spiritual power—power to decide law, create theology, and chart a path for the community—was not very popular in the Talmudic era or in the Middle Ages. However, the image of queen began to creep into stories about God. Many rabbinic parables speak of God and the Shekhinah as a king and queen. The Talmud also refers to the Sabbath as a queen: "Rabbi Hanina used to wrap himself in a garment, stand close to sunset as the Sabbath entered, and say, Come, let us go out to welcome Sabbath the queen!"[13]

The image of the Sabbath as queen continues to exist in the imagination of the kabbalists. The Shekhinah, who doubles as Sabbath, Torah, and bride of God, becomes a queen in Jewish mythology. The Zohar tells the following parable:

There was a king among his people,
But the queen was not with the king.
As long as the queen was not with the king,

> *The people did not feel secure,*
> *And could not dwell in safety.*
> *As soon as the queen came,*
> *All the people rejoiced and dwelled safely.*[14]

One of the names of Shekhinah in kabbalistic literature is Matronita—the Lady. A *matronita* is an aristocratic woman—the word is a direct translation of *gevirah*. The Zohar writes about Shabbat:

> *The Sabbath is a queen and a bride. This is why the masters of the Mishnah used to go out on the eve of the Sabbath to receive her on the road... One must receive the Lady with many lighted candles, many enjoyments, beautiful clothes...*

The Shekhinah as queen is protector of her people, interceding with the Divine masculine as king, and also defending the Jews from attack. She is a regal warrior:

> *What shall I do for Her? Well look! My entire household is in Her hands. He issued a proclamation: "Henceforth all affairs of the King are entrusted to Matronita [the Lady/the Queen]." He placed in Her control all His weapons: lances, swords, bows, arrows, catapults, fortresses, stones... In front of Her would appear warriors, catapultiers, lancemen, swordsmen—since other camps were coming to wage war against Israel from above."*[15]

The Zohar depicts the Shekhinah with Kali-like ferocity, saying: "We have learned that a thousand mighty mountains standing before her are just one bite for her. A thousand great rivers she swallows in one gulp."[16] When a person is traveling, the Shekhinah stands by as a guardian.[17]

As noted in the introduction to this book, the Frankists of the seventeenth century use the term Gevirah, lady or queen, to refer to Jacob Frank's wife Sarah and daughter Eva, and they also use the term to refer to the Tarot card known as the High Priestess.[18] Thus, they resurrect the title of the queen mother to describe a woman who brings with her the presence of Shekhinah.

On Friday night, when many Jews around the world rise at the end of the mystical poem Lecha Dodi, turn to the back of the room, and bow. They are greeting the Sabbath queen. While the worshippers may not know it, this invisible queen is directly connected to the divine queen and to the queens of ancient Israel.

Queen-Priestess Incarnations

The notion that spiritual women can be powerful, and that powerful women can be spiritual leaders, is still dissonant in contemporary Jewish society, as it is in many societies. In the United States, women rabbis continue to have smaller congregations and lower pay than male rabbis, and high-ranking Jewish communal professionals still tend to be men.[19] In Israel, women can serve at every level of government, but the official rabbinate is entirely male. Even in supposedly egalitarian societies, there is often a bias against the powerful feminine.

The queen-priestess archetype invites women to break down this bias within themselves. While hierarchy, particularly the rigid hierarchies of the ancient world, makes many women uncomfortable, imagining the queen as a holy figure challenges us to find the power center in our own souls. A Kohenet Institute graduate, Sheva Melmed, writes:

> *The Queen is an archetype I feared but wanted to learn how to embody. My way into this was through very powerful goddess figures. In my mid-20s I discovered goddess figures that were powerful but not in a way that embodied hierarchy.*
>
> *We think of destructiveness and creativity as masculine. For me, that there could be a feminine way to destroy and end things meant there was a feminine way to begin and create things. Destroying old systems makes way for the new.*

Like other women of her generation, Elisheva is seeking a way to claim her power within society. She is looking for faces of women and God that empower her and invite her to step into her fullest self.

> *I meet the Queen in assertive women, women who use power for the benefit of the community, and not only for themselves. I meet her in women who know how to take care of themselves and not deplete their energy sources while taking care of everyone else. I am seeing her in myself over time, as I speak truth to power and stand up for myself.*
>
> *The Shekhinah is not powerful enough for me. I see Shekhinah as a weeping woman or as a bride, connected to male deity but not embodied in Herself. I understand her value as an expression of the immanent, but I connect Jewishly through [names like] Elat and El Shaddai because they embody full power. I don't reject Adonai [Lord], but I need this balance.*

Another way the Kohenet Institute community engages the archetype of queen-priestess is as ritual guardian. Just as Judith was a guardian of her city, we appoint some participants in ceremonies to be spiritual guardians. We understand this as a necessary part of creating a ritual container: a space within which ritual participants feel safe enough to be comfortable.

One Kohenet ordinee, Erev Richards, has taken the role of ritual guardian at many of our ceremonies, and educates others on how to take on this role. She understands herself as being a guide to the powerful energies that must enter and leave during the ceremony. Erev also teaches our community (as well as other women) archery, inviting women to claim our power in the physical world.

Erev speaks of her lifelong calling to the role of guardian:

> *I dedicate my life on a daily basis to provide safety, nurturing and guidance to women, children and creatures. The guardian's sacred rites are providing safe, secure, sacred space for women to worship; serving as an intermediary to and teacher of the elements and the portals to the next realm; providing guidance to those who journey so that they may return safely to their own healthy shape.*
>
> *Women must be reunited with our past, with our ancestors and with our power. As a guardian I dedicate myself to bringing women closer to Her ancient ways. We each carry the knowledge of our ancestors, guardians just help to unlock the gate or to provide Her daughters the tools to unlock the gate to where that knowing is held.*

Spirit Journey The Queen

You find yourself in a mountainous landscape. Begin climbing. You will come to a high place. The wind whistles around you. There is a stone throne here, carved with animals. Sit on the throne. Look out at the valleys below. Do you feel powerful? Small? Important? Serene? Anxious?

Three regal figures appear before you. They could be queen mothers of ancient Israel. They could be the three patriarchs Abraham, Isaac, and Jacob. They could be anyone you imagine—or three aspects of yourself. Greet them. See them as clearly as you can. "We have come to help you claim your throne," one of them says.

The three will now have a conversation about you, which you will witness. They will discuss your strengths and weaknesses, and the ways you can stand fully in your power. When they are finished with their discussion, each of the three steps forward with a gift for you. You may take one or all of these gifts, or you need not take any. Remember that all kinds of power have a double edge. Choose only those kinds of power that you believe you can wield justly and properly. When the three gifts have been presented, the three advisors disappear.

As you descend from the throne, you notice that one of the animals carved into the throne has come alive. "I am the guardian of your power," the animal says. "I will be with you whenever you need me." Ask the animal for his or her name, and then ask for a way that you can call her or him again when you are in need.

Descend from the high place. As you leave, your animal spirit calls out a farewell to you. Continue until you return to the place of your waking self.

She Who Embraces Her Power:
The Practice of Shadow Integration
by Taya Shere

The queen-priestess protects and channels power. Becoming a queen-priestess requires coming to terms with our power and the fullness of our selves. Integrating shadow-qualities supports us in being at home in our challenges and our gifts. Shadow-work is a practice of seeing, claiming and integrating the aspects of our self that we keep hidden.

We may keep these aspects hidden because we are ashamed of them, judge them, or dislike them. We may repress them because we are afraid of our own power or greatness. Excepting situations of abuse or misuse of power, what we fear, judge, or dislike in others can give us important information about shadow aspects of ourselves.

When we are gripped by the need to judge another, particularly if our emotion feels excessive given the situation, we are blessed with an opportunity to engage in shadow-work. In such a situation you might ask yourself: What about this person do I find distasteful? What am I judging? What about them angers or frightens me? What is my relationship to the quality they are displaying? For example, if you are angered by a friend's carefree attitude toward making plans, explore your own attitude toward making plans, scheduling, or control. What angers you about their carefree attitude? In your mind, what would happen if you were as carefree as they? What would it mean, or how would it affect your life, or at least your self-conception, if you acted or made choices as they did?

Shadow-work asks us to integrate aspects of ourselves that we judge as negative. It invites us to acknowledge and claim positive qualities as well. In his book *Shadow Dance*, David Richo suggests that many of us often fear full expression of our positive qualities or power, possibly even more than the negative qualities we try to hide. As Marianne Williamson teaches, "Our deepest fear is not that we are inadequate. Our deepest fear is that we are powerful beyond measure. It is our light, not our darkness that most frightens us. We ask ourselves, 'Who am I to be brilliant, gorgeous, talented, fabulous? Actually, who are you *not* to be?'"

To uncover the positive shadow aspects not yet integrated, look at your s/heros, the people in your life or in the wider world who you admire. Who do you dream of being like? Toward whom do you feel jealous? Perhaps there is someone you long to be around, to a degree that outweighs the reality of your relationship with them. What do they represent for you? What dreams of yours are they bringing forth into the world?

Over a decade ago, I became focused on a musician I encountered at a festival. I found him inordinately compelling, and listened to his music incessantly. The intensity of my desire to connect with him far surpassed the reality of our initial contact. I struggled to unhook from this longing. Eventually, I uncovered what he represented for me — a devotional musician whose voice becomes a portal for the divine. I was longing not for this man I barely knew, but to share my own devotional music with the world.

In subsequent weeks and months, when his face and voice began cycling in my mind, I entered into my own chant practice, or visioned steps for sharing my music. My thoughts of him waned and my chants grew in frequency, power, and beauty. In time, I began to share my music widely and to record and release CDs. Now whenever I find myself gripped by thoughts about someone that are intense beyond the reality of our connection, I identify what this person represents for me, and work to engage my "inner them."

Shadow-integration work can be informative, rewarding, and transforming. Find a friend, partner, or circle of people with whom you can explore shadow integration practices. Welcome intense emotion and energy as it moves through you. Cultivate yourself as an aligned, clear, and strong vessel for the gifts that uniquely enter the world through you.

Resources

Shadow Dance: Liberating the Power and Creativity of Your Dark Side by David Richo (Shambhala, 1999), *Practically Shameless: How Shadow Work Helped Me Find My Voice, My Path and My Inner Gold* by Alyce Barry (Practically Shameless Press, 2008), *Seeing in the Dark: Myths and Stories to Reclaim the Buried, Knowing Woman* by Clarissa Pinkola Estes (audio CD), (Sounds True, 2010).

Chapter 10:
Midwife-Priestesses

When I was in college, I discovered midrash: creative interpretation of sacred text. For as long as there have been stories in the world, there has been interpretation of those stories, but I had been unaware that this was "kosher" in a sacred context. I read brilliant masters of this genre: Marge Piercy and Alicia Ostriker, Yehuda Amichai and Howard Schwartz, each of who were employing this ancient tradition—part exegesis and part creative writing—to read their own voices into sacred text. By the time I was in graduate school, I had begun to write my own midrash.

In my twenties, I was reading a biblical genealogy that mentioned Elisheva, the wife of Aaron, brother of Moses, future high priest of the Hebrews. I discovered that very little was said about Elisheva in the Bible or in midrash, but that one talmudic source claimed she was a midwife.[1] Inspired by this, I wrote a story called *The Tenth Plague*.

In my story, an impoverished Egyptian woman is giving birth to her firstborn son on the night of the tenth plague. The Egyptian midwives are afraid to deliver her baby. The laboring woman's young sister runs to Elisheva, a Hebrew midwife, and asks for her help. After initial reluctance, Elisheva agrees to deliver the baby. Later that night, when the Angel of Death comes to the door, Elisheva has the choice to flee, but she defends the mother and her child, sending the Angel of Death away. Because of her brave act, God/dess rewards Elisheva by making her the mother of the priesthood. The mother and her child, along with the little girl who summoned Elisheva, come along on the Exodus and become free.[2] The story became the seed for my first book.[3] I still occasionally receive phone calls asking for the ancient source of the midrash about Elisheva and the Angel of Death, and this feels to me like an even more gratifying reward.

Looking back, I now see that the essence of my story was the archetype of a midwife-priestess: a skilled healer, a defender of the life-force, an ancestor of the priestly tribe. Midwives are mediators of the sacred through their work of aiding birth. They are servants and guides of creation: They help to bring new things into being.

The Biblical Period: Midwife as Savior

The most prominent of the biblical midwives, and the only ones with names, are Shifrah and Puah. They serve the enslaved Hebrew women in Egypt. Because of an ambiguity in the biblical Hebrew that describes them, we do not know if they are Hebrews themselves, or Egyptians who supervise the birthing of Hebrew slaves. We also do not know their relationship to one another. Are they sisters, friends, co-workers, lovers, mother and daughter?

We do know that in ancient Egypt midwifery was priestess work, most probably done by servants of Heqet, frog-goddess of birth.[4]

We meet Shifrah and Puah in the throne room of Egypt. Pharaoh is in a rage at the frightening fertility rates of the Hebrews: they breed like rats, lice, locusts. He is convinced they are plotting to take over the country. Enslaving the Hebrews is not enough for Pharaoh; he orders the two chief midwives to kill all male Hebrew infants at birth.

> *When you assist the Hebrew women in giving birth, look at the birthstones. If it is a boy, kill him. If it is a girl, let her live. The midwives revered Elohim, and they did not do as the king of Egypt had told them; they let the boys live.*
> —Exodus 1:15

The midwives bow to Pharaoh's command, but when they leave the throne room, they do not carry it out. They fear God, or the gods—the Hebrew word Elohim can mean both. They midwives create a conspiracy—one by one the Hebrew boys slide through their hands and live. Shifrah and Puah are midwives not only to the Hebrew women but to the coming Exodus.

> *The king of Egypt summoned the midwives and asked them: "Why did you do this thing, letting the children live?" The midwives answered Pharaoh: "The Hebrew women are not like Egyptian women; they are like wild animals! Before the midwife comes to them, they give birth." Elohim rewarded the midwives, and the people became many and multiplied greatly. Because the midwives revered Elohim, he made houses for them. Then Pharaoh commanded his people: "Every son that is born, throw him into the Nile, but let every daughter live."*
> —Exodus 1:18-22

When Pharaoh demands to know what happened, the midwives play on Pharaoh's own prejudices. They reply slyly that the Hebrew women are like animals who give birth without a midwife. This answer is brilliant because it has a double meaning. *Ki chayot heina* means "they are wild beasts" but it also means "because they are alive." The midwives brazenly hint to Pharaoh that they respect the children of the Hebrew women simply because they are alive, and for no other reason. Pharaoh must turn elsewhere to carry out the murder of children.

The Holy One looks kindly on Shifrah and Puah, and rewards them by making houses for them. Houses can mean dynasties—God grants the midwives children. "Houses" can also mean shrines. This reading fits with what we know of ancient Egyptian birth practices, where a small house or room, like a shrine, served as a birth chamber. In later Egyptian civilization, a birth-house was attached to a temple. How powerful to imagine these revolutionary women as elder teachers, passing on their wisdom and courage to a new generation of midwife-priestesses.

Shifrah and Puah are ethical and religious revolutionaries. They defy a living god, Pharaoh, in order to fight for slave women and children. A rabbinic legend imagines them as healers and Robin Hoods, taking food and water from wealthy women to sustain the new mothers and infants in the slave quarters.[5]

In a number of scenes in the Bible, a midwife appears at the moment of birth to speak words of comfort to the mother and/or provide oracles about the child. As helpers in the difficult work of labor, midwives wait to learn what the fates have brought. Midwives to Rachel and to the wife of Pinchas the high priest reassure dying mothers that they have borne sons and that their children will survive them. In Genesis 38, a midwife delivers the twins of Tamar (Tamar's story appears in Chapter 1):

> *At the time of her giving birth, there were twins in her womb! As she was laboring to give birth, a hand appeared, and the midwife tied a red thread on that hand, saying: "This one came out first." Yet he drew back his hand, and his brother came out. The midwife said: "How you have made a breach for yourself!" So he was named Peretz [breach]. Then his brother came out, whose hand bore the red thread, and he was called Zerach [shining.]"*
> —Genesis 38:27-29

The midwife uses a red cord to indicate the twins' birth order—but then the first one pulls back and the other comes out first. The midwife's comment of surprise—"How you have made a breach for yourself!" becomes a key factor in the child's name, Peretz, meaning "breach." While the midwife does not give the name, she speaks the oracle that the name reflects. Peretz will be the ancestor of David, the man who makes a breach in the House of Saul and becomes king himself. Oracular work is the work of priestesses, and midwives bearing oracles could be regarded as holy women.

God too does holy midwife-work. Prophetic descriptions of the redemption, the age of perfect peace and unity, invoke the image of rebirth, with the Infinite as midwife to the future age. The prophet Isaiah exclaims in God's voice:

> *Before she labored she gave birth; and before her pangs came upon her, she delivered a son. Whoever heard such a thing? Who ever saw such a thing? Can a land labor in a single day? Can a people be born in a single moment? Yet Zion labored and gave birth to her children. Shall I who bring on labor not bring to birth? And shall I who cause birth shut [the womb]?"*
> —Isaiah 66:7-9

Isaiah predicts the return of the Israelite people to the land of Israel by imagining that, in a single day, the land/nation "gives birth" to hordes of returning exiles. The Divine is a midwife, speeding along labor and drawing countless children from the womb of the land itself. At the end of the passage, God indignantly asks: "Shall I who aid in conception not also aid in birth?" Midwifery is the natural perogative of a Creator. Indeed, in the mind of the Psalmist, God watches over individual births as well:

> *You drew me from the womb*
> *and placed me safe at my mother's breast.*
> —Psalms 22:9-10

Similarly, many have noted the resemblance of the Exodus to a birth—the nation passes through homes with bloody doorposts and crosses over an immense watery canal to freedom. God is the midwife to the people at that moment as well. Centuries later, a rabbinic midrash comments:

> *Like one who pulls a fetus from the womb of a mother animal,*
> *God took Israel out of Egypt.*
> —Yalkut Shimoni 828

The Rabbinic Period: Midwife as Wise Woman

Many rabbinic texts indicate the respect with which midwives were viewed. The rabbinic title for a midwife was *chachamah*—wise woman. This is actually the feminine of the masculine term for sage: *chacham*. A related teaching from Pirkei Avot says: "Who is wise? One who sees what is born [one who knows the future]."

Midwives received certain spiritual prerogatives. Midwives' testimony was accepted by talmudic sages, though ordinary women could not be witnesses in a rabbinic court.[6] The laws of the Sabbath were strict, but they were relaxed for midwives because the midwives were involved in life-saving work: A midwife could light a lamp, tie the umbilical cord, and perform other tasks on the Sabbath.[7]

> *[For a woman in labor] a midwife may be called to come from anywhere. Even if it is a midwife who is giving birth, a midwife may be called, and we profane the Sabbath for her—we light a bonfire for her even if it is summer.*
> —Jerusalem Talmud, Shabbat 65b

Certain rabbinic *midrashim* identify Shifrah and Puah with the mother and sister of Moses, Yocheved and Miriam.[8] These midrashim show the respect that the rabbis had for midwives: Miriam, a prophetess, and Yocheved, the mother of Moses, receive praise as excellent midwives who could revive a nearly-dead child:

> *Who were these midwives?...Rabbi Samuel bar Nachman said: A mother and her daughter; Yocheved and Miriam. Miriam was only five years old... and she would help her mother Yocheved, seeing to all her needs. She was an energetic child. Yocheved was called Shifrah... because the Israelites multiplied (paru) because of her, and Puah, because when others said the child was dead, she would revive it [meifiah oto].*
> —Exodus Rabbah 1:13

Midwives as Healers and Ritualists

Jewish women continued to be active as midwives in the Middle Ages. Certain halakhic and medical texts in thirteenth century Germany speak of midwives, informing us that midwives provided care from early in the pregnancy until several weeks after the birth, and were not simply called in for labor. These texts also mention that circumcisers (*mohalim*) and midwives (*meyaldot*) worked closely together to preserve the health of infants, and that circumcisers often learned their remedies and healing techniques from midwives. One text includes the phrase: "Thus say the *rofot* and *chachamot*" (the women healers and the wise women). Most midwives of this period were widows with grown children, who had apprenticed to midwives while younger and learned the art of midwifery, and had begun to practice once their own children were grown. These German Jewish midwives received the title of Meyaledet/Midwife in community lists and on gravestones.[8a]

Throughout Jewish history, midwives' work was understood to be spiritual as well as physical. A fourteenth-century text recommends that midwives be "God-fearing, respectable, learned, wise, intelligent, clean, innocent, strong, skillful, and patient."⁹ In Ashkenazi Europe in the Middle Ages, a room for sick people and birthing women was known as a *hekdesh* or "sanctified place."¹⁰ Through this shared root for holiness, (k-d-sh), healers and midwives can be connected to priests.

In eighteenth century Constantinople, a book of ethical sermons included a prayer for midwives on their way to a delivery, asking God that the midwife should cause no harm, and praying for compassion for the birthing woman. The midwife was instructed to help the birthing woman pray, and to inform her that safe delivery depended solely on divine mercy. An Italian woman's prayer-book records a similar prayer.¹¹

Ashkenazi midwives were also master chanters of incantations, and creators of charms. A midwife might pierce the ears of a baby girl and tie a red thread through the holes, or tie a red thread around the baby's wrist. This was to keep away Lilith, the baby-stealing demon.¹² Sometimes a midwife would save the after-birth for use as a charm for curing barrenness in other women, or to rub on the chest of a newborn to stimulate breathing.¹³

In Morocco in the early twentieth century, Jewish midwives would take the newborn infant to the doorpost and touch their hands to the mezuzah. She would then deliver a spontaneous prayer of thanks. This ritual is extraordinary for its clarity about birth as a literal 'rite of passage'. The midwife takes the child, who has just passed through the birth canal, to the mezuzah, a ritual marker that invokes God's presence in the liminal space of the doorway. Here, the midwife ritually welcomes the child through the door of life and into the world of human beings.

In eighteenth century London, the Jewish community continued to support midwives in ways that were unusual among their neighbors. The birth ward in the Sephardic Jewish hospital was the first of its kind anywhere in England in that only female midwives were allowed into the birthing ward. In the rest of England, male midwives and obstetricians were trying new and unproven technologies, often to the detriment of women. Tellingly, the gravestones of midwives in the Sephardic Jewish community of London bore the title *matrone*, lady or motherly one, as a sacred title—just as rabbis and priests/*kohanim* did and still do bear such titles.¹⁴

Modern society frequently paints midwives as less competent than doctors —in many states a midwife cannot practice. However, in the last fifteen years there has been a growth in the number of women turning to midwives for their prenatal care and delivery, and more insurance companies are covering their services. Midwifery in Europe has been demonstrated to lead to healthier mothers and babies than the physician-based care women receive in the United States.¹⁵ We are still learning to respect the legacy of the priestess-midwives and their modern sisters.

Midwife-Priestess Incarnations

Midwife and *kohenet* Paula Freedman works in a New York City hospital. She describes her mission as a modern priestess-midwife:

> *It has always been my desire to empower women to have the experience they need and want. My work also entails well woman care, family planning, and counseling for women who choose not to keep pregnancies. I am always looking for alternatives to the medical model using herbs, homeopathy, etc. I see my role as somewhat subversive and alternative to the medical and patriarchal models. Part of my role as midwife is to teach and mentor midwifery students and younger women.*

Elsa Asher, a student in the Kohenet program, is a doula. Her role is to offer physical, emotional, and spiritual assistance to women giving birth, and often to post-partum mothers as well. She writes: "As an aspiring midwife, I learn at the feet of birthing women and midwives, and I feel blessed to be part of this ancient lineage."

> *When I attend a birth, I am present as a resourced person to hold space for the mother's experience. This takes many forms. In one moment a soothing massage, in another, words to summon strength in the last pushes. Though sometimes I am at work in the foreground, and other times I stand to the side, my job throughout is the encourage her to take responsibility for herself in her own decisions.*
>
> *Having clarity of purpose demands strenuous spiritual work. I have witnessed women's experiences of sadness, frustration, disappointment, joy, love, and awe of their own power. It is my focused path to hold space for all of this. My passion for this work was ignited by my own experiences in my early twenties of a first trimester miscarriage and a second trimester stillbirth. My journey of grieving and integration has offered itself as a deep well of inspiration for the healing process. I have engaged in a range of therapeutic practices, including the poetic and the narrative, and draw upon these traditions to serve others.*

Literal midwifery is not the only way modern women can be midwives. Priestess and healer Tiana Mirapae sees her counseling work, as well as her doula work, as midwifery:

> *As a psychotherapist, healer, and teacher, I am midwifing people through their healing into who they are becoming. I am holding sacred space for people to do whatever they need to do, in order to grow, release, change, and emerge into their wellness. I have felt like a midwife, as well, when helping people to cross over in their dying process. I have felt like a midwife when I witness my students becoming the priestesses and healers that they are. I feel like a midwife whenever I see a woman or man I've worked with become empowered to be, and be, happy and well.*
>
> *I loved the childbirth experience so much I became a natural childbirth teacher and coach working with pregnant teenagers and women with high risk pregnancy at Baystate Medical Center. Now I doula for friends and have assisted at countless births.*

Sacred artists can also see themselves as midwives, bringing new forms into the world. Working with raw substance to make an as-yet-unknown thing can feel like assisting God/dess to create. Jess Schurtman, a Kohenet initiate, uses clay to create ritual objects:

> *Art is my spiritual practice and so I approach the clay as a partner. I try to honor the integrity of the clay. I don't try to make the clay just do what I want. I try to listen to the clay and be in tune with it, not impose my will on it. When I'm able to honor the clay, the most delightful and honest things come forth. I think of it as being like a midwife, in that a midwife uses her hands and her intuition and tries to bring forth a being.*
>
> *I'm partnering with the Shekhinah and I try to surrender as much as possible. In the beginning, I am still in my conscious process, but then it's just me and the clay with the Shekhinah. I feel like I'm being guided. When I'm using my hands to do the Shekhinah's work, it's effortless. When I'm in my own head, it's like trying to catch a baby when the contractions haven't started.*

Midwifery is also a metaphor for the spiritual work of helping people negotiate the liminal realms: the places of transformative change in their lives. When they aid in the process of rebirth for individuals and communities, spiritual leaders are also midwives.

Ritual midwifery is also an important part of Kohenet work. Through ritual, we aid people to pass into a new chapter of their lives. For example, it often happens that during the Kohenet program, a woman decides that she needs a new name. Through ritual, we grant this new name and with it, new growth.

At a 2015 Kohenet retreat, we created a ritual for naming a student, Judith Wouk. She had chosen a new middle name, Maeryam. Judith is a sacred drummer, so we used rhythm to "write" the new name into being. We inscribed the name in earth, drumming its syllables into the ground. We inscribed it in water, having Judith write the name in a bowl of water. We inscribed the name in air through singing the name with our voices, and we inscribed it in the fire of the spirit. With each inscription, we layered on a new meaning of the name, invoking Judith's ancestors, the prophetess Miriam, and the sea. This kind of ritual is a rebirth ritual, in which those who participate are midwives, helping the celebrant to birth a new self.

> *Midwifery, whether for birth or for death, is in the realm of Goddess work. As kohanot, we have the skills to deal with the liminal spaces between worlds. This is part of what we are trained for and one of our great strengths.*
> —Yocheved Landsman

Spirit Journey
The Midwife

You are standing on a beach, looking out to the sea. You can catch a glimpse of dry land on the sea's distant other side. The beach is crowded with many people. You hear a sound like the cry of a ram's horn, or a conch. Men, women, children and animals begin running toward the sea.

At the edge of the beach, a few people are splashing into the waves. To your amazement the sea begins to part. Dark roiling water surrounds an empty, gaping tunnel of air. The people on the beach stare. Notice your feelings as you witness the movement within the sea.

You begin to coax people into the sea with song, words, gestures, and incantations. You are a midwife, aiding the birth of each person here. You pass through the crowd encouraging everyone to move forward. As each person passes into the dark tunnel, you see waves shaped like hands reaching out to grab each shirt, dress, or cloak and pull the people along through the passages.

Now you too are swept into the dark passage. Reach out to touch the walls of water. Feel their texture. Push your hands into the walls. Feel, see, or hear a blessing being bestowed on your hands, that they may bring new things into the world.

You have the sense that there are enemies behind you: maybe your old fears or resentments. The sea crashes down on these enemies and they are washed away, giving you strength to move into the future. Notice what, if anything, changes around you as this happens.

Ahead of you, you see light. The tunnel suddenly opens out. It is dawn, and you are on the other shore. It is time for you to arise from your meditation.

She Who Supports Transformation:
The Practice of Being With What Wants To Be Born
by Taya Shere

The midwife-priestess draws forth through her presence. The literal meaning of the word midwife is "with-woman." The path of the midwife is one of presence: being fully with one who is birthing. A midwife-priestess shows up to support new life coming into the world. Midwife-priestesses teach us to stand by friends, lovers, and family in moments of profound transition. We cultivate ourselves as midwife-priestesses when we serve as allies, coaches, guides, empowering friends, and mentors.

Midwife-priestesses show up when the moment is ripe. When friends or mentees are ready to birth, or when they are in need of a support team, be present for them. Listen to what the person you are supporting communicates, verbally and non-verbally. Listen on practical, emotional, cognitive, or spiritual levels. Listen with as many senses as you are able to engage. Listen as prayer.

When you see clearly the gifts and dreams of people you champion, let them know it. Be clear, direct, and generous with your praise. Tell them what is unique and amazing in their particular offerings.

When you perceive the strengths and challenges in how they grow and create, share with them what you understand as the gifts in their particular process. Express to them the ways you feel their distinct characters, experiences, and skill sets serve in being able to bring their creations into the world.

Some people prefer to offer support that is passive, relying on the guidance and desires of the one being supported. Some give support that is directive, firmly holding and steering the supportee. A midwife-priestess knows that in any given situation multiple kinds of support can be resonant, and that often, a combination of steering and surrender is what is called for.

As you support those you love or are mentoring, bring yourself into deep presence. Be in the moment. Pay attention to your intuition, to Spirit, or the cues you receive. As you practice offering support, your skill will build in trusting yourself to know what is needed and offer it effortlessly.

A good midwife knows when to call for back-up and additional resources. Even when you offer your best, it may not always be exactly what your supportee needs. Sometimes, bringing in additional friends or colleagues is necessary. Other times, relying on a wider or more skilled support-network is called for. This could mean connecting your friend with therapeutic contexts or communities of people with similar healing needs or experiences. In creative realms, this could be connecting your artist-friend to a recording studio with more equipment or expertise or with a kindred spirit in her discipline.

Even the most dedicated, compassionate support person can only be truly fulfilled when she is living in alignment with her own dreams. Make sure you are giving yourself time for self-nurturance and that you are receiving an abundance of support in your own life. What are the ways you are brings forth all you dream of? How are you being nourished? What supports you in growing, creating and thriving? We give best when we are at our most whole.

Resources:

For a playful practical map of manifesting creative dreams, read *Make Your Creative Dreams Real: A Plan for Procrastinators, Perfectionists and People Who Would Really Rather Sleep All Day* by Susan Ariel Rainbow Kennedy (Touchstone, 2009). For expanded ways of viewing and experiencing what is possible in friendship, read *Fabulous Friendship Festival: Loving Wildly, Learning Deeply, Living Fully With Our Friends*, also by Susan Ariel Rainbow Kennedy (Harmony, 2007).

Chapter 11: Wise-Woman-Priestesses

A few years ago I had a dream that I have learned from ever since. In the dream, I had come to a house of priestesses—nothing grand, a little two-story house with white siding and a front and back door, and a nice lawn outside. Inside, there was a staircase with a banister, a front desk, and many rooms for the priestesses who were living or visiting there.

I asked the priestess at the front desk about my room, and was directed to the second-best room. "Why not the best room?" I wanted to know indignantly. "It is standing empty." There was indeed a beautiful room on the first floor with lots of light: the high priestess's room. I had been a teacher to my community for many years; I felt I deserved the high priestess's room. The priestess at the desk informed me: "That room is reserved for your teacher." I experienced instant relief and peace. Of course that room was for my teacher. And I gladly went to take another room.

I learned from the dream how badly we need teachers, even when we ourselves are teachers of others. There is a psychic space in our minds for the elder, the master, the sage—or the wise woman. This is the person who challenges us to grow beyond where we currently are. Without these mentors and advisors, we have to struggle through our life lessons as orphans, without the benefit of the experiences of others.

Wise-woman-priestesses are mentors, storytellers, conflict mediators, and interpreters of tradition and law. They bring insight, prudence, and skill to any profession they may engage in—whether leader, healer, midwife, singer, or teacher, to name but a few. The Wise Woman can be experienced as a face of God.

The Biblical Period: At the Crossroads

Does not Wisdom call,
and Understanding raise her voice?
At the heights, by the road,
At the crossroad she stands,
Near the gates, at the city's door she cries.
O people, I call to you
And my voice is for humankind.
You who are simple, understand cleverness,
And fools, understand with your hearts!
—Proverbs 8:1-5

In the Book of Proverbs, Wisdom (*Chochmah*) is a semi-divine female figure who appears as a woman standing at the crossroads. In ancient Greece, the crossroads was a place sacred to Hecate, crone-goddess of magic. Indeed, the Talmud tells us that two women sitting opposite one another at a crossroad are surely doing magic.[1] According to William Dever, the gates of the city were once places of worship for a number of deities, before the monotheistic reforms of King Josiah and the Deuteronomic school.[2] Wisdom has a shrine at the gates, where she calls to the masses, inviting them to learn. She does not suffer fools.

As we noted in chapter 2, the Lady Wisdom figure has much in common with Asherah: Proverbs calls her a tree of life, which is a title of Asherah, and her followers are frequently described as happy: One Hebrew root for happiness, *aleph-shin-reish*, sounds very similar to Asherah. The Lady Wisdom who cries at the crossroads may represent the goddess in her new biblical form. She may also represent a human priestess—a priestess of knowledge.

In Proverbs, the wise woman is often associated with a house. As we have noted elsewhere, *bayit* or house also means "shrine." The word *bayit*/house, and the word *mezuzot* or doorposts, may hold the meaning "sacred place" in the following texts:

> *The wise woman builds her house, but the foolish one tears it down with her own hands.*
> —Proverbs 14:1

> *Wisdom has built her house; she has hewn her seven pillars...*
> *She has sent her maidens to call at the heights of the town:*
> *Let the simple enter here!*
> —Proverbs 9:1,3-4

> *Happy is the man who listens to me,*
> *Coming early to my doors each day,*
> *Keeping vigil at my threshold,*
> *For he who finds me finds life*
> *And obtains favor from YHWH.*
> —Proverbs 8:34-36

This shrine to Wisdom may be a metaphor—a way of speaking about dedication to prudence and good sense. The shrine may also represent an oracle-shrine: a place where one receives divine wisdom. The shrine could represent one's mother's house, and the learning and growth of one's formative years. Proverbs 1:8 teaches: "Listen to the discipline of your father and don't forsake the Torah of your mother." The shrine might be a place of learning, represent-

CHAPTER 11: WISE-WOMAN-PRIESTESSES

ing a gathering around a teacher or a scribe reading a text (such as the Torah). There are so many layers of meaning, and at its source the true meaning is most likely a blend.

Jeremiah speaks of "Torah from the priest, advice from the wise-man (*chacham*), speech from the prophet." These may have been three different categories of sacred person. Were there wise-women in ancient Israel? One can't tell from the book of Proverbs, because the language is so abstract. In the book of Samuel, though, there are two biblical stories of wise women that may be able to shed more light.

In II Samuel 20, a Benjaminite named Sheva ben Bichri encourages the Israelite population to reject King David and rebel against him. David sends his wily and ruthless general, Yoav, after Sheva. Yoav pens Sheva inside the city of Avel, in the region of Beit Maacah, and prepares to destroy the city.

> *A wise woman called from the city: "Listen, listen! Ask Yoav to come here so I can speak with him." He approached her, and she said: "Are you Yoav?" and he said "I am." She said, "Listen to the words of your maidservant," and he said: "I am listening." In ancient days it was said, 'Go and ask of Avel,' and so people would do. I am [one of] the faithful peaceful folk of Israel. You are seeking to destroy a city and a mother in Israel! Why should you swallow up God's possession?"*
> —II Samuel 20:16-20

The wise woman (*chachamah*) in this passage, known as the wise woman of Avel, comes to the city wall to speak to the king's general. This implies that she is not just a sensible person but someone of importance in the city. She informs Yoav that Avel is a place where people sought knowledge—in other words, the city was the site of an oracle. The Hebrew used for "go ask" is *sha'ol yishalu*, a phrase that sounds like She'ol, the underworld or "place of questions". The oracle may have been connected to She'ol and the ancestors.

The wise woman identifies herself oddly as *anochi shelumei emunei Yisrael*—literally, I am the peaceful faithful ones of Israel, as if she is a composite person, or a representative who speaks for others. She calls the city (and perhaps herself) a mother in Israel. The only other time this phrase appears is in reference to Deborah the prophet. The wise woman seems to be claiming for herself the mantle of the oracle of the city—which, if so, would make her the keeper of an oracular shrine.

One must understand when reading this story that no one negotiates with Yoav: He kills mercilessly over and over again in David's name. It is a mark of her respected position that Yoav listens to the wise woman of Avel.

> "God forbid I should swallow or destroy! A certain man from the mountains of Ephraim, called Sheva ben Bichri, has raised his hand against the king, against David! Hand him alone over, and we will go from the city." The woman answered Yoav: "His head will be thrown to you over the wall." The woman went to all the people with her wisdom, and they cut off the head of Sheva ben Bichri, and threw it to Yoav. He blew the shofar, and the soldiers went back to their tents, and Yoav returned to Jerusalem, to the king.
> —II Samuel 20:20-22

The wise woman negotiates the execution of the traitor in return for the city's safety. Perhaps she simply wants to save other lives, or perhaps she holds Sheva guilty for rebelling against the king. Or perhaps she has him killed so Yoav will not have the chance to torture him or humiliate him. She has no doubt that the cityfolk will obey her. "She went to the whole people with her wisdom" in Hebrew is *vatavo ha'isha el kol ha'am bechachmatah*. A more literal translation would be "she went to the whole people in her wisdom"—perhaps in her role as city oracle, and they obey—even to the extent of killing a man at her request.

The reader knows that Yoav has prior experience with wise women; earlier in the book of Samuel he himself has hired one. In I Samuel 14, David and his son Absalom are estranged—Absalom has killed his elder brother Amnon, because Amnon raped Absalom's full sister Tamar. Yoav sends a messenger to the town of Tekoa to bring a wise woman. He tells the wise woman to dress like a woman in mourning, go to the king, and tell the king a story: One of her sons has murdered the other one. Her town now wants to execute her remaining son and leave her childless, "to quench my coal which is left."

The king listens to the wise woman and promises her son absolution. The woman asks the king for an oath, which he grants. The woman then says to the king: "Why then have you planned the like against God's people?" and reproaches him for banishing his own son. King David summons Yoav and tells him to bring Absalom back from exile.

The text tells us no less than three times that Yoav conceived of the speech that the wise woman gives. Yet the speech is complex; she must be the author of much of it. If she is just any woman, why does Yoav need to send to Tekoa to fetch her to Jerusalem? Clearly she is a person of some renown. Like the wise woman of Avel, the wise woman of Tekoa negotiates a political conflict and saves lives.

The scholar Michael Moore sees the role of the Israelite wise woman as mediator of spiritual and political conflicts. Both the wise woman of Avel and the wise woman of Tekoa function in this role.³ Abigail, wife of Nabal, is also called wise, and she also is a mediator of conflict. She prevents King David from attacking her husband Nabal and his estate, by bringing David gifts and negotiating a peace with David herself.⁴ This suggests a unique role for the wisdom-priestess as conciliator of community conflicts. The presence of wise women in the Bible is echoed in other Near Eastern texts. Ninsun, queen, priestess, and mother of Gilgamesh, is described as "one of the wise gods" and gives her son an oracle by interpreting his dream. In Anatolia, a wise woman was an exorcist, purification priestess, and incantation-reciter.⁵ Michael Moore also notes the wise woman as teller of homeopathic stories: stories that grant the listener perspective and bring healing and peace.

"Wisdom" can also refer to craft or skill. The Bible uses the term *chachamah*, wise woman, to refer to women skilled in mourning.⁶ Similarly, the book of Exodus refers to skilled weaver-women as *chachmot-lev*, wise of heart. The *chachamah* is a woman with practical skills as well as intellectual or spiritual knowing.

The Talmudic Era: Keepers of Knowledge

By the Talmudic period, *chachamah* meant "midwife" and referred to the midwife's technical skill. However, in other rabbinic texts, *chachamah* meant a pious, prudent, and knowledgeable woman. One midrash calls Queen Esther an *ishah chachamah*, a wise woman.

Another midrash refers to the daughters of Zelophehad, five biblical women who demand to inherit their father's land-rights because he has no son to inherit, as *chachamot*, wise women. In Tractate Bava Batra 119b, the Talmud relates: "The daughters of Zelophehad were wise women, exegetes, and virtuous." Their wisdom consists in that they wait for Moses to discuss a related legal case before bringing theirs to him—they are good reasoners and lawyers (in other words, they are like rabbis).⁷ Interestingly, both Esther and the daughters of Zelophehad are negotiators and conflict mediators—Esther negotiates a reprieve for the Jews of Persia, and the daughters of Zelophehad negotiate inheritance rights for themselves.

Some Talmudic era women, like the learned Beruria, are depicted as wise women: "Beruria learned from the rabbis 300 halakhot (laws) on a single cloudy day."⁸ (More on Beruria in the chapter on trickster-priestesses.) The rabbis are often being confronted by a *matronita*—an aristocratic Jewish or Roman lady with very difficult questions. This is another manifestation of the wise woman—the woman with knowledge and skill.

The quintessential mythic wise woman of the rabbinic era is Serach bat Asher, Serach the daughter of Jacob's son Asher. She appears in the Torah in two geneaologies: Genesis 46:17 and Numbers 26:46. In both texts, she appears as a daughter in a list that contains only sons. The two lists are four hundred years apart; how can she appear in both?

In a midrash, Serach is a girl at the time her uncles go down to Egypt to find food during a famine. They meet their brother Joseph, whom they previously had sold into slavery—Joseph has become the governor of Egypt. After hiding his identity from them, Joseph reveals himself and demands that his brothers bring their father. Afraid their father will have a heart attack, the brothers ask Serach, Jacob's granddaughter, to tell Jacob. Serach is a wise woman, and the brothers believe that she alone will be able to break the news to him gently.

> *They summoned Serach the daughter of Asher, a wise and beautiful maiden who was skilled at playing the harp. She sat down before Jacob while he was in prayer and sang, "Joseph is alive…" Jacob's joy awakened the holy spirit in him, and he knew she spoke the truth… Jacob rewarded her with the words: "My daughter, may death never have power over you, for you have revived my spirit." And so Serach never died…*
> —Louis Ginzberg, *Legends of the Jews*[9]

Serach uses poetry and song to slowly awaken Jacob to his new reality. In return, Jacob blesses Serach with eternal life. She becomes like Elijah the Prophet, eternally walking the earth with the Jewish people.

The children of Jacob go to Egypt to live with Joseph, and Serach becomes a slave along with the other Israelites. Hundreds of years later, Moses is born. He grows up in Pharaoh's palace and later goes into exile. When he returns from the wilderness, he claims to be a messenger of God who has come to free the slaves. The people do not know whether to believe Moses. Here, again, the midrash fills in gaps in the text. They go to Serach to ask if he is telling the truth.

> *The Israelites believed because they heard, not because they saw the signs. What made them believe? The sign of redemption. They had this sign as a tradition from Jacob… Asher, the son of Jacob, had handed down the secret to his daughter Serach, who was still alive. This is what he told her: "Any redeemer that will come and say to my children* pakod yifkod *("he will surely remember you") shall be regarded as a true deliverer. When Moses came and said these words, the people believed him at once.*
> —Exodus Rabbah 5:13

The password *pakod yifkod* can also mean "will remember." It is the word Joseph uses when he promises his family that God will remember them and take them out of Egypt: "God will surely remember you and take you up from here."[10] *Pakod* is also the word for God's remembering of Sarah when she becomes pregnant with Isaac. This password names the continuity of God's connection with the Hebrews. Serach holds the password to redemption: She knows how to identify a hero and when liberation must begin.

When Joseph, vizier of Egypt, lies dying, he instructs his brothers to bury him in the land of Canaan, but not right away. Joseph will be buried in Egypt, and in a later generation, when the Israelites leave Egypt, they will carry Joseph's bones with them. Jewish legend holds that the Egyptians hid Joseph's coffin in the Nile so the Israelites would not be able to retrieve it and fulfill the promise to Joseph. Only one descendant of Jacob knows where the coffin is: Serach, the daughter of Asher, Jacob's granddaughter. She preserves the knowledge of the location of his coffin for four hundred years, and she presides over the return of Joseph's bones to his people.

> *They say that only Serach daughter of Asher had survived from that generation, and she revealed to Moses where Joseph's grave was located. The Egyptians had made a metal coffin for him and then sunk it into the Nile. Moses went to the bank of the Nile… and called out, "Joseph, Joseph, the time has come for the Holy One to redeem his children. The Shekhinah and Israel and the clouds of glory await you. If you will reveal yourself, good, but if not, we shall be free of your vow that we should carry your bones with us to Canaan." Joseph's coffin floated to the surface.*
> —Midrash Tanhuma Beshalach 2

In the fourth century Samaritan version of the story, Tibat Markeh, the people try to leave Egypt without the bones, and a pillar of fire blocks their way. Serach is the only one who knows why God is preventing the people from leaving: She reminds them that they have forgotten Joseph's bones. Moses praises Serach and follows her to the bones' hiding place.

> *The great prophet Moses said to her: "Worthy are you, Serach, wisest of women. From this day on will your greatness be told." Serach went with all the tribe of Ephraim around her, and Moses and Aaron went after them, until she came to the place where he was hidden.*[11]

Michael Moore relates that in Anatolia, near ancient Israel, wise women were responsible for "preserving, interpreting, and applying the myths of antiquity to the needs of real people."[12] Serach preserves, interprets, and applies her forebears' tales of liberation to the needs of the Hebrews in her own day. Even though it is probable that she is an invention of the sages of the Talmud, her character is consistent with ancient images of the Wise Woman.

The Middle Ages and the Modern Era

In the Middle Ages, *isha chachamah* or "wise woman" was sometimes a word for a woman doctor. Professional female healers were not uncommon throughout Europe and North Africa. In thirteenth century Germany, a wise woman known as Marat Yuska (Mistress Yuska) recorded a recipe for an eye medicine.[13] Midwives also retained the title of *chachamah*.

However, in the Middle Ages, Torah study was the defining quality of a wise person. While most Jewish women did not have access to higher learning, a few became scholars. For example, Bellette, daughter of Rabbi Menachem and sister of Rabbi Elijah the Elder (LeMans, France, eleventh century) was an expert in Jewish law and a teacher of Torah to women.[14]

Asnat Barzani, a learned Jewish woman in Kurdistan who lived from 1590-1670, gained wide renown for her knowledge of Torah, Talmud, Jewish law, and kabbalah. Her father was Samuel Barzani, a Torah scholar, and his fellow scholars were her tutors and guides. Barzani's wedding contract (she married a cousin who headed a Torah academy) stipulated she was not to be saddled with housework.

> *Never in my life did I step outside my home. I was the daughter of the king of Israel... I was raised by scholars; I was pampered by my late father. He taught me no art or craft other than heavenly matters.*[15]

When her husband died, Asnat Barzani became a *rosh yeshivah*, or head of an academy of Torah. Historical information about her comes partly from fund-raising letters she wrote to raise funds for her yeshiva, in which she argued passionately for Jews' support of Torah learning. Barzani's knowledge of practical kabbalah was considerable, and the Kurdish Jews credited her with working many miracles. She was also a poet, one of the very few women who could write literary works in Hebrew. The title her community gave her was *tanna'it*, meaning a female Talmud scholar. *Tanna* is a term for a scholar from the earliest times of Talmud study, and is not feminized, except in the case of Barzani centuries later.[16]

There were a number of eighteenth-century Jewish women who became learned in Torah, usually by studying with a father or husband. Moses Sofer (1762-1839), a scholar known as the Hatam Sofer, studied Torah with his daughters. The Hatam Sofer made the statement that Jewish learning had to be available to women, or else women would be drawn after secular learning and values. Many fields of study were opening to women, and the Hatam Sofer saw that women would pursue other opportunities if Jewish learning was closed to them. His opinion became widespread over time, leading to Torah education for girls in many Jewish communities. Today, there are many learned Jewish women: Torah scholars as well as women knowledgeable in secular fields and professions.

There also were and remain wise women who are keepers of tradition. One woman tells of the girls of her family gathering around her grandmother in the *shtetl* to say their morning prayers.[17] The elderly Yemenite and Kurdish women Susan Sered studied in her book (mentioned in Chapter 9) are ritual experts and instruct the family in how ceremonies should occur.

> *The old women... consider themselves to be the spiritual guardians of their extended families. The women understand the concept of family in an extraordinarily broad sense, indicating descendants and ancestors, both biological and mythical. Seeing themselves as the link between the generations, old women are responsible for soliciting the help of ancestors whenever their descendants are faced with problems...*[18]

Like Serach bat Asher, these modern wise women carry forward the tradition of wise women being keepers of ancestral knowledge, "applying the myths of antiquity to the needs of real people."

Wise-Woman-Priestess Incarnations

At one Kohenet retreat, the group held a *simchat chochmah*, a wise-woman ritual, for an elder student, Nancy Handwerger. Savina Teubal, a foremother of Jewish feminist ritual and priestess work, innovated this ceremony, and today it is sometimes used as a Jewish "croning" ritual. During the ceremony, led by Sharon Jaffe, we seated Nancy at the center of the room in a throne, sang, and crowned her with flowers, just as Proverbs 16:31 says: "Gray hair is a crown of splendor." Then we all asked for blessings from the *chachamah*, the wise woman. How rare it is in our society to see aged women honored in this way! We need to see our elders as sacred, to discover in them the Wise Woman as priestess and teacher of the community.

Yet the Wise Woman manifests in many stages of life. Some contemporary Hebrew priestesses identify with the ancient tradition of wise woman/priestess as mediator and resolver of conflict. Rabbi Melissa Weintraub, the founder of

Encounter, an organization dedicated to creating dialogue between Jews and Palestinians, taught a course called "Priestess Peacemaking" during the first Kohenet retreat in 2004. Yocheved Landsman, a Kohenet graduate who took that initial course, writes:

> *I believe being a kohenet implies a commitment to promoting and modeling peaceful and sacred ways, and to providing space for meaningful reconciliation. This is what Aaron the high priest did.*

Others identify with the Wise Woman as teacher. Gail Tishman is a retired physician, a former president of her synagogue, a Hebrew priestess, and a student of Torah and kabbalah. Our community knows her as Ma'ayana, which means "wellspring."

Shortly after beginning the Kohenet Institute training program, Ma'ayana gave a sermon at her synagogue. She spoke passionately about the divine feminine as manifested through the biblical matriarchs. Her rabbi spontaneously chose to initiate her (his choice of words) as *Morat Shekhinah b'Yisrael*, a teacher of Shekhinah to the Jewish people. He handed her the Torah and gave her this title. "It took my breath away and left me changed," Ma'ayana later said. "[During the initiation] I felt separate from the world, a bit outside of everything, as something unnameable shifted in and around me. One of the greatest gifts of my initiation was that I had to acknowledge my own gift of the ability to teach."

Still others identify with the aspect of wise woman as chanter of incantations, spiritual mentor, and initiator. Shoshana Jedwab, the shamanic drummer of the Kohenet Institute, describes this ritual role:

> *I was the Wise Woman when I chose to take on the role of a fearsome she-bear at our initiation in the dead of winter, wearing fur and sheepskin. Where the presiding priestesses' role was to offer structure, validation and even comfort through the ritual of the initiation, I needed to hold and express the urgency of the mission. Why become a priestess of the divine feminine? The she-bear had an urgent, direct, even frightening message for each of the initiates.*
>
> *I growled to a woman: "Do something." I told her what she was already telling herself, but I amplified it, spoke it in a fiery voice.*
>
> *The God of many Western religions these days is quite tame. But the divine feminine is not a controlled experiment. When you are a devotee of the divine feminine, She can manifest as a fierce she-bear.*

Often in fairy tales, the wise woman in the woods has animal characteristics or is accompanied by geese, deer, wolves, or other animals. Shoshana used this mythic resonance to create her own Wise Woman persona. "Do something"—this was Shoshana's message to us that our life-work is needed, precious, and all too fleeting.

Spirit Journey
The Wise Woman

You find yourself on a cliff above a river. Below you is a cave into which the river flows. The mouth of the cave is wide and around it you see carved symbols or words, though you cannot make them out. A wooden boat, with a guide standing in it, is moored at a dock nearby. You step into the boat and your guide releases it. The boat is carried by the river current toward the entrance to the cave.

You pass beneath the carved signs above the entrance to the cave but still cannot decipher them. The river sweeps you into the darkness. The river widens and you come to a lake with many islands. On each island is a palace. You ask your guide which palace is your destination. Your guide says: "You must choose."

You select one of the palaces and your guide brings the boat to rest near a dock. You climb up a staircase and step through a door. Inside the palace, you see treasures: gold, jewels and silk. You may see the bones of your ancestors, or of the ancient priestesses. You may see books or chalices or seeds of rare trees. Do not take any of these treasures. Keep walking.

You will come to a room. Inside this room is the Wise Woman as you need to imagine her: wizened, strong and middle-aged, or a child. She will ask you which of the gifts you have seen is most precious to you. Think carefully before you reply. You must pass her test in order to become one of the wise ones yourself. Once you have chosen, the Wise Woman may be pleased, or she may shake her head and invite you to choose again. When you have made your final choice, receive what the Wise Woman gives. She tells you: "Know that this is a gift that is meant to be shared with others."

Your guide is waiting for you. Return to the boat and head past the place where the river forks, back toward the entrance to the underground river. As the boat passes the rocks near the cave's mouth, you can now make out the words, symbols, or images carved into the stone above you. The boat will pull up on shore. Thank your boat-guide. Climb back up to the path and return to your waking self.

She Who Knows and Guides:
The Practice of Initiation
by Taya Shere

The wise-woman-priestess meets us at the crossroads and illuminates the way. She shepherds us through initiations in which we begin familiar to ourselves, we enter the mystery and we emerge transformed.

Initiation is a transformation from one state of being to another—physically, emotionally, mentally and spiritually. An initiatory experience may gradually shift us or suddenly catapult us into becoming our new or next selves. Initiations are rites of passage that carry us to where and who we have never been before, and away from where we can never fully return. Initiation can be carefully crafted or it can be thrust upon us. The Wise Woman is a bearer of initiation. She is a servant to and a guide of this sacred and potent process.

Stages of Initiation

There are three stages in any initation: Separation, Ordeal, and Return. On the surface, the manifestation of these stages may look quite different across time and culture. On a deeper level, these building blocks remain similar even in diverse contexts.

Separation is a moment when one is split off—from wider community, from family, from old patterns of being. Ordeal is a trial by fire, the intense training, the moment when we are out beyond all we know, and must find a way to navigate something we never before thought possible. Return is a moment when we come back to solid ground and share our gifts. We are received, witnessed and celebrated as our new selves by our community.

Consciously-held initiation rituals and experience often have been lost in modern-day society and Western culture. Yet we find and innovate ways—consciously and unconsciously—to recreate this profound experience the body, soul, and psyche crave. In her book *The Language of Emotions*, Karla McLaren draws on the work of initiation theorist Michael Meade to suggest that many of us may have experienced unconscious partial initiations (into adulthood, womanhood, tribal identity, etc.), where we move through the stages of separation and ordeal, but never fully return or are welcomed by community. We may cycle and recycle through the first two stages, repeating patterns or re-enacting traumas that we are desperately seeking to resolve.

Initiation Reflection and Journaling

Take time to reflect on your personal initiation journey by engaging the following questions through journaling. Recall initiations that you have experienced throughout your life—both initiations that were conscious/chosen, and those that were unconscious or in which you were compelled into the initiation. In what ways were the stages of separation, ordeal, and return/recognition present or absent in each?

Initiation at Adolescence

What did your initiation look like during adolescence? What were your separations, your ordeals, your returns? Was your physical entry into puberty, or bat/bar mitzvah, or your first blood, a part of this? What was your first experience of sexual expression?

How did you separate from your family or friends so that you had enough space around you to become a new person? In your moments of ordeal, were you alone or did you have guidance? What did your recognition or welcoming look like? Who was or became your tribe and how did they receive you? Were there ways in which your initiation experience as a teen was incomplete? What is needed to bring healing and completion?

Further Initiations

Choose another initiation experience and trace its stages, its successes, and its challenges and gifts. What did it cost you? What did it bring you? What did you learn and how did you grow and transform from the experience? In what way has your life been different, or larger, since this experience?

Current or Upcoming Initiations

Are there initiations that you still need to complete? Is there an initiation you are in the midst of or that is on the horizon for you? If so, what do you need at your current stage, or what are next steps for you in your initiatory process as you move toward another initiation cycle?

Mentors and Guides

Who have been wise ones for you during your initiations and beyond? Who supported, mentored, and guided you, particularly during initiatory experiences? What did they offer you that gave them in this role? If you were lacking Wise Women or supports to guide you through your initiation, what were the challenges in being on your own? What were the gifts you received from this?

You as Mentor and Guide

Who in your life have you guided through initiation experience? Who have you supported while they were in the throes of transformation? How have you mentored or guided them through this experience? What are the gifts that you have brought them?

Resources

For further reading on initiation experience, try *Rites and Symbols of Initiation* by Mircea Eliade (Spring, 1998), *The Water of Life: Initiation and the Tempering of the Soul* by Michael Meade (Greenfire Press, 2006), *The Language of Emotions* by Karla McLaren (Sounds True, 2010), *Deeply into the Bone: Re-Inventing Rites of Passage* by Ronald Grimes (University of California Press, 2000), and *Ritual: Power, Healing, and Community* by Malidoma Patrice Some (Penguin Books, 1997)

Chapter 12:
Mourning-Woman-Priestesses

On Tisha b'Av, the summer night when Jews mourn the destruction of the Temple, the Kohenet Institute led a service for the entire community at the Isabella Freedman Jewish Retreat Center. We appointed some of our students as spiritual guardians. They stood at the door of the synagogue, served bread made with ashes that we had just baked (a traditional Ashkenazi dish for Tisha b'Av), and anointed everyone who entered with the ashes that had been mixed with the bread. The reading of the Book of Lamentations began.

At the center of the room was a pattern constructed of river stones: a kind of mandala. We invited everyone present to come and take a stone at some point during the reading. This represented the destruction of Jerusalem: the removal of its walls, foundations, inhabitants. The stones were also a reminder of present reality: people starving, enslaved, at war, expelled from their homes.

Surrounding the mandala were four women, covered in tallitot and shawls, who acted as our *mekonenot*, our mourning women. As the reading began, the women keened and vocalized. Most of us have never heard professional lamenting women, but these women gave us some of that experience. Their voices blended with the voices of the violated girls and bereaved mothers of the Book of Lamentations itself. As the stones began to disappear, the women's voices grow louder. The last of the stones was taken away, the reading ended, and the center of the room was empty.

Nearly twenty-four hours later, we re-gathered for a ceremony to end Tisha B'Av. The center of the room was still empty. A single stone was at the center of the empty floor. We began a chant:

> *What is gone*
> *We build upon*
> *Stone by stone*
> *Tear by tear*
> *We release*
> *And create right here*[1]

As we sang, the community came forward to replace their stones. Priestesses began to arrange the stones in spirals and vine-shapes; a new pattern, not the old. The mourning women watched and slowly removed the shawls from their heads. Some of us began to weep.

We were seeing the rebuilding of Jerusalem, of the world, of our own hearts. Later, we broke our fast together.

The mourning woman is the keeper of grief and also the bringer of comfort. She acknowledges the seasons of loss and prepares us for what will come. Mourning-priestesses give voice to the love we have for what once was, and teach us ways to carry that love into the future.

The Biblical Period: Ritual Grief

As the Babylonian empire grows and the exile of Judea looms, Jeremiah instructs the women of Israel: "Call the mourning women [*mekonenot*], and let them come; send for the wise women, and let them come: let them set up a wailing over us, so that our eyes run with water… let them teach their daughters weeping, and their companions lamentation…"[2] A *mekonenet* is a professional wailing woman at a funeral. She is a ritual expert at grief.

Lamentation is a ritual performed by mourning women from Korea to Egypt to Chile. The biblical Book of Lamentations speaks of women weeping for the lost Jerusalem, and weeping for their own lost spouses and children. Some believe this ancient book was written or spoken at least partly by women, who had a tradition of performing grief-poems after a death.[3] Men also recited mourning songs and poems in ancient Israel. King David's lament over Jonathan is only one example. II Chronicles 35:25 reports that *hasharim vehasharot*, male and female singers, recited laments for King Josiah, and these laments became a fixed custom.

In the book of Judges, there is a ritual involving the grief of young women. In the story of Jepthah's daughter, a chieftain named Jephthah is about to go into battle. He makes the foolhardy vow that if God grants him victory, he will sacrifice the first creature to come toward him out of the door of his house. This is lethal stupidity, as we know from the rest of the Bible that *mevasrot*, female dancers, frequently come out of towns and cities to welcome returning warriors. Jephthah's daughter comes out to greet him, and his response is to blame her for causing his suffering: He now must sacrifice her to God.

> When Jephthah arrived at his home in Mizpah, there was his daughter coming out to meet him with timbrel and dance. She was his only child, he had no other son or daughter. On seeing her, he rent his clothes and said: "Woe, daughter! You have brought me low, you have become a trouble to me. For I have made a vow and I cannot retract."
>
> She said, "Father, do to me as you have vowed."… Let this be done for me: leave me alone for two months, and I will go down upon the hills and weep for my maidenhood, I and my companions. He said: "Go." He sent her away for two months, and she and her

CHAPTER 12: MOURNING-WOMAN-PRIESTESSES 175

> *companions went and wept for her maidenhood on the mountains. After two months, she returned to her father and he did to her as he had vowed. She had never known a man.*
>
> *It became a law in Israel: Every year, for four days of the year, the maidens of Israel went to sing mourning songs for Jephthah's daughter.*
> —Judges 11:34-40

Jephthah's daughter asks permission to "bewail her virginity" or "her maidenhood" before her father kills her as a sacrifice. She does this among other young woman, though the nature of the lamentation they perform is unclear, After the grisly deed occurs, it becomes an annual ritual for girls to go into the mountains and ritually grieve (*letanot*) for the daughter of Jephthah.

It may be that the ritual of mourning predates the story of Jephthah's daughter. An annual ritual of mourning may have been a seasonal lamentation for a dying and reborn god or goddess. The story of the maiden sacrificed by her father might be a later tale, meant to provide a "legitimate" explanation for the ritual. The phrase "they went down upon the hills" is strange. The usual prhrase would be "they went *up* upon the hills." This might indicate some sort of cave/underworld descent ritual similar to the one performed as part of the Eleusinian rituals for Demeter and Persephone. The girls who enacted these rites would have been lay priestesses of a sort, similar to the girls who participated in the annual dances at Shiloh.

In the Bible, there is no cycle of mythic life and death, no dying goddess or resurrected Osiris. Yet there does seem to be a relationship between some Israelite women in Babylonia and the god Tammuz, a dying and resurrected God of ancient Canaan. Tammuz, or Dumuzi, is the Sumerian/Babylonian shepherd-god, husband of Inanna. In the myth known as *The Descent of Inanna*, Dumuzi is condemned to live in the underworld. His devoted sister Geshtinanna volunteers to substitute for him half of every year. Like Persephone, Tammuz must return to the underworld at a specific time each year, and there is ritual mourning for him. The prophet Ezekiel complains that women are ritually weeping for the god Tammuz in the Temple itself:

> *Next he brought me to the entrance of the north gate of the house of the Lord, and there sat the women wailing for Tammuz. He said to me: Have you seen, mortal? You will see even greater abominations than these.*
> —Ezekiel 8:8

This text suggests that the prophet knew of Jewish women who were mourning not only for humans but for deities. They may have been priestesses of Tammuz or simply been part of an annual festival observance. Their weeping would have served to honor the spirit of the grain, and the sunlight that grows and diminishes. Like the tears of Geshtinanna, the women's tears assure that Dumuzi will return to the world in his proper season. Demeter, Cybele, Isis, and other weeping goddesses in other myths also play this role.

The prophet Jeremiah also alludes to the ritual weeping of women and goddesses. Jeremiah invokes the spirit of Rachel, wife of Jacob: the matriarch who died in childbirth and was buried by the road near Bethlehem. Jeremiah transforms Rachel into a mythic figure weeping for Jewish exiles:

> *A voice is heard in Ramah, lamentation and bitter weeping, Rachel weeping for her children, refusing to be comforted for her children, for they are not. Thus says God, Refrain your voice from weeping and your eyes from tears, for there is a reward for your labor. There is hope for your future, God says, and your children will return to their borders.*
> —Jeremiah 31:15-17

Jeremiah, well aware of the myths in which mothers weep for their suffering offspring, depicts Rachel as an eternally compassionate mother, praying for the return of her people. Justin Lewis has suggested that Jeremiah is telling the people Israel that they have a Spirit Mother (just as they did in the form of the Goddess Asherah). This Spirit Mother pleads for them before the angry God, and her compassion will rescue them from exile.

In the Second Temple period and beyond, there continue to be figures of women mourning. In II Maccabees, as Syrian-Greek soldiers defile the Second Temple, Jewish women tie sackcloth around their breasts and raise their hands toward heaven. This is an act of mourning and a prayer to God to help the people. The Christian depiction of Mary grieving for Jesus, accompanied by female companions, also is very much in the tradition of the mourning woman.

The Mythic Mourning Woman in the Post-Temple Period

By the rabbinic period, Shekhinah, the numinous Divine Presence, begins to appear in the role of God's estranged wife. She takes a particularly strong role as mourning woman, grieving for the Temple's destruction. Shekhinah's "Husband" is the transcendent aspect of the Divine, who has withdrawn into the heavens in anger. As enemies destroy the Temple—the home of Shekhinah—she weeps and reluctantly flees from Jerusalem:

CHAPTER 12: MOURNING-WOMAN-PRIESTESSES

> *When the Shekhinah went forth from the Temple, she returned and hugged and kissed its walls and pillars and wept, and said: "Goodbye [shalom], my Temple, goodbye, my royal dwelling, goodbye, my beloved house! From now on, let there be peace!"*
> —Lamentations Rabbah, Petichta 25

In this midrash, the word *"shalom,"* which is "goodbye" but also "peace," expresses the Shekhinah's suffering and her hope in a single breath. Another midrash tells how Jeremiah meets Mother Zion on a mountain near Jerusalem. In this midrash, the Jewish people itself is depicted as a mourning woman.

> *Jeremiah said: When I went up to Jerusalem, I saw a woman sitting on the mountain top, dressed in black with disheveled hair, and she was weeping and wailing: "Who will comfort me?" I approached her and said to her: "If you are a woman, speak to me, and if you are a spirit, flee before me." She said to me: "I am your mother Zion." I said to her: "In time to come I will build you up."*
> —Pesikta deRav Kahana 166

Much later, the kabbalists integrate the weeping Shekhinah into their vision of God. They imagine exile as a cosmic disaster that affects all of creation. For the kabbalists, the passage in Jeremiah where Rachel weeps becomes a depiction of Shekhinah mourning her children's exile. Her grief is so great that it shakes the entire world. Her mourning nearly turns the universe back into chaos and void.

> *R. Yose then discoursed on the verse: "A voice is heard in Ramah, lamentation and bitter weeping; Rachel weeping for her children, for they are not." He said: We have learned that on the day that the Sanctuary on earth was laid waste and Israel went into captivity with millstones on their necks and their hands bound behind them, and the Shekhinah was banished from the house of her Husband to follow them...*
>
> *She said: I will weep for my home and my children and my Husband. When she came down and saw her home devastated and the blood of saints spilled in its midst and the holy shrine and temple burnt, She lifted up her voice, and the higher and lower angels quaked and fell. The voice ascended to the place of the King, and the King wanted to turn the world into chaos again. Many armies and hosts of angels went down to meet her, but she would*

> *not accept consolation... She went all around the land of Israel and then into the wilderness...*
> —Zohar I, 203a

The weeping Shekhinah, like the weeping goddesses of the ancient Near East, is not only a lamenter. She is a healer. Her tears inspire God's mercy. So too, the grief of lamenting women was a way to ask God to console and heal mourners—mourners of individuals, mourners of community disasters, and mourners for the brokenness of God.

The Talmud, the Middle Ages, and the Modern Era

The Mishnah (second century CE) mentions mourning women as a standard part of Jewish funerals. We learn about mourning women because the Mishnah mentions they are restricted from performing certain kinds of laments at funerals that take place on minor holidays.

> *On the new moon, on Chanukah, and on Purim, women may cry out and pound their hands [in grief]. They may not wail (mekonenot). Once the deceased is buried, they may not cry out or pound their hands. What is "crying out"? When they all sing together as one. What is "wailing"? When one speaks and they all answer after her.*
> —Mishnah, Moed Katan 3:9

The Talmud notes that it was the custom of women to walk before the funeral bier, heads covered.[4] The text suggests that this is because "women brought death into the world" (because of the sin of Eve), but the real reason may be that women were the chief lamenters of the community. The procession of women before a funeral bier may be a continuation of the customs of mourning women from the biblical period. It may also indicate the continuing sense of women's power in the realm of death. Women, who birth human beings into the world, have the role of escorting them out of the world again.

Maimonides, the twelfth century Jewish philosopher of Cairo, writes in a similar vein to the Talmud:

> *During [the intermediate days of Passover] women cry out, but they may not pound their hands on each other in grief or ritually mourn. Once the corpse is buried, they may not lament. On Rosh Chodesh, Chanukah, and Purim, they may cry out and pound*

their hands on each other in grief before the corpse is buried, but they may not wail.

What is meant by crying out? That they all lament in unison. What is meant by wailing? That one recites [a dirge] and the others respond in unison.[5]

This passage shows that from second century Israel to twelfth century Cairo, Jewish women served as sacred mourners, singers and poets, giving vent to the feelings of mourners by expressing grief in sound and gesture. This was probably one of the few rituals women were permitted to perform in public in that time period. This text, and others like it, preserve a variety of women's mourning traditions: call and response poetry, pounding of the hands, and vocalizing or singing in unison. While women did not say kaddish for the dead, they were intimately involved in the mourning process—particularly those professional women who specialized in grief ritual. A sixteenth century Yiddish manuscript called *Many Pious Women* describes mourning women who sew shrouds while wailing, wearing special mourners' headdresses. "They stare out from their mourners' headdresses like owls, they bawl and cry for the deceased so sorrowfully, and stir up pity beyond telling."[6]

However, in other Jewish sources, women's involvement in mourning is discouraged. Women are a danger at a funeral, the Zohar says, because "the Angel of Death dances before them."[7] The Zohar further instructs that men and women should not walk near each other at a funeral lest harm come to the men. Other texts claim that a spirit of uncleanness clings to women at a funeral. The folklorist Joshua Trachtenberg reports that in Worms "men turn their faces to the wall when the women walk by" on their way home from a funeral.[8] These sources indicate a growing desire to take the public rituals of mourning away from women. However, many women retained their own customs around death: Sephardic women had a tradition of mourning songs, and Ashkenazi women recited *tekhines* at graves.[9]

After the fourteenth century, women became involved in the *chevra kadisha*: the burial society, with its washing and garbing ceremonies. This secret society maintained elaborate traditions and customs, and every community had one. In Jewish law, only women are allowed to prepare a female for burial, and so this practice was and remains open to women—though women were not considered full members of the burial society until the modern period.[10]

Though by the seventeenth century a few women were reciting kaddish, women continued to be barred from most public mourning practices.[11] The refusal, even in twentieth century America, to allow women to say kaddish was a major catalyst for Jewish feminism in the 1970s and 1980s. Women like Letty Cottin Pogrebin and Susannah Heschel were galvanized by their mourning experience. In liberal Jewish communities around the world, women have claimed the right to say kaddish and publically mourn, and women rabbis and cantors lead funerals. Modern Orthodox Jews have also loosened some of the strictures around women's mourning. In contrast, contemporary ultra-Orthodox practice bars women from attending burials, saying kaddish, or participating in many other kinds of mourning practices. There has been recent controversy in Israel because some rabbis are forbidding women from giving eulogies even if it is their family custom to do so. Millennia after Jeremiah reported the first lamenting women, the role of women in mourning practices remains controversial.

Mourning-Woman-Priestess Incarnations

Amy is a practicing Jew, a DJ, and a promoter of Rastafarian music. An initiate of the Kohenet Institute, Amy identifies as a mourning priestess. She has lost many relatives in her life: Her father died when she was eleven, and in recent years she has lost her mother and aunts. Amy is devoted to the memories of her loved ones, honoring their death-dates and saying kaddish for them all.

> *Every time we do a mitzvah, every time we say a blessing or give charity, we are participating in* aliyat neshamah, *in the raising of a beloved deceased person's soul. Everything we do can be dedicated to those we love on the other side.*

When asked to define the Mourning Woman, Amy replies:

> *She is the priestess who is grieving, and because of her own personal experience with grief, she is there for those in mourning. Because of whatever loss she has experienced, she's been altered, and that alteration defines her. You lose a part of yourself; there's a sadness.*
>
> *My personal experience enables me to comfort others. There's something so wonderful about Shekhinah Goddess energy, nurturer, healer, tender, the gift of life. Whatever life cycle event is going on, the rituals we [priestesses] create are there to strengthen them, acknowledge whatever has occurred, and pray for the future.*

Kohenet graduate Ri J. Turner is studying for the rabbinate. A composer of sacred chant, she understands the role of priestess as integrator of many kinds of experience, including sorrow. She reports the following vision of the Mourning Woman:

CHAPTER 12: MOURNING-WOMAN-PRIESTESSES

> *In the moments between being awake and asleep, I saw all of us kohanot in a room, at a festive gathering, a New Year's gathering. Then another woman entered the room—the New Year herself, embodied as a woman. She was clad half in black, half in white. She was veiled. There was the sense that she bore great grief, but she carried it sacredly. She was welcomed into the room by the kohanot, with great warmth and love, and she seemed comforted.*
>
> *Grief Herself is just another woman in need of our love, support, and welcome. In our circle, the love that we offer to each other, and to the Grieving One herself, makes it possible for grief to coincide with fullness, and for life to go on, for all of us together.*

This vision is similar to visions of the weeping Shekhinah in ancient midrash and mystical sources—only this Shekhinah is surrounded by women who support her and comfort her. At a Kohenet Institute retreat, Jess Schurtman created a papier-mâché mask of Shekhinah weeping, with crystal tears dangling down Her cheeks. Performing while wearing the mask, Shekhinah invited the audience to tell their sorrows so that She could mourn them. As we shared, She wailed out our grief in a loud voice. At morning prayer the next day, just before Kaddish, we passed around the mask, this time as a bowl full of blue ribbons. Everyone took a ribbon as a reminder of our mourning with Shekhinah. We recited the names of our loved ones and told their stories, bound together by the blue thread.

Spirit Journey
The Mourning Woman

You find yourself on a hill overlooking a ruin. It may be a building, or even a city. It looks as if the place is abandoned. You feel you are searching for something.

You wander through the ruin. In an open space or clearing you find a tree. The tree has charred, cracked skin. Its limbs are burned away. It bears a single flower. Compelled by a strong impulse, you pluck this flower. As you do so, your heart is pierced with a great grief. You hear the weeping of a woman. You feel invisible arms embracing you, and you too begin to weep or express your grief in some way.

You look down at the blossom in your hands. As you watch, the blossom shrivels, dries up, and blows away. In its place is a seed. You search for a place to plant this precious seed.

When you find the right place, dig a hole and plant the seed. Wait to see what emerges. Perhaps the seed will produce a seedling, a temple, a baby, or a fiery phoenix. Whatever grows, nurture the new thing and interact with it. It will grow to maturity in a brief span of time. Notice what it feels like to do this work of tending, and what you learn from it.

As the new thing grows and thrives, notice what happens to the ruin. It may completely transform as the new entity grows. See what unfolds. When you feel the process of growth and renewal is complete, depart the ruin (or whatever it has become). Return up the hill and toward your waking self.

She Who Remembers and Releases:
The Practice of Mourning as Transformation
by Taya Shere

> *You turn my mourning into dancing.*
> —Psalm 30

The mourning-priestess embraces transformation through remembering and release. The practices in this section include memory, pilgrimage, and an exploration of meeting death with embrace.

Yahrtzeit: Practices of Remembering

There are many Jewish practices of mourning, such as the seven-day ritual of *shiva* following a funeral, the ritual of *shloshim* thirty days after a death, and yearly *yahrzeit* (year-time) observances marking the death anniversaries of loved ones. Traditional Jewish *yahrzeit* observance includes the recitation in synagogue of mourner's kaddish and the lighting at home of a twenty-four hour remembrance candle. It also may include a visit to the burial location.

If you are aware of the death dates of loved ones or those you are mourning, the *yahrzeit* is a time to open to remembering. If you are mourning, remembering or honoring those whose death anniversary you do not know, or if you find yourself mourning even though it is not near a death anniversary, give yourself the gift of mourning ritual practice whenever it is needed.

Coming together in community—in worship space, in nature, or on a conference call—allows us to connect with the person who we are remembering. Recite mourner's kaddish. Share stories about your loved one. Share art or music or food that was loved by the person you are remembering. Open to celebrating that life and spirit.

Whether you are in community or remembering alone, light an extended (twenty-four hour) candle. Gather items of meaning and relevance around your candle. Recite prayers and poems. Sing sacred songs. Place pictures of your loved one around the candle or around your space. Bring natural elements onto your *yahrzeit* altar, such as a plant, a bowl of water, or a feather.

Mourning as Pilgrimage

There is a Jewish custom of celebratory pilgrimage, or *hillula*, on the death anniversary of *tzaddikim*, holy teachers. A lesser known holiday, Lag B'Omer, is the yahrzeit of mystic Shimon Bar Yochai; pilgrims from around the world journey to celebrate at his grave. Among Moroccan Jews, pilgrimage has been and remains a primary practice of remembering. All over the world, Jews pilgrimage to the gravesites of rebbes and *tzaddikim* (holy people) on the anniversaries of their deaths.

You might journey to the burial site of a loved one, or you might journey to a place that was one of their favorite spots, or was somewhere you frequented together when they were alive. For me, *yahrzeit* pilgrimages have included Shabbat morning flea markets to remember my Grandma, and to the Korean Spa to remember a priestess sister who loved soaking in spa waters.

All Kinds of Death

If you are marking the dying not of a beloved being, but of a part of yourself or a relationship or a way of being, consider how yahrzeit practice or pilgrimage might serve this process. Perhaps make an altar that represents the gifts of what you received from a situation that no longer serves you, so it can be honored and fully released. Consider a celebratory pilgrimage—what journey might you make to support the new life that is coming through through as what is no longer aligned falls away?

Embracing Death

Death is an emergence, not an emergency.
Death is ordinary and utterly acceptable and filled with awe.
—Susan Ariel Rainbow Kennedy

Years ago, during a seminar called The Practice, I experienced an exercise on how we perceive the process of dying. Seated in groups of ten or so, in family pods or circles scattered throughout the large room, we were told that Death would be coming into the room to select folks from each pod to join Her. If she came for us or touched us, we had to respond.

"Death" entered the room, robed and blindfolded, with attendants to help guide her. Her attendants steered her to each pod and then released her for her encounter with that circle. Death came near some people who moved to avoid her touch. Others softened their bodies and relaxed their breath, closing their eyes as she neared. On occasion, she physically touched participants. More than one person she touched struggled with her, resisting. They received support from others in the circle to follow Death, yet they often cried out along the way. Waves of wails among the family pods filled the room as their circle-mates were guided away from the circle.

At some point during the exercise, a shift occurred. Death entered a circle, and rather than dodging, a woman in the circle held out her hands. As Death approached her, the woman linked arms with Death and began to dance. She whooped and hollered and let out calls of celebration and praise. The tension in her circle softened and her pod-mates joined her in ululations and cheers. One woman even began to softly stroke Death's hair. This exercise was the first time I understood the possibility of death as something other than something to fear, resist, and avoid at all costs.

Members of the Kohenet community witnessed and supported our sister Yosefa Strauss as she priestessed her own dying from a place of presence and possibility. Yosefa approached dying as she had approached everything else in her life, with presence, humor, creativity, and wild grace. In the final months of her life, she had at most a few hours of energy amidst severe pain each day. In the wee hours of each morning, she sat with the question, "What is the most important thing for me to do today?" She considered this question with much care, because even on a good day, there was generally only one thing she could do.

That August, one day she bought and mailed chai to her sister for her birthday. Another day, she tattooed my hip. One day, she cooked mung beans and brown rice for her caregiver husband. Another day, she met with me about her funeral: "Make it a celebration. Make sure they know I was one of the luckiest people who ever lived." That November, one day she priestessed a funeral for a Jew in her recovery community—the ceremony exhausted her but she did it because he was not well-liked and she was the only one who would. Another day, she taught a workshop on Spirituality and Kink at a BDSM conference. One day, she attended the opening of the Women's Tattoo Forum Art show, in which she exhibited new work. The last day that month, the most important thing for her to do was to die.

In accordance with Yosefa's wishes, some of her priestess sisters sat by bed serving as *shomrot*, guarding her body in the hours after she died. Traditionally, this is a time of solemn recitation of psalms. We tried to pray in this way, but it wasn't what her spirit wanted. Yosefa wanted celebration. She lived free and she would die free. We sung our hearts out offering praisesongs she loved. I swayed and prayed at the foot of her bed with a fervor and a fierce joy that I never imagined in a house of mourning. Yosefa was my teacher in the practice of becoming a mourning-priestess.

Resources:

Saying Kaddish: How to Comfort the Dying, Bury the Dead, and Mourn as a Jew by Anita Diamant, (Schocken, 1999), the section on grief in *The Language of Emotions: What Your Feelings Are Trying to Tell You* by Karla McLaren, (Sounds True, 2010)

Chapter 13:
Seeker-Priestesses

Sometimes at a Kohenet retreat, we build a labyrinth. The labyrinth is a dedicated space-form that appears all over the world, in lands from Ireland to India. It is a long and winding path that curves around and back on itself until it finally comes to a sacred center. The labyrinth is an ancient spiritual tool, a representation of birth, death, and rebirth. It is not a maze: There is a no way to get lost in a labyrinth as long as you keep walking.

The Temple in Jerusalem had at its heart a kind of labyrinth. In Mishnah Yoma, from the 2nd Centuary CE, the text describes the high priest wending his way toward the Holy of Holies for a once-a-year encounter. He walks down the length of one sacred curtain, then turns and walks between the two sacred curtains, then turns again and walks along the length of the inner curtain until he comes to the incense altar: winding back on himself several times. So too, when we walk a labyrinth, we are taking a slow journey to a holy center, and then a journey back to the entrance, which becomes a gateway to the next part of our lives. Like the high priest, we use this journey as a meditation on what in our lives needs to be made new.

During one labyrinth walk, we left a ball of red yarn at the entrance, to remind us of the red thread of life, of the yarn Theseus and Ariadne used in the archetypal Greek labyrinth, and of the cord that (Talmudic legend relates) the high priest tied to his ankle on Yom Kippur in case he was stricken inside the Holy of Holies and had to be pulled out. I touched the yarn as I went in, and felt the power of choice mixed with fate: What is my destiny? Will I find the courage to follow the thread of my life? Will I walk the long path to the sacred center, which is the place of the Loving Presence? When I came upon the center at last and found a copper bowl full of water, I felt refreshed and strengthened, guided by a love I was beginning to learn how to feel.

I came back to the entrance of the labyrinth and bowed down in thanks and reverence. A number of my sisters who had finished their journeys were standing with their ritual shawls over their heads, waiting for each person who exited the labyrinth. As I rose and joined them, they looked at me with such love that I felt I truly had been reborn, that I had made a pilgrimage into my heart and had found Shekhinah there. In space and time, I had not traveled far, but in my soul, I had come to a new land.

Pilgrims go to a sacred place, often a distant one, in the hope of answering a prayer, fulfilling a dream, or finding a truth. Monastics are pilgrims on the inside: They stay in one place and live a simple life, in the hope of answering an inner prayer for grace, stillness, or enlightenment. Priestesses are sometimes one or both of these. Seeker-priestesses are on a quest toward the eternal center, a quest to find the place where their prayers are answered.

Inner Pilgrims: Jewish Women Monastics in Alexandria and Ethiopia

Ancient Sumerian culture dates back to almost 6000 BCE. Ancient Sumer had female monastics who were priestesses. The *naditu*-priestesses lived in a *gagam* or walled cloister; some were scribes or writers. For example, the scribe Amat-Mamu lived in the *gagam* at Sippar in ancient Babylonia. The cloistered *naditu*-priestesses were expected to be celibate, but could adopt children.

Despite the connection between Sumerian and biblical culture, there is no direct evidence of female monastics in the Bible. However, one could conjecture that the Temple weavers or the *tzovot*/shrinekeeper-priestesses who worked in the shrine at Shiloh might have lived monastic lives—just as in the book of Samuel, some priests live in a monastery-like enclave called Nob. Also in the book of Samuel, prophets live and roam in ecstatic bands—women like Devorah could have lived in community as well.

The Jewish women known to live in monastic communities did so outside the land of Israel. In the first century CE, Philo records the existence of Jewish women monastics, part of a contemplative order living outside Alexandria, Egypt, that included both men and women. Philo himself may have been a member of this order. These Jewish monastics were known as the Therapeutrides. They lived separately in small cells, spending their days in study and prayer, eating little. They pondered the allegorical meanings of Torah, and composed hymns. The community came together on Shabbat, though the women gathered behind a partial wall in order to preserve their modesty.

> *This common sanctuary in which they meet every seventh day is a double enclosure, one portion set aside for men, the other set aside for women. For women customarily form part of the audience with the same zeal and the same sense of calling.*[1]

The Therapeutrides must have been educated in order to engage in their scholarly practices. They were probably women of means: widows, or those who had never married. Once a year, on Shavuot, the men and women gathered together and sang the Song of the Sea, in memory of Moses and Miriam, who sang the Song together. Philo writes:

> *The feast [of Shavuot] is shared by women also, most of them aged virgins who have kept their chastity not under compulsion, like some of the Greek priestesses, but of their own free will in their*

CHAPTER 13: SEEKER-PRIESTESSES

> *ardent yearning for wisdom. Eager to have Wisdom for their life mate, they have spurned the pleasures of the body and desire no mortal offspring, but only those immortal children which only the soul that is dear to God can bring to the birth unaided because the Father has sown in her spiritual rays enabling her to behold the verities of wisdom... The order of reclining is so apportioned that the men sit by themselves on the right and the women by themselves on the left.*[1a]

Philo goes to great pains to imagine that the Therapeutrides have become "male" by pursuing prayer and philosophy and putting aside family concerns. He sees these "male" women as married to Wisdom, a female figure. We cannot know if the Therapeutrides themselves would have agreed with this assessment. It is interesting that Philo compares the Therapeutrides to Greek priestesses. He finds the Therapeutrides morally superior in that they have chosen chastity rather than having to submit to it because of their lot in life. Yet priestesses and the Therapeutrides have a similar way of life in that they live among women, pursuing religious tasks. In a sense, the Therapeutrides were the *naditu*-priestesses of the Jewish people.

Philo mentions that the Therapeutrides have chosen "immortal children" over earthly ones. Elsewhere, Philo describes Wisdom as a mother who is always "sowing and begetting in souls aptness to learn, discipline, knowledge." This suggests that the Therapeutrides may be considered mothers to new ideas. Sharon Lea Mattila writes that the Therapeutrides might have found contemplative life an antidote for the stigma of not having children.[2] As spiritual seekers, they no longer needed to judge themselves by the standards of society. The Therapeutae prized "knowledge, philosophy, chastity, the solitary life, and the spiritual quest of the individual soul."[3]

European and Middle Eastern Jewish women in the Middle Ages did not have access to monastic life as Christian women often did. There is no Hildegard of Bingen or Julian of Norwich in Jewish tradition—women were by and large expected to marry and raise families. However, from the fifteenth century to the beginning of the twentieth, Ethiopian Jewish women did have access to the monastic life.

Jews came to Ethiopia sometime between the first and sixth century CE. Isolated from other Jewish communities, they had a distinct religious tradition that included a tradition of priesthood—priests gave blessings, made sacrifices, and settled disputes, just as they did in ancient Israel. In the mid-fifteenth century, an Ethiopian monk named Abba Sabra tried to convert the Jews of Ethiopia, and ended up converting to Judaism himself. He introduced the monastic tradition to the Jews. The Jewish monks of Ethiopia became custodians of the liturgical tradition and educators of priests.[4] The festival of Sigd, which celebrated the giving of the Torah and the renewal of the covenant, often focused on monastic sites or on sacred place associated with the founder of Jewish monasticism.[5]

The Jewish monastic tradition of Ethiopia included nuns, who according to one source were called *batiwa*. For hundreds of years there were secluded monastic communities of Jewish women in Ethiopia, dedicated to prayer and good works and using strict rules of ritual purity. By the late nineteenth century there were few Ethiopian Jewish nuns.[6] Contemporary Qes (priest/spiritual leader) Efraim Zion-Lawi of the Ethiopian Jewish community of Israel confirms that there were Jewish nuns, and says they were called *melekuse*, just like male Jewish monks, and that they studied and prayed in community just as Jewish monks did. He relates that if a man wanted to learn from a female melekuse, she would teach him from behind a screen to preserve her modesty. The Ethiopian Jewish women's monastic tradition is no longer practiced, but their example of the inner pilgrim remains.

Women Pilgrims in the Biblical Period

Rebecca, daughter of Bethuel, makes two pilgrimages. The first is her marital pilgrimage. Abraham's servant arrives in Rebecca's city and asks her to give him some water. Generously, she draws water for him and also for his thirsty camels. It turns out this is the sign of God the servant has been awaiting, and he asks Rebecca's family to allow her to go with him to marry Isaac in the land of Canaan.

The family asks Rebecca what she wants to do, and she announces: *elekh*, I will go. This is the echo of God's command to Abraham: Go/*lech lecha*—Abraham himself is a pilgrim from his own land to the place God has indicated. The linguistic connection to the call of Abraham makes Rebecca's journey a pilgrimage. When she arrives, Isaac brings her into the tent of Sarah his mother—her spiritual destination as a future matriarch.[7]

Rebecca's second pilgrimage is during her pregnancy:

> *The children struggled in her womb, and she said: "If so, why do I exist?" And she went to inquire of [lit. "seek"] God. God said to her: Two nations are in your womb, and two peoples will separate from your belly. One nation will be stronger than the other nation, and the older shall serve the younger."*
> —Genesis 25:22-23

The phrase *vatelekh lidrosh* (she went to seek/inquire) suggests that Rebecca makes a pilgrimage to an oracle (an individual prophet/ess or a temple). She receives a cryptic and poetic message concerning the fate of her twin sons.[8] We hear no details of where or how her pilgrimage took place, but Rebecca spends the rest of her life trying to make the message come to pass. When a blind Isaac wants to bless his elder son Esau, Rebecca devises a scheme which will enable Jacob, the younger son, to receive Isaac's blessing and become the spiritual heir of the patriarchs.

In tribal Israelite society, pilgrimage was one of the religious obligations of male Israelites: "Three times in the year shall all your males appear before the face of Adonai your God—on Pesach, Shavuot, and Sukkot—and they shall not appear before God empty-handed, but each with a gift out of God's bounty."[9] Women were not obligated to make this pilgrimage, but we know from the biblical text that some women journeyed as pilgrims to sacred places.

In I Samuel 1, Hannah and her husband and his other wife Peninah go to the shrine at Shiloh every year. Shiloh is one of the many shrines in the land of Israel, but Shiloh is special because it contains the Tabernacle. One year at the shrine, Hannah is so desperate to have a child—she has been barren for many years—that she makes a vow to donate the child to the shrine if she becomes pregnant. She prays to God, weeping. The high priest Eli complains that she is drunk, but Hannah defends herself, saying: "I have drunk no wine... I have been pouring out my heart before God." The high priest replies: "Go in peace, and may the God of Israel grant what you have asked." Hannah then eats of the ritual sacrifice, which she had been unable to eat earlier because of her depression.

Once her son Samuel is born, Hannah does not make another pilgrimage until Samuel is weaned. Then she brings her son to become a servant of the shrine. Each year, Hannah comes to the shrine at a certain season—she makes offerings with her husband, brings Samuel the gift of a coat, and receives a blessing of fertility from the high priest. She subsequently has many more children. Samuel becomes a judge, and the anointer of Israel's kings.

Hannah and Rebecca are exemplars of pilgrims whose prayers are answered. Their stories suggest that the female pilgrim was a known and respected figure in the biblical spiritual landscape. While she was not part of the clergy, she had the power, through her passion, to directly communicate with God and have God answer her. These divine answers to women pilgrims then became the ground for transformation of the women and their society. In that sense, the pilgrims themselves are channels for the divine to enter the world.

Not all pilgrim-women are successful. King Jeroboam's wife also goes on a pilgrimage to Shiloh, bearing offerings, to consult with the prophet Ahijah. She is disguised, but the prophet recognizes her and prophesies the death of her husband. He also prophesies the death of her child, the king's heir, as soon as she sets foot in her home. This harsh story indicates that Israelites continued to make pilgrimages to oracles as well as to the priestly ritual sites.[10]

Women might have had other important pilgrimage sites in addition to the Tabernacle and the Temple: the *bamot* or mountain-shrines, the *bamot she'arim* or gate-shrines outside Jerusalem, the *asherot* and *matzevot* (sacred trees and pillars), the sacred wells such as the one at Beersheva, and the shrines King Jeroboam built at Bethel and Dan. Oracles like the one that may have been located at the city of Avel might also be sites of pilgrimage.[11]

The Talmud records a number of instances of women going on pilgrimage to the Second Temple. This historical memory is likely to have been accurate, since the Talmud does not lean toward describing women's religious observances. The Talmud writes:

> *The rejoicing during the pilgrimage festivals applied both to men and to women.*
> —Babylonian Talmud, Chagiga 6b

> *A man once said to his children: I am slaughtering this Passover offering on behalf of whoever of you goes on pilgrimage to Jerusalem first. The daughters outdistanced the sons, for they were enthusiastic for the pilgrimage, while the sons displayed apathy.*
> —Babylonian Talmud, Pesachim 89a

The journey to Jerusalem would have allowed women a chance to see the world and be away from home, something they ordinarily would have been unable to do. It would also have been an opportunity to experience the strong emotions of being at the national shrine. The Talmud records that the wife of Jonah went on pilgrimages to the Temple and the sages did not object.[12]

Women may have had an important role in the annual harvest celebration of Sukkot. The festival of the water-drawing, a joyful festival that took place on the second night of Sukkot, celebrated the end of the harvest cycle and asked God for rain in the coming autumn. At the end of the ceremony, priests poured water on the altar to rededicate it for the new year.

> *One who has not seen the rejoicing in the water-drawing ceremony has never seen joy in his life. At the end of the first festival day, they descended into the women's court, where great renovations were made. Golden candelabra were placed there... Pious and distinguished men danced before the people with lit torches, and sang hymns, and the Levites accompanied them with harps and cymbals... In ancient times the women sat on the inside*

and the men on the outside, and they engaged in frivolity. They arranged that the women would sit on the outside and the men on the inside, but still they engaged in frivolity. They arranged that the women would sit above in a balcony, and the men below.
—Babylonian Talmud, Sukkah 51a

A number of elements in this description suggest that women pilgrims played a special role. The ritual took place in the Women's Court. *Barishonah*, at first (a phrase that means "long ago"), women sat on the inside, where they would have been closest to the dancing, singing, water libations, etc. This might have meant a special role for women as celebrants, singers, water-bearers, pilgrim-priestesses of the harvest—similar to the dancing maidens at Shiloh. The text does not tell us anything about their role—only that later generations remembered that women once sat in front.

Over time, women were moved to the outside of the celebration, and then into a balcony. This might have been because the Temple priests became uncomfortable with the erotic overtones of the festival, or the accusation of frivolity may have been an excuse to remove women from the harvest rites. If there were women serving as pilgrims and priestesses (as there are today in Nepal, for example),[13] it is hard to tell from this text.

The sages did borrow the idea of the female pilgrim or seeker to talk about the feminine face of God. Shekhinah often appears as a Seeker who searches for Her people throughout the world. She will return to the sacred center as a pilgrim only when the people can return with Her in joy.

> *Rabbi Shimon bar Yochai said: Come and see how beloved are Israel in God's eyes, for to every place that they were exiled the Shekhinah went with them... And when they will be redeemed in the future, the Shekhinah will be with them, as it says: "Then God will return [with] your captivity." This teaches that the Holy One of Blessing will return with them from the places of exile...*
> —Babylonian Talmud, Megillah 29a

Women Pilgrims in the Middle Ages and Beyond

In the Middle Ages, Jewish women in the land of Israel made pilgrimages to the tomb of the patriarchs and matriarchs in Hebron, sometimes dressing like Muslim women in order to gain entry (in some eras, Jews were forbidden to enter the tomb). European Jewish women made pilgrimages to the land of Israel—the financier and philanthropist Dona Gracia Nasi, and the Maiden of Ludomir (Hannah Rachel Werbermacher) are only two examples. From North

Africa to Russia, Jewish women made pilgrimage to the graves of saints and rebbes. Pilgrimage gave these women an opportunity to see something new, seek blessings, and be in community with other Jews.

Tunisian Jewish women still make pilgrimages to a synagogue-shrine in Djerba, La Ghriba, that is said to hold a stone from the Temple in Jerusalem. They light candles and fill the shrine with eggs to ask for fertility.[14] Iranian Jewish women make pilgrimages to the tomb of Esther, bringing colorful cloths as offerings to place on the tomb. The cloth is then made into garments that hold blessing. In 1925, Touba Somekh, a young Iranian Jewish woman, galvanized her women's prayer group to raise the funds to preserve Esther's tomb, and today Jewish and Muslim women pray there.[15]

Jewish women in the land of Israel visit the holy sites of Jerusalem and Hebron, as well as the graves of wonder-workers, holy women, and biblical figures. Susan Sered writes of elderly Jewish Kurdish and Yemenite women in Jerusalem: "Most of the women believe that pilgrimage is the preferred, that is, the most efficacious, ritual." Their pilgrimages are called *ziara*, an Arabic word for visit. Palestinian and other Arab women also make such pilgrimages.

Contemporary Jewish women around the world may make pilgrimages to the land of Israel, to sacred sites from other traditions like Macchu Picchu, to ancestral villages in "the old country," or even to Auschwitz. Some still sometimes see the Shekhinah as a pilgrim. In Alicia Ostriker's poem, "The Shekhinah as Exile" follows Jewish exiles into many new lands, suffers with them, and shares their journey:

> *you folded wings patched coats*
> *dragged mattresses pans in peasant carts, lived your life*
> *laboring praying and giving birth, you also*
> *swam across the hard Atlantic*
> *landed in the golden land*
> *they called you greenhorn*
> *you danced in cafes*
> *bargained pushcart goods ice shoes Hester Street*
> *put on makeup threw away wigs*
> *and you learned new languages…*[16]

This poem brings together the pilgrim Shekhinah with her emigrant and immigrant daughters, who journeyed from their homes to find new lives. Whether or not immigrant women saw these wanderings as sacred, they were making a transformative pilgrimage to the future. So too, modern Jewish women who move from one place to another shift the future for themselves and their people.

Seeker-Priestess Incarnations

Margie Klein, a rabbi and Kohenet graduate, now works as a congregational leader. She is the founder, and a former resident, of Moishe Kavod House, a living space dedicated to Judaism, social action, and community. While the house she founded is not a monastic space, living there has aspects of the monastic life. While at Moishe Kavod House, Margie dedicated herself to good works, learning, relative poverty, and service to the community, just as many monastics have done.

> *I welcomed people into my home, thinking of hospitality as a kind of divine invitation. I welcomed all different kinds of people, even people who were lonely and socially awkward, living out the idea that "the earth is the Lord's" and nothing is really yours. My room was mine, but in terms of the house, there was a sense that my life was shared with the community. I was cooking all the time and giving away my stuff.*
>
> *My organizing theory was that I couldn't do that much myself, but I could encourage other people to pursue their own passions in combination with the community. They could form teams to work on issues they cared about: housing foreclosure, environmental sustainability, Jewish spiritual practice, artistic creativity.*
>
> *A community is a holy and vibrant network: the more one engages, the stronger the community gets, and the more one gets out of it. As more people interact in a variety of settings, the community becomes a safer place for people to try on different identities, try out different activities, take risks and learn new skills. Though we have power in working together, the source of power is bottom up, in the community, which is in a continual process of acting and reflecting.*

Margie's dedication comes from early childhood experiences with women activists in her family:

> *Growing up I lived in a one-bedroom with a big living room. I slept on a futon behind the couch and grew up listening to my mother lead activist meetings as I fell asleep. I have lived in community my whole life.*

Annie Matan, a Kohenet Institute graduate, rabbinical student, poet, and singer who lives in Toronto and sometimes Jerusalem, has been on the pilgrim side of the Seeker. Annie spent a year studying in Jerusalem at the Pardes Institute. Part of this experience was encountering the pilgrimage sites of Israel and Jordan.

Annie describes three visits to the Western Wall over the course of her life.

> *The first time I came to the kotel [Western Wall] was weird. I sang the Shema and put my note in the wall. It was very scripted. When it was done, I turned and walked away. I didn't know you weren't supposed to turn your back on the Wall.*
>
> *The second time I went, I had a very strong feeling of coming home. I felt that my prayer was more improvisational, more inspired.*
>
> *When I came this year, I didn't have awe. The Kotel looks like an amusement park. People walk through turnstiles and gates. The big wooden walkway to the Temple Mount looks like construction. I felt the mechitzah [divider between men and women] very strongly. It was uncomfortable for me. It felt foreign.*

Uncomfortable with the Western Wall experience, Annie eventually concluded that she had to redefine her idea of pilgrimage.

> *I went on the tunnel tour and got a sense of the scope of the Temple Mount. This little piece of the wall that I've been fighting over is nothing. Anybody can stand in the spot that is a 93 feet straight shot to the Holy of Holies anytime they want.*
>
> *There's a sign as you approach the Kotel that tells you: please be respectful, you are entering a place where the Divine Presence always rests. But I don't believe God is any more present at the Kotel than anywhere else. It's powerful to be close to the Holy of Holies because there are centuries of energy around that space, but it's not about where God is; it's about what we've done there.*

Annie described another pilgrimage during her year of study that had power for her: a visit to Petra, the ancient Jordanian city carved out of stone canyons. Aaron the high priest, founder of the priestly line, is said to be buried there. Annie sees Aaron as an ancestor and a role model for modern priests, priestesses, and peacemakers.

> *I went to Petra and I got to see the peak where Aharon haCohen [Aaron the high priest] is buried. That was much more powerful to me than going to the Western Wall. Aaron is the model of the*

first priest and the first rodef shalom [pursuer of peace]. He is important for the kohen/kohenet line. Seeing his burial place was very powerful.

Suzanne Stier is a spiritual director (*morah derech*) and a student of Mussar, the Jewish ethical tradition. Suzanne's spiritual search began early in her life and has led her to many places, including Jewish feminism. Suzanne's discovery of the Goddess in the 1970s galvanized her as a feminist and a spiritual person, but she received backlash from her community, so much so that she felt as if she were going crazy.

> *I was in the Yale co-op one day, and a book fell out of a stack, and it was called "When God Was a Woman," by Merlin Stone. I read the book and realized I wasn't crazy. There was at least one other person saying: "This God can't be my god." Stone showed historical precedent for the divine feminine. When I spoke about Stone's book to my rabbi and his wife, the rabbi scolded me. "Everybody knows that God has no gender. You're only saying these things because you have a weak father." I left crying.*
>
> *I called my dissertation "The Patriarchal Prism." It was about the way that our organizational systems arise out of patriarchy. With a monotheistic male god, there is a hierarchical structure, and all of our organizations are modeled on that. I posited that we needed a new model. The few people I let read it accused me of being anti-Semitic, of being an angry feminist.*
>
> *I knew archaeologists and sociologists were talking about Venus figures and how women were worshipped and had power, but I couldn't put that knowledge together with my Judaism. When I finished my dissertation, I never wanted to see it again.*

When Suzanne walked the labyrinth walk at a Kohenet Institute retreat, she experienced our winding labyrinth of stones as a Seeker's path, allowing her to reawaken her long-standing conversation with the Goddess. Her pilgrimage to the labyrinth succeeded in integrating her spiritual search.

> *I entered the labyrinth with the intention "What's next?" I walked, and along the path there was a white smooth stone, and on top of it a smaller stone, and on top of that an even smaller stone. I looked at this, and said to myself, "This is a Goddess figure." I kept walking and came around again, and bent down and caressed her.*

And what came to me was "You abandoned me." It was like a stab in my heart.

I continued walking, and I saw a rock out of line with the perimeter, and I put it back in the perimeter. A few steps later I saw an acorn out of line, and I put it back. What came to me was: "Stay on the path."

Later, I wanted to take the stone home, but I couldn't do that. It belonged where it was. She doesn't belong to me; she belongs to the world. That labyrinth was her home. I had to force myself not to take her.

Now I am able to think about the Goddess as a feminine figure. Sometimes she comes to me as a young woman in flowing robes and no feet—floating in space. Sometimes she comes to me as a grandmother figure. The male God forms human beings out of clay. The female Goddess gives birth. That's organic; it's part of our body. If we are part of God's body, then being like God is a natural process.

These contemporary seekers are doing what their priestess ancestors did: engaging in ritual journey and community living for the purpose of transformation. Like pilgrims before them, they are using once-in-a-lifetime journeys to observe and shift the patterns of their everyday lives.

Spirit Journey The Seeker

You see before you a wall: a hedge, a stone cliff, some other sort of barrier. You walk along it looking for an opening, but find none. As you continue to search, you see a keyhole within the wall. Lean down to the ground. You will find a very small thing: a nut, a pine cone, a gold coin, a hairpin. This is the key to the Labyrinth. Put the key into the keyhole and open the door. The door opens, and you see a passage into the heart of the Labyrinth.

Begin to walk the path of the Labyrinth. It is a single path so you cannot get lost, though there may be many turns or obstacles. You may meet others, or you may find yourself walking for a long time in solitude and silence. This is your journey inward. Be mindful of what arises for you. What are you seeking?

You come to the center of the Labyrinth. Notice what is here: an altar, a tree, a statue, a book, a fountain, a single flower, nothing special at all? Reflect. Have you found what you are seeking? What would it mean to find it? What would it mean to let go of finding it?

As you reflect, you notice that someone else has been sitting here with you all along, so still and quiet you did not see her. She stirs, rises, and comes to stand before you. See her as clearly as you can. "I am the Seeker of Names," she says. "It is my work to give a name to all who find the center of the Labyrinth."

The Seeker of Names may speak a name you already have, or she may give you a new name. She may give you a Hebrew name if you do not have one, or she may give you a name that reflects something you love in the natural world. You and the Seeker of Names hear the name echoing all around you.

Receive the name with humility. Thank the Seeker of Names. Return along the path until you come to the door by which you entered. Close the door behind you. Retrace your steps along the wall until you come to your newly-named waking self.

She Who Seeks:
The Practice of Pilgrimage
by Taya Shere

A good traveler has no fixed plans and is not intent on arriving.
—Lao Tzu

The seeker-priestess journeys and questions. She practices pilgrimage of the body, heart, mind, and spirit. Physical pilgrimage can take us around the world and to the most remote or revered of sites, and it can also simply carry us around the corner or to that sweet hidden spot just downstream. While pilgrimage can be weeks or months or years in duration, it can also be an overnight, or even an afternoon. Many kinds of places can be a focus for pilgrimage.

Visioning Pilgrimage

If embarking on pilgrimage is resonant for you, sit with the following questions and reflections: What places are you drawn toward? Do you need ancestral or divine guidance? Is there a particular wisdom you seek?

Perhaps your body is yearning to be near a natural space—a place where spring water emerges from the earth, a remote mountain range, ancient caves. Perhaps you have received a summons in a dream or a vision. Perhaps you need to connect more deeply with a particular aspect of the Goddess, or a particular aspect of yourself. There are few, if any, coincidences on the pilgrim's path. If multiple signs portend in the same direction, follow the openings. When an angel shows up, in the form of an unexpected new friend, or a bus or train missed, receive her with grace.

Manifesting Pilgrimage

Craft an itinerary that has the right balance of structure and flexibility. Do you need pilgrimage that is open-ended and flexible, or do you need clear parameters inside of which to unfold? If you drive everywhere at home, take buses or trains instead of renting a car. Take the subway instead of a taxi. Borrow a bike. Walk wherever possible. Choose methods of transport that allow you to connect with the land, local people and your body.

Preparing for Pilgrimage

If you don't know you'll need it, leave it at home. Pack the smallest, lightest bag possible, and be prepared to let go of what you bring. Turn on your email vacation reply and commit to staying offline. Clearing away as many ties to home as you can allows space for freedom.

On The Journey

You've stepped out of the house with your pack on your back. You found your seat on the bus. Your plane has taken off. You are on the water, oars in hand. However you are traveling, you are on your way. These moments are as important as any other moment on your pilgrimage. Allow yourself to unfold into the adage "The journey is the destination."

Sensory Awareness

Let yourself be led by senses that usually take a back seat. In an open air market, let your hands run over tapestries. In a cathedral, explore the carved lines of the pews. In the forest, get to know the bark of the trees. If you don't tend to notice smells, make a conscious effort to let your olfactory sense guide you. If you don't often take time to appreciate the tastes in what you eat, partake in delicacies with spices that are entirely new to you, or seek out favorite treats and notice how their flavors expand with added consciousness. Pay deeper attention to the senses of sight and hearing and see what new things you discover.

At the Destination

For some, the intent of the pilgrimage is to experience a particular place that holds sacred energy. For many, the journey itself is the destination. And for those who are open to it, the pilgrimage can end up being about a place or experience that we were not even aware of at the start of the journey.

When you arrive at the place that is the pinnacle of your pilgrimage, whether by design or by grace, give thanks. You are here! Breathe. Center. Orient. Let yourself fully appreciate this place. Be led by your senses, your intuition, the energy of the place. Take your time leading up to your power spots or people. Allow time for integration as a practice of respect for your body and the place. What does it feel like to be at home in this place? What does it feel like to be in awe in this place? Allow yourself to be touched by the gifts of your destination, and to open to the gifts that it holds for you.

Leaving Your Destination

Whether you leave your destination site for external reasons (the site is closing, the bus is leaving in twenty minutes), or because you know it is time, give thanks: speak words, make a gesture, place a stone. Focus not just on what you are taking from this place, but also on offerings or prayers for the place, its inhabitants, and its caretakers. Remember that a pilgrimage is not just the journey to a place, but also the journey back home or to wherever is next.

Coming Home

Build in quiet time for introspection or grounding at home at the end of your journey. Build an altar with stones you collected, spices you purchased or anything that was gifted to you. Make a collage from your ticket stubs and brochures. Frame and hang a photo from the trip. Enter contact information from kindred spirits you met along the way into your address book and be in touch not long after your return.

May you journey far and deep and may all of your pilgrimages bring you ever closer to your most vibrant self and to the Goddess.

Resources

For Jewish resources on Pilgrimage, explore *Pilgrimage and the Jews* by David Gitlitz and Linda Kay Davidson (Praeger, 2005), *Saint Veneration Among the Jews in Morocco* by Issachar Ben-Ami (Wayne State University Press, 1998), and the section on Pilgrimage in *Jewish Passages: Cycles of Jewish Life* by Harvey Goldberg (University of California Press, 2003). Books about inspirational women's pilgrimage include *Traveling With Pomegranates: A Mother and Daughter Journey to the Sacred Places of Greece, Turkey, and France* by Sue Monk Kidd and Ann Kidd Taylor (Penguin Books, 2010), and *Eat, Pray, Love: One Woman's Search for Everthing Across Italy, India, and Indonesia* by Elizabeth Gilbert (Riverhead Books, 2007). A powerful resource on sacred natural sites across the world is *Sacred Earth: Places of Peace and Power* by Martin Gray (Sterling, 2007), or his website, www.sacredsites.com.

Chapter 14:
Lover-Priestesses

In the summer of 2013, at the Kohenet Hebrew Priestess Summer Retreat, the retreat participants led a Tu b'Av ritual for the community. Tu b'Av, an ancient grape harvest festival mentioned in Chapter 7, was once celebrated by women in white dresses dancing under the full moon. During the dancing, men would seek romantic partners from among the dancers. The Talmud relates that each woman borrowed a dress from another one, so that all would be equal. While this ritual is not observed often today, it is a reminder of folk rituals of ancient Israel where women would have been prominent participants and leaders.

At our ritual, we began indoors, telling the story of Tu b'Av and reminding everyone that this day was halfway between summer and autumn, just as Tu b'Shevat, festival of the trees, falls between winter and spring. We told the story of the women and their dancing, and of rituals that honored the earth with the drumming of feet and the meeting of potential lovers. Then women in white, singing and ululating, led us out into a field. As we gathered, the women fed us grapes and other fruit, inviting us into a rich experience of the senses. They invited us to greet one another, meeting the Divine in each person. Then they led us in a circle dance beneath the moon. Finally, we recited a blessing over the moon and over the summer.

The evening reminded me of a Tu b'Av in 2001, at an event called the Festival of Miriam at a retreat center known as Elat Chayyim. At the retreat, we held a Saturday night full-moon celebration of the life of the prophetess Miriam. It was also Tu b'Av, and we danced and drummed beneath a glorious full moon. It was at that festival that I began to realize that the ancient priestesses had been real women—and that we could follow in their footsteps. Now, at a Tu b'Av thirteen years later, I was seeing the fruit of the seed that had been sown—as we all became priestesses and priests of love for one another.

Lover-priestesses, like all priestesses, connect worlds, bringing together human and divine. They do this through the uncanny, unique vehicle that is eros. Sexuality is a potent force, still untamed after millennia of human existence. Lover-priestesses use this force as an entering-place for God. Though often maligned, the lover-priestess appears from the Bible to the kabbalah and around the world. She appears in us whenever we find the sacred in our intimate relationships.

The Biblical Period: On the Threshing Floor

In Chapter 8 of the book of Isaiah, the prophet makes a cryptic statement: "I approached the prophetess, and she conceived and gave birth to a son, and God told me: Name him Maher-Shalal-Hash-Baz." (Isaiah 8:3) The name of the child is an oracle-name meant to predict coming events in the land of Israel. But who is the prophetess? Most commentators assume this is Isaiah's wife, but it is also possible that Isaiah goes to a holy woman to lie with her, as part of his prophetic mission. The Hebrew reads: *"va'ekrav el haneviah,"* "I came close to the prophetess." This is not the usual term for a husband's relations with his wife—in fact, the root *krv* is also used to mean "make an offering" or "come near God." Isaiah may be engaging in sacred sexuality, with his wife or with a prophetess he visits.

Sacred sexuality is a powerful undercurrent in the Bible, even as the Bible condemns it. In Numbers 25, the Israelites are worshipping Baal-Peor with a Midianite tribe they have met in the desert; this worship includes sex acts. When Zimri, a prince of the tribe of Simon, brings Cozbi, daughter of a Midianite chieftain, to his brethren, the word used in the text is *vayakrev*, the same root we find above in the story of Isaiah's prophetess. Zimri leads Cozbi "into the chamber (*kubah*)"—possibly into a shrine, or even into the Tabernacle. Cozbi may be acting as a priestess of Baal-Peor. Pinchas, grandson of Aaron, becomes enraged, follows the two, and stabs them to death. God rewards Pinchas with an eternal priesthood. This ritual of sacred sexuality clearly takes on the tinge of corruption, otherness, and foreign worship. Other texts depict priestesses as lewd prostitutes, and men as their dupes.

Yet there are other passages where the Bible seems to allude to ritual sexual union as if it is acceptable and even crucial. In the introduction, we examined the story of Tamar and Judah, in which the widowed Tamar garbs herself as a *zonah/kedeishah* (prostitute/holy woman), seduces her father-in-law, and becomes pregnant. Tamar's act produces children who are the ancestors of King David. The image of the king lying with the priestess is a very old one from the ancient Near East, and continues to hold power in the Bible itself.

Consider the events in the book of Ruth. An Israelite family travels to Moab because of a famine. While they are there, the father of the family, Elimelekh, dies. The two sons marry Moabite women. The two sons both die, and their mother, Naomi, is left a widow and childless. Naomi wants to go back to her home, Bethlehem (the name means "house of bread," which is a central theme of the story). Naomi discourages her daughters-in-law from following her, saying that she has no more sons for them to marry. One of her daughters-in-law, Ruth, ignores this pragmatic advice in favor of the bonds of family loyalty she still feels for her mother-in-law and chooses to go with Naomi.

Once they arrive in Bethlehem, Ruth offers to glean among the ears of grain to sustain herself and Naomi. It just so happens that the man whose field she chooses is the redeemer for her and Naomi.[1]

The field's owner, Boaz, takes a liking to Ruth and orders his staff to treat her well. He asks her to glean among his female workers so she will be safe. This is very kind, and it is also revealing: We see that Boaz is making sure that the boys stay away from Ruth. It is his seed he wants her to glean, with all the Shakespearean double-entendre that implies. The text gets even more suggestive later in the story, when Ruth sits beside Boaz at lunch and he keeps handing her handfuls of grain until she is satisfied. Then he orders the reapers to drop even more seed for her to pick up. When Ruth gets home, and Naomi sees the barley for herself, she cries: "Blessed is he of God, who has not failed in his kindness (*chesed*) to the living or the dead. The man is close to us, he is one of our redeemers."[2]

Naomi now has a problem. Harvest is over, and it is not seemly for Ruth to go and knock on Boaz's door. She must stay at home and wait for him to come to her, and since she is a poor girl, a visit from a wealthy landowner is unlikely. So, Naomi conceives of a mythic drama, a sacred marriage in the grand traditions of the ancient Near East. She asks Ruth to dress up, anoint herself, and go down to the threshing floor. Boaz will be sleeping alone there to protect the harvest. Ruth is to uncover his feet (or his genitals) and lie down, and follow the man's instructions.

Inanna was the goddess with whom the ancient kings of Sumer perfomed the sacred marriage. She was first and foremost a storehouse goddess, protector of the harvest grain. The king's sexuality was a metaphor for the seed, and the priestess who stood in for the goddess represented the earth. In the ancient mind, their union was identical with the land's fertility.[3] To have sexual relations on a threshing floor is to evoke this tradition of the kings of old. Boaz is a king in potential, since he is about to father the Davidic line.

> *She went down to the threshing floor and did all that her mother-in-law had instructed. Boaz ate and drank and his heart was happy. He came to lie down beside the grainpile. She went over quietly and uncovered [revealed] his legs, and lay down. In the middle of the night, the man trembled and flinched—and there was a woman lying at his feet!*
>
> *"Who are you?" he asked. She said: "I am Ruth your handmaid. Spread your wings over your handmaid, for you are a redeemer [goel]."*
>
> —Ruth 3:6-9

"Who are you?" Boaz asks, as if Ruth is not herself, as if she is the grainpile come to life. Ruth is standing in for a priestess or goddess here—but in a particularly Israelite way. Like a priestess, Ruth is not there only for sexual fulfillment. Metaphysically, her dead husband Machlon is within her, waiting for a redeemer to give his seed life. Through levirate marriage, the dead "return to life" in a spiritual sense. The *goel*, the redeemer of the dead husband, ritually brings the dead seed back to life and transmits it to the widow, as if resurrecting the dead for a single night. So too, the king and priestess unite for one night to bring renewed life to the grain and the land.

Boaz agrees to be Ruth's redeemer, but he also notes that a closer relative might want to be the *goel* and that this person must be consulted before Boaz and Ruth can wed. It is unclear whether the couple have intercourse on the threshing floor or not. Boaz's command to Ruth: "Lie down until morning," probably means that they did not, though it could also mean that they did. However, when Ruth leaves the threshing floor at dawn, Boaz places six measures of seed on her back. This is a token of harvests and pregnancies to come. By the end of the story, Ruth has given birth to a son, Obed, the founder of the Davidic line. Naomi has a grandson, even though she thought that was impossible.

The story of Ruth and Boaz, read in its literary and theological context, is the story of a priestess and a king. The extraordinary thing about the story is that it is less a story of sex than it is a story of love. The word *chesed*, lovingkindness, repeats over and over again throughout the book. The night on the threshing-floor is a ritual of *chesed*—deep love between people, between generations, between humans and the divine.

The Song of Songs

The Song of Songs is a series of love poems, with little gender hierarchy or anxiety about sexual mores. The heart of the Song is a duet between two lovers, one male and one female. The female describes her lover as king, running deer, apple tree, and shepherd. The male describes his lover as friend, bride, dove, garden, and palm tree. The non-linear, almost dreamlike text brings nature, eros, and love together into a mysterious work that hints at love as a sacred act.

> *Who is she who looks forth like the dawn, beautiful as the moon, bright as the sun, awesome as bannered hosts? I went down to the nut grove to see the valley budding, to see if the vine had flowered and the pomegranate had blossomed. Before I knew it, my lover placed me in a princely carriage…*
> —Song of Songs 6:10-12

The "princely carriage," according to Chana and Ariel Bloch, is the woman herself, who carries the man into the throes of love. She is dawn, moon, sun, vine, and pomegranate—all images of the Goddess. God is never mentioned in the Song, except in one brief and ambiguous phrase that describes love as a "Divine flame."

One traditional reading of the Song is that the male character represents God, while the female character represents the people of Israel. Another viewpoint, more common today, sees the Song of Songs as a beloved collection of love songs, so precious to the Israelite people that it was canonized. A third interpretation sees the Song of Songs as related to pagan literature—a paean to sacred sex similar to Sumerian and Egyptian love poetry. Scholars in this camp point out the similarities between the Song of Songs and other love songs of the region. For example, in the love story of the goddess Inanna and her shepherd lover Dumuzi, Inanna sings of her lover as king, apple tree, and burgeoning garden:

> *At the king's lap stood the rising cedar.*
> *Plants grew high by their side.*
> *Grains grew high by their side.*
> *Gardens flourished luxuriantly.*
> *Inanna sang:*
> *"He has sprouted; he has burgeoned;*
> *He is lettuce planted by the water...*
> *My apple tree which bears fruit up to its crown.*[4]

Compare these verses from the Song of Songs:

> *Like an apple tree among the trees of the wood, so is my beloved among men. I delighted in his shade, and his fruit was sweet to my mouth.*
> Song of Songs 2:3

> *Your stature is like the palm, and your breasts are clusters. I say: Let me climb up the palm, I will take hold of its branches, and may your breasts be like grape clusters, and your breath like fragrant apples.*
> Song of Songs 7:8-9

Scholars note that a name or epithet of the woman in the Song of Songs—Shulamit, the peaceful one—is almost identical to the Canaanite word Shulmanitu, or "She of the Peace-Offering", a name of the Goddess Ishtar.[5] The Song of Songs could possibly contain liturgy from a period when Israelites still revered goddesses and priestesses.

Dvorah Klilah bat Shachar (see Lover-Priestess Incarnations) reads the song as an epic cycle where the male figure represents the tribal king, and the female figure represents the Goddess, or a priestess playing the role of the Goddess. "The king has brought me into his chambers" would refer to the entry of the priestess to the king's bedroom, where the union of male and female would strengthen the fertility of the land. "Behold the winter is past, and the rains have gone away" would indicate that the Song is a springtime ritual.

Julia Watts Belser, a rabbi and contemporary devotee of the Goddess, also proposes an alternate way of reading this text. Belser notes that if one imagines the female figure in the Song as Goddess, and the male figure as human, one comes to a new perspective. In Belser's reading, "Let him kiss Me with the kisses of his mouth," comes from the desirous Goddess and not from the human partner of an erotically pursuing God.

> *When we read the feminine speaker in the Song as an expression of God's voice, we meet Her as a God turned toward us. While classical theology has sometimes depicted God as without need or desire, a theology centered in the Song of Songs suggests that one of God's most profound self-expressions comes through Her yearning. She reveals herself not as the God who has everything, but the God who wants something from you and from me, from the grasses and the birds, from the wind and the wild doe. We hear Her voice in the voice of the waiting Lover, we hear her desiring us. "Kiss Me," She calls. "Draw Me," She commands, and together, "Let us run."*[6]

Belser also invites us to transform the language of royalty in the Song, where the male lover is described as king. "By naming him king, Goddess imagines Her beloved as one centered in his own power, brimming with vitality and concern. The use of kingship in a feminist reading of the Song of Songs emphasizes that kingship is granted to a king, that this act of 'crowning a king' through desire and delight acknowledges not the power of the king himself, but the power of relationship." The Goddess and Her lover experience love and trust for one another, modeling a relationship in which both parties can love, enjoy, give, and receive.

Cherubim: The Second Temple Period and the Talmud

The Talmud, like the Bible, is not supportive of sexuality as an avenue to channel the divine presence, though sex is regarded as healthy and acceptable within marriage. The Talmud is full of stories of sages resisting the sexual powers of women. Sometimes, midrashim refer to women such as Tamar, and even

Potiphar's wife, pursuing sexuality "for the sake of heaven"—a kind of sacred sexuality.[7]

The Talmud contains one astonishing reference to sacred lovemaking within the Temple. To understand this story, one must note that inside the Holy of Holies, two golden cherubim—guardian creatures like winged lions—faced one another, their wings sheltering the holy Ark within the shrine. A talmudic tradition held that these creatures were gendered; that one was male and one female.

> When Israel would go up on pilgrimage, [the priests] would draw back the curtain of the Holy of Holies and show them the cherubim in intimate embrace, and tell them: "See how great is God's love for you, like the love of a man and a woman."
> —Babylonian Talmud, Yoma 54a

According to this text, the creatures who guard the Holy of Holies are male and female beings in sexual congress. The priests show them to the people once a year as a sign of God's love for them—expressing the connection between God and the people as multi-faceted—not simply spiritual, but also erotic and physical. This tradition seems to be enfolding the vivid imagery of priest and priestess as vehicles for the love of the divine in the cloak of ancient Temple rite, perhaps by way of retaining the power of the passion without straying into the area of forbidden worship.

While this report of what happened in the Second Temple was written centuries afterward and is probably fanciful, the story may encode a certain cultural memory about the centrality of sexuality in the sacred realm. If we remember that the harvest pilgrimage was a time when the sages worried about "frivolity" between men and women and that women had played a central role in that festival at one time, we may get the faint outlines of an Israelite harvest tradition that included sexuality or lovemaking in some way. This Talmudic myth may be a vestige of a harvest ritual in which women served as priestesses of love.

Sacred Marriage: The Mystics

The kabbalists of the Middle Ages believed that men and women could channel the masculine and feminine divine, and create cosmic healing through sexual intimacy. "When does the Shekhinah reside with a man? When he marries… The Supernal Mother is with the male only when the male and female are conjoined.[8] Nachmanides, a biblical commentator and mystic, wrote in his Iggeret haKodesh, a letter on sexual matters: "When a man cleaves to his wife in holiness, the Divine Presence is manifest."

For the mystics, the Friday night sexual union of a husband and wife reflected the union of the Holy One of Blessing with the Shekhinah. Other *mitzvot* (commandments) could also effect the union of God and Shekhinah. Special prayers called *yichudim* asked that the commandments be a vehicle for union between sacred He and sacred She. This worldview made all Jews priests and priestesses, in the sense that their actions drew the worlds together and created cosmic order.

Humans could also be sacred attendants at the divine wedding. The Zohar writes about Shavuot, the grain festival and holiday of the giving of the Torah, as a wedding:

> *R. Shimon was sitting and studying the Torah during the night when the bride was to be joined to her husband. For we have been taught that all the "members of the bridal palace" during the night preceding the Shekhinah's espousals are in duty bound to rejoice with her in her final preparations for the great day: to study all branches of the Torah… for these represent her adornments. The bride with her bridesmaids comes up and remains with them, adorning herself at their hands and rejoicing with them all that night, and on the following day She enters the chuppah in their company*
> —Zohar I, 8a

The male Torah scholars are the priestesses! They accompany the divine bride, who is Shekhinah and the Torah at the same time, as bridesmaids. The sages/bridesmaids make ornaments for the bride by discussing Torah and giving creative interpretations for its meanings. At dawn, the bridesmaids lead the bride to the wedding canopy.

The kabbalists saw their daily study of Torah as a kind of eroticism with a text that is an embodiment of Shekhinah. Here, the Shekhinah is the priestess/goddess who calls to her devotees to come and experience revelation through Her in the most intimate sense.

> *The Torah… discloses her innermost secrets only to them who love her. She knows that the one who is wise in heart hovers near the gates of her dwelling place day after day. What does she do? From her palace, she shows her face to him, and gives him a signal of love, and forthwith retreats back to her hiding place. Only he alone catches her message, and he is drawn to her with his whole heart and soul, and with all of his being… And when he arrives, she commences to speak with him, at first from behind the veil that she has hung before the words… When, finally, he is on near*

terms with her, she stands disclosed face to face with him, and holds converse with him concerning all of her secret mysteries, and all the secret ways that have been hidden in her heart from immemorial time.[9]

We don't know a great deal about how women experienced the "priestesshood" of uniting with their husbands on Friday night. We also do not know much about same-sex sexuality or same-sex spiritual experience among the mystics, though there are a variety of homoerotic images in the mystical literature. However, we do know that from biblical times, Jewish sexuality was surrounded by a great deal of ritual. Women observed laws of purity such as abstaining from sexual relations with their husbands during and after menstruation and immersing in a ritual bath prior to resuming relations. While these laws were demanding and difficult, they may have given some women the sense that their sexual relationships were sacred.

The Frankists, eighteenth-century antinomian kabbalists, were particularly explicit in regarding women as priestesses of the divine union. There is some evidence that, in secret Frankist rituals, sexual congress occurred in order to channel the presence of the Shekhinah/the Divine Maiden. Frank cautioned his followers not to be sexually jealous of their wives, in order to allow these rituals to occur.[10] The Frankists were widely accused of depraved orgies, but the truth of what happened in these rituals is unknown.

Contemporary Jewish mystics Dawn Cherie Ezrahi and Ohad Ezrahi have founded the organization Kabalove and the sacred sexuality school *haGan*/The Garden. These modern shamans see sacred sexuality as part of a re-invigorated mystical practice. They lead rituals that invite safe exploration of eros as a spiritual experience. Dawn writes: "If you desire to deepen your connection to God, then loving… is the best way to bring heaven down to earth."[11]

Lover-Priestess Incarnations

Ariel Vegosen, a Kohenet graduate, is a social justice activist and conflict resolution specialist. She is also a devotee of sacred sexuality. In a poem, she writes:

> *My sexuality is sacred*
> *is a pool of water*
> *I dip into gleefully emerging closer to the universe*
> *to the whole*
> *to the Goddess*
> *who dwells deep within me*

within the waters
within us all
The act of love
of sex of desire
is holy
is an awakening
is a ritual
my connection to spirit
to higher power
to earth
to the wind
to this moment.

Ariel believes that viewing sexuality as sacred is a radical act against an American culture devoid of eros and constrained by notions of "ideal" forms of relationship. She comments:

> *I, like many Americans, grew up believing sex to be taboo, secretive, and maybe even a little dirty. I was raised on myths of purity and virginity as ways to be closer to God. I was told girls don't masturbate. Neither my parents nor my friend's parents ever really talked about sex. In school our health classes scared us with pictures of diseases and intense videos of giving birth. No one told me about sacred sexuality, queerness, self-love, cosmic-love, polyamory, abundant love, and sex positivity until I was an adult.*
>
> *When I was a child I didn't even know the words for my identity. Now I have words to share my truth: I am a queer, multi-gendered, poly, cosmic, sacred lover. I enjoy myself, other humans, and I am in love with the earth, the divine universe. My sexuality is an act of resistance, a pathway to newness, a direct cord to universal connection.*
>
> *I do not look like a typical girl and I do not make-love like the movies. I make-love like my ancient ancestors, like my foremothers who tore off their white frocks and ran naked in the woods on Tu B'Av—only I don't believe they were just seeking husbands. I imagine there were women who found lovers just for the night and were present with them deeply and in the morning left because they valued their independence. I imagine there were women who found men, and women who found other women, and women who found people who had gender expressions we have since forgotten.*

Ariel emphasizes the multiplicity of sexual experience and affirms all wanted sexual encounters as sacred.

> *I am a supporter of love, safe sex, expanding boundaries, diving deeply into playful waters, and seeing where skin touching skin becomes light touching light. I believe all love and all healthy consensual sex is sacred because I think the Goddess wants us to enjoy ourselves! I know so many people that have been hurt by the myth that God only values heterosexual married love. I hope to give the gift of knowing that God/Goddess/Divine (insert what word works for you) loves love—all kinds of love.*

Taya Shere, Kohenet co-founder, has devoted herself to the art of erotic healing. For years, she identified as a *kedeisha*, a holy woman, and is committed to cultivating herself as a channel for the transformative power of the Goddess.

> *In my mid-twenties, I awakened to the mysteries of sacred sexuality in a tantric context. My initiatory experience included days of riding and being ridden by an energy of bliss, of perceiving each other as Goddess/God in myself, in another and all around. I opened to the possibilitiy of individual and collective healing through transcendent erotic connection. I dreamed of co-creating a temple where priestesses would be nurtured by each other and our community in our path of erotic healing, and visioned a Judaism that celebrated sensuality as a primary expression of the sacred.*
>
> *Eros is at the heart of my experience of embodied divinity. Through practices of dance, chant, somatic awareness and sex as prayer, I devote myself to the art of erotic presence, engaging sensually in all of life.*

D'vorah Klilah bat Shachar is a graduate of the Kohenet program, a science teacher, and a self-taught scholar of sacred marriage in the Bible. She believes that many of the biblical kings would have received their sovereignty through sacred sex with priestesses.

> *In all of the stories of Genesis and Kings, women had an important part in establishing who was and wasn't king. I think those women were priestesses of Asherah. When David proposes to Abigail, the text says that "Abigail rose quickly and mounted a donkey… and she became his wife." (I Samuel 25:42) The image of Anat [the goddess] is right there.—Anat is the one who stands on*

> the horse [in Canaanite iconography Anat is depicted as a naked woman on a horse¹²]. Abigail is the priestess, Anat incarnate, and if David marries her he marries Anat.
>
> In a sacred marriage, the woman would have relations with the man at a shrine, and say: This is your destiny, I confer these blessings on you; you are my chosen and now you will be king. This is the same concept as the Jews being the chosen of YHVH, and is probably why David is named David (beloved).

When asked how this ancient sovereignty rite manifests in her own life, Dvorah describes her connection to the ritual of sacred marriage as personal and immediate. She believes that women's contemporary sexual relationships have the potential to grant power in the same way as did those of the ancient priestesses.

> If I look back on my sexual relationships with several men, they mirrored those sacred marriage rites. I notice that when I develop a sexual relationship with a man, it's a way of supporting him in the world.

Nathan Tamar Pautz, who as a woman completed a two-year Kohenet training, is a transgender man who has dedicated hirself[13] to love of the Goddess. This contemporary mystic has committed to the ancient notion of sacred marriage, in which the priestess, priest, or mystic is wedded in some way to the Divine. One of hir beliefs is that this commitment to love for an ultimate beloved should not remove one from physical reality, but rather enhance physical reality. Nathan Tamar sees hir partner as the world itself: God/dess embodied in the universe.

> Even in love-mysticisms expressed in highly erotic imagery, this love is usually directed toward the Deity in a non-material manner rather than toward people and the earth in a more sensual, human manner. I would like, in my own spirituality, to apply the imagery of Lover and Beloved toward that which we can see, feel, and touch, and to develop a contemplative paneroticism toward the world. I would like to see the ordinary world, the earth, the human, and the material, through contemplative eyes, and to love that which is known through the senses.
>
> I desire to relate to the Lover within, to fan the flames of that love, and also to live in some way as a lover of the world around me.

One symbol that I find inspiring is the troubadour. The troubabour, a wandering minstrel, went about romancing, courting, serenading, and serving the chosen object of love, even when, in many cases, the beloved was unresponsive or unattainable. Similarly, I find inspiring the idea of an everyday life of courting, romancing, appreciating, and serving people, other creatures, and the earth, and in this way, becoming oneself a lover to the world as a beloved.

I feel that as long as one is alive and has human consciousness, this power to love is always ours to exercise, no matter what the circumstances of life may bring.

Spirit Journey
The Lover

You find yourself in a garden. It is late afternoon in midsummer. You can hear bees buzzing and birds singing. Flowers are blooming. Scents fill the air. A path leads through the flower beds. Follow it. Pay attention to each of the lush plants and flowers.

It feels as if this garden has been designed especially for you. In fact, you get the sense that the garden itself is attracted to you. The garden is erotically alive. Allow this aliveness to awaken your senses and your desires.

You come to a grassy hill surrounded by cedar trees. Waiting for you on this hill is God/dess in the form of the Lover. This Lover greets you and invites you to make yourself comfortable on the soft grass. The cedar branches seem to dip down over you like a canopy. You and the Divine Lover share a kiss.

Allow this journey to unfold as deeply as you are willing to go. If you are able to imagine it, visualize making love with this divine being. Feel yourself to be perfectly loved and desired. Feel the genuine passion of God/dess for you. If discomfort arises, note what triggers the discomfort.

Later, you sit on the grass while God/dess makes a crown for you out of flowers and branches. Accept this crown. If you wish, you may make a crown in return for your divine beloved. Say farewell to the Lover and ask how you can meet him/her/it again in the future.

Follow the path back through the garden. As you return to your waking self, fragrances follow you from the realm of the Lover.

She Who Loves:
The Practice of Erotic/Sexual Healing
by Taya Shere

The lover-priestess heals herself, her lovers and the world through sacred sensuality and intimacy. Erotic/sexual healing is a process of becoming whole, present and free, and deeply connected with spirit. On a basic level, sexual healing brings corrective experience when trauma has impacted one's ability to be present in the body and one's availability to sexual energy and expression. On an esoteric level, sexual healing can be an experience of transformation that occurs while making love or sharing sensual or sexual intimacy with another or oneself.

Every one of us can priestess our own sexual healing, invoke transformation, and embody divinity through erotic exploration. We can practice erotic healing through self-pleasure, loving ourselves as we would the Goddess. Many lover-priestesses explore healing with intimate partners, worshipping the Divine through embodied devotion. Some sexual healers focus beyond emotionally intimate contexts, working with transpersonal aspects of erotic connection. Sexual healing can also be pursued through talk therapy or body or energy work that is not explicitly sexual.

Cultivating the Sacred

If you desire to embody the Lover as sexual healer—sacred harlot, temple prostitute, or *kedeisha*—first explore close to home. Invite the Goddess into your self-loving sessions. Create a sacred, sensual environment with scents and candles. Adorn yourself as a lover of the Goddess or as the Goddess herself. Feel the energy of Shekhinah course through you as you stroke your own skin. Experience your body as a temple. Become aware of your pelvic space as a portal of the Divine Mother.

Approaching the Lover

Embrace the Goddess/God in yourself. Perceive Goddess/God in another. Allow abundant time to explore. Slow your movements, touch, and breath, until desire will allow for slow no more. In partner-play, bring mouths close to each other and simply breathe until you can distinguish neither sound nor pace nor smell; until your breath becomes one. Touch even more slowly, welcoming boundaries between skin to blur. Let mingling sweat become a salty stream of healing. Give voice to the divinity that you embody and receive, sounding the song of the sacred through you.

Play and delight in the sensuality and pleasure that is possible being in a body. Healing through sexual intimacy can be powerful. Taking ourselves too seriously, trying too hard, or forcing things is the surest way to cut off from the flow. Erotic healing is served by joy, laughter, devotion, and humility. Experiment with what works for you. Discover what awakens you to the divinity in your own skin, what allows you to find the sacred in your partner and in the connection between you. Talk about, or whisper to each other, ways you experience the Goddess through sexual expression and pleasure.

Returning

Cultivate structures that support grounding and integration after erotic healing experiences. It can be tempting to merge indefinitely. Whether your sexual healing practice is one of union with the Source through a beloved or through self-loving, allow time and space to come back to yourself. Put your hands in the earth. Prepare and partake in a delicious meal. Do laundry or scrub the bathtub, all the while knowing that erotic presence is readily available and awaits your return again and again.

May you revel in the Goddess as She appears inside of you and those you love.

Resources for Further Study

For further sexual healing inspiration, read *Wild Feminine: Finding Power, Spirit and Joy in the Root of the Female Body* by Tami Lynn Kent (Atria Books, 2011), *Urban Tantra: Sacred Sex for the Twenty-First Century* by Barbara Carrellas (Celestial Arts, 2007), *Tantric Sex for Women: A Guide for Lesbian, Bi, Hetero and Solo Lovers* by Christa Schulte (Hunter House, 2005), *Women's Anatomy of Arousal: Secret Maps to Buried Pleasure* by Sheri Winston (Mango Garden Press, 2011), *Healing Sex: A Mind-Body Approach to Healing Sexual Trauma* by Staci Haines (Cleis Press, 2007), and the accounts of sexual healing rituals in *The Fifth Sacred Thing* by Starhawk (Bantam, 1994)

Chapter 15:
Fool-Priestesses

In the spring of 2011, during a Kohenet Institute retreat, we assigned our students the task of building a sacred shrine. We divided participants into four groups, each one dedicated to a priestess path: Wise Woman, Shrinekeeper, Mother, and Fool. Each group was given a room in a dormitory to transform into a sacred space.

The members of the Mother group covered their walls in colorful construction paper and wrote words about mothers. They created a womb-nest on a bed for everyone to cuddle in. The Shrinekeeper group created a spiritual spa with essential oils, cushions, and meditative music. The Wise Woman group created a divination space with mirrors set up for us to reflect on our inner selves, and silent guardians to witness our meditations.

The tone of the Fool shrine was a little different. We were greeted at the door with "I'm sorry, but our mezuzah[1] is out of order." A welcome banner called out "Bend or Break." The priestesses of the Fool shrine went on to invite us to purge all of our unwanted spiritual issues in the sacred toilet. They had each of us stand in the shower to receive a wish from a fairy with a magic wand. We made extravagant wishes. (Give me great sex! Make me twenty years younger!) Occasionally the fairy's wand went on the fritz if she thought our wish was truly impossible. We expressed our fears about love, death, ambition, and trauma. Shrieks and giggles echoed from the shower's walls, filling the hallways of the dormitory. The Fool shrine was a meditation on the slightly crazed, playful exuberance of telling the truth.

Fools give us strange ideas to contemplate, make fun of our assumptions, and express desires we hadn't been able to speak. They can be entertainers and transgressive challengers of tradition. They make the invisible visible and the unsayable sayable. And, of course, they make us laugh.

The Biblical Period: Tricksters

The priestly cults of the Bible do not have sacred fools. There is no King Lear's jester to be shockingly honest, no Hopi clown to make fun of the priests as part of the ritual, no masked animals or demons to dance and scare children as part of a harvest festival. The prophets and priests of the Bible are a rather serious species. The book of Proverbs says: "The foolish woman bustles about; she is simple and knows not a thing..."[2] Proverbs defines "foolish" as corrupt and lacking wisdom, not as role-challenging or laughter-bringing.

Though there are no 'sacred fools' in the bible, there are many tricksters to be found, recognized, and reckoned with: Rebecca and Jacob maneuver Isaac into giving Jacob a blessing, by covering Jacob's arms with goatskin and disguising him as Esau. Jacob convinces Esau to give up his birthright, using a pot of lentils. Laban deceives Jacob into marrying his older daughter Leah rather than his younger daughter Rachel. Samson fools his wedding guests by telling unsolvable riddles. These tricksters are frequently, though not always, carrying out God's will through their trickery.

One of the tricksters is Rachel. After serving his father-in-law Laban for fourteen years, Jacob decides to flee with his four wives and twelve children and much of the wealth of Laban's household. As the family treks into the wilderness, Rachel takes with her the *terafim*, the family's household gods/ancestor spirits. (These may be hers by right—another time *terafim* appear in the custody of a biblical character, they are with a younger daughter, Michal daughter of Saul.) Laban gathers a raiding party and chases after Jacob and his household.

When Laban catches up with them, he indignantly asks Jacob why he stole Laban's gods. Jacob, unaware of Rachel's actions, insists that he has done no such thing and that furthermore anyone who is found to have Laban's gods will die. Laban searches through the family's tents. Rachel takes the *terafim*, places them in the camel-riding-cushion, and sits on them. When he comes to Rachel's tent, she declines to rise, saying: "The way of women is upon me." Laban departs, frustrated in his efforts to find the *terafim*.

This is deeply funny, and it is also profound. Laban's gods are being bled on by a woman—from the biblical perspective, that makes them impure, and certainly not divine. Yet, Rachel claiming to bleed on the gods reminds us of exactly what the old goddesses were for—sexuality, fertility, and women. Rachel "hiding" the old gods in an "impure" place is exactly what patriarchy has done to the goddesses. A sacred fool reveals something that seems funny and incongruous but is deeply true—Rachel does this by sitting on the *terafim*. She is acting as a fool-priestess: a comedienne, yet also a guardian of the sacred.

The Talmudic Period: Breaking the Jars

> *Clowns are the only ones who can "ask why" of dangerous subjects or "ask why" of those people who are specialist in advanced sacred knowledge. They ask in their backwards language, through their satire, and their fooling around. They ask the questions others would like to say; they say the things others are afraid to speak...*"[3]

There are a few sacred fools mentioned in the Talmud. At the Sukkot festivals, sages juggle torches and entertain the crowd.[3a] Rabbi Meir tells fox-fables (probably Aesop's fables).[4] There are also women who use humor to resist their

CHAPTER 15: FOOL-PRIESTESSES

own oppression. Yalta and Beruria, two brilliant learned women, are limited by their social constraints as women and wives. Each uses humor to point out prejudice against women and to vent their frustration at their limited wifely roles.[5] Their stories can be read as stories of sacred fools—challengers of the unexamined assumptions of society.

According to the Talmud, the fiery Yalta is a Jewish aristocrat; the daughter of a *reish galuta* (exilarch or head of the Jewish community in exile). She is known for her sharp tongue and her wisdom. Her learned husband, the sage Rabbi Nachman, asks for her advice, sometimes on humorous matters (such as what to do if you develop a deep desire for non-kosher food). The Talmud mentiones that she is knowledgeable about healing and compassionate toward the ill. She lived sometime around 250 CE. This is a time when the priestesshood was ending in the West, and when Jewish women's leadership was diminishing as well.

In one story in the Talmud (Berachot 51b), Rabbi Nachman is having a meal with a sage named Ulla. Yalta is nearby, perhaps dining in another room, or at the other end of the table. Yalta's husband asks Ulla to include Yalta in the closing ritual of the meal, which involves drinking from a blessed cup of wine:

> *Ulla was once at the house of Rabbi Nachman. They had a meal and Ulla said the blessing after the meal, and he handed the cup of blessing to Rabbi Nachman. Rabbi Nachman said to him: Please send the cup of blessing to Yalta.*

The cup of blessing represents the divine gifts bestowed upon a house. Nachman expects that Yalta will be included in this symbol of divine abundance. (It's clear Nachman thinks highly of his wife: In another story, Nachman allows Yalta to be carried in a palanquin on the Sabbath, contrary to custom.) Ulla doesn't think much of women. He uses the blessing-cup to display his contempt.

> *Ulla said to him: "Thus said Rabbi Yochanan: The fruit of a woman's body is blessed only from the fruit of a man's body, since it says, 'He will also bless the fruit of your body.' (Deut. 7:13) It does not say 'the fruit of her [fem.] body,' but 'the fruit of your [masc.] body.'"*

Ulla refuses to send the blessing-cup to Yalta. Ulla argues that the real "womb" belongs to men, who receive God's gift of life directly, while women are only vessels for the male life-force. By using a prooftext from the Bible, Ulla implies that women's ability to bear children is only a secondary gift to the male gift of generation. Secondary as it may be, the gift of children is women's only blessing; there are no spiritual blessings that apply to them.

This reasoning, in a nutshell, is how women lost the priestesshood. The ruling social and religious powers began to say that women were not a source of life, but only a secondary vessel for God's blessings and men's procreation. At the same time, women began to be viewed as secondary in spiritual life, rather than as crucial facilitators of spiritual experience. Women's secondary place in fertility was linked to their secondary place in spiritual and intellectual community. This denigration would have been occurring in Yalta's Jewish world and in the larger world as well.

Ulla has the powers that be on his side: the Bible, social convention, and presumably God. But Yalta doesn't give up so easily.

> *Yalta heard, and she got up in a passion and went to the wine store and broke four hundred jars of wine.*

Yalta reverses Ulla's statement and turns it back on him. Ulla says that the cup (fertility) belongs to men. So Yalta goes to the wine cellar and breaks the containers of wine that fill the cup. Where will you get your blessing-wine from with no jars to hold the wine in? Yalta's action asks. Where will you get the gift of life, without wombs? The red of the wine further evokes the bodies of women, bodies that Ulla is trying to discount. Yalta is acting the sacred fool by reversing the sacred ritual in order to expose its inequality. She is doing something "foolish" that exposes the truth.

> *Rabbi Nachman said to Ulla: "Let the Master send her another cup." He sent it to her with a message: "All that wine can be counted as a blessing.' She answered: "Gossip comes from peddlers and vermin from rags."*

Rabbi Nachman tries to smooth things over. He doesn't want to insult his guest, but he doesn't approve of Ulla's nastiness, and he probably doesn't like seeing Yalta destroy the wine cellar. He asks Ulla to send Yalta a different cup of wine as a substitute for the blessing-cup. Ulla complies, but he makes another wisecrack: The wine Yalta spilled can be counted as the blessing-wine, so she has no need of what he sends. Or, perhaps he means something even nastier: The wine he sends her may as well be spilled because it will do her no good.

Yalta's final words are a dig at Ulla's high-and-mighty attitude toward his own male fertility. You are indeed fertile and creative, Yalta implies, but what you create are foul words and pests! Like the culture around him, Ulla tries to make Yalta invisible. Yalta challenges this view of women by asserting herself as a "cup of blessing": a source of wit, intellect, creativity, and the life-force.

Beruria, the best-known woman scholar of the Talmudic age, matches Yalta in her sharp wit. Beruria is the wife of Rabbi Meir, a Jewish scholar of the second century. She is known for her outstanding Torah learning. Sages often consult her. Like Yalta, Beruria shows frustration with the gender prejudice of the sages around her. One story about Beruria goes as follows:

> *Rabbi Yose the Galilean was once on a journey when he met Beruria. He asked her: "By what road do we go to Lydda?" She replied: "Foolish Galilean, did not the sages say: 'Do not talk too much with women?' You should have asked: 'By which to Lydda?'"*
> —Babylonian Talmud, Eruvin 53b

Rabbi Yose is known for his negative attitudes toward women. However, this doesn't stop him from asking Beruria for directions when he finds himself at a loss. Beruria sees her chance to embarrass Yose, and mockingly replies that he has used too many words in speaking to her. Surely, since she is a woman, he should have used fewer words.

Beruria too uses ironic reversal to make her point. Normally, it is men who invoke the principle that men should not spend too much time talking to women, presumably because the men might be seduced. For example, Pirkei Avot 1:4 cautions: "He who talks too much with women brings evil on himself." But here, Beruria invokes the same principle to tell Yose he is talking too much. Now the shoe is on the other foot. It's Yose, not women, who stands accused of being garrulous and silly. It's he who is the "fool."

We cannot know to what extent these stories reflect a real Yalta or a real Beruria. We do know that Yalta and Beruria lived in an age from which we have archaeological evidence of women's leadership in synagogues and communities. We see in the Yalta/Beruria stories that the sages knew of women who could turn the commonly-held beliefs about women's place in the universe upside-down.

The Middle Ages and Beyond: Jesters

One role of the sacred fool is to bring sexuality into the public sphere—to take hold of that which usually occurs in private in the dark and bring it into the public conversation in the light. At the ancient celebration of the Eleusinian mysteries, women celebrated Demeter and Persephone by telling licentious and lustful jokes and stories. In Japan, the goddess Uzume lured the sulking sun goddess Amaterasu out of her cave by telling lewd jokes and dancing lasciviously—thus saving the world from chaos and darkness. In sixteenth century Europe, Jewish women would tell bawdy jokes to the bride on the night before her wedding. The bride would sit with a bowl in her lap, and as her hair was braided, people would throw money and presents into the bowl. Women would sit around the bride, "chatting with her to make her merry and telling her about naughty things to make her laugh." This ritual would have defused the bride's fear and tension and perhaps also taught her something about the sexual realm.[6]

At the wedding, the foolery continued. The *koyletch tanz* (challah dance) might be performed by the grandmother of the bride—she would dance with loaves of bread and ask the groom: "What do you want, the challah (bread) or the kallah (bride)?" Another wedding custom was the dance of the mothers-in-law, who pretended to fight with one another and then make up.[7]

In another humorous ritual, performed on the Sabbath after the wedding, the bridegroom would throw the bride his prayer shawl after morning services. She would throw it back to him. In some communities, many other women would join in tugging and throwing the prayer shawl. Again, this was a way of defusing the tension between the newlyweds and bringing the bride into the community of married women.[8]

In medieval Europe, the fool was an important part of Jewish weddings, in spite of the disapproval of rabbis. The *marshallik* was a humorous master of ceremonies. The *letz* was a clown: a juggler, acrobat, and entertainer. A *badchan* or jester performed at Jewish weddings to delight the bride and groom, and acted as a dance leader, encouraging the guests to dance before the bride. Sometimes the *badchan* composed satirical verses about the guests to make the bride and groom laugh. These sacred fools performed in *tanzhausen* or dance-houses, buildings built especially for weddings. Sometimes male fools dressed as women.[9] These traditions date back to the 1300s, and to the troubadours who entertained at medieval Jewish weddings.[10] Most were men, but some were women.[11] Jewish women even formed their own klezmer bands and would go to weddings to "contribute to the festivities."[12] The fool was a much more popular figure at the wedding than the rabbi or cantor.

We can see a female *badchan* (a *badchanit*) in the wedding scene of the movie *The Dybbuk*. In 1914, S. Ansky, a Yiddish playwright, published a play called *The Dybbuk*.[13] In this play, a bride, Leah'le, is possessed by a *dybbuk*, a spirit that houses itself in a human body. The *dybbuk* is actually the spirit of Hannan, who was destined to marry Leah'le. Leah'le's father Sender had promised Hannan's father that their children would wed. However, Leah'le's father reneges on this deal and plans to marry Leah'le to a wealthy man instead. Hannan, who loves Leah'le, dies upon hearing this news. At her wedding, Leah'le becomes possessed. A Chassidic sage conducts a grand exorcism ritual, during which

Sender's treachery is exposed and the souls of Hannan and his father are propitiated. The *dybbuk* is supposedly appeased—but then the bride Leah'le sees Hannan appear before her, and steps out of the magical protective circle to reunite with her beloved in death.

The movie version of this play, filmed in 1937 in Poland, is a window into eastern European Jewish culture before the Holocaust.[14] We see the guests entertaining the bride on the day of the wedding. A *badchanit* encourages the guests to frighten the bride by pretending to be ghosts, demons, and zombies. Judith Berg, who is also the choreographer of the movie, plays the *badchanit*.

The Dance of Death (*toytntants*) in the movie is preceded by a cantor's incantation of a Yiddish prayer admonishing the wedding guests that they all must face death: 'From dust you came and to dust you will return… in the end your bones will be carried to the grave. Everything which lives must finally pass away." As the Dance of Death begins, the guests bob up and down, their erratic moves lending eeriness to the scene. The *badchanit*, dressed in a skull mask and a garment with white wing-like sleeves and a striped overtunic, cavorts and gestures before the terrified-looking bride. The women guests look on, entertained, as Death reaches out again and again to try to touch the bride. Finally, Death takes Leah'le's hands and dances with her, while the bride imagines the face of her true bridegroom, Hannan. The bride puts her head on Death's shoulder and is led away in a dreamy embrace.

According to Berg's biographers, this Dance of Death is a traditional Jewish wedding dance that Judith Berg choreographs for the movie. In its usual context, the dance would have served, in some way, to remind the couple of the reality that life leads to death, and also to propitiate death and keep it away from the wedded couple. In that sense, although the dance was meant to entertain, it had a magical purpose.

Judith Berg is acting as a priestess: a sacred fool who frightens the bride and also presumably offers protection from the forces of death. The dance of the woman Death with the woman Bride is a folk representation of the repressed sacred feminine, which encompasses creative and destructive forces. In the end, Life and Death dance together and are merged.

This theme emerges in other Jewish weddings as well. In some Ashkenazi weddings, musicians played Kol Nidre (the most solemn Yom Kippur liturgy) as the groom walked to the chuppah, and then a "light" piece for the bride, while wealthy women of the town danced around her. The combination of death and sex, the two untouchable topics (and from earliest time, subjects connected to women), was often the province of the Fool.[15]

The "sacred fool" tradition is preserved today in the "shtick" or funny dancing that still occurs at some Jewish weddings to entertain the bride and groom, and also in the "tisch," a table where a groom, or both members of a couple, attempt to give a sermon while the guests laugh and sing silly songs. All this foolishness helps the couple not to feel nervous, which is part of its intent.

The fool's job is to mention the unmentionable: to call to mind the "elephant in the room." At a wedding, the elephant in the room is death. Weddings are about joy, love, hope, and the future. Death is the guest no one wants to invite. So it makes a great deal of sense that one role the *badchan* played was that of Death. The Fool enacts Death to release the tension inherent in a ritual creating an "eternal bond" between mortal people.

The custom of the Jewish sacred fool gave rise to Yiddish theater (in which many women actors thrived), Jewish Borscht Belt entertainers, and eventually modern Jewish comedians and comediennes. In the modern synagogue humor is often confined to costumes and plays on the holiday of Purim, but the tradition of sacred foolery is still alive and well in Jewish performers.

Fool-Priestess Incarnations

Nancy Handwerger, a Kohenet Institute graduate, is a healer, and one of the ways she heals is with humor. She sees the Fool as the one who helps us appreciate the unexpected and contradictory nature of our lives.

> *A Fool exudes joyfulness and happiness for no apparent reason......only because she is alive. This laughing and joyful behavior sparks others to lighten up and see situations with a fresh approach. The Fool arises from looking at oneself and at life from a slant. It's the ability to enjoy the unexpected.*
>
> *Personally, when I become overly serious about something, at a certain point I break into laughter at my attempts to figure things out and control the outcome. The signature of Shekhinah is surprise.*

Sharon Jaffe, also a Kohenet graduate, is an activist and a feminist. Her friends describe her as "a shamanic Jewish priestess." Sharon is often laughing with or at her women's community; her humor gives perspective and also enjoyment. Her laughter comes from her sense of hope that women do not have to go it alone as they discover sexism in the world, but rather can be part of liberating communities, and can offer a vision of hope.

> *There's always the possibility that all of what happened, all the advances around women could disappear. There's grace in seeing others take up the work, and not having to worry about it or carry it. It's like laying down a wonderful burden.*

CHAPTER 15: FOOL-PRIESTESSES

I have joy that second wave feminists don't have to reinvent the wheel; third-wave and fourth wave feminists don't have to reinvent the wheel and rediscover all the problems. We are circling around, we are spiraling, we are building on each other. The garden is growing, the perfume is there; it's full summer. You don't have to worry about winter and survival in the same way.

Sharon expresses astonishment that, since her Kohenet ordination, her local women's spiritual group has been designing her a priestess business card. "I laugh," she says, "because this is so great and unexpected. That's the Fool laughing!"

DJ and Kohenet Institute initiate Amy Wachtel adds:

I call myself the Fool, but it's the Holy Fool! It used to upset me when people called me flaky or crazy. It's taken me a long time to realize that the holy Fool is part of our tradition—though I was often taught that the Fool is bad. The Fool gives the world a chance to laugh at themselves or at the other.

If someone's laughing, it can knock them off their guard and open up the space for another perspective, a way to look at something differently. It can bring comfort to an otherwise tense situation. We need to release and smile!

At a teaching, I was asking questions about a midrash; a Talmud text connecting Torah study to the kidneys. People across the room were cracking up. I wasn't asking my question to get the laugh—but my question exposed the silliness and creativity of the midrash.

Shoshana Jedwab, a Kohenet core teacher and sacred drummer, identifies herself as a Sacred Fool. She uses humor in her teaching and her musical performance to keep her audience off guard and to offer penetrating words of wisdom. As Kohenet faculty, Shoshana is the one to inject sacred foolery into teaching and ritual. Like Nancy and Amy, Shoshana sees the sacred clown as the one with the truest gift of perspective.

A sacred clown is a person who is aware of the great forces arrayed against the individual, who can smile about it and ride on the surf of laughter to new possibilities. The sacred fool is a priest of belief in a god other than fear.

The sacred clown lives in a tragic, broken world where everything is lost, all ethics, all tradition, all convention. Yet the other side of this is that through the truths the sacred clown tells, the community is reborn, and life goes on. This paradox also runs through the story of Purim. Because Esther hides herself and nearly loses her identity, we survive as a people. Purim is the holiday of the sacred fool.

I'm the child of a Holocaust survivor. Without Purim, I can't be a Jew. The fact that there is Purim helps me to trust my religion. It means my religion is aware that genocide is part of human experience, and we have ancient wisdom to deal with it. I'm a sacred clown in part because I am a child of survivors. But then, aren't we all?

Spirit Journey
The Fool

Your spirit guide leads you through the gate, which has been festooned with balloons and ribbons. You are in a ballroom where many people are dancing, eating hors d'oeuvres, and laughing loudly with one another. There are many kinds of lamps, and tables with wine and food. At the center of the room is a tree.

You will notice that everything and everyone you see has a shadow that reveals its opposite. The shadow of a rich-looking man might be a poor old woman, the shadow of a mouse might be a bear or wolf, the shadow of a lamp is a splotch of deep darkness. Even the central tree has an upside-down tree beneath it. Walk around and observe. You may see people you know, as well as their shadow-opposites.

If you look down, you will see your own shadow-companion as well. Note its appearance and what it teaches you. Allow your shadow to lead you to a table. There is an object on it. Pick up the object. It is a mask. This mask reveals a side of you that you do not often show. It may be "you" at your fullest potential, or the "you" you do not want to recognize. It may be an angelic being, mythical creature, or animal representing your spirit.

Put on this mask and exit the gazebo. Dance and cavort with the others. If this is a face you like, revel in it. If it is a face you do not like, see if you can find something in it that teaches you or attracts you. Look down at your shadow. What is it doing?

At some point you will see the Sacred Fool herself as she jests and makes merry for the crowd. She may be a rapier-tongued hostess, a Columbine-like clown, an acrobat, or a Yiddish *badchanit*. As she passes you, she smiles, takes off your mask, turns it over, and hands it back to you.

This side of the mask reveals something else about you, perhaps something completely different from the first face of the mask. Put this mask on and move through the crowd. See how your dance is different. Then put the mask back in its place.

Your shadow will lead you back to where you entered. As you follow your shadow, you will pass the central tree and its shadow-opposite. Take a careful look at this upside-down tree and see what you learn. Then thank your guide, and leave the ballroom, returning through the gateway to your waking self.

She Who Shatters:
The Practice of Embracing Change
by Taya Shere

The fool-priestess lives at the place of beginnings and endings. The fool-priestess turns things upside down and relishes the unknown. When we are feeling stagnant or stuck, invoking the fool-priestess or the trickster can jolt us free from familiar patterns and launch us into the next step of possibility. Practices of the fool-priestess include shattering—destroying to allow space for the creation of something new—and embracing change.

Chronicle Change

Take stock of big changes you have experienced over the course of your life. Choose a few changes to chronicle, giving attention to how you approached them before, during, and after they occurred. What was lost in these changes? What gifts did these changes bring?

Notice your typical patterns around change. What are your knee-jerk reactions? Do you resist? Do you waver? Do you jump in? What emotions emerge for you in moments of change? Fear and anxiety? Excitement? Anger? Do you tend to integrate change slowly over time, or do you prefer to move quickly in moments of transition?

In what ways have you taken care of yourself during times of change? What has been missing from your self-care? What do your body, heart, mind and spirit need to integrate change? How can you apply this wisdom to current changes in your life?

Meet Change

Get clear about what isn't working in your life. This may be a friendship, pattern, or commitment. Be honest about what needs to shift. Reflect on it. Invoke support around it. Communicate it. It can be scary to say 'no' to things or to choose endings. Shift your focus away from what you are saying 'no' to. Become aware of what you are saying 'yes' to through that same choice. The more you move toward and celebrate your 'yes'es, the more easily things that are a 'no' will fall away.

Be Willing to Know Nothing

Discern what is needed and open to new possibilities by stepping out of habit. Go somewhere- or to a kind of place- you have never been before, with no expectations. See what calls to you or who shows up to teach you. Listen with a different kind of ear. Let it be possible that the way you have always made decisions or done things no longer fits. What would a totally new way of choosing or acting look like for you? Try this.

Break Something

When something shatters, energy is freed up and can reconfigure. Break something on purpose. Choose an old wine glass or thin ceramic dish that you no longer need. Smash it against the wall, or place it on the floor and stomp on it (while wearing shoes). Consider shattering something while holding an intention around an issue or situation you want to release. You can choose to break something simply because you are in a stuck place and need to free up energy, even if you are not cognizant of the content of what is needed to shift.

In the novel *Broken for You* by Stephanie Kallos, the main characters intentionally shatter antique-ware as a practice of healing and transforming old wounds. As each piece is thrown against the floor, the broken vessels become small tiles that are then brought together to make new creations.

Whether we want to or not, we all experience breaking points throughout our lives. Cultivating a relationship with change, and practicing the art of shattering well, is a skill that serves us in many contexts. May we learn to surrender.

Resources

For a novel approach to the practice of breaking, read *Broken for You* by Stephanie Kallos (Grove Press, 2004). For wisdom and inspiration on reframing your relationship with material things, read *Clutter-Busting* by Brooks Palmer (New World Library, 2009). For spiritual wisdom on letting go, read *When Things Fall Apart: Heart Advice for Difficult Times* by Pema Chodron (Shambhala 2000) or *Comfortable with Uncertainty: 108 Teachings on Cultivating Fearlessness and Compassion* by Pema Chodron (Shambhala, 2003). For science fiction and poetic approaches to embracing change read *Parable of the Sower* by Octavia Butler (Grand Central Publishing, 2000) or Mary Oliver's poem "The Journey."

Chapter 16:
The Future of the Hebrew Priestess

> *The true mysteries of the Sacred Feminine are not about cryptic codes, secret messages, or hidden hoards of treasure. They are the most ordinary, everyday things of life, which we all experience: birth, growth, death, and regeneration.*
> —Starhawk[1]

> *The problem of truthfulness becomes one of being true to a complexity.*
> —Avivah Zornberg[2]

The shrines and altars at which Hebrew priestesses once served, danced, divined, and drummed are now available to us only through archaeology, fragments of text, and imagination. Some of us live in traditional Jewish communities, and some do not. Yet contemporary Hebrew priestesses are choosing to serve in new ways that echo the old ones: by creating prayer language that invokes Goddess; by building altars and making sacred art; by drumming and dancing; by spirit journeying; by dreaming and divining; by burning incense, baking bread, and lighting candles; by honoring the earth and the body as sacred; by scholarship that treats the history of priestesses as relevant for the modern age. What lessons about how to live and worship can we learn from Hebrew priestesses, ancient and modern, as we move into the future?

Readers of this book likely come from many different points along the social and spiritual continuum. Some of us live in communities where men and women are free to pursue spiritual and communal leadership. Some of us may not. Some of us continue to work for an egalitarian age in which gender roles do not define our lives. Some of us may be seeking a spiritual relevance and resonance as yet unnamed. There is a great deal to be gained by introducing priestess practices into our contemporary spiritual landscape. These practices can be useful to communities of women, mixed-gender communities, communities of men, and communities with other definitions. Here are thirteen gifts we can all take from Hebrew priestess practice as we continue on our path.

I - The Weaver-Priestess: Reverence for the Web of Life

> *As far back as I can remember, I have had a feeling of interconnection and wonder in nature... The texture of the desert has always been to me like the Grandmother. The flow of water*

to the Ocean, and her waves. And then, the intersection of the intangible with the physical. These are my encounters with the Divine.
—Toby Eliana Shulruff

I pray because I believe there is something inside of me—and inside of every other human being—that is holy, and that the holiness in me is connected to the holy in everything else.
—Margie Klein[3]

I'm on the fence about deity. Life itself is sacred.
—Sharon Jaffe

When the Temple weavers wove sacred fabrics for the shrine, they were also modeling weaving as a way of understanding the world. We are beings merged and intertwined with others, the way the weavers' threads merge and intertwine. The interdependence of life is at the core of the truths we can derive from weaver-priestesses.

In the Western world, we tend to see creation as a completed action. We view plants and animals as lesser beings. We perceive our will as separate from the forces that exist outside of us. Our ancestors did not live this way: for them, creation was ongoing, and the world was full of spirits and living presences that affected the human community. In the Bible, plants and animals might be signs or messengers, like the burning bush or the ravens who feed Elijah. For kabbalists, every substance has divinity in it, and every positive action has the potential to aid the cosmos.

This interconnected worldview is similar to the thinking of shamans and mystics around the world, and also to the relational ethics proposed by modern feminist and ecological thinkers. Luce Irigaray notes that the dividing line between self and other may be biologically and psychologically more porous for women than it is for men[4]—but the boundary is diffuse for everyone to some degree. Ova are formed in most girl babies before they are born; that means all of us have some part of us that was inside our grandmother's body. Our bodies blend. So too, we aren't separate from the ecosystems around us.

In biblical priestly ritual, every act that anyone in the community performed had not only an ethical but an energetic impact on the whole. Certain sacrifices were a clean-up of any spiritual residue left over from wrong action. Shrine ritual was meant to keep the cosmic order free from damage and spiritually up and running. Priests and priestesses were guardians of this process. Developing a priestess or priest consciousness today can mean taking one's place as a guardian and transmitter of an ecological understanding of our place in the world, and celebrating rituals that speak to the interwoven nature of things.

II - The Prophetess-Priestess: Modes of Revelation

> *I view Torah as a skeleton framework upon which all ages throughout time can build. I also feel dismayed that we continue to meet many of the same unresolved issues.*
> —Nancy Handwerger

> *As a woman, accessing my fierce self, taking up space, and speaking with a full and deep voice is a radical act. When one woman does this, she inherently makes room for others to do so.*
> —Elsa Asher

In the summer of 2010, at the Isabella Freedman Jewish Retreat Center, Kohenet Institute participants were sharing a Shabbat morning service with others at the retreat. When the time came for the Torah reading, we brought the Torah outside to a grove of pine trees. Worshippers sat on benches shaded by green branches. We carried the Torah through the group, and then unwrapped the scroll in preparation for reading. Instead of placing the Torah on a table or lectern, we wrapped a tree in prayer shawls and supported the Torah upright against the tree.

I explained to the community that our Torah portion contained the verse: "You shall not set up an Asherah (a sacred tree of the Goddess) beside the altar." Rather than ignore this verse, I used it to invite the community to consider how we felt about sacred trees. I invited the Torah to "speak" to the tree and the tree to "speak" to the Torah, each sharing its unique wisdom about God. We read a part of the weekly portion, including the verse about the Asherah. Then, I spoke a prayer that the tree and the Torah would be reconciled; that we would learn how to see nature and sacred text as different aspects of one tree of life. When I looked around, I saw people weeping.

The prophetesses and prophets of the ancient world did not rely on a single sacred text to connect them to God. For them, the divine spoke all the time, through dreams, visions, signs, and oracles. Many cultures today continue to utilize prophecy, poetry, ecstatic speech, dance, spirit journey, and other modalities to experience revelation. The moment of placing the Torah in contact with the tree was a moment of bridging the Jewish faith that the Torah speaks, and the ancient tradition that the tree speaks.

Sacred text and its interpretation have been the primary mode for Jews (and many others) to connect with the will of the Creator, and this interpretive system has been creative, dynamic, and enduring. Some modern Hebrew priestesses have a traditional theology about the primacy and divinity of Torah. Others have adopted a hermeneutic of suspicion toward the Bible, seeing in the removal of priestesses and the Goddess from the Temple a political and theological agenda expressed by one part of Israelite society. For these priestesses, the Torah may be a connection to the ancestors and even to the divine, but it cannot speak as a sole authoritative voice, because there is too much that has been stifled.

I remember an interfaith conference I attended, where the following conversation took place. A Talmud scholar said to a witch: "I don't believe in the efficacy of prophecy in the contemporary world," and the witch snapped back: "I don't believe in the efficacy of sacred text!" This is the crux of the contradiction between prophecy and textual revelation. Perhaps ancient and modern Hebrew prophetesses and prophets can teach us how to bring sacred text and ecstatic prophecy together. What if we could hold sessions where we listened to and could truly hear how each community member experiences the sacred? What if we took dance, drum, and song seriously as a way to communicate with the divine? How would we change and grow? This is the challenge of the prophetess-priestess.

III - The Shrinekeeper-Priestess: Temple Consciousness

Shekhinah is home and hearth, root and rug,
the altar on which we light our candles.
We live here, in her body.
—Lynn Gottlieb[5]

For me personally, the altar is more welcoming than a traditional synagogue setup. The altar is a universal spiritual space.
—Rachel Koppelman

I started being visited by a woman in my dreams. She would take me to see these places I couldn't even understand. The sea and the mountains were so vivid in them. Temples.
—Erev Richards

At a Sukkot holiday retreat known as Sukkahfest,[6] I taught a joint class with Rabbi Ezra Weinberg, who is a *kohen*, a member of the priestly tribe. The class explored ancient and modern models of priesthood and invited the participants to share their thoughts about how they felt the priest/esshood could contribute to spirituality today. Many of them spoke about a longing for sacred

CHAPTER 16: THE FUTURE OF THE HEBREW PRIESTESS

space of the kind that once existed—the kind of sacred space that represents the cosmos and draws pilgrims to its doors. This kind of sacred space may use the elements and directions, the altar and inner sanctum, or features of the land, to symbolize the universe as a whole. Shrinekeeper-priestesses once watched over such spaces, at the holy city of Shiloh, at the hill-shrines, and perhaps even in the Temple in Jerusalem.

Today, at Kohenet Institute retreats, we use an altar at the center of the room to make our space sacred, rather than a podium or ark at one end of the room. This too is Temple consciousness—a return to an older form of organizing spiritual space. Our altar contains one or more of the four elements, and is organized according to the four directions. It may have stones painted with the letters of the Hebrew alphabet, or linen from an unmarried woman's dowry (kept for a generation in a chest of drawers), or a circle of pine cones, or a bowl with water from twenty different holy sites, or the skull of a cow who had twelve calves during her lifetime. The altar is a home for the divine to dwell with us.

This practice arises out of modern feminist Goddess practice, and is consistent with many indigenous practices around the world. It is also deeply Jewish. The *bamot*, altars, pillars, and sacred trees of the land of Israel were a time-honored and deeply valued way for our ancestors to connect with God. Modern Hebrew priestesses, and many others, are teaching the community ways of re-incorporating Temple consciousness into our spiritual practices.[7] These ritualists not only see traditional Jewish holy sites as sacred—they understand that the earth itself is holy, and anywhere can be a shrine. Altars are not restricted to ancient temples or modern prayer spaces—they can exist in homes, forests, campgrounds—anywhere people gather together with sacred intent.

At a Shavuot retreat, Kohenet graduate, environmental activist, and earth-based practitioner Sarah Shamirah Chandler created a harvest procession reminiscent of the one that the Mishnah describes as part of the springtime celebration in the Temple. Goats, farmers dressed as goats, drummers, and dancers moved forward in a procession, surrounded by onlookers and well-wishers. Someone blew a shofar. There was a sacred platter of vegetables from the farm, beneath a wedding canopy that represented the union of heaven and earth. Someone held two loaves of bread, reminiscent of the two loaves of bread offered in the Temple on Shavuot. When we reached our destination, a rabbi stood under the canopy and sang the blessing over wine and bread—joining Temple consciousness with rabbinic daily practice. We lunched on creamy goat cheese made from the milk the goats that had been part of our procession, and delicious fresh vegetables from the farm. This kind of ritual is one way of introducing the work of the shrinekeeper-priestess into a contemporary age.

IV - The Witch-Priestess: Taking Spirit Seriously

Priestesses have an understanding of the dual nature of reality: that unseen reality is operating at the same time as the seen. They understand how the two realities interact; they can see them both at the same time.
—Dvorah Klilah bat Shachar

When someone comes to the gateway [between worlds], the baalat ov [sorceress] can be the conduit for them to receive wisdom, truth, and healing.
—Juna Madrone

My ancestors are instructing me to continue my explorations of their knowledge and wisdom.
—Leah Chava Reiner

I was once at a seminar for rabbis where Chava Weissler, a scholar and anthropologist, was teaching about Ashkenazi women's candle rituals. When she explained that these rituals were meant to contact dead souls and acquire their aid, the rabbis around me giggled.

These same rabbis would never giggle to hear that their ancestors believed God dictated a sacred document to Moses on Mount Sinai. They might choose to reframe that belief, or see it as a metaphor, but it certainly would not be cause for humor. I suspect that they also would not have giggled if Weissler had been teaching about kabbalists contacting angels or the souls of previous kabbalists. Because Weissler was teaching about women's "folk ritual" that is ordinarily labeled superstitious and foolish, my colleagues felt uncomfortable and therefore they laughed.

Yet our ancestors strongly believed they shared the human community with the spirits of those who had gone before. The witch-priestess teaches us about tending relationships with our ancestors. For many of us, that may mean honoring their cultural and spiritual traditions—lighting Shabbat candles and remembering the women who did it before us, or making amulets as our great-grandmothers in many lands have done throughout history.

During one Kohenet Institute prayer service in the spring of 2011, Kohenet Tiana Mirapae led us in making an ancestor cord. This ritual involves making a braided cord that represents the past generations of our individual lineages, which also holds all of the built-up energy, fate, and tradition that has come from those ancestors. We chanted and purified ourselves, then tied a bundle of three cords to our big toe and carefully braided it while singing. The yarn was black and coarse and felt like wool our great-grandmothers might have used.

Some of us ended up with a neatly braided cord. Others ended up with a knotted mess. Tiana suggested that the knots could represent traumatic incidents in the lives of our ancestors that we are still working out. As a Jewish shamaness, Tiana studies and teaches about the Holocaust, and helps Jews acknowledge, heal, and integrate the trauma of our ancestors' suffering. She says: "I became a shamaness so that I could heal people at the level of the soul."

Tiana invited us to keep the cords we braided on our personal altars and use them as we work with our ancestral lines. Some people found the spiritual power of this exercise overwhelming. Others were left puzzling about how their distant ancestors relate to their own lives.

The witch may also be open to elemental energies and angelic spirits, which Adin Steinsaltz defines as "gloves for the fingers of God." During another Kohenet Institute ritual, we adapted a traditional Jewish bedtime ceremony invoking the four angels at the four corners of the bed and the Shekhinah above the bed. We sealed our ritual space using an ancient mystical formula from the Sefer Yetzirah, inviting female and male angelic energies to surround us, and the Divine to shelter us above and below. After the ritual, we felt protected within our space, and connected to one another in a new and powerful way. The witch-priestess invites us to acknowledge our relationships with other souls, and with the great energies of the universe. She asks us to take spirit seriously. Hebrew priestesses are finding ways to be open to the unseen.

V - The Maiden-Priestess: Creating Safe Space

> *Women in women's space are funny, embodied, musical. They can put heart with mind and mind with heart. I feel safe in women's space to access my gifts and powers. I don't feel like I need to edit myself. It's healing for culture when "outsiders"—and women are still outsiders—do concentrated work together.*
> —Shoshana Jedwab

> *Though we are each very different, I swear I see myself in all of their eyes.*
> —Yosefa Strouss

Priestesses who work in, or who create, women's communities may receive criticism for being separatists. In a world where women can be rabbis, why would women need to go off on their own to do spiritual work? Indeed, why even use the term "priestess" instead of "priest"? Maiden-priestesses who danced together at Shiloh, Kurdish Jewish women who went off together for a spring Shabbat, might today be criticized for not including men in their ritual.

Many women and girls still need separate space, in order to talk about how spirit looks from inside a woman's body. This is a discourse that is difficult to have around men, or indeed around most people. The body is aggressively secularized in modern society. The idea that the body is a temple is a slogan used to cover up society's obsession with women's weight and shape. Women's voices and life experiences have been systematically excluded from many dominant belief systems until recently. Women and girls need space to discuss these things with a level of privacy and intimacy, and accept or reject ideas based on women's experience, not based on society's shame about the feminine. They need space to open up about their spiritual lives as women, space to dance without feeling self-conscious or self-protective. Many men also crave separate space to feel the energy of men together. Changing views of gender identity, and the presence of transgender people in our community, may make the creation of separate spaces more complex, but with care, separate space can be created that includes transfolk and those with non-traditional gender identity.

Girls' and boys' rituals and sacred spaces can fill similar needs. Girls' coming-of-age programs like 'Rosh Chodesh: It's a Girl Thing!', facilitated by the organization Moving Traditions, and *bat mitzvah* programs that take place in natural settings, like the program Bat Briyah mentioned in Chapter 7, have an important role to play in letting Jewish girls explore themselves as spiritual beings dwelling in a diverse world.

Women also need to be honest about the ways conventional sacred text and prayer is painful for them, as well as the ways their tradition has affirmed them. Often they are reluctant to criticize Torah or Jewish law in front of men lest their comments be perceived as shrill or shaming. As feminism becomes more widespread and accepted, even in more traditional Jewish communities, times for separate women's space are more important, not less. The time and space needs to be an environment of affirmation, rather than embarrassment. A safe place to move from anger to creativity can allow women to return to the greater community with renewed resources, more positivity, and fresh inspiration for the future.

Spiritual work has always included healing, and some kinds of healing may take place most effectively in same-gender contexts. At a recent retreat, Kohenet Institute students spontaneously created a ritual for sexual abuse survivors, taking many women to immerse in the lake nearby as a sign of healing. At another retreat, we created boxes that contained gifts to our inner child-selves. The maiden-priestess is just as vulnerable—and just as powerful and holy—as she has always been. Hebrew priestesses are creating safe spaces for women to gather together.

VI - The Mother-Priestess: Speaking about Goddess

Focusing on the cycle of my breath, the moon, the seasons, and the Torah reminds me that only change endures. Just when I hunger for permanence and linear motion with some end in sight, I am reminded that the cycle of creation is proof of God's love for me. She is forever pregnant, forever birthing, forever dying, and forever being reborn. What endless grace and mercy!
—Rinah Rachel Galper

At the end of the day, G-d(dess) is who She is regardless of what I call Her, but my relationship to Her and to Her world are created over and over again every day through language.
—Annie Matan

The Jewish community has struggled with God-language, and language about mothers, for decades. While many synagogues include the names of the foremothers along with the names of the forefathers in their prayer, this is still a controversial liturgical issue. Many liberal prayerbooks retain traditional masculine-gendered language for God in Hebrew while referring to God with gender-neutral pronouns in the English. A few prayer communities, such as Chavurat Shalom in Boston, P'nai Or in Philadelphia, Congregation Romemu in New York, and the Kohenet Institute community use feminine God-language, but for the most part, imagining deity in the feminine is still off-limits. The awareness that conception and pregnancy once were metaphors for how God/dess made the world is missing from our discourse.

It is an inescapable mammalian truth that all of us get here in a biologically female body. Perhaps this is why the Divine Mother continues to inhabit the human imagination. We can let God take on the role of mother in our lives, and let our caregiving to others be the actions of the divine made actual through our hands. The mother-priestesses who lit Shabbat candles as an echo of the Shekhinah kindling souls—they teach us of the possibility of connecting to the Divine Mother in our prayers and deeds.

Yet the mother-priestesses also remind us not to stereotype the Mother as eternally self-sacrificing and benevolent. Mothers can be fierce, lonely, desirous, angry, and a host of other things. And the feminine is not always a mother at all. As we find ways to speak about the Divine, it is important that any gendered language we use, male or female or other, not reify our biases about gender. If we speak about Goddess as mother, we should also speak about Goddess as activist, scholar, hermit, crone, or little girl—and we should speak about male and other faces of God in similarly diverse ways. God-language, and Goddess-language, should challenge, surprise, and mystify us, not box us in. Modern Hebrew priestesses can be innovators of new ways to see God.

VII - The Queen-Priestess: Sharing Power

> *Cultivating... awareness of group dynamics can help us to look for or cultivate other roles in other participants.*
> —Juna Madrone

> *Something that has been a struggle for me is that I try to take on too many [spiritual leadership] roles at once, especially when I am leading. Taking on all these roles at once has left me feeling depleted. It's so helpful to remember that others are already taking care of the group in [other] ways.*
> —Annie Matan

> *The guide sees and nurtures the potential of the whole and the capabilities of each part.*
> —Rabbi Shefa Gold

Convening ritual, creating meaning, holding sacred space, teaching knowledge: These things mean using our power and strength. The queen mothers of ancient Israel exercised religious and temporal authority, and they remind us that power is one of the tools of a Hebrew priestess. In the modern age, we can and must use an egalitarian ethic to inform our power. The most powerful leader is the one who empowers others.

We live in an age of professionalized spiritual roles, where a few people (rabbi, cantor, chaplain) are supposed to do all the "spiritual work," and other people are the followers, customers, or audience. Burnout among religious professionals is common, and many speak about feeling overworked and disillusioned. This is partly because the community expectation of them is too high. Meanwhile, the role of the non-professional Jews (social justice worker, donor, giver of hospitality, learner, Torah reader, fervent pray-er, yoga teacher, etc.) are underplayed but of crucial importance to the community. Diversifying our definition of clergy may be a necessary paradigm shift. This paradigm shift to community leadership may also work in other realms—the academy, the workplace, the political sphere.

At a recent retreat of the Academy for Jewish Religion, I heard Shefa Gold speak about the different roles people play in ritual—not only the leader, but the person who exudes celebration, the person who observes, the one who is a guardian for the group, etc. Everyone participating in a sacred space has a role and a function. This gave me more insight into how the different priestess roles work together—no one role is sufficient to meet the needs of a community. This is the priestly model—a temple that has ritual officiants, Levites, oracles, weavers, prophet-poets, etc.—and it is a healthier model than the one we now have. Modern queen-priestesses are teaching their communities how to claim and share power in ways that give everyone renewed energy.

VIII - The Midwife-Priestess: Holy Transformation

I am committed to being there with women for the experience of birth.
—Paula Freedman

I am... the midnight doula,
gently rocking the precious baby redemption
in my grandmother's rocking chair...
—Ilana Streit[8]

Midwife-priestesses are helpers at birth: a person, an idea, a passion, an organization, a new identity. The midwife-priestesses Shifra and Puah supported the Hebrews in birthing, and through their resistance to Pharaoh, they also aided the Hebrews in leaving Egypt. So too, modern midwife-priestesses guide individuals and groups through transitions.

At a summer 2011 retreat at the Isabella Freedman Jewish Retreat Center, the participants all met by Skype with Rabbi Zalman Schachter-Shalomi, of blessed memory, known affectionately as Reb Zalman to the members of the movement he founded—the Jewish Renewal movement. Reb Zalman had asked for questions prior to the call, and someone had asked him: what should the role of a *kohenet* be?

Reb Zalman answered the question in two ways. First, he asked the organizers of Kohenet to sit in the front row so he could see us, and he transmitted to us and our community the priestly blessing, spreading his hands in the traditional gesture. Reb Zalman is himself a *kohen*, a member of the priestly caste. Many of us took this to mean that he wanted to give assent to our endeavor, to give us a connection to the traditional priesthood.

Reb Zalman gave his second answer by offering many examples of spiritual events where a *kohenet*'s presence could be useful. Some of the examples were: bringing a bride to the ritual bath and teaching her about the consciousness of sacred sexuality; guiding *b'not mitzvah* (adolescent girls); aiding the dying; midwifery; helping people in a shiva house to be in communion with the spirit of their loved one; and circumcision (Reb Zalman pointed out that one of the people to circumcise a baby in the Bible is a woman: Zipporah, wife of Moses).

Priestesses have many roles that Reb Zalman did not mention, but most of the roles he did mention have something in common: they are a kind of spiritual midwifery: birthing a person from one state into the next. Reb Zalman was suggesting to us that priestesses have a role in giving meaning to moments of transition and transformation. Reb Zalman was inviting us to teach others to look at their own life transitions—weddings, births, deaths, entry into the covenant—as offerings to the Holy One. He was naming us as midwives of spirit.

Contemporary priestesses are celebrants of life cycle ritual. They perform weddings with a Goddess consciousness. They conduct bat mitzvah rituals that have a consciousness of indigenous initiation rites. They invent rituals for menarche, aging, adoption, menopause, surgery, gender transition, miscarriage—many events for which there are no traditional rituals. Midwife-priestesses are enriching the ritual language of their tribe. And, of course, midwife-priestesses are still delivering babies.

IX - The Wise-Woman-Priestess: Creating Lineages

I am a bat kohen but felt excluded from participating in the privileges/responsibilities of the kohanim .... I only had a vague sense of what the priestly class was all about. One reason I decided to pursue Kohenet training was to reclaim the priestess role for myself and my female ancestors.
—Celia Strickler

My grandfather was from a secretive line of Jewish mystics. I have his hand-written parchment Zohar. There were no boys to claim it, and I was the oldest grandchild, although grandpop never spoke of Cabala to me. I was a girl—much loved by him, but still, a girl... Now our magic circle of sisters continues to open me to the voice of Shechina growing ever stronger and sweeter... The secrets are coming out and inviting us to share them.
—Judi Dash

I co-create the culture we live in and speak in the circle.
—Rebecca Lemus

My wife Shoshana's father is an Auschwitz survivor. He comes from a long line of learned Jews and is very proud of his ancestry. He often tells Shoshana that she comes from seventeen generations of rabbis. Shoshana sometimes feels torn between all the rabbinic expectations implied by that long lineage and her spiritual calling as a shamanic drummer and priestess. Once, after hearing "I come from seventeen generations of rabbis" one too many times, I exclaimed, "Shoshana, you come from seventeen generations of *women*!"

I can still remember the dumbfounded shock on her face, then the dawning enlightenment. We don't often think of lineages of women. The wise women of the Bible and Talmud don't have female students, or even daughters. The statement in the Mishnah that "Moses received Torah from God at Sinai, then transmitted it to Joshua; Joshua transmitted it to the elders, the elders to the prophets, the prophets to the men of the Great Assembly..."[9] doesn't contain a single woman. Many women's traditions, from household rituals to healing cures, are lost, because no one made a permanent record of them.

It is radical to name oneself a Hebrew priestess—it would be much more theologically acceptable, from a conventional point of view, to study them. Claiming the priestesses as a lineage, rather than a relic of antiquity, implies an emotional and spiritual connection that reaches from past to future. It means inviting priestesses out of the past to be teachers and wise women in the present.

Calling oneself a priestess in the absence of a lineage makes it more difficult to pass down that identity to someone else; being in learning and teaching community makes women accountable to one another. It is important that Hebrew priestesses be part of a community, and that there be ceremonies and traditions of ordination. Wise-woman-priestesses teach us to create lines of connection from one woman to another, and from one generation to the next.

X - The Mourning-Woman-Priestess: Rethinking Death

True wisdom is that which can hold the dark and the light.
—Dvorah Klilah bat Shachar

Being a priestess involved in chevra kadisha *feels scary and right."*
—Ryan Erev

Traditionally, Hebrew priests (*kohanim*) do not attend funerals or go to cemeteries, except for a very close relative. This custom is related to the ancient taboo that kept priests away from human death. In the Kohenet Institute's priestess community, the question has frequently arisen as to whether Hebrew priestesses also should refrain from attending funerals. We have debated this vigorously, and the general conclusion has been that we should not avoid death—mourning women throughout Jewish history approached death as sacred, and so should we. Hebrew priestesses have counseled the dying, officiated at funerals, washed the dead (*chevra kadisha*), guided prayers at houses of mourning, and been part of the end of life in many other ways.

This is not a leniency but a statement of philosophy. The circle of life and death is sacred. Biblical laws kept the Temple free of birthing women, menstruants, men who had emitted semen, and people in mourning. We want to do differently. Hebrew priestesses are placing experiences of liminality, ephemerality, and transition at the center of our ritual lives, not keeping them outside. This perspective has much to offer the Western world, which often fears and ignores death, and it has much to offer Jewish culture as well. Mourning-Woman-Priestesses are teaching us to re-envision the Jewish culture and rituals surrounding the life cycle in ways that embrace and include.

XI - The Seeker-Priestess: Becoming Spiritual Pilgrims

As a Kohenet,
may I help others to see
the Divine Presence in all
and in themselves.
—Blessing for women's tefillin, created by Ahava Lilith EvershYne

May we reject all ways that are destructive to ourselves, each other and the earth. Let's regenerate our sacred connections with ourselves, the earth and all beings... I am praying to pray no longer, but to simply live the prayer.
—Miriam Rubin

In 2009, the Sacred Circles conference gathered at the National Cathedral in Washington, D.C. It was an extraordinary gathering of women. There was a Lakota shaman, a Sufi dervish, and a Tibetan Buddhist teacher and former nun. There were ministers, women priests, sheikhas and rabbis. Taya and I conducted a workshop on Hebrew priestessing. A hundred women showed up, most of them Episcopalian. I found the gathering very special in that it was free of fear. The Lakota shaman invoked the four directions from the altar of the National Cathedral, and everyone watched in rapt attention. We each had our separate identities, but no one was overly concerned about boundaries. We were women meeting the spirit together.

Judaism is an indigenous tradition formed in the land of Israel/Canaan thousands of years ago. Yet many modern Jews think they have much more in common with Christians and Muslims—other text-based monotheists—than with Native Americans, African diaspora religions, or Celtic shamans. The assumption is that a non-monotheist, or a monotheist who is not text-based, is less connected to us than a Catholic, a Mormon, or a Pentecostal Protestant. This attitude prevents us from identifying with cultures that have been demonized, demeaned, and nearly destroyed, as Judaism has been. It prevents us from seeking out the commonalities with the spiritual histories of many peoples of color. It prevents us from identifying with priestesses.

We learn from seeker-priestesses—ancient women on pilgrimage, women monastics listening to the inner voice—to search for truth in new places. Contemporary Hebrew priestesses are listening to their counterparts in the Goddess movement, to developments in pagan spirituality, to indigenous priestesses in Africa and Asia, to Christian and Muslim women exploring the sacred feminine in their own traditions, and also to Jewish mystics in other sectors of Jewish life. This is a different conversation than the general, and somewhat superficial, interfaith conversations Jews usually have, and it allows us to see new aspects of ourselves and our traditions. From these encounters has come theology and ritual—not borrowed from others, but developed in response to the holy encounter with the other.

The seeker-priestesses of old went to pilgrimage sites, not because they couldn't encounter the divine at home, but because journey itself is a spiritual practice. Being challenged and enriched by the perspectives of others does not erase the self. Contemporary seeker-priestesses—and all who encounter and dialogue with other faiths around the world—are teaching us to live in curiosity, and to explore without fear.

XII - The Lover-Priestess: Intimate Priestessing

Ah, lover, ah, beloved,
Together we may yet fill up this earth
So lost, so ravishingly lovely
With the sweet and mighty melody
From which flows
Every song
—Diane Eliot, "Song of the End and of the Beginning"

Sex can be healing, fun, connection to higher power, self-love, a one-night stand, a chance to play, an exploration, meaningful and anything in between as long as it happens between adults who are consenting.
—Ariel Vegosen

> *Eros is a sacred force that calls the opposites to passionately merge.*
> —Felice Winograd Holt

The lover-priestesses, some believe, could anoint kings through their lovemaking. They could also be ordinary lovers on Friday night in any Jewish town throughout the world. Lover-priestesses teach us that creating a channel for the divine can occur in the most intimate settings. One doesn't have to be a leader of an institution, or an extrovert, to be a priestess.

Priestessing can mean guiding a ritual for hundreds or convening a small new moon circle in your living room. You can also be a priestess for yourself and/or your most intimate circle. Priestesses of love treat the beings they love—gardens, lovers, children, elders, friends, themselves—as if they are deity incarnate. They pursue their passions—knowledge, art, literature, work, body practices, prayer, humanitarian action—with devotion and eros, knowing that human passions are gifts of the Goddess. They create their home and work spaces as shrines for conversation, ceremony, creative work, lovemaking, parenting.

Some Hebrew priestesses may see romance and sexuality as part of their relationship with the Goddess. Others may be "lovers" in different ways. Lover-priestesses can also devote themselves to the freeing of the power of love by working against sex slavery and forced marriage. The contemporary Hebrew priestess, whether or not she is sexually active, comes to us bringing her desire to engage the world, and to fully meet the people in her life. Living with an ethic of love is one calling of the Hebrew priestess.

XIII - The Fool-Priestess: Not Knowing

> *Come be our Shekhinah we are your glory*
> *We believe that you live*
> *Though you delay we believe you will certainly come*
> —Alicia Ostriker[10]

> *The Trickster is waiting to see if we'll ask the right questions.*
> —Carly Lesser

Hebrew priestesses today have to live with a great deal of not knowing. Sometimes we can tell from the evidence what women spiritual leaders have been doing in centuries prior to this one, but often, we can't know for sure. As important as it is to document women's religious history as fully as possible, we cannot always draw clear conclusions. We also may not be able to draw clear conclusions about how to fit priestess work together with traditional religious practice. In such an environment, our questions are as important as our answers.

Fortunately, uncertainty is an important part of priestess practice. A contemporary Goddess chant says: "She changes everything she touches and everything she touches changes." Cataclysm can be holy. When our assumptions and ideas are most challenged, we can be most open to new revelations and integrations. Improvisation is sacred: it makes room for surprise, humility, humor, and even mystery. The Goddess enters when we loosen our assumptions and make room for things we've never seen or known.

The fool-priestesses, with their laughter and their rebels' challenge to the status quo, remind us to go on being open to the future. Being a conduit for the divine to enter the world sometimes means doing the work of the day, without assumptions about what that work will be. The path of the priestess is to take the next step forward.

Chapter 17:
Epilogue

It is July 2009. Family and friends gather for the ordination of the first class of Hebrew priestesses trained by the Kohenet Institute. From one perspective, this hasn't happened in two or three thousand years. From another, it has been happening all the time, unnoticed by history.

Guests wash their hands before entering. Led by a flute player, accompanied by the drum, women in white procede past an altar abundant with pomegranates. They take their place at the front of the room. The three teachers, Jill, Taya, and Shoshana, enter and take their places.

We invoke Shekhinah:

> Blessed Wisdom
> Pool of Blessing
> Spirit of the World
> North, South, East, and West
> Tree of Life
> Evergiving Well
> Divine Weaver
> Knower of Secrets
> come![1]

We make a meal offering, as priests did in the Temple. We make a formal invitation to the ancestors. We invite the thirteen priestess paths to manifest for us. We tell the story of the ancient priestesses and of our community in the present. We express our gratitude. We sing.

Now it is time for anointing. We summon each woman using her Hebrew name, and also name her with her own particular title, representing her priestess path in the world: kedeisha (holy woman), m'agelet (circlemaker), maggid (storyteller), and others. Then each one steps forward to become a kohenet, a Hebrew priestess.

Shoshana stands behind each woman who is becoming a *kohenet*. "From before," she says. She invokes the blessing of past Hebrew priestesses on this ceremony.

"From above," Jill says, invoking the blessing of the Universe, the Cosmic Mother of the stars. She anoints the forehead of the new priestess.

Taya crouches. "From below," she calls, inviting the grace of the deep underbelly of the world, the embodied Presence of Shekhinah dwelling in the Earth. She anoints the feet of the new priestess.

All the ordinees say together: "And from this moment forward…" They speak for the present, the community that witnesses and agrees to this new identity, and for the future—as yet unknown.

All together, we say: "You are a *kohenet*."

We have a few pictures of these anointings. The expression on each face, in each moment, is different, yet there is so much surprise and gratitude. There is even humor, as if each of us is saying: "Who could have imagined such a thing?"

Mei Mei Miriyam Sanford, who was ordained that day, later recalls: "Even though it was repeated with everybody, I remember feeling the particularity of my own. My teachers' gestures and tones of voice were a kind of naming: some depiction of them and me and the beyond."

Near the end of the ritual, current Kohenet students come to the front of the room to receive blessings from and give blessings to the ordinees. This is the passing of the torch. This part of the ceremony represents our hope that what we have reclaimed will not be lost again, and that what we have summoned will find its place in our larger community and in the world.

We cannot know fully what it was like to be a Hebrew priestess in ancient times. We cannot know whether this tradition will continue after us, or how it will evolve. The priestesshood has been born and has been lost many times, in many cultures. We make this leap of faith: that there is a thread joining what was, what is, and what will be. We are repairing this thread as best we can. The rest is up to God/dess.

Appendix: MotherLine Ritual Materials

MotherLine Healing Divining Quotes

What would healing be if it did not begin and end with talk about our mothers?
—Kim Chernin, *The Woman Who Gave Birth to Her Mother*

Every mother contains her daughter in herself and every daughter her mother, and every woman extends backward into her mother and forward into her daughter.
—Carl Gustav Jung, "The Psychological Aspects of the Kore"

Each person enters the world by virtue of three mothers: the literal birth mother, who lends her body to the matter at hand; the psychological complex of mother, which forms between the psyches of human mother and child; and the spiritual or mythic mother, who stands behind the entire process of birth and growth and death. Taken together, the three levels of mother shape the mother complex and weave the great complexities of one's fate and one's potentials in life.
—Michael Meade, *The Water of Life: Initiation and the Tempering of the Soul*

The materialism and literalism of modern cultures intensifies the fixation of the human mother with Great Mother. The loss of vital connections to Mother Nature and absence of rituals that indicate the psychic and mythic aspects of motherhood leave human mothers in a heavily conflicted place. When the image of the Great Mother as the womb of life and the tomb at death gets condensed into a literal mother, the personal mother becomes the focus of unreal expectations, surreal fears, and tragic disappointments.
—Michael Meade, *The Water of Life: Initiation and the Tempering of the Soul*

Teaching (allowing) the mother to become a mother—this is one sense in which a daughter gives birth to her own mother. It is an act that requires an enormous maturity on the daughter's part, an ability no longer to be bound by the conflicts and disappointments of the past, a recognition that change between mother and daughter is still possible although both the child and the mother of childhood have long since vanished.
—Kim Chernin, *The Woman Who Gave Birth to Her Mother*

Giving birth to one's mother... belongs to a stage when a woman takes re-

sponsibility for the relationships and circumstances that will advance her development. Here the past has begun to release her. What she is becoming matters more than what she has been. If circumstances are not right for her development, she will create them.... It is a breakthrough moment when a pattern is relaxed, a self-authority is assumed, a deliberate act of self-creation is launched, through the establishment of a new relationship to a symbolic mother.
—Kim Chernin, *The Woman Who Gave Birth to Her Mother*

There is nothing in human nature more resonant with charges than the flow of energy between two biologically alike bodies, one of which has lain in amniotic bliss inside the other, one of which has labored to give birth to the other. The materials are here for the deepest mutuality and the most painful estrangement.
—Adrienne Rich, *Of Woman Born*

To carry our mothers forth in our bellies is to know them in our own bodies and souls, in the life they gave us and the life they denied us, in their pain, their labor, their love and their hate. We must face with them the dark passageways through which they passed to bring us here, and which we face again in the end of our days.
—Naomi Lowinsky, *The Motherline*

Like those old pear-shaped Russian dolls that open at the middle to reveal another and another, down to the peasized, irreducible minim, may we carry our mothers forth in our bellies. May we, borne onward by our daughters, ride in the Envelope of Almost-Infinity, that chain letter good for the next twenty-five thousand days of their lives.
—Maxine Cumin, *Tangled Vines: A Collection of Mother and Daughter Poems*

[The Mother] is the bed we are born in, in which we sleep and dream, where we are held, love and die. In her wisdom we remember days' broken images and carry them down into dreams where their motions roll into shadows and root, grown into stories. My imagery originates here... in the pulse beat I learned from her body and the beat of her dark imagination that I still feel in the natural world.
—Meinrad Craighead, *The Mother's Songs: Images of God the Mother*

"Who is your mother?" is an important question. At Laguna, one of several

of the ancient Keres gynocratic societies... your mother's identity is the key to your own identity... Failure to know your mother, that is, your position and its attendant traditions, history and place in the scheme of things, is failure to remember your significance, your reality, your right relationship to earth and society. It is the same as being lost—isolated, abandoned, self-estranged and alienated from your own life.
—Paula Gun Allen, *The Sacred Hoop*

So many of the stories that I write, that we all write, are my mother's stories. Only recently did I fully realize this: That through the years of listening to my mother's stories of her life, I have absorbed not only the stories themselves, but something of the manner in which she spoke, something of the urgency that involves the knowledge that her stories—like my own—must be recorded.
—Alice Walker, *In Search of My Mother's Garden*

Mother is the first word we know, the source of our lives and stories. Embodying the mysteries of origin, she connects us to the great web of kin and generation. We are so full of judgments about what mother ought to be, that we can barely see what mother is.
—Naomi Lowinsky, *The Motherline*

The Motherline is the embodied experience of female mysteries... Every woman alive is connected to all the women before her through the roots of her particular family and culture. We all emerge out of the ancient line of mothers... We all participate in the human drama; our personal Motherlines connect us to universal myths.
—Naomi Lowinsky, *The Motherline*

The Motherline is not a straight line, for it is not about abstract geneological diagrams; it is about bodies being born out of bodies. Envision the ... line as a cord, a thread, as the yarn emerging out of the fingers of the woman at the spinning wheel.
—Naomi Lowinsky, *The Motherline*

Mothers are seen as all-powerful in psychology but are personally disempowered.
—Naomi Lowinsky, *The Motherline*

We live in a culture of object-mothers. The subject-mothers, culturally silenced for millennia, are only just beginning to speak.
—Nancy Mairs, *Plaintext: Essays*

We have a great difficulty sorting out the limited human power of an individual mother from the Great Mother archetype because we don't want to believe that much of what happens to us in life is beyond the control of mere mortals. Mothers get blamed because we refuse to face our fates, which must be suffered. Thus, mothers are used, indeed abused, as stand-ins for the gods.
—Naomi Lowinsky, *The Motherline*

MotherScroll

by Taya Shere with Indigo Bacal

Do you know anything about the Divine Mother?
Well, let me tell you something about her.
She is known in one of her aspects as _____
This form of the Divine Mother is also called _____
and by sincere devotees, simply, _____
This is the Divine Mother in her _____
She is sometimes invoked _____
She can often be found _____
She helps remind us as women to _____
She teaches us to _____
She helps us explore our inner relationship to _____
She can be called upon for _____
and she teaches about _____
She is the patron Goddess of _____
She is one of the most _____ aspects of the Goddess.

Bibliography

Adrienne Rich, *Of Woman Born* (W.W. Norton, 1976).

Alice Walker, *In Search of My Mother's Garden* (Harcourt, Brace, Jovanovich, 1983).

C.G. Jung, "The Psychological Aspects of the Kore," in *Essays on a Science of Mythology* (Princeton University Press, 1959).

Kim Chernin, *The Woman Who Gave Birth to Her Mother* (Viking, 1988).

Maxine Kumin, *Tangled Vines: A Collection of Mother and Daughter Poems*, ed. Lyn Lifshin (Beacon Press, 1978).

Meinrad Craighead, *The Mother's Songs: Images of God the Mother* (Paulist Press, 1986).

Michael Meade, *The Water of Life: Initiation and the Tempering of the Soul* (Greenfire Press).

Nancy Mairs, *Plaintext: Essays* (The University of Arizona Press, 1986).

Naomi Ruth Lewinsky, *The Motherline: Every Women's Journey to Find Her Female Roots.* (Fisher King Press, 1992/2009).

Paula Gunn Allen, *The Sacred Hoop: Recovering the Feminine in American Indian Traditions* (Beacon Press, 1986).

Appendix: Kohenet Biographical Statements

Kohenet Core Faculty:

Rabbi Jill Hammer, PhD (Ye'ilah) is an author, educator, midrashist, and ritualist. She is the co-founder of the Kohenet Institute, and the Director of Spiritual Education at the Academy for Jewish Religion, a pluralistic Jewish seminary in Yonkers, NY. Rabbi Hammer is the author of five other books: *Sisters at Sinai: New Tales of Biblical Women*, *The Jewish Book of Days: A Companion for All Seasons*, *The Omer Calendar of Biblical Women*, *The Garden of Time*, and *Siddur haKohanot: A Hebrew Priestess Prayerbook*, which she co-authored with Taya Shere. She is a poet, scholar, and essayist; her work has been published in many journals and anthologies. She has been an educator and scholar-in-residence in a variety of contexts, and a ritualist of traditional and non-traditional Jewish ceremonies. She holds a doctorate in social psychology from the University of Connecticut and received rabbinical ordination from the Jewish Theological Seminary in 2001. She and her wife Shoshana and daughter Raya Leela live in Manhattan. More information is at kohenet.com, ajrsem.org, and rabbijillhammer.com.

Shoshana Jedwab *(BatShemesh)* is the Jewish Life Coordinator at the A.J. Heschel Middle School in NYC. She is the founding facilitator of the Makom Drum Circle at the JCC in Manhattan and is a percussionist and performance artist who has trained in bibliodrama and psychodrama. Shoshana has performed with: Storahtelling, Chana Rothman, Debbie Friedman, Kirtan Rabbi Andrew Hahn, and Tel Shemesh seasonal events. She is Kohenet's ritual drummer and serves on the Kohenet faculty. Her first album is titled *I Remember*. She is also a ritual percussionist and singer at Congregation Romemu in New York, NY. More information is at www.shoshanajedwab.com.

Taya Shere (Taya Ma) plays passionately in the realms of transformative ritual and embodied vocalization. Taya is co-founder and co-director of the Kohenet Institute. Her chant albums *Wild Earth Shebrew*, *Halleluyah All Night*, *Torah Tantrika* and *This Bliss* have been heralded as "cutting-edge mystic medicine music." She is co-author, with Jill Hammer, of *The Hebrew Priestess* and *Siddur HaKohanot: A Hebrew Priestess Prayerbook*. Trained in the folklore of religion at the University of Pennsylvania and as a Somatic Experiencing Practitioner, she is Spiritual Leader Emeritus of a Washington D.C. area Jewish congregation. Taya now leads spiritual community, teaches at Starr-King Seminary, offers mentorships, and makes home, music, and other magic in Oakland, California.

Learn more about her offerings at holytaya.com

Kohenet Graduates and Participants:

The following women are current students, initiates (two-year graduates), or ordinees (three-year graduates, called Kohenet) of the Kohenet Hebrew Priestess Institute. Names in parentheses indicate Hebrew and/or priestess names.

Kohenet **Elsa Asher** works in the intersection of birth, medicine, ritual, and narrative. She writes poetry and fiction, and has a Master's degree in Narrative Medicine from Columbia University. Her website is www.elsaasher.com

Kohenet **Ellie Barbarash** (Alitza Ma'ayan) has initiated groups devoted to creative anti-oppression consciousness-raising, facilitated joint union-management endeavors to improve workplace safety, offered conflict mediation and facilitation services to women's groups and unions, and, most recently, has advocated for the disabled in federal employment. Her writing has been published in *Bridges, Off Our Backs,* and *Jewish Book World.* Raised in Brooklyn, she prays, parents, works, wrestles with sacred text, and makes music in Philadelphia.

Kohenet **Shoshana Bricklin**, *Oreget bachochim* (knitter in the thorns/thornweaver), is a legislative attorney for a Philadelphia City Council member. She focuses her priestessing on speaking truth to power through the creation of haftarot that raise social justice issues of the day. She studies voice and is an avid knitter and crocheter. She views her textile work as part of her spiritual practice.

Kohenet **Sarah Shamirah Chandler** is a Jewish experiential educator, community activist, and earth-based spiritual leader. She recently served as the Director of Earth Based Spiritual Practice for Hazon's Adamah Farm, responsible for Food, Farm and Forest Jewish Educational Programming. Sarah holds a M.A. in Jewish Education and a M.A. in Hebrew Bible from the Jewish Theological Seminary, and a certificate in Non-Profit Management and Jewish Communal Leadership from Columbia University. She teaches, writes, and consults on a national level on issues related to Judaism, earth-based spiritual practice, the environment, mindfulness, food values, and farming.

Kohenet **Judi Dash** is a travel journalist who never imagined her most amazing journey would be this inner one. She lives on Lake Erie in Huron, Ohio, and is a member of the Reconstructionist Community of Cleveland and Temple Oheb Shalom in Sandusky, Ohio. Her deeply Foolish spirit has fallen/risen passionately in love with Jewish Renewal and the feminine face of God/dess.

Kohenet **Ryan Rebekah Erev**, a Kohenet graduate, is a queer, Jewish, feminist priestess and artist. She is the author of the Moon Angel / Malakh Halevanah divination deck and book. You can learn more about her work at: ryanrebekaherev.com

APPENDIX: KOHENET BIOGRAPHICAL STATEMENTS

Kohenet **Ahava Lilith EvershYne** (ALY) is an activist & artist, full-loving heart-ist, circle caster, reiki master, healing healer, social work student returning to school, joy squad faery fool, keeper of gates, reader of fates, meowmama & magick maven, hostess of a faery haven, Rosh Chodesh facilitatress, singer, songcrafter & enchantress, ritualist, feminist eclectic witch, shebrewer of blessings, midwife of bliss, loving partner of Larry, word weaver, faery G!d/ G!ddus mother, vegan mamaearthlover, spiritual~journey guide, womyn who is fully alive!

Kohenet **Paula Freedman** (Puah) is a nurse midwife who lives and works in Brooklyn, NY. She is actively involved in various congregations in New York City, and is committed to alternative loving relationships. Her Kohenet goal is to create and facilitate innovative rituals for life transforming events while nurturing and supporting the Kohenet Movement.

Kohenet and Rabbi **Sarah Bracha Gershuny** is a UK-born spiritual seeker, musician and educator. She received rabbinic ordination at the Hebrew College rabbinical school in Boston, Massachusetts, and currently serves as the spiritual leader of Congregation Nevei Kodesh in Boulder, Colorado.

Kohenet **Rachel (Rinah) Galper** is a healer, *maggid* (spiritual storyteller and guide), art educator, and spirit dancer. She loves Divine work and play and is devoted to teaching and learning with others along their faith journeys. She is the founder of the Mamash Rainbow Brigade. Rinah is in a training program to help children connect more deeply with nature and is gearing up to enter seminary to become an interfaith rabbi.

Kohenet **Nancy Handwerger** is a lifelong learner, enjoying her rejuvenation as a Jewish woman. For 25 years as a LCSW she has served in private practice integrating psychotherapy with hands-on healing. More recently, through study, meditation, and teaching she draws upon the energies of the Hebrew letters to paint them on paper and on silk. In 2013, she published the book *The Hebrew Letters Speak*.

Kohenet **Judith Porges Hollander** earned her PhD in Nursing Science from Indiana University in 1997. She had her jubilee bat mitzvah in 2005 and she is committed to continuing her Jewish education in whatever form it presents itself. She is a mother, a partner, a grandmother, and a retired nursing informatist who forgot and continues to work.

Felice Winograd Holt is a lawyer and fundraiser, and has studied yoga, meditation, and dance. She is deeply committed to creating environments where women can explore through meditation, movement, and sisterhood.

Kohenet **Sharon Jaffe** lives in Minnesota and practices grassroots community organizing for collective responsibility for a just society based on respect. Wonder, integrity, and love are core values. She enjoys inter-generational and cross cultural creative work and honors her lesbian feminist roots daily.

Rabbi and Kohenet **Margie Klein Ronkin** is a passionate activist and religious leader. Founder and director of Moishe House Boston: Kavod Jewish Social Justice House, she is a graduate of the Rabbinical School of Hebrew College. She is the founder of Project Democracy, a program that mobilized 97,000 students to vote in the 2004 election. She is the rabbi of Sha'arei Shalom in Ashland, Massachusetts.

As a Bat Mitzvah, Kohenet **D'vora K'lilah** was the first female to read from the Torah in her childhood synagogue. By receiving ordination as a Kohenet with the first cohort, she hopes to continue expanding the boundaries of contemporary Judaic practices. She is currently involved in researching the supposed boundary between science and spirit, and is curious as to how this project will manifest in her own practices. She leads Rosh Chodesh, Pesach, and Sukkot celebrations with a focus on the ancient Israelite and pre-Israelite local practices, writes liturgy that encompasses her knowledge of Ancient Near Eastern history, and has her work featured in several devotional anthologies.

Rachel May Koppelman lives a life of service as a practitioner of the healing arts, including vibrational medicine, massage, herbalism, and holistic nutrition. She is deeply devoted to the creative arts, especially music; the creative process is an important part of her spiritual path, through which she strives to embody the values of beauty, balance, harmony, and simplicity. Rachel lives to serve, learn and love; and loves life.

Kohenet **Yocheved Landsman** is a peace worker, dance artist, choreographer, and improviser, as well as a mother, tai chi practitioner, and perpetual student of mysticism. She holds a B.A. in dance from Naropa University, where she honed her awareness and improvisational skills, and has an MFA from CU Boulder. Yocheved has worked actively for peace since 2004 between Israelis, Palestinians, and Jews. Presently, she is a facilitator in an ongoing dialogue group with local Palestinians and Jews of all genders, and operates on the premise that women and women's ways will be and are the harbingers of world peace and sustainability. Curerently, Yocheved teaches and is working on the Big Heart Project, a multidisciplinary performance project about empathy and conflict.

Kohenet **Rebecca Lemus** is a classically trained clarinetist, a jazz improviser and klezmer enthusiast, an energy healer, and an environmental activist.

Kohenet **Carly (Ketzirah) Lesser** is a Priestess, M'agelet, Artist, and Guide. Her mission is to help others experience the best life possible by connecting fully with the Divine Presence, the resources they consume, personal expression, and communal ritual experience. Her web site is ketzirah.com.

Mother, entrepreneur, organic homesteader, activist and Hebrew priestess, Kohenet **Juna Berry Madrone** (Tamar) lives simply in the alternate reality of the Mateel in the Humboldt Nation, behind the Redwood Curtain. Called to a spiritual mission at age eleven, she currently manifests her love affair with

Shekhinah through facilitating two-way conversations with the Divine, using Tarot imagery. Present passions include cutifying the world through accessories; orchid cultivation; her Akita, the Queen of Sheba; mahjong; and Reggae music.

Kohenet **Annie Matan** shares her passion for infusing Jewish ritual, music, and prayer with meaning, intention and soul as a facilitator of women's Rosh Hodesh circles, chanting and liturgy workshops, and Shabbat services. Her priestess path has led her to communities in Toronto, Boston, Connecticut, and Jerusalem where she sings light into the dark corners of the world as an artist, spiritual leader, and rabbinical student. She recently founded Matanot Lev (Gifts of the Heart), a Goddessy, inclusive, and earth-based Jewish Renewal prayer community in downtown Toronto, and is the Jewish Life Program Coordinator at the Miles Nadal JCC.

Kohenet **Sheva Melmed**, LCSW-C, Kohenet, has been working with her own dreams and those of others for fifteen years. Her dreams have always been a source of guidance and creativity in her life journey. Sheva received her MSW from Smith School for Social Work and was ordained at the Kohenet Hebrew Priestess Institute. She practices as a psychotherapist and Kohenet in the Washington Metro area.

Kohenet **Tiana Mirapae** is an Integrative Psychotherapist and Wholistic Medicine Practitioner, specializing in healing trauma, dis-ease, and relationships; and teaching sacred sexuality. She is a master herbalist, consultant of classical homeopathy, Shamanic Healer, and WisdomKeeper of the Munay Ki. Lady Tiana is Ordained Clergy as a Priestess of the Well of Avalon and is the founder and director of S.O.P.H.I.A., a Mystery, Wisdom School for Shamans, Oracles, Priest/esses, Healers, Intuitives & Alchemists. More information is at www.schoolofsophia.com

Nathan Tamar Pautz was born in 1950 and resides in The Villages, Florida. Shortly before being initiated as a Tzovah in January 2008, Nathan Tamar began a transgender transition from female to male/genderqueer, and sees hir desire to express the feminine Divine in mixed-gender form as being in the spiritual tradition of third gender persons of many cultures throughout history. He/ze has had a lifelong interest in mystical spirituality and dreams of connecting with others of all faiths and genders who wish to dedicate themselves to the Goddess experienced as immanent in the world.

For 35 plus years, Kohenet **Leah Chava Reiner** engaged in in-depth study and practice of Taoist, Shamanic, and Wiccan traditions. With the help of her shamanic ancestor work, she has been called to return to her Judaic spiritual foundation to combine and expand her spiritual practice and share it with her extended tribes.

Kohenet **Erev Richards** is a graduate of the Spiral Door Women's Mystery

School of Magick and Ritual Arts. She has studied with guardian priestesses Falcon River and Firehawk and serves the Goddess community as Guardian Priestess of Her Daughters, Children, and Creatures. Erev runs a small nonprofit animal sanctuary with her life partner Sarah Esther is devoted to the art of Dressage and training her equine partners in mounted archery, and spends all of her time away from work with her three children who are the light of her life.

Kohenet **Sarah Richards** holds a B.A. in Jewish Studies from Emory University and an M.A. in Religion from the University of Georgia. She works as a Jewish educator and as a counselor to individuals and families dealing with interfaith or spiritual issues. She and her spouse, Erev, have two beautiful children and a menagerie of pets.

Joy Rosenberg is a Jewish educator, artist and writer living in Santa Fe, New Mexico. Joy works with calligraphy and natural materials, creating art such as Faith Rocks: powerful Hebrew and English words inscribed on stones.

Kohenet **Ashirah Marni Rothman** (Smith College 1995, California Institute of Integral Studies 2010) is an artist, psychotherapist, and co-founding editor and designer of the Irish journal *Spiorad: Exploring the Sacred in Words and Images*. Originally from the New York metro area, she now lives in Dublin, Ireland, with her partner. She recently launched a website of her artwork: ashirahmarni.com

Miriam Rubin is a doula, permaculture designer, and environmental activist. She describes herself as a seeker, a warrior of love, a child of the earth, an explorer, a dreamer, an artist, a canvas, a healer channeling love.

Kohenet **Mei Mei Miriyam Sanford** received her doctorate in Religion and Society, and she teaches Africana Studies at the College of William and Mary. She is the Iyalode Osun of Iragbiji, Nigeria, and the author of numerous articles about Yoruba religion. She is the *maggid*/storyteller of her shul, a midrashist, *charash*, and carver of staffs and Torah pointers.

Jessica Schurtman (Emunah Noa) practices the skills of listening, nurturing, healing, and making meaning as a Keeper of Sacred Time and Space which manifests in her work as an artist, therapist, teacher, and steward of the Earth. She was initiated by Kohenet as a Tzovah in 2010.

Kohenet **Terri Schuster** (Alumah) lives in the woods of Wisconsin, where she weaves her studies of yoga, Jewish Spirituality, comparative literature and aromatherapy into both her practices and the different venues of her teachings. She is ever grateful to be part of Kohenet and experience the wisdom, deep caring and rootedness of all her teachers. To be part of this group is to be held truly in the womb of the mother.

Toby Shulruff (Eliana) makes her blessings amidst the tall trees of the Pacific Northwest. She has co-led a Rosh Chodesh Circle, Shabbat services, mikveh and other spaces for her community to connect through meaningful

Jewish practice. She has been initiated as a Tzovah.

Suzanne Stier is a Goddess-oriented wife, mother, daughter, sister, and friend. She is a Spiritual Director, an organizational consultant to family businesses and synagogues, a psychotherapist, an executive coach, and a lifelong journeyer and learner.

Kohenet **Ilana Streit** is an experiential educator, ritual innovator and Jewish life coach. She is a member of the Kohenet Institute's third cohort.

Kohenet **Celia Vine Strickler** is a licensed clinical social worker residing in Baton Rouge, Louisiana. She was born a *bat kohen*, and is interested in reclaiming the role of priestess for herself and her female ancestors.

Kohenet **Yosefa Strouss** (of blessed memory) was a tattoo artist, an organizer of women's art, and a dedicated believer in healing and recovery from addiction. She graduated with the first Kohenet class of 2009. She is survived by her husband Charles Strouss. Her art continues to grace our sacred space, and the Kohenet scholarship fund is known as the Yosefa's Colors Fund. She is dearly missed.

Kohenet **Gail Tishman** (Ma'ayana) is *Morat Shekhinah B'Yisrael* / Teacher of the Shechina, the Divine Feminine face of God. She leads Jewish life-cycle rituals, teaches feminine *midrash* (women's stories in Judaism), and guides people to greater connection with the Divine Feminine in Jewish tradition. Her website is www.moratshechina.com.

Kohenet **Ri J. Turner** began their Jewish journey at the Los Alamos Jewish Center in Los Alamos, New Mexico. Since then, they have deepened their spiritual path primarily through Renewal Judaism (especially at the Isabella Freedman Retreat Center), meditation practices learned through the Art of Living Foundation, and leftist, queer, and/or songful Jewish communities. Their participation in Kohenet has provided an invaluable preparation for stepping into spiritual confidence and leadership. Currently, they are pursuing a rabbinical degree at Hebrew College.

Kohenet **Ariel Vegosen** is a writer, educator, performer, activist, and Hebrew priestess. Ariel co-founded the Gender Blender Collective and is committed to creating safe spaces to explore gender. She is also a conflict resolution specialist, professional dialogue facilitator, ropes course instructor, youth educator, media wizard, organic therapist, and world traveler.

Amy Wachtel is a native New Yorker. While her Kohenet name is Amy Orah Joy & Light, she's known in reggae music circles as "The Night Nurse." She loves to dance, chant, laugh, and listen to and play music. She's fascinated with pop culture and has an ever-growing collection of vintage toys. As part of her Kohenet project prior to her initation, Amy came up with a Barbie-themed series of the 13 Netivot, as well as "Initiation" and "Ordination" Barbie.

The Kohenet Institute thanks all current and former students. Many of our students are not quoted in this book, but all of their spirits helped to inform it.

Endnotes

Prologue

[1] Leonard Shlain, *The Alphabet Versus The Goddess: The Conflict Between Word and Image* (Compass, 1999)
[2] Rachel Adler, "Second Hymn to the Shekhinah," in *Women Speak to God: The Prayers and Poems of Jewish Women*, ed. Marcia Cohn Spiegel and Deborah L. Kremsdorf, (Women's Institute of Continuing Jewish Education, 1987).
[3] Z. Budapest, "We All Come from the Goddess" (Chant).
[4] Jill Hammer, *Sisters at Sinai: New Tales of Biblical Women* (Jewish Publication Society, 2001).
[5] Jill Hammer, "Holle's Cry: Unearthing a Birth Goddess in a Jewish Naming Ceremony," in *Nashim: A Journal of Jewish Women's and Gender Studies*, number 9 (Indiana University Press, Spring 2005), p. 62-87.

Chapter 1

[1] Mishneh Torah, Laws of the Sabbatical and Jubilee Year 13:13.
[2] Joan Breton Connelly, *Portrait of a Priestess; Women and Ritual in Ancient Greece* (Princeton University Press, 2009); Norma Lorre Goodrich, *Priestesses* (Perennial, 1990); C. Scott Littleton, *Shinto: Origins, Rituals, Festivals, Spirits, Sacred Places* (Oxford University Press, 2002); Jane Hirshfeld, *Women in Praise of the Sacred: 43 Centuries of Spiritual Poems by Women* (HarperCollins, 1994); Betty DeShong Meador and Judy Grahn, *Inanna, Lady of Largest Heart; Poems of the Sumerian High Priestess* (University of Texas Press, 2001); Patricia Monaghan, *The Red-Haired Girl from the Bog: The Landscape of Celtic Myth and Spirit* (New World Library, 2004); Joseph Murphy and Mei Mei Sanford, *Osun Across the Waters: A Yoruba Goddess in Africa and the Americas* (Indiana University Press, 2001); Layne Redmond, *When the Drummers were Women: A Spiritual History of Rhythm* (Three Rivers Press, 1997).
[3] Susan Ackerman, *Warrior, Dancer, Seductress, Queen: Women in Judges and Biblical Israel* (Yale University Press, 1998), p. 138-154; Lynn Bellair. "History of Egyptian Medicine and Philosophy," http://www.realmagick.com/7108/history-of-egyptian-medicine-and-philosophy/; Geoffrey W. Bromiley, *International Standard Bible Encyclopedia*, p. 88; Joan Breton Connelly, *Portrait of a Priestess; Women and Ritual in Ancient Greece* (Princeton University Press, 2009); Henny J. Marsman, *Women in Ugarit and Israel: Their Social and Religious Position in the Context of the Ancient Near East*, (Brill, 2003), chapter 3; Jacobine Oudshoorn, *The Relationship Between Roman Law and Local Law in the Babatha and Salome Komaise Archives: General Analysis and Three Case Studies on Law of Succession,*

Guardianship, and Marriage (Koninklijke Brill, 2007), p. 256-259; Elna Solvang, *A Woman's Place is in the House, Royal Women of Judah and their Involvement in the House of David* (Sheffield Academic Press, 2003), p. 76; Akhet Hwt-Hrw: An Educational Resource for Ancient Egyptian Religion & Esoteric Studies www.Hwt-Hrw.com.

[4] Exodus 2:16; 18:1

[5] Genesis 41:45

[6] Ann Jeffers, *Magic and Divination in Ancient Palestine and Syria* (Brill, 1996), p. 52.

[7] Sarah Iles Johnston, *Religions of the Ancient World: A Guide* (Belknap Press, 2004), p. 296.

[8] Edward Lipinski, *The Aramaeans: Their Ancient History, Culture, Religion* (Peeters Publishers and Booksellers, 2000), p. 508.

[9] Exodus 4:24-26

[10] Mark Leuchter, "The Priesthood in Ancient Israel," *Biblical Theology Bulletin*, vol. 40 no. 2, pages 1-11.

[11] Exodus 15:12, Numbers 12:1-9

[12] Mark Leuchter, scholar of the levitical role in the Bible and later Jewish culture, lecture in Philadelphia, April 28, 2013.

[12a] Deuteronomy 26:14

[13] Alexei Kondratiev, "Thou Shalt Not Suffer A Witch to Live," in *Enchante*, vol. 18, p. 11-15; www.draknet.com/proteus/Suffer.htm; ; Ismar J. Peritz, "Women in the Ancient Hebrew Cult," *Journal of Biblical Literature*, vol. 17 (1898), p. 137-138.

[14] Deuteronomy 23:18

[15] Hosea 4:13

[16] Marten Stol, *Birth in Babylonia and the Bible: Its Mediterranean Setting* (Brill Academic Publishers, 2000), p. 173, p. 186.

[17] William Dever, *Did God Have a Wife? Archaeology and Folk Religion in Ancient Israel* (Eeerdmans Publishing Co., 2005).

[18] Gen. 38:6-26

[19] Jerusalem had gate shrines (II Kings 23).

[20] Mark Leuchter, "The Priesthood in Ancient Israel," *Biblical Theology Bulletin*, vol. 40 no. 2, pages 1-11.

[21] The idea that Judah is playing the role of a king in this scene was first suggested to me by Dvorah Klilah bat Shachar, whose ideas appear in Chapter 14.

[22] Savina Teubal, *Sarah the Priestess: The First Matriarch of Genesis* (1984).

[23] See I Kings 15:13, II Kings 10:13, II Chron. 15:16, Jer. 13:18, 29:2

[24] Zafrira Ben-Barak. "The Status and Right of the Gebirah." *Journal of Biblical Literature*, 110/111 (1991), p. 23-34.

[25] Ackerman, Susan. "The Queen Mother and the Cult in Ancient Israel." *Journal of Biblical Literature*, 112/3 (1993), 385-401; Terrien, S. "The Omphalos Myth and Hebrew Religion," *Vetus Testamentum* 20, (1970), 315-338; N.E.A. Andreasen, "The Role of the Queen Mother in Israelite Society," *CBQ* 45 (1983), 179-194.

[25a] P. Bird. "The Place of Women in the Israelite Cultus." In P.D. Miller, P. D. Hanson,

and S.D. McBride (eds.), *Ancient Israelite Religion: Essays in Honor of Frank Moore Cross* (Fortress Press, 1987), p. 397-419.

[26] Nehemiah 7:67

[27] The first century CE Jewish philosopher Philo also alludes to the geneaological/familial status of priestess, saying that a high priest must marry "a priestess born of priests." (*De Specialibus Legibus* 1:110).

[28] Mishnah Sotah 3:7

[29] Pesachim 49a

[30] *The Cambridge History of Judaism: The Early Roman Period*, eds. William Horbury, W.D. Davies, John Sturdy (Cambridge University Press, 1999), p. 80.

[31] David Noy, *Jewish Inscriptions of Western Europe: The City of Rome*, (Cambridge University Press, 1995), p. 18.

[32] Bernadette J. Brooten, *Women Leaders in the Ancient Synagogue* (Brown Judaic Studies, 1982), p. 73-74, 88-90.

[33] Bernadette J. Brooten, *Women Leaders in the Ancient Synagogue* (Brown Judaic Studies, 1982).

[34] Klaas A. D. Smelik, G. I. Davies (Translator), *Writings from Ancient Israel: A Handbook of Historical and Religious Documents* (Westminster John Knox Press, 1992).

[35] J.M. Modrzejewski, *The Jews of Egypt from Rameses II to Emperor Hadrian* (Clark, 1995).

[36] Nehemiah 7:46 and 7:72 note the presence of Temple servants or *netinim* in the Second Temple; perhaps their roles were similar.

[37] Betzalel Porten and J. J. Farber. *The Elephantine Papyri in English: Three Millenia of Cross-Cultural Continuity and Change* (Brill Academic, 1996), p. 80.

[38] C.C. Torrey, "More Elephantine Papyri," in *The Journal of Near Eastern Studies*, vol. 13, no. 3 (1954).

[39] Bernadette J. Brooten, *Women Leaders in the Ancient Synagogue* (Brown Judaic Studies, 1982), p. 75-76.

[40] Maimonides, *Mishneh Torah, Hilchot Melachim uMilchamoteihem* (Laws of Kings and their Wars) 1:5.

[41] D. Nirenberg, "A Female Rabbi in Fourteenth Century Zaragoza?" *Sefarad*, Vol. 51, No. 1, (1991), pp. 179-182; Emily Taitz, "Women's Voices, Women's Prayers: The European Synagogues of the Middle Ages," In *Daughters of the King: Women and the Synagogue*, eds. Susan Grossman and Rivka Haut. Philadelphia: Jewish Publication Society (1992), p. 59-72.

[42] Jeffrey Howard (Yossi) Chajes, *Between Worlds: Dybbuks, Exorcists, and Early Modern Judaism* (University of Pennsylvania Press, 2003), p. 97-118.

[43] Ada Rapoport-Albert, *Women and the Messianic Heresy of Sabbatai Zevi, 1666-1816* (Littman Library of Jewish Civilization, 2011), p. 67.

[44] Conversation with Catherine Shainberg, a student of Colette Aboulker-Moscat and an inheritor of her meditative tradition, April 2013.

[45] Tracy Klirs, *The Merit of our Mothers: A Bilingual Anthology of Jewish Women's Prayers* (Hebrew Union College, 1992), p. 22.

[46] Devra Kay, *Seyder Tekhines: The Forgotten Book of Common Prayer for Jewish Women* (Jewish Publication Society, 2004), p. 83.

[47] Ibid., p. 37.

[48] Ibid., p. 26.

[49] Zalman Schachter-Shalomi, *A Heart Afire: Stories and Teachings of the Early Chasidic Masters* (Jewish Publication Society, 2009), p. 107-126.

[50] Jenna Weissman Joselit, *New York's Jewish Jews: The Orthodox Community in the Interwar Years* (Indiana University Press, 1990), p. 97; Jenna Weissman Joselit, "The Jewish Home Beautiful," in Jonathan Sarna, *The American Jewish Experience* (Holmes and Meier, 1997), p. 236-244; Steven M. Cohen and Paula E. Hyman, *The Jewish Family: Myths and Reality* (Holmes and Meier, 1986), p. 62-81; Maria T. Baader. "From the Priestess of the Home to the Rabbi's Brilliant Daughter: Concepts of Jewish Womanhood and Progressive Germanness," in *die Deborah and the American Israelite, 1854-1900*; Nahida Remy, *The Jewish Woman* (C.J. Krehbiel and Co.; 1895), p. 17.

[51] Sarah Cohen Berman, manuscript, about 1943, The Jewish Historical Society of the Upper Midwest.

[52] Jewish Women's Archive: http://jwa.org/womenofvalor/frank/jewish-womens-congress/women-in-synagogue.

[53] Nina Amir, *The Priestess Practice: 4 Steps to Creating Sacred Space and Inviting the Divine to Dwell within It*, http://www.purespiritcreations.com/The-Priestess-Practice.html.

[54] Jewish Women's Archive: http://jwa.org/thisweek/feb/28/1935/jeannette-miriam-goldberg.

[55] "Gemara Sota," essay by Rav Mosheh Lichtenstein, www.vbm-torah.org/sota/23a.doc.

[56] See Rabbi Joel Roth, "The Status of Daughters of Kohanim and Leviyim for Aliyot", *Proceedings of the Committee on Jewish Law and Standards of the Conservative Movement, 1986-1990*. For Conservative positions prohibiting ritual activity by bnot kohanim, see http://www.faqs.org/faqs/judaism/FAQ/04-Observance/section-51.html.

[57] Rabbi Gershom Sizomu, leader of the Abayudaya, lecture in Minneapolis, April 26, 2013.

[58] Starhawk, *The Spiral Dance: A Rebirth of the Ancient Religion of the Goddess* (HarperOne, 1999).

[59] The Elat Chayyim Center for Jewish Spirituality is part of Hazon and is physically housed at the Isabella Freedman Jewish Retreat Center in Falls Village, CT.

[60] http://wjudaism.library.utoronto.ca/index.php/wjudaism/article/view/3545.

[61] http://www.jewishsightseeing.com/louis_rose_historical/honorees/dosick_wayne_rabbi/2006-06-16-new_rabbi.htm.

[62] This is particularly true in the Jewish Renewal movement.

[63] Brochure describing Rabbi Gershon Winkler and Rabbi Miriam Maron's visit to

Ojai, CA, March 23, 2012.
[64] http://www.rainewalker.com/book-page.htm.
[65] Shonna Husbands-Hankin, "Eshet Chazon: Woman of Vision," in *New Menorah* 4 (1983); Hanna Tiferet Siegel, "Eshet Hazon Ceremony Honors Eight Women at 2011 Aleph Kallah," *Kol Aleph*, no. 21, 2011, p. 8.

Chapter 2

[1] John Day, *Yahweh and the Gods and Goddesses of Canaan* (Bloomsbury T&T Clark, 2002), p. 13-41; Tikvah Frymer-Kensky, *In the Wake of the Goddesses: Women, Culture, and the Biblical Transformation of Pagan Myth* (Ballantine Books, 1993), 14-31, 153-161.
[2] Layne Redmond, *When the Drummers Were Women: A Spiritual History of Women* (Three Rivers Press, 1997), 94-97, 109-111.
[3] Betty DeShong Meador, *Inanna, Lady of Largest Heart* (University of Texas Press, 2001), p. 128-130.
[4] Tablet I:1-20. Translation by E.A. Speiser, in *Ancient Near Eastern Texts Relating to the Old Testament*, ed. J.B Pritchard (Princeton University Press, 1958), p. 60-61.
[5] George Barton, *Archaeology and the Bible* (American Sunday School Union, 1946), p. 303-305.
[6] Deuteronomy 4:12
[7] Exodus 24:10
[8] Deuteronomy 12:2, 3
[9] II Kings 23:4-7
[10] William G. Dever, "Asherah, Consort of Yahweh? New Evidence from Kuntillat-Ajrud, *Bulletin of the American Schools of Oriental Research*, vol. 255 (1984), p. 21-27.
[11] William G. Dever, *Did God Have a Wife?: Archaeology and Folk Religion in Ancient Israel* (Eeerdmans Publishing Co., 2005), p. 121.
[12] Jenny Kien, *Reinstating the Divine Woman in Judaism* (Universal Publishers, 2000), p. 106.
[13] Jeremiah 7:18; 44:17; Hosea 3:1
[14] http://www.jehovahs-witness.net/watchtower/bible/73244/1/The-Tree-of-Life-Asherah-and-Her-Snakes
[15] From a Ugaritic text, documented in the KTU (*Die Keilalphabetischen Texte aus Ugarit* (M. Dietrich, O. Loretz and J. Samartín, editors). See Jesús-Luis Cunchillos, Juan-Pablo Vita, José-Ángel Zamora, *The Texts of the Ugaritic Data Bank* (Gorgias Press, 2003).
[16] Mark S. Smith, *The Origins of Biblical Monotheism: Israel's Polytheistic Background and the Ugaritic Texts* (Oxford University Press, 2001), p. 172.
[17] Kaya Stern-Kaufman, "Between Heaven and Earth: Revisioning Synagogue Space" (Rabbinic thesis, Academy for Jewish Religion).
[18] Ant. 3:179-187, cited in Tessel Marina Jonquier, *Prayer in Josephus* (Brill, 2007), p.

157.

[19] Bonna Haberman, "The Yom Kippur Avodah within the Female Enclosure," in *Beginning Anew: A Woman's Companion to the High Holy Days*, eds. Gail Twersky Reimer and Judith A. Kates (Touchstone, 1997), p. 243-257.

[20] Sarit Paz, *Drums, Women, and Goddesses: Drumming and Gender in Iron Age II Israel*, (Orbis Biblicus et Orientalis, 2007), 118-124.

[21] Rachel Elior, *The Three Temples: On the Emergence of Jewish Mysticism* (Littman Library of Jewish Civilization, 2005).

[22] Howard Schwartz, *Tree of Souls; The Mythology of Judaism* (Oxford University Press, 2004), p. 54.

[23] Amichai Lau-Lavie, in Jay Michaelson, "The Jewish Goddess Past and Present, *The Forward*, May 5, 2005.

[24] Babylonian Talmud, Yoma 56b, Shabbat 12b, Megillah 29a, among many other references.

[25] Leah Novick, *On the Wings of Shekhinah: Rediscovering Judaism's Divine Feminine* (Quest Books, 2008), p. 61.

[26] Daniel Matt. "Beyond the Personal God," in *God and the Big Bang: Discovering Harmony Between Science and Spirituality* (Jewish Lights, 1998).

[27] Raphael Patai, *The Hebrew Goddess* (Wayne State University Press, 1990), cf. p. 96.

[28] Shulchan Aruch, Yoreh Deah 335

[29] Raphael Patai, *The Hebrew Goddess*, p. 204.

[30] Raphael Patai, *The Hebrew Goddess*, p. 215.

[31] David Biale, *Eros and the Jews: From Biblical Israel to Contemporary America* (University of California Press, 1997), p. 144.

[32] Hayim Nachman Bialik and Atar Hadari, *Songs from Bialik: Selected Poems of Hayim Nachman Bialik* (Syracuse University Press, 2000), p. 52.

[33] Alicia Ostriker, *The Volcano Sequence* (University of Pittsburgh Press, 2002), p. 64.

[34] Julia Watts Belser, "Making Room for the Divine She" (*Zeek*, August, 2007).

[35] Rami Shapiro, *The Divine Feminine in Biblical Wisdom Literature* (SkyLight Illuminations, 2005), p. xiv.

[36] Marcia Falk. *The Book of Blessings: New Jewish Prayers for Daily Life, the Sabbath, and the New Moon* (Beacon Press, 1999), p. 471.

[37] Lecture, Teva Conference, Cold Spring, NY, May 2008.

[38] Ellen Umansky, "Re-imagining the Divine," cited in Sylvia Barack Fishman, *A Breath of Life: Feminism in the American Jewish Community* (Free Press, 1993), p. 239.

[39] Elizabeth Davis and Carol Leonard, *The Women's Wheel of Life* (Penguin, 1997).

Chapter 3

[1] Thacher Hurd, *The Weaver*, illustrated by Elisa Kleven (D&M Publishers, 2010).
[2] The Elijah stories suggest that priests of Asherah functioned in Judea as part of the royal cult (supported by Ahab and Jezebel). These priests may not all have been male.
[3] Ismar J. Peritz, "Women in the Ancient Hebrew Cult," in *Journal of Biblical Literature*, 17 (1898), p. 121.
[4] Savina Teubal, *Sarah the Priestess: The First Matriarch of Genesis* (Ohio University Press, 1984), p. 102. Teubal also suggests that the tents of the matriarchs in Genesis may represent abodes of the Goddess as well.
[5] Susan Ackerman, "Asherah, the West Semitic Goddess of Spinning and Weaving?", *Journal of Near Eastern Studies*, Vol. 67, no.,1, p. 1-30.
[6] G.R. Driver, *Canaanite Myths and Legends* (T and T Clark, Edinburgh, 1971), 37-45.
[7] Gillian Alban, *Melusine the Serpent-Goddess in A.S Byatt's Possession and in Mythology* (Lexington Books, 2003), p. 158.
[8] Mishnah Middot 1:1
[9] The names here are somewhat suspicious. Elazar and Pinchas are names of the son of Aaron and Aaron's grandson. The other names in the passage tend to have patronymics attached and are more redolent of the Mishnaic time period (Ben Achiyah, Matityah ben Shmuel, Hugros ben Levi, etc.) One wonders if the biblical names are tacked on here to an existing text, perhaps replacing the names of women the Tosefta preferred to omit.
[10] Tal Ilan, *Mine and Yours Are Hers: Retrieving Women's History from Rabbinic Literature* (Brill, 1997), p. 139-140.
[11] Ibid., p. 142.
[12] Ross Shepard Kraemer, *Her Share of the Blessings: Women's Religions Among Pagans, Jews, and Christians in the Greco-Roman World* (Oxford University Press, 1992), p. 81.
[13] Miriam Peskowitz, *Spinning Fantasies: Rabbis, Gender, and History* (University of California Press, 1997), p. 164-166.
[14] Jerusalem Talmud, Pesachim 4:1.
[15] Midrash Tanhuma Buber, Kedoshim 10.
[16] Judith R. Baskin, *Jewish Women in Historical Perspective* (Wayne State University Press, 1998), p. 101.
[17] Ibid., p. 119.
[18] Elisheva Baumgarten, *Mothers and Children: Jewish Family Life in Medieval Europe* (Princeton University Press, 2004); Hayim Schauss, *The Lifetime of a Jew Throughout the Ages of Jewish History* (UAHC, 1950), p. 79.
[19] Jill Hammer, "Holle's Cry: Unearthing a Birth Goddess in a German Jewish Naming Ritual" in *Nashim: A Journal of Jewish Women's Studies and Gender Studies*, 2005).
[20] Menachem Brayer, *The Jewish Woman in Rabbinic Literature: A Psychohistorical Perspective* (1986), p. 119.

[21] Ibid., p. 120.
[22] Rosemary Skinner-Keller, Rosemary Radford Ruether, Marie Cantlon, *Encyclopedia of Women and Religion in North America*, vol. 2 (Indiana University Press, 2006), p. 802.
[23] Shoshana Jedwab, "The Whole Wide World/Shirat haParochet." Lyrics appear in *Siddur haKohanot: A Hebrew Priestess Prayerbook*, on p. 38.
[24] Jill Hammer, "The Unfolding One," in *Siddur haKohanot: A Hebrew Priestess Prayerbook*, on p. 10.
[25] In the Talmud, Honi the Circlemaker is a master shaman and bringer of rain.

Chapter 4

[1] Ismar J. Peritz, *Woman in the Ancient Hebrew Cult*, in *Journal of Biblical Literature*, vol. 17 (1898), p. 111-148.
[2] Scholar Mark Leuchter notes that mythic stories about kinship may represent the creation of tribal bonds among people who once were a class or guild. It seems clear from the story of Samuel and elsewhere in the Bible that "Levite" was not originally a familial or tribal term but a term for a class of priests and prophets—the term took on tribal dimensions later in Israelite history (Lecture at Limmud Philadelphia, April 2013).
[3] Numbers 13:14
[4] Leviticus 8, Leviticus 14
[5] Micah 6:4
[6] Babylonian Talmud, Taanit 9a; Numbers Rabbah 1:2; Song of Songs Rabbah 4:14; and elsewhere.
[7] While there is no mention of goddesses in the Biblical story, it should be noted that the palm tree was sacred to Asherah and marks Deborah, perhaps, as a holy woman.
[8] Genesis 25:22-24
[9] Prologue to the Sibylline Oracle, lines 190-209. See: Milton S. Terry, *The Sibylline Oracle, Annotated Edition*, (e-book). For more information, see: http://www.jewishvirtuallibrary.org/jsource/judaica/ejud_0002_0018_0_18450.html.
[10] Ross Kraemer, *Her Share of the Blessings: Women's Religions among Pagans, Jews, and Christians in the Greco-Roman World* (Oxford University Press, 1992), p. 90.
[11] Babylonian Talmud, Megillah 14a
[12] ibid.
[13] Babylonian Talmud, Megillah 14b
[14] Babylonian Talmud, Yoma 9a
[16] J.H. Chajes, *Between Worlds: Dybbuks, Exorcists, and Early Modern Judaism* (University of Pennsylvania Press, 2003), p. 114.
[17] Ibid., p. 106.
[18] Ibid., p. 109-110.
[19] Album: Sephardic Songs in the Hispano-Arabic tradition of Medieval Spain, 1997.

http://www.jaro.de/php/endex.php3/page/content:flypage/cd_id/74/artist_id/da743e8e075da235b176afc1f8dc6b0f

[20] Ada Rapoprt-Albert, *Women and the Messianic Heresy of Sabbetai Zevi 1666-1816*, Litman Library of Jewish Civilization, 2011), p. 16-27.

[21] http://www.jewishgen.org/yizkor/Sochaczew/so079.html
http://www.breslev.co.il/articles/breslev/customs_and_thought/feige_the_prophetess.aspx?id=9521&language=english.

Chapter 5

[1] Ismar J. Peritz, "Women in the Ancient Hebrew Cult," in *Journal of Biblical Literature*, vol. *17* (1898), p. 119, 145.

[2] Rabbi Moses ben Nachman Girondi, 1194-1270—a great exegete and mystic, he lived most of his life in Gironda, Catalonia.

[3] Theresa C. Dintino, "Amazons with Mirrors: Mirror Divination Throughout the Ages," http://www.ritualgoddess.com/the2012vortex/?tag=amazons&paged=2

[4] II Kings 23:4

[5] I.S.D. Sassoon, *The Status of Women in Jewish Tradition* (Cambridge University Press, 2007), p. 120.

[6] II Kings 23:8

[7] I Kings 11:4-8

[8] William Dever, *Did God Have a Wife? Archaeology and Folk Religion in Ancient Israel* (Eeerdmans Publishing Co., 2005).

[9] Genesis 31:19

[10] I Samuel 19:13

[11] Tirzah Firestone, *The Receiving: Reclaiming Jewish Women's Wisdom* (HarperOne, 2003), p. 142.

[12] Richenza and Urania are mentioned in many surveys of Jewish medieval women; cf. Emily Taitz, *The JPS Guide to Jewish Women: 600 BCE to 1900 CE* (Jewish Publication Society, 2003), p. 85 and 101.

[13] For mention of Guta bat Nathan and Anna d'Arpino, as well as other aforementioned women who served as *firzogerin*, see: "Firzogerin," http://www.jewishvirtuallibrary.org/jsource/judaica/ejud_0002_0007_0_06498.html

[14] D. Nirenberg, "A Female Rabbi in Fourteenth Century Zaragoza?" *Sefarad*, Vol. 51, No. 1, (1991), pp. 179-182.

[15] Aviva Ben-Ur, "Still Life: Sephardi, Ashkenazi, and West African Art and Form in Suriname's Jewish Cemeteries," in *American Jewish History*, vol. 92, number 1 (March 2004), pp. 31-79.

[16] Mark Zborowski, *Life is with People: The Jewish Little-Town of Eastern Europe* (International Universities Press, 2005).

[17] From a conversation with Roiza's son Cwi Jedwab.

[18] Joyce Antler, *The Journey Home: Jewish Women and the American Century* (Simon and Schuster, 1997), p. 40.
[19] The Kohenet Institute performs an initiation for women who have been in the program for a year and a half, and grants them the title *tzovah*, or shrinekeeper.
[20] Zohar II, 24a

Chapter 6

[1] Ezekiel 13:17-23
[2] II Kings 9:22
[3] Jeremiah 29:8,9
[4] Alexei Kondratiev, "Thou Shalt Not Suffer A Witch to Live," in *Enchante*, vol. 18, p.11-15; www.draknet.com/proteus/Suffer.htm.
[5] Deuteronomy 26:14
[6] Ismar J. Peritz, "Women in the Ancient Hebrew Cult," *Journal of Biblical Literature*, vol. 17 (1898), p.137-138.
[7] Carol Meyers, *Households and Holiness: The Religious Culture of Israelite Women* (Augsburg Fortress, 2005), p. 14.
[8] I Enoch 7:1
[9] Jerusalem Talmud, Sanhedrin 6:6
[10] Nachmanides on Genesis 4:3
[11] Meir Arama, *Sefer Me'ir Tehillot* 91b
[12] Zohar III, 69a13
[13] In Sephardic homes Isaac Jack Levy and Rosemary Zumwait Levy, *Ritual Medical Lore of Sephardic Women: Sweetening the Spirits, Healing the Sick* (University of Illinois Press, 2001), p. 25.
[14] Susan Sered, *Women as Ritual Experts: The Religious Lives of Elderly Jewish Women in Jerusalem*, p. 18-20.
[15] Isaac Jack Levy and Rosemary Zumwait Levy, *Ritual Medical Lore of Sephardic Women: Sweetening the Spirits, Healing the Sick*, p. 28.
[16] Brenda Sirotte, *The Fortune Teller's Kiss* (American Lives, 2006), p. 5.
[17] Jennifer Hunter wrote the book *Magickal Judaism*; Carly Lesser and Liorah Lleucu are both blog authors (www.peelapom.com and walking-on-fire.blogspot.com).
[18] Rachel Pollack, *The Shining Tribe Tarot: Awakening the Universal Spirit* (St. Paul, MN: Llewellyn Publications, 2001), p. 258.

Chapter 7

[1] Ismar J. Peritz, "Women in the Ancient Hebrew Cult," in *Journal of Biblical Literature*, 17:2 (1898) p.147.
[2] For a full discussion of this story, see Phyllis Trible, *Texts of Terror: Literary-Feminist*

Readings of Biblical Narratives (Fortress Press, 1984), p. 82-83.

[3] Charlene Spretnak, "The Myth of Demeter and Persephone," in *Weaving the Visions: New Patterns in Feminist Spirituality*, eds. Judith Plaskow and Carol Christ (HarperCollins, 1989), p. 72-77.

[4] Mishnah Shekalim 8:5

[5] Philo, De Specialibus Legibus, ii, 56-58. Cited by Raphael Patai, *The Hebrew Goddess* (Wayne State University Press, 1990), p. 258.

[6] *Teezaza Sambat* in Patai, *The Hebrew Goddess*, p. 261.

[7] *Ibid.*, p. 263.

[8] Diane Wolkstein and Samuel Noah Kramer, *Inanna, Queen of Heaven and Earth: her Stories and Hymns from Sumer* (Harper Perennial, 1983), p. 14; Callimachus Hymn III.

[9] Susan Berrin, *Celebrating the New Moon: A Rosh Chodesh Anthology* (Jason Aronson, 1996).

[10] Susan Sered, *Women as Ritual Experts: The Religious Lives of Elderly Jewish Women in Jerusalem* (Oxford University Press, 1996), p. 132.

[11] Ada Rapoport-Albert, *Women and the Messianic Heresy of Sabbatai Zevi, 1666-1816*, p. 184.

[12] Jay Michaelson, "'I do not look to heaven, but at what God does on earth': Materialism, Sexuality, and Law in the Jagellonian Manuscript of Jacob Frank's Zbior *Słow Panskich*." (PhD diss., Hebrew University, 2012).

[13] From a private communication by Sarai Shapiro. Also see: "A Critical Time for Jewish Youth: Rethinking the Bar and Bat Mitzvah," by Sarai Shapiro and Zelig Golden, http://zeek.forward.com/articles/117847/

[14] Deborah J. Grenn, "Metaforms of a Monotheistic Religion: The Menstrual Roots of Three Jewish and African Rites of Passage: Khomba, Bat Mitzvah, and the Mikvah," published in the online journal Metaformia; http://www.metaformia.org/articles/metaforms-monotheistic-religion/

[15] From a paper by Liz Sternlieb for the Academy for Jewish Religion, which won a prize in creative ritual.

[16] At Kohenet Institute retreats, students not only participate in group ritual but are invited to request personal rituals for healing and transformation.

[17] Sanhedrin 42a

Chapter 8

[1] Judges 5:7; II Samuel 20:19

[2] Story of Kirta, Ugarit tablets found in Ras Shamra. See Michael David Coogan, *Stories from Ancient Canaan* (The Westminster Press, 1978).

[3] Tilde Binger, *Asherah: Goddesses in Ugarit, Israel, and the Old Testament* (Bloomsbury T&T Clark, 1997), p. 46.

[4] Savina Teubal, *Sarah the Priestess: The First Matriarch of Genesis* (First Swallow Press, 1984), chapter 3.
[5] Rashi to Genesis 21:7
[6] John H. Walton, Victor Harold Matthews, Mark William Chavalas, *The IVP Bible Background Commentary* (Intervarsity Press, 2000), p. 408.
[7] Pesikta Rabbati 43:23
[8] Simcha Fishbane, *Deviancy in Early Rabbinic Literature: A Collection of Socio-Anthropological Essays* (Brill, 2007), p. 23.
[9] Babylonian Talmud, Nedarim 9a-b
[10] I Samuel 1-2
[11] Mishnah Nazir 1:7
[12] Mishnah Nazir 3:6; Josephus, Bellum Judaicum, II, xv.
[13] Genesis Rabbah 82, end of passage.
[14] Zohar I, 25b
[15] Zohar I, 48a
[16] Zohar II, 24b
[17] Michele Klein, *A Time to Be Born: Customs and Folklore of Jewish Birth* (Jewish Publication Society, 2000), p. 206-207.
[18] Chava Weissler. *Voices of the Matriarchs: Listening to the Prayers of Early Modern Jewish Women* (Beacon Press, 1999), p. 107.
[19] Devra Kay, *Seyder Techines: The Forgotten Book of Common Prayer for Jewish Women* (Jewish Publication Society, 2004), p. 24.
[20] In *The Merit of Our Mothers: A Bilingual Anthology of Jewish Women's Prayers*, compiled and introduced by Tracy Guren Klirs, translated by T. G. Klirs et al. (Hebrew Union College Press: 1992), 12–45.
[21] Hila Tucherman-Mishali, private conversation regarding her research into North African Jewish women's rituals.
[22] Michele Klein, *A Time to Be Born: Customs and Folklore of Jewish Birth* (Jewish Publication Society, 2000), p. 149.
[23] Harry Fox and Justin Jaron Lewis, *Many Pious Women: Edition and Translation* (Degryter, 2011), p. 236.
[24] Lawrence Hoffman, *Covenant of Blood; Circumcision and Gender in Rabbinic Literature* (University of Chicago Press, 1996), p. 196.

Chapter 9

[1] See I Kings 15:13. II Kings 10:13, II Chron. 15:16, Jer. 13:18, 29:2.
[2] Tilde Binger, *Asherah, Goddesses in Ugarit, Israel, and the Old Testament* (Bloomsbury T&T Clark, 1997), p. 79; CTA 6.1.39-55.
[3] Susan Ackerman, "Out of Her Window She Peered: Sisera's Mother, Queen Mothers, and the Gods," in *Warrior Dancer Seductress Queen* (Doubleday, 1998), p. 136.

⁴ II Kings 18:1; II Kings 22:1
⁵ Ezekiel 19:10
⁶ I Kings 19
⁷ I Kings 21, II Kings 9
⁸ Numbers 21:8-9; II Kings 18:4
⁹ Zohar III, 169b
¹⁰ Kenneth Atkinson, *Queen Salome: Jerusalem's Warrior Monarch of the First Century B.C.E.* (McFarland, 2012); Charles Peter Mason, "Alexander, Jannaeus" in William Smith, *Dictionary of Greek and Roman Biography and Mythology* 1 (Little, Brown and Company, 1867), p. 117.
¹¹ Elna Solvang, *A Woman's Place is in the House: Royal Women of Judah and their Involvement in the House of David* (Sheffield Academic Press, 2003).
¹² Helen Efthimiadis-Keith, "On the Egyptian Origin of Judith, or Judith as Anathyahu," *Journal for Semitics*, vol. 20 (2011), p. 300-322.
¹³ Babylonian Talmud, Shabbat 119a.
¹⁴ The Zohar, trans. Daniel Matt (in *The Zohar, Pritzker Edition.* Stanford University Press, 2003), Chapter 79.
¹⁵ Zohar II, 51a
¹⁶ Zohar I, 223a
¹⁷ Moses Cordovero, *Tomer Devorah*, Chapter 9.
¹⁸ J.H. Laenen, *Jewish Mysticism: An Introduction* (Westminster John Knox Press, 2001), p. 208. Laenen notes that Jacob Frank's wife and later his daughter were also venerated as *gevirah* by Frank's disciples.
¹⁹ *Listen to Her Voice: The Ma'yan Report. Assessing the Experiences of Women in the Jewish Community and their Relationships to Feminism.* January, 2005; Jane Eisner and Maia Efrem, "Gender Equality Still Elusive in Forward Survey of Top Jewish Leaders," *The Forward*, Dec. 16, 2011, p. 1.

Chapter 10

¹ Babylonian Talmud, Sotah 11b
² Jill Hammer, "The Tenth Plague," in *Sisters at Sinai: New Tales of Biblical Women* (Jewish Publication Society, 2001), p. 107-113.
³ Jill Hammer. *Sisters at Sinai: New Tales of Biblical Women* (Jewish Publication Society, 2001).
⁴ Norman Bancroft Hunt, *Living in Ancient Egypt* (Chelsea House Publications, 2008), p. 76. There is some controversy around the idea that midwife-priestesses served Heqet, as there is no ancient Egyptian word for midwife. However, given that many priestly classes in Egypt had specialized skills, and given Heqet's role as patroness of laboring women, it makes sense that her priestesses would be midwives.
⁵ Exodus Rabbah 1:15

⁶ Babylonian Talmud, Kiddushin 73b; Mishnah Rosh haShanah, chapter 2.
⁷ Babylonian Talmud, Shabbat 128b
⁸ Babylonian Talmud, Sotah 11b and elsewhere.
⁸ᵃ Elisheva Baumgarten, "Thus Sayeth the Wise Midwives: Midwives and Midwifery in Thirteenth Century Ashkenaz," *Zion*, 65/1 (2000), p. 45-74.
⁹ Michele Klein, *A Time to Be Born: Customs and Folklore of Jewish Birth* (Jewish Publication Society, 2000), p. 124.
¹⁰ Michele Klein, *A Time to Be Born: Customs and Folklore of Jewish Birth* (Jewish Publication Society, 2000), p. 132-133.
¹¹ Michele Klein, *A Time to Be Born: Customs and Folklore of Jewish Birth* (Jewish Publication Society, 2000), p. 125.
¹² Ibid., p. 125.
¹³ Ibid., p. 193.
¹⁴ Presentation of ongoing research, Sarah Kelly, Spring 2010, Academy for Jewish Religion.
¹⁵ Jane Sandall, Hora Sultani, Simon Gates, Andrew Shennan, and Declan Devane. "Midwife-led continuity models versus other models of care for childbearing women." Published by The Cochrane Collaboration (2013).

Chapter 11

¹ Babylonian Talmud, Pesachim 111a
² William G. Dever, *Did God Have a Wife? Archaelogy and Folk Religion in Ancient Israel* (Eerdmans Publishing Company, 2005), p. 160-162.
³ Michael S. Moore, "Wise Women or Wisdom Woman? A Biblical Study of Women's Roles," in *Restoration Quarterly* 35.3 (1993), p. 156.
⁴ I Samuel 25
⁵ Michael S. Moore, "Wise Women or Wisdom Woman? A Biblical Study of Women's Roles," in *Restoration Quarterly* 35.3 (1993), p. 147-158.
⁶ Jeremiah 9:17
⁷ Babylonian Talmud, Bava Batra 119b
⁸ Babylonian Talmud, Pesachim 62b
⁹ Louis Ginzburg, *Legends of the Jews, vol. II* (Jewish Publication Society, 1911) p. 115-116. Ginzburg is summarizing a version of the story from Sefer haYashar, a medieval novel-like midrash.
¹⁰ Genesis 50
¹¹ Z. Ben-Hayyim, ed. *Tibat Markeh; A Collection of Samaritan Midrashim* (Jerusalem: Academy of Science, 1998), p. 98. Cited and translated in Leila Leah Bronner, "Serach and the Exodus," in Athalya Brenner (ed), *Exodus to Deuteronomy; A Feminist Companion to the Bible* (Sheffield Academic Press, 2000), p. 192. The reference to Serach as "wisest of women" echoes the book of Proverbs, where Lady Wisdom is called "wisest of women."

¹² Michael S. Moore, "Wise Women" or Wisdom Women: A Biblical Study of Women's Roles. *Restoration Quarterly* 35.3 (1993), p. 147-158.
¹³ Elisheva Baumgarten, *Mothers and Children: Jewish Family Life in Medieval Europe* (Princeton University Press, 2007).
¹⁴ http://jwa.org/encyclopedia/article/torah-study
¹⁵ Tirzah Firestone. *The Receiving: Reclaiming Jewish Women's Wisdom* (HarperOne, 2004).
¹⁶ http://judaism.about.com/od/womenrabbis/a/asenathbarzani.htm
¹⁷ Isaac Jack Levy and Rosemary Levy, *Ritual Medical Lore of Sephardic Women: Sweetening the Spirits, Healing the Sick* (University of Illinois Press, 2001), p. 23.
¹⁸ Susan Sered, *Women as Ritual Experts: The Religious Lives of Elderly Jewish Women in Jerusalem* (Oxford University Press, 1992), p. 18.

Chapter 12

¹ © Taya Shere, 2011
² Jeremiah 9:16
³ Nancy C. Lee, *The Singers of Lamentations: Cities Under Siege, from Ur to Jerusalem to Sarajevo* (Brill Academic Publishing, 2002), chapters 1 and 3.
⁴ Babylonian Talmud, Berachot 51a
⁵ Maimonides, Laws of Rest on the Festivals 6:24.
⁶ Harry Fox and Justin Jaron Lewis, *Many Pious Women: Edition and Translation* (Degryter, 2011), p. 234.
⁷ Zohar II, 194b (Vayakhel), quoting Babylonian Talmud, Berachot 51a.
⁸ Joshua Trachtenberg, *Jewish Magic and Superstition* (University of Pennsylvania Press, 2004), p. 179.
⁹ Jennifer Breger, "Women at the Cemetery: Historical Notes," in *The Orthodox Jewish Woman and Ritual: Options and Opportunities: Death and Mourning* (JOFA, 2000), p. 12.
¹⁰ "A Short History of the Chevra Kadisha," in *The Orthodox Jewish Woman and Ritual: Options and Opportunities: Death and Mourning* (JOFA), p. 7.
¹¹ Barbara Gaims-Spiegel, "Women and Kaddish," in *The Orthodox Jewish Woman and Ritual: Options and Opportunities: Death and Mourning* (JOFA), p. 9.

Chapter 13

¹ Ross Kraemer, "Monastic Jewish Women in Greco-Roman Egypt: Philo Judaeus on the Therapeutrides," in *Signs*, Winter 1989, p. 342.
¹ᵃ Ibid.
² Sharon Lea Mattila. "Wisdom, Sense Perception, Nature, and Philo's Gender Gradient, "in *Harvard Theological Review*, vol. 89, no. 2 (April 1996), p. 103-129.
³ Ross Shepard Kraemer, *Her Share of the Blessings: Women's Religions among Pagans, Jews,*

³ª Mishnah Sukkah 5:4.

⁴ Baruch Kimmerling, *The Invention and Decline of Israeliness: State, Society, and the Military* (University of California Press, 2001), p. 153.

⁵ Alex Weingrod and Michael Ashkenazi, *Ethiopian Jews and Israel* (Transaction Publishers, 1987), p. 145.

⁶ Stephen Spector, *Operation Solomon: The Daring Rescue of the Ethiopian Jews* (Oxford University Press, 2005), p. 7.

⁷ Genesis 24

⁸ The Delphic Oracle was also known for giving cryptic prophecies, sometimes ones that were not decipherable until they had been fulfilled.

⁹ Deuteronomy 16:16

¹⁰ I Kings 14

¹¹ II Samuel 20:14-22

¹² Babylonian Talmud, Eruvin 96a

¹³ Miranda Shaw, "Living Goddesses: Embodying the Divine in Buddhist Nepal," lecture at the conference of the Association for the Study of Women and Mythology," March 12, 2011.

¹⁴ http://www.whatsonwhen.com/sisp/index.htm?fx=event&event_id=43284

¹⁵ Helen Eliassian, "Esther's Iranian Tomb Draws Pilgrims of All Stripes," Ha'aretz, March 22, 2005.

¹⁶ Alice Ostriker, *The Volcano Sequence* (University of Pittsburgh Press, 2002), p. 25-26.

Chapter 14

¹ Portions of this chapter are adapted from: Jill Hammer, "Ruth and Naomi: The Return of the Seed," in *G'vanim: The Journal of the Academy for Jewish Religion*, vol. 7 no. 1 (2011), p. 9-20.

² Ruth 2:20

³ Samuel N. Kramer, *The Sacred Marriage: Aspects of Faith, Myth and Ritual in Ancient Sumer* (Indiana University, 1969).

⁴ Diane Wolkstein and Samuel Noah Kramer, *Inanna, Queen of Heaven and Earth: Her Stories and Hymns from Sumer* (HarperPerennial, 1983).

⁵ See H.H. Rowley, "The Meaning of the Shulammite," in *The American Journal of Semitic Languages and Literatures*, vol. 56 no. 1, p. 84-91.

⁶ Julia Watts Belser, "Speaking of Goddess: Finding the Sacred Feminine in the Song of Songs," *Zeek*, Spring 2009, p. 43.

⁷ Rashi on Genesis 38 and 39

⁸ Zohar I, 101b

⁹ Zohar II, 99a

¹⁰ Jay Michaelson, "I Do Not Look to Heaven, but at What God Does on Earth":

Materialism, Sexuality, and (A)Theology in the Jagellonian Manuscript of Jacob Frank's Zbior Słow Panskich." (Dissertation, Hebrew University, 2013).

[11] Dawn Cherie Ezrahi, "Surrendering to Love," http://eolife.org/articles/beliefs/Surrendering_To_Love.aspx

[12] Izak Cornelius, *The Many Faces of the Goddess: The Iconography of the Syro-Palestinian Goddesses Anat, Astarte, Qedeshet, and Asherah c. 1500-1000 BCE* (Academic Press Freibourg, 2004), p. 42.

[13] Nathan Tamar uses the gender-neutral pronouns ze and hir.

Chapter 15

[1] A scroll in an ornamental case placed on the doorpost of Jewish homes to fulfill the biblical commandment: "You shall write them [God's laws] on the doorposts of your house and on your gates."

[2] Proverbs 9:15-17

[3] http://cometogetherarticles.yolasite.com/heyoka-clowns.php; also see www.redelk.net.

[3a] Mishnah Sukkah 5:4

[4] Babylonian Talmud, Sanhedrin 38b

[5] Tal Ilan: *Mine and Yours are Hers: Retrieving Women's History from Rabbinic Literature*, (Brill Academic Publishers, 1997) p. 57-58, 121-129; Tal Ilan, *Jewish Women in Greco-Roman Palestine* (Hendrickson Publishers, 1996) p. 197-200.

[6] Harry Fox and Justin Jaron Lewis, *Many Pious Women: Edition and Translation* (De Gruyter, 2011), p. 232.

[7] Yale Strom, *The Book of Klezmer: The History, The Music, the Folklore from the Fourteenth Century to the Twenty-first* (A Cappella Books, 2002), p. 94.

[8] Harry Fox and Justin Jaron Lewis, *Many Pious Women: Edition and Translation* (De Gruyter, 2011), p. 232.

[9] Yale Strom, *The Book of Klezmer: The History, The Music, the Folklore from the Fourteenth Century to the Twenty-first* (A Cappella Books, 2002), p. 44.

[10] Judith Brin Ingber, "Dancing Despite the Scourge: Jewish Dancers During the Holocaust." (2005). Web essay: www.jbriningber.com/Dancing_Despite_the_Scourge.pdf

[11] Yale Strom, *The Book of Klezmer: The History, The Music, the Folklore from the Fourteenth Century to the Twenty-first* (A Cappella Books, 2002), p. 37.

[12] Yale Strom, *The Book of Klezmer: The History, The Music, the Folklore from the Fourteenth Century to the Twenty-first* (A Cappella Books, 2002), p. 17.

[13] S. Ansky, *The Dybbuk, or Between Two Worlds* (1914).

[14] *The Dybbuk*, 1937 Yiddish language film, directed by Michael Waszynski.

[15] Yale Strom, *The Book of Klezmer: The History, The Music, the Folklore from the Fourteenth Century to the Twenty-first* (A Cappella Books, 2002), p. 15.

Chapter 16

[1] Starhawk, "Is the DaVinci Code Good for the Pagans?", Beliefnet, http://www.beliefnet.com/Entertainment/Movies/The-Da-Vinci-Code/Is-The-Da-Vinci-Code-Good-For-The-Pagans.aspx

[2] Aviva Zornberg, *The Murmuring Deep: Reflections on the Biblical Unconscious* (Schocken Books, 2009), p. 285.

[3] Margie Klein, "Praying to Pray with my Feet," in *Tikkun*, no. 22 vol. 2 (2007), p. 53.

[4] Luce Irigaray, *This Sex Which is Not One* (1977, Cornell University), p. 23-33.

[5] Lynn Gottlieb, *She Who Dwells Within: A Feminist Vision of a Renewed Judaism* (HarperOne, 1995), p. 27.

[6] One of the most popular retreats at the Isabella Freedman Jewish Retreat Center.

[7] Other examples of this include Reb Zalman Schachter-Shalomi's ordinaton of a sacred Temple drummer, Akiva Wharton, who in turn ordained Shoshana Jedwab as a Baalat haTof, a drum master.

[8] Ilana Streit, "How Are You, or the Midwife Poem" (unpublished poem)

[9] Pirkei Avot 1:1

[10] Alicia Ostriker, *A Prayer to the Shekhinah*, in *The Nakedness of the Fathers: Biblical Visions and Revisions* (Rutgers University Press, 1997), p. 253.

Chapter 17

[1] Yocheved Landsman, "Invocation," printed in the *Kohenet Siddur* (2nd ed., 2010).

References

S. Ansky, The Dybbuk, or Between Two Worlds (1914).

"A Short History of the Chevra Kadisha," in *The Orthodox Jewish Woman and Ritual: Options and Opportunities: Death and Mourning* (JOFA), p. 7.

Susan Ackerman, "Asherah, the West Semitic Goddess of Spinning and Weaving?" in *Journal of Near Eastern Studies*, Vol. 67, no. 1, p. 1-30.

Susan Ackerman, "Women and the Worship of Yahweh in Ancient Israel," in *Confronting the Past: Archaeological and Historical Essays on Ancient Israel*, William Dever, Seymour Gitlin, J. Edward Wright, J.P. Dessel (Eisenbrauns, 2006).

Susan Ackerman, *Warrior, Dancer, Seductress, Queen: Women in Judges and Biblical Israel* (Yale University Press, 1998).

Gillian Alban, *Melusine the Serpent-Goddess in A.S Byatt's Possession and in Mythology* (Lexington Books, 2003).

N.E.A. Andreasen, "The Role of the Queen Mother in Israelite Society," *Catholic Biblical Quarterly* 45 (1983), 179-194.

Nina Amir, *The Priestess Practice: Four Steps to Creating Sacred Space and Inviting the Divine to Dwell Within It*, booklet, 2012.

Joyce Antler, *The Journey Home: Jewish Women and the American Century* (Simon and Schuster, 1997).

Kenneth Atkinson, *Queen Salome: Jerusalem's Warrior Monarch of the First Century B.C.E.* (McFarland, 2012).

Maria T. Baader. "From the Priestess of the Home to the Rabbi's Brilliant Daughter: Concepts of Jewish Womanhood and Progressive Germanness," in *die Deborah and the American Israelite, 1854-1900*.

M. Bar-Ilan, "Witches in the Bible and in the Talmud," in Herbert W. Basser and Simcha Fishbane (eds.), *Approaches to Ancient Judaism V* (Scholars Press, 1993).

Judith R. Baskin, *Jewish Women in Historical Perspective* (Wayne State University Press, 1998).

George Barton, *Archaeology and the Bible* (American Sunday School Union, 1946).

Elisheva Baumgarten, *Mothers and Children: Jewish Family Life in Medieval Europe* (Princeton University Press, 2007).

Elisheva Baumgarten, "Thus Sayeth the Wise Midwives: Midwives and Midwifery in Thirteen Century Ashkenaz," *Zion*, 65/1 (2000), p. 45-74.

Julia Watts Belser, "Making Room for the Divine She," (*Zeek*, August 2007).

Julia Watts Belser, "Speaking of Goddess: Finding the Sacred Feminine in the Song of Songs," *Zeek*, Spring 2009.

Zafrira Ben-Barak, "The Status and Right of the Gebirah." *Journal of Biblical Literature*, 110/111 (1991), p. 23-34.

Z. Ben-Hayyim, ed. *Tibat Markeh: A Collection of Samaritan Midrashim* (Jerusalem: Academy of Science, 1998).

Aviva Ben-Ur, "Still Life: Sephardi, Ashkenazi, and West African Art and Form in Suriname's Jewish Cemeteries," in *American Jewish History*, Vol. 92, no. 1 (March 2004), pp. 31-79.

Susan Berrin, *Celebrating the New Moon: A Rosh Chodesh Anthology* (Jason Aronson, 1996).

David Biale, *Eros and the Jews: From Biblical Israel to Contemporary America* (University of California Press, 1997).

Hayim Nachman Bialik and Atar Hadari, *Songs from Bialik: Selected Poems of Hayim Nachman Bialik* (Syracuse University Press, 2000).

Tilde Binger, *Asherah: Goddesses in Ugarit, Israel, and the Old Testament* (Bloomsbury T.&T. Clark, 1997).

P. Bird, "The Place of Women in the Israelite Cultus," In P.D. Miller, P. D. Hanson, and S.D. McBride (eds.), *Ancient Israelite Religion: Essays in Honor of Frank Moore Cross* (Fortress Press, 1987).

Menachem Brayer, *The Jewish Woman in Rabbinic Literature: A Psychohistorical Perspective* (1986), p. 119.

Jennifer Breger and Lisa Schlaff, *The Orthodox Jewish Woman and Ritual: Options and Opportunities: Death and Mourning* (JOFA, 2000).

Marc Bregman, Serah bat Asher: Biblical Origins, Ancient Aggadah and Contemporary Folklore, The Bilgray Lectureship, booklet published and distributed by the University of Arizona, 1997 [reprinted in *New Harvest* (The Brodsky Library Press, St. Louis, 2005).

Athalya Brenner (ed.), *Exodus to Deuteronomy; A Feminist Companion to the Bible* (Sheffield Academic Press, 2000).

Geoffrey W. Bromiley, *International Standard Bible Encyclopedia* (Eerdmans Publishing Co., 1995).

Bernadette Brooten, *Women Leaders in the Ancient Synagogue: Inscriptional Evidence and Background Issues* (Scholars Press, 1982).

Jeffrey Howard (Yossi) Chajes, *Between Worlds: Dybbuks, Exorcists, and Early Modern Judaism* (University of Pennsylvania Press, 2003).

Steven M. Cohen and Paula E. Hyman, *The Jewish Family: Myths and Reality* (Holmes and Meier, 1986).

Joan Breton Connelly, *Portrait of a Priestess; Women and Ritual in Ancient Greece* (Princeton University Press, 2009).

Michael David Coogan, *Stories from Ancient Canaan* (The Westminster Press, 1978).

Izak Cornelius, *The Many Faces of the Goddess: The Iconography of the Syro-Palestinian Goddesses Anat, Astarte, Qedeshet, and Asherah c. 1500-1000 BCE* (Academic Press Freibourg, 2004)

Jesús-Luis Cunchillos, Juan-Pablo Vita, José-Ángel Zamora, *The Texts of the Ugaritic Data Bank* (Gorgias Press, 2003).

Geoffrey Dennis, *Encyclopedia of Jewish Myth, Magic, and Mysticism* (Llewelyn, 2007).

Elizabeth Davis and Carol Leonard, *The Women's Wheel of Life* (Penguin, 1997).

John Day, *Yahweh and the Gods and Goddesses of Canaan* (Bloomsbury T&T Clark, 2002).

William G. Dever, "Asherah, Consort of Yahweh? New Evidence from Kuntillat-Ajrud," in *Bulletin of the American Schools of Oriental Research*, Vol. 255 (1984), p. 21-27.

REFERENCES

William G. Dever, *Did God Have a Wife?: Archaeology and Folk Religion in Ancient Israel* (Eeerdmans Publishing Co., 2005).

Irene Diamond, *Fertile Ground: Women, Earth, and the Limits of Control* (Beacon Press, 1994).

G.R. Driver, *Canaanite Myths and Legends* (T.&T. Clark, Edinburgh, 1971).

The Dybbuk, 1937 Yiddish language film, directed by Michael Waszynski.

Helen Efthimiadis-Keith, "On the Egyptian Origin of Judith, or Judith as Anath-yahu," *Journal for Semitics*, Vol. 20 (2011), p. 300-322.

Jane Eisner and Maia Efrem, "Gender Equality Still Elusive in Forward Survey of Top Jewish Leaders," in *The Forward*, Dec. 16, 2011, p. 1.

Helen Eliassian, "Esther's Iranian Tomb Draws Pilgrims of All Stripes," in *Ha'aretz*, March 22, 2005.

Rachel Elior, *The Three Temples: On the Emergence of Jewish Mysticism* (Littman Library of Jewish Civilization, 2005).

Clarissa Pinkola Estes, *Women who Run with the Wolves* (Ballantine, 1996).

Marcia Falk, *The Book of Blessings: New Jewish Prayers for Daily Life, the Sabbath, and the New Moon* (Beacon Press, 1999).

Tirzah Firestone, *The Receiving: Reclaiming Jewish Women's Wisdom* (HarperOne, 2004).

Simcha Fishbane, *Deviancy in Early Rabbinic Literature: A Collection of Socio-Anthropological Essays* (Brill, 2007).

Sylvia Barack Fishman, *A Breath of Life: Feminism in the American Jewish Community* (Free Press, 1993).

Harry Fox and Justin Jaron Lewis, *Many Pious Women: Edition and Translation* (Degryter, 2011).

Tamar Frankiel and Judy Greenfeld, *Minding the Temple of the Soul: Balancing Body, Mind, and Spirit through Traditional Jewish Prayer, Movement, and Meditation* (Jewish Lights Publishing, 1997).

Tikvah Frymer-Kensky, *In the Wake of the Goddesses: Women, Culture, and the Biblical Transformation of Pagan Myth* (Ballantine Books, 1993).

Barbara Gaims-Spiegel, "Women and Kaddish," in *The Orthodox Jewish Woman and Ritual: Options and Opportunities: Death and Mourning* (JOFA), p. 9.

Louis Ginzburg, *Legends of the Jews* (Jewish Publication Society, 1911).

Elyse Goldstein, *Revisions: Seeing Torah through a Feminist Lens* (Jewish Lights Publishing, 1998).

Lynn Gottlieb, *She Who Dwells Within: A Feminist Vision of a Renewed Judaism* (Harper San Francisco, 1995).

Norma Lorre Goodrich, *Priestesses* (Perennial, 1990).

Bonna Haberman, "The Yom Kippur Avodah within the Female Enclosure," in *Beginning Anew: A Woman's Companion to the High Holy Days*, eds. Gail Twersky Reimer and Judith A. Kates (Touchstone, 1997), p. 243-257.

Jill Hammer, "Holle's Cry: Unearthing a Birth Goddess in a German Jewish Naming Ritual" in *Nashim: A Journal of Jewish Women's Studies and Gender Studies* (no. 9, 2005), p. 62-87.

Jill Hammer, *The Jewish Book of Days: A Companion for All Seasons* (Jewish Publication Society, 2004).

Jill Hammer, "Ruth and Naomi: The Return of the Seed," in *G'vanim: The Journal of the Academy for Jewish Religion*, Vol. 7 no. 1 (2011), p. 9-20.

Jill Hammer, *Sisters at Sinai: New Tales of Biblical Women* (Jewish Publication Society, 2001).

Jill Hammer and Taya Shere. *Siddur haKohanot: A Hebrew Priestess Prayerbook* (Kohenet Institute, 2013).

Jill Hammer, "The Unfolding One," in *Siddur haKohanot: A Hebrew Priestess Prayerbook*. Jill Hammer and Taya Shere, eds. (Kohenet Institute, 2013), on p. 10.

Abraham Joshua Heschel and Gordon Tucker, *Heavenly Torah as Refracted through the Generations* (Continuum International Publishing Group, 2006).

H. W. Hirschberg, *A History of the Jews in North Africa: From Antiquity to the Sixteenth Century*, vol. 1 (Brill, 1974).

Jane Hirshfeld, *Women in Praise of the Sacred: 43 Centuries of Spiritual Poems by Women* (HarperCollins, 1994).

Lawrence Hoffman, *Covenant of Blood: Circumcision and Gender in Rabbinic Literature* (University of Chicago Press, 1996).

William Horbury, W.D. Davies, John Sturdy eds. *The Cambridge History of Judaism: The Early Roman Period* (Cambridge University Press, 1999).

Norman Bancroft Hunt, *Living in Ancient Egypt* (Chelsea House Publications, 2008).

Jennifer Hunter, *Magickal Judaism: Combining Pagan and Jewish Practice* (Citadel, 2006).

Thacher Hurd, *The Weaver*, illustrated by Elisa Kleven (D&M Publishers, 2010).

Shonna Husbands-Hankin, "Eshet Chazon: Woman of Vision," in *New Menorah* 4 (1983).

Tal Ilan, *Jewish Women in Greco-Roman Palestine* (Hendrickson Publishers, 1996).

Tal Ilan, *Mine and Yours Are Hers: Retrieving Women's History from Rabbinic Literature* (Brill, 1997), p. 139-140.

Luce Irigaray, *This Sex Which is Not One* (Cornell University, 1977).

Ann Jeffers, *Magic and Divination in Ancient Palestine and Syria* (Brill, 1996).

Shoshana Jedwab, "The Whole Wide World/Shirat haParochet." (Song) Lyrics appear in *Siddur haKohanot: A Hebrew Priestess Prayerbook*. Jill Hammer and Taya Shere, eds. (Kohenet Institute, 2013), p. 38.

Sarah Iles Johnston, *Religions of the Ancient World: A Guide* (Belknap Press, 2004).

Tessel Marina Jonquier, *Prayer in Josephus* (Brill, 2007).

Jenna Weissman Joselit, *New York's Jewish Jews: The Orthodox Community in the Interwar Years* (Indiana University Press, 1990).

Jenna Weissman Joselit, "The Jewish Home Beautiful," in Jonathan Sarna, *The American Jewish Experience* (Holmes and Meier, 1997), p. 236-244.

Carl Jung, *Memories, Dreams, Reflections* (Vintage, 1989).

Jenny Kien, *Reinstating the Divine Woman in Judaism* (Universal Publishers, 2000).

Baruch Kimmerling, *The Invention and Decline of Israeliness: State, Society, and the Military* (University of California Press, 2001).

Devra Kay, *Seyder Techines: The Forgotten Book of Common Prayer for Jewish Women* (Jewish Publication Society, 2004).

Sarah Kelly, dissertation research into Anglo-Jewish midwives in eighteenth century London, University of Cambridge.

A. D. Klaas, G.I. Smelik, and G. I. Davies (Translator), *Writings from Ancient Israel: A Handbook of Historical and Religious Documents* (Westminster John Knox Press, 1992).

Tracy Klirs, *The Merit of our Mothers: A Bilingual Anthology of Jewish Women's Prayers* (Hebrew Union College, 1992).

Margie Klein, "Praying to Pray with my Feet," in *Tikkun*, Vol. 2, no. 22 (2007), p. 53.

Michele Klein, *A Time to Be Born: Customs and Folklore of Jewish Birth* (Jewish Publication Society, 2000).

Samuel N. Kramer, *The Sacred Marriage: Aspects of Faith, Myth and Ritual in Ancient Sumer* (Indiana University, 1969).

Ross Kraemer, *Her Share of the Blessings: Women's Religions among Pagans, Jews, and Christians in the Greco-Roman World* (Oxford University Press, 1992).

Ross Kraemer, "Monastic Jewish Women in Graeco-Roman Egypt: Philo Judaeus on the Therapeutrides," in *Signs*, Winter 1989.

J.H. Laenen, *Jewish Mysticism: An Introduction* (Westminster John Knox Press, 2001), p. 208.

Amichai Lau-Lavie, cited by Jay Michaelson, "The Jewish Goddess Past and Present," in *The Forward*, May 5.

Emma Lazarus, "The New Colossus" (1883).

Nancy C. Lee, *The Singers of Lamentations: Cities Under Siege, from Ur to Jerusalem to Sarajevo* (Brill Academic Publishing, 2002).

Mark Leuchter, "The Priesthood in Ancient Israel," in *Biblical Theology Bulletin*, vol. 40 no. 2, pages 1-11.

Isaac Jack Levy and Rosemary Zumwait Levy, *Ritual Medical Lore of Sephardic Women: Sweetening the Spirits, Healing the Sick* (University of Illinois Press, 2001).

Edward Lipinski, *The Aramaeans: Their Ancient History, Culture, Religion* (Peeters Publishers and Booksellers, 2000).

C. Scott Littleton, *Shinto: Origins, Rituals, Festivals, Spirits, Sacred Places* (Oxford University Press, 2002).

Betty DeShong Meador and Judy Grahn, *Lady of Largest Heart: Poems of the Sumerian High Priestess Enheduanna* (University of Texas Press, 2000).

Henny J. Marsman, *Women in Ugarit and Israel: Their Social and Religious Position in the Context of the Ancient Near East*, (Brill, 2003).

Daniel Matt, "Beyond the Personal God," in *God and the Big Bang: Discovering Harmony Between Science and Spirituality* (Jewish Lights, 1998).

Sharon Lea Mattila, "Wisdom, Sense Perception, Nature, and Philo's Gender Gradient," in *Harvard Theological Review*, Vol. 89, no. 2 (April 1996).

Ma'yan: The Jewish Women's Project at the JCC in Manhattan. *Listen to Her Voice: The Ma'yan Report. Assessing the Experiences of Women in the Jewish Community and their Relationships to Feminism.* January, 2005.

Betty DeShong Meador, *Inanna, Lady of Largest Heart* (University of Texas Press, 2001).

Carol Meyers, *Households and Holiness: The Religious Culture of Israelite Women* (Augsburg Fortress, 2005).

Jay Michaelson, *God in Your Body* (Jewish Lights, 2009).

Jay Michaelson, *I Do Not Look to Heaven, but at What God Does on Earth: Materialism, Sexuality, and (A) Theology in the Jagellonian Manuscript of Jacob Frank's Zbior Słow Panskich.* (Dissertation, Hebrew University, 2013).

Jay Michaelson, "The Jewish Goddess Past and Present, *The Forward*, May 5, 2005.

Goldie Milgram, *Living Jewish Life Cycle: Creating Meaningful Rites of Passage for Every Stage of Life* (Jewish Lights, 2008).

Edna St. Vincent Millay, "Prayer to Persephone," in *Second April* (1921), p. 90.

Patricia Monaghan, *The Goddess Companion: Daily Meditations on the Feminine Spirit* (Llewelyn, 2000).

Patricia Monaghan, *The Red-Haired Girl from the Bog: The Landscape of Celtic Myth and Spirit* (New World Library, 2004).

Michael S. Moore, "Wise Women" or Wisdom Women: A Biblical Study of Women's Roles. *Restoration Quarterly* 35.3 (1993), p. 147-158.

J.M. Modrzejewski, *The Jews of Egypt from Rameses II to Emperor Hadrian* (Clark, 1995).

Joseph Murphy and Mei Mei Sanford, *Osun Across the Waters: A Yoruba Goddess in Africa and the Americas* (Indiana University Press, 2001).

D. Nirenberg, "A Female Rabbi in Fourteenth Century Zaragoza?" in *Sefarad*, Vol. 51, no. 1, (1991), pp. 179-182.

Leah Novick, "Encountering the Shechinah, The Jewish Goddess," in *The Goddess Re-Awakening: The Feminine Principle Today*, Shirley Nicholson ed. (Theosophical Publishing House, 1983), p. 204-14.

Leah Novick, *On the Wings of Shekhinah: Rediscovering Judaism's Divine Feminine* (Quest Books, 2008).

David Noy, *Jewish Inscriptions of Western Europe: The City of Rome* (Cambridge University Press, 1995).

Alicia Ostriker, *The Nakedness of the Fathers: Biblical Visions and Revisions* (Rutgers University Press, 1994).

Alicia Ostriker, *The Volcano Sequence* (University of Pittsburgh Press, 2002).

Jacobine Oudshoorn, *The Relationship Between Roman Law and Local Law in the Babatha and Salome Komaise Archives: General Analysis and Three Case Studies on Law of Succession, Guardianship, and Marriage* (Koninklijke Brill, 2007).

Raphael Patai, *The Hebrew Goddess* (Wayne State University Press, 1990).

Sarit Paz, *Drums, Women, and Goddesses: Drumming and Gender in Iron Age II Israel* (Vandenhoeck & Ruprecht, 2007).

Ismar J. Peritz, "Women in the Ancient Hebrew Cult," in *Journal of Biblical Literature*, Vol. 17 (1898), p. 111-148.

Miriam Peskowitz, *Spinning Fantasies: Rabbis, Gender, and History* (University of California Press, 1997).

Marge Piercy, "The Low Road," from her work *The Moon is Always Female* (Alfred A. Knopf, 1980).

Judith Plaskow and Carol Christ, eds, *Weaving the Visions: New Patterns in Feminist Spirituality* (HarperCollins, 1989).

Rachel Pollack, *The Shining Tribe Tarot: Awakening the Universal Spirit* (St. Paul, MN: Llewellyn Publications, 2001).

Betzalel Porten and J. J. Farber. *The Elephantine Papyri in English: Three Millenia of Cross-Cultural Continuity and Change* (Brill Academic, 1996).

Ada Rapoport-Albert, *Women and the Messianic Heresy of Sabbatai Zevi, 1666-1816* (Littman Library of Jewish Civilization, 2011).

"Ella's Song." Composed by Bernice Johnson Reagon, Songtalk Publishing Co.

Layne Redmond, *When the Drummers were Women: A Spiritual History of Rhythm* (Three Rivers Press, 1997).

Nahida Remy, *The Jewish Woman* (C.J. Krehbiel and Co., 1895).

Sarah Richards, *Spiralinear Time: Religious Calendar Formation, Momentum, and Change within a Dynamic Time Structure* (Masters Thesis, University of Georgia, 2008).

Joel Roth, "The Status of Daughters of Kohanim and Leviyim for Aliyot", *Proceedings of the Committee on Jewish Law and Standards of the Conservative Movement*, 1986-1990.

H.H. Rowley, "The Meaning of the Shulammite," in *The American Journal of Semitic Languages and Literatures*, Vol. 56 no. 1.

Janice Rubin and Leah Lax. *The Mikvah Project* (2001).

Muriel Rukeyser, "Akiba," in *Telling and Remembering: A Century of Jewish American Poetry*, Steven J. Rubin ed. (Beacon Press, 1997).

Jane Sandall, Hora Sultani, Simon Gates, Andrew Shennan, and Declan Devane. "Midwife-led continuity models versus other models of care for childbearing women." Published by The Cochrane Collaboration (2013).

I.S.D. Sassoon, *The Status of Women in Jewish Tradition* (Cambridge University Press, 2007).

Zalman Schachter-Shalomi, *A Heart Afire: Stories and Teachings of the Early Chasidic Masters* (Jewish Publication Society, 2009).

Howard Schwartz, *Tree of Souls; The Mythology of Judaism* (Oxford University Press, 2004).

Susan Sered, *Women as Ritual Experts: The Religious Lives of Elderly Jewish Women in Jerusalem* (Oxford University Press, 1992).

Rami Shapiro, *The Divine Feminine in Biblical Wisdom Literature* (SkyLight Illuminations, 2005).

Leonard Shlain, *The Alphabet Versus The Goddess: The Conflict Between Word and Image* (Compass, 1999).

Hanna Tiferet Siegel, "Eshet Hazon Ceremony Honors Eight Women at 2011 Aleph Kallah," *Kol Aleph*, no. 21, 2011, p. 8.

Brenda Sirotte, *The Fortune Teller's Kiss* (American Lives, 2006).

Rosemary Skinner-Keller, Rosemary Radford Ruether, Marie Cantlon, *Encyclopedia of Women and Religion in North America*, vol. 2 (Indiana University Press, 2006).

Rivkah Slonim, ed. *Total Immersion: A Mikvah Anthology* (Jason Aronson, 1997).

Mark S. Smith, *The Origins of Biblical Monotheism: Israel's Polytheistic Background and the Ugaritic Texts* (Oxford University Press, 2001).

William Smith. *Dictionary of Greek and Roman Biography and Mythology* vol. 1. (Little, Brown and Company, 1867).

Elna Solvang, *A Woman's Place is in the House: Royal Women of Judah and their Involvement in the House of David* (Sheffield Academic Press, 2003).

Stephen Spector, *Operation Solomon: The Daring Rescue of the Ethiopian Jews* (Oxford University Press, 2005).

Marcia Cohn Spiegel and Deborah L. Kremsdorf. *Women Speak to God: The Prayers and Poems of Jewish Women* (Women's Institute of Continuing Jewish Education, 1987).

Charlene Spretnak, "The Myth of Demeter and Persephone," in *Weaving the Visions: New Patterns in Feminist Spirituality*, Judith Plaskow and Carol Christ eds. (HarperCollins, 1989).

Starhawk, *The Spiral Dance: A Rebirth of the Ancient Religion of the Goddess* (HarperOne, 1999).

Starhawk and Hilary Valentine, *The Twelve Wild Swans: A Journey to the Realm of Magic, Healing, and Action* (HarperCollins, 2000).

Adin Steinsaltz, *The Thirteen-Petalled Rose: A Discourse on the Essence of Jewish Existence and Belief* (Koren Publishers, 1980).

Kaya Stern-Kaufman, "Between Heaven and Earth: Revisioning Synagogue Space" (Rabbinic thesis, Academy for Jewish Religion, 2012).

Marten Stol, *Birth in Babylonia and the Bible: Its Mediterranean Setting* (Brill Academic Publishers, 2000).

Ilana Streit, "How Are You, or the Midwife Poem" (unpublished poem).

Yale Strom, *The Book of Klezmer: The History, The Music, the Folklore from the Fourteenth Century to the Twenty-first* (A Cappella Books, 2002).

Emily Taitz, *The JPS Guide to Jewish Women: 600 BCE to 1900 CE* (Jewish Publication Society, 2003).

Emily Taitz, "Women's Voices, Women's Prayers: The European Synagogues of the Middle Ages," *In Daughters of the King: Women and the Synagogue*, Susan Grossman and Rivka Haut eds. (Jewish Publication Society, 1992), p. 59-72.

Joan Taylor, "The Asherah, the Menorah, and the Sacred Tree," *Journal for the Study of the Old Testament* 66 (1995), p. 29-54.

S. Terrien, "The Omphalos Myth and Hebrew Religion," *Vetus Testamentum* 20, (1970), 315-338.

Milton S. Terry, *The Sibylline Oracle, Annotated Edition* (e-book).

Savina Teubal, *Ancient Sisterhood: Lost Traditions of Hagar and Sarah* (Swallow Press, 1990).

Savina Teubal, *Sarah the Priestess: The First Matriarch of Genesis* (First Swallow Press, 1984).

C.C. Torrey, "More Elephantine Papyri," in *The Journal of Near Eastern Studies*, vol. 13, no. 3 (1954).

Joshua Trachtenberg, *Jewish Magic and Superstition: A Study in Folk Religion* (University of Pennsylvania Press, 2004).

Phyllis Trible, *Texts of Terror: Literary-Feminist Readings of Biblical Narratives* (Fortress Press, 1984).

Ellen Umansky, "Re-imagining the Divine," cited in Sylvia Barack Fishman, *A Breath of Life: Feminism in the American Jewish Community* (Free Press, 1993).

John H. Walton, Victor Harold Matthews, Mark William Chavalas, *The IVP Bible Background Commentary* (Intervarsity Press, 2000).

Rivkah Walton, "The Rock," in *Living Text* 1 (1997), p. 22.

Arthur Waskow, *Seasons of our Joy: A Modern Guide to the Jewish Holidays* (Jewish Publication Society, 2012).

Arthur Waskow and Phyllis Berman, *A Time for Every Purpose Under Heaven: The Jewish Life-Spiral as a Spiritual Path* (Farrar, Straus and Giroux, 2003).

Alex Weingrod and Michael Ashkenazi, *Ethiopian Jews and Israel* (Transaction Publishers, 1987).

Chava Weissler, *Voices of the Matriarchs: Listening to the Prayers of Early Modern Jewish Women* (Beacon Press, 1999).

Gershon Winkler, *Magic of the Ordinary: Recovering the Shamanic in Judaism* (North Atlantic Books, 2003).

Elliot Wolfson, *Circle in the Square: Studies in the Use of Gender in Kabbalistic Symbolism* (State University of New York Press, 1995).

Diane Wolkstein and Samuel Noah Kramer, *Inanna, Queen of Heaven and Earth: Her Stories and Hymns from Sumer* (HarperPerennial, 1983).

Mark Zborowski, *Life is with People: The Jewish Little-Town of Eastern Europe* (International Universities Press, 2005).

Aviva Zornberg, *The Murmuring Deep: Reflections on the Biblical Unconscious* (Schocken Books, 2009).

Web References

Akhet Hwt-Hrw: An Educational Resource for Ancient Egyptian Religion & Esoteric Studies www.Hwt-Hrw.com

Lynn Bellair. "History of Egyptian Medicine and Philosophy," http://www.realmagick.com/7108/history-of-egyptian-medicine-and-philosophy

http://cometogetherarticles.yolasite.com/heyoka-clowns.php; also see www.redelk.net.

Theresa C. Dintino, "Amazons with Mirrors: Mirror Divination Throughout the Ages," http://www.ritualgoddess.com/the2012vortex/?tag=amazons&paged=2

Dawn Cherie Ezrahi, "Surrendering to Love," http://eolife.org/articles/beliefs/Surrendering_To_Love.aspx

http://www.rainewalker.com/book-page.htm

"Firzogerin," http://www.jewishvirtuallibrary.org/jsource/judaica/ejud_0002_0007_0_06498.html

http://www.jehovahs-witness.net/watchtower/bible/73244/1/The-Tree-of-Life-Asherah-and-Her-Snakes

Jane Enkin, "Soul Candles," http: telshemesh.org/tishrei/soul_candles_.html

Deborah J. Grenn, "Metaforms of a Monotheistic Religion: The Menstrual Roots of Three Jewish and African Rites of Passage: Khomba, Bat Mitzvah, and the Mikvah," Metaformia; http://www.metaformia.org/articles/metaforms-monotheistic-religion/

Judith Brin Ingber, "Dancing Despite the Scourge: Jewish Dancers During the Holocaust," www.jbriningber.com/Dancing_Despite_the_Scourge.pdf

http://www.jewishsightseeing.com/louis_rose_historical/honorees/dosick_wayne_rabbi/2006-06-16-new_rabbi.htm

http://judaism.about.com/od/womenrabbis/a/asenathbarzani.htm

http://jwa.org/encyclopedia/article/torah-study

http://www.mnsu.edu/emuseum/prehistory/egypt/dailylife/midwifery.htm

Anne Hamre, "Hebrew Priestess," Minnesota Women's Press, http://www.womenspress.com/main.asp?FromHome=1&TypeID=1&ArticleID=3706&SectionID=1&SubSectionID=20

Alexei Kondratiev, "Thou Shalt Not Suffer A Witch to Live," in *Enchante*, vol. 18, p. 11-15; www.draknet.com/proteus/Suffer.htm

Sephardic Songs in the Hispano-Arabic tradition of Medieval Spain, 1997. http://www.jaro.de/php/endex.php3/page/content:flypage/cd_id/74/artist_id/da743e8e075d-a235b176afc1f8dc6b0f

Sarai Shapiro and Zelig Golden, "A Critical Time for Jewish Youth: Rethinking the Bar and Bat Mitzvah", http://zeek.forward.com/articles/117847/

Starhawk, "Is the DaVinci Code Good for the Pagans", Beliefnet, http://www.beliefnet.com/Entertainment/Movies/The-Da-Vinci-Code/Is-The-Da-Vinci-Code-Good-For-The-Pagans.aspx

Starhawk (Miriam Simos), "Religion from Nature, not Archaeology," http://www.starhawk.org/pagan/religion-from-nature.html

http://www.whatsonwhen.com/sisp/index.htm?fx=event&event_id=43284

Citations of Ancient and Medieval Works

Ancient Jewish Sources

The Bible
The Apocalypse of Baruch
The Book of Enoch
The Book of Judith
Josephus, Wars of the Jews

Philo, Specialibus Legibus
Testament of Reuben

Talmudic Sources

Mishnah
Tosefta
Jerusalem Talmud
Babylonian Talmud

Midrashic Sources

Alphabet of Ben Sira
Genesis Rabbah
Exodus Rabbah
Lamentations Rabbah
Mekhilta deRabbi Ishmael
Midrash Tadshe
Midrash Tanhuma
Otzar haMidrashim
Pesikta deRav Kahana
Pesikta Rabbati
Pirkei deRabbi Eliezer

Medieval Law Codes:

Joseph Caro, Shulchan Arukh
Moses Maimonides, Mishneh Torah

Medieval Exegetes:

Meir Arama
Moses ben Nachman Girondi
Rashi (Rabbi Shlomo Yitzchaki)
Maimonides
Nachmanides
Meir Arama, Sefer Me'ir Tehillot

Chasidic Exegetes:

Mordechai Yosef Lainier of Ishbitz (Mei haShiloach)

Mystical Sources:

Or haHammah (Moses Cordovero)
Sefer Yetzirah
Shi'ur Qomah
Tomer Devorah (Moses Cordovero)
The Zohar

Other Jewish/Semitic Sources:

Teezaza Sambat (Ethiopian)
Testament of Reuben
Tibat Markeh (Samaritan)

Other Ancient Works Cited:

Callimachus Hymn III
The Descent of Inanna
Enuma Elish
The Louvre Stele
Prose Edda
Protoevangelium of James
Story of Kirta
Tao Te Ching
Ugaritic cuneiform text KTU- Die Keilalphabetischen Texte aus Ugarit (M. Dietrich, O. Loretz and J. Samartín, editors)

Index

Aaron, 62, 79
Aaronide line, 82
Abaye, 96
Aberlin, Rachel, 68
Abigail, 66
Aboulker-Moscat, Colette, 26, 74
Absalom, 162
activists, Jewish women, 69
Adam and Eve, 37, 124
Adler, Rachel, 4–5
adolescence, initiation at, 171
Adonai. *See* God; YHWH/Yahweh
Agrippa, 124–126
Akkadian culture, 17, 79
Alexandria, 24, 188–190
altar-craft, 87–90
altars, 6–9, 11–12; home, 81; home tables as, 82, 83; keeping/care of, 89–90; as sacred spaces, 236–237; *yahrzeit*, 182
Amnon, 162–163
amulets, 99
Anani, 24
Anat, 34, 135, 139
Anatolia, 163, 165–166
ancestors: connection to, 236; creating lineage, 244–245; keeper of well of, 93; relationships with, 238–239; spiritual relationship with, 99; tribes of Israel, 19, 63, 106, 204
ankh symbol, 78
Anna, 65–66
anointment, 63
Ansky, S., 224
Anubis, 79
Apocalypse of Baruch, 50–51
Arabic language, 62
archetype altars, 89
archetypes: Crone, 45; existence in Bible of, 17, 31; Great Mother, 256; Greek labyrinth, 187; human/divine, 4; king's mother, 21; Lover, 45; Maiden, 45; Matriarch, 45; midwife-priestesses, 147; Mother, 45; Priestess, 45; queen-priestess, 142–143; Sorceress, 45; types of, 12
Ark (Holy Ark), 39; cherubim guarding, 209; rituals of shrinekeeper-priestesses, 77–78; sacred curtain of, 126; sacred fabric creation for, 53; sacred fabric for, 53, 126; *See also* Torah
art/artists, 154
Artemis, 109
Asa, King, 135
Asher, Elsa, 153
Asherah, 20, 21, 34, 35, 37, 48
Ashkenazi Jews, 126, 152
asking a dream question, 73–74
Avodah service, 77–78
Ba'alat Chalom (Dream Priestess), 73
Baal-Peor, 204
Baal Shem Tov, 41, 69
Babylonia, 21–22, 175
Babylonian Talmud, 22, 66, 67, 95–97, 108, 192–193, 223
baby-naming ceremonies, 52–53
Barak, 19, 64
Barbarash, Ellie, 71
bar/bat mitzvah, 111, 171, 240, 244
Barzani, Asnat, 166
Bat Briyah program, 111
baths, ritual, 91, 98, 211
Bat-Shalom, Dorit, 29
Batsheva, 134–135
beauty, attributions of, 78
bedtime ceremonies, 239
Beit Shearim, inscriptions in, 22–23
Berenice, 124–126
Berg, Judith, 225
Bernaldez, Andres, 68
Beruria, 163, 223
Beta Yisrael traditions, 109
Bethlehem, 204–205
Bible, 68: circumcision by women, 244; condemnation of witches, 19; consecrated persons, 122; depictions of God in, 33; dying and resurrection, 175; evocations of Goddess in, 35; female dancers, 174; female monastics in, 188; gatekeeping priests in, 79; goddess images, 31; goddess-related objects, 38; images of divine feminine, 32; kings of Judah, 135; lover-priestess in, 203; midwives in, 149–150; missing letter in, 61; oracular speeches in, 68; priestesses in, 17, 31; priestesshoods documented in, 45–46;

Bible (*continued*)
  references to wisdom, 159–160, 161, 163; removal of Asherah-objects, 48; sacred spaces, 80; sexuality in, 204, 209; shrines described in, 37; sovereignty of kings, 213–214; tricksters, 219–220; view of creation in, 234; weaver-priestesses, 47–49; whoredom, 81; wisdom/wise women, 163; wise women, 245; witches/witchcraft, 92–95; women who perform priestess roles, 21; words for holy woman in, 20; worship of Goddess in, 35; *See also* Torah
Bichri, Sheva ben, 161–162
birth. *See* childbirth; pregnancy/pregnant women
bleeding Sabbath, 116
blessed women, 99
blood wisdom, 115–117
Boaz, 205–206
breaking of something, 220–223, 230, 231
breasts/breastfeeding, 120–121
Bricklin, Shoshana, 71
Broken for You (Kallos), 230
burial practices: eulogies, 180; funerals, 178–180; gravestones of midwives, 152; Kazakh, 78; pilgrimages to graves, 193; *See also* death
burial society, 179
candle-lighting ceremonies, 83, 124–125
candlemaking rituals, 26, 125
cantors/cantorate, 28, 29, 83, 84
Cardozo, Abraham, 27
Caro, Joseph, 41
Catholic devotional images, 133
caves as sacred spaces, 9–11
celebrations/ceremonies, 106: baby-naming, 52–53; bar/bat mitzvah, 111, 171, 240, 244; bat mitzvah, 111; bedtime, 239; blessings of past Hebrew priestesses, 252; of *chevra kadisha*, 179; circumcision, 18, 124–125, 126, 244; dance in, 74, 113–114; of death, 185; end of Sukkot, 192; end of Tisha B'Av, 173; fertility, 108; Festival of Miriam, 203; festival of Sigd, 190; funeral ceremonies, 113–114; grape-harvest festival, 107–108; harvest, 107–108, 192, 209; initiation, 170–172; instructions for, 167; mourning, 173–174; ordination ceremonies, 245; ritual guardians for, 143; transformation, 112

celebrations/ceremonies (*continued*)
  victory, 139; women's placement in, 193; *See also* ritual practices
Ceti of Zaragoza, 25
Chandler, Sarah Shamira, 54–55, 237
change: breaking/reconfiguring, 230; chronicling, 229–230
chants/chanters, 6, 15, 100–101, 145, 152, 168, 173, 213, 249
Chanukah, 9, 110
charms, 97, 152
Chasidic movement: origin and focus of, 28; Shekhinah as eminine form of God, 41; women in early, 69–70
Chava, Leah, 100
cherubim, 208–209
chevra kadisha, 179
childbirth, 97: being with what wants to be born, 156–157; circumcision ceremony, 124–125; Jewish customs, 52–53, 126; story of Sarah, 120–121; witchcraft performed during, 98; *See also* midwife-priestesses; pregnancy/pregnant women
childlessness, 120–121
Chochmah (Wisdom), 35–36, 37, 38, 124. *See also* wise-woman-priestesses
Christianity, elevation of Mary in, 21
Christian texts, 51
Christian women with divine force, 68
circumcision, 18, 124–125, 126, 244
cleansing rituals, 91
clothing, 65, 137, 179, 193, 203
clothing/garments, 108
commandments: divine commandments (*mitzvot*), 26–27, 39, 125, 180, 210; God's, to Abraham, 190; in Judges, 64; obeying God's, 3; Sabbath, 109
community, 55, 74, 239–240
confirmation ritual, 111
Conservative Jews, 28–29
Constantinople, 152
contemporary Hebrew Goddess, 41–44
contemporary priestesses, 28–30
conversion to Judaism, 29
Cozbi, 204
creating personal prayers, 57–60
Creation, 37, 96: creation stories, 47, 124; cycle of creation, 241; exile's effect on creation, 177; Goddess birthing scene, 34; in Middle Ages, 124–125;

Creation (*continued*)
  source of all creation, 109; Sumerian, 49; the Weaver, 58; Western view of, 234
Crone archetype, 45
croning ritual, 167
crossroads, 160
cults: Asherah, 34; Divine feminine, 135; Israelites (*See* Israelite cult); priestly, 66, 219; Temple cult, 22, 23–24; weaving of cult objects for Asherah, 48
cultural memory, 209
cures for the sick, Turkish, 99
curtain makers, 50
cycle of life and death, 175
dance, 213: in ceremonies/rituals, 74, 113–114; maidens' roles in, 106; ritual, 80, 108; victory celebrations in, 139; at weddings, 224, 225–226
daughter of Anav (prophetess), 68–69
Daughter-Sabbath, 109
David, King, 81, 134, 149: ancestors of, 204, 205; lament over Jonathan, 174; rejection of, 161; story of Absalom, 162–163
the dead/spirits: communication with, 91, 92, 99; household, 34; keeper of, 93; reborn souls, 113; relationships with ancestors, 238–239; spiritual connections with, 19
death: burial of Joseph, 165; as defilement, 63; dying process, 184–185; embracing, 183–185; entering the world of the dead, 79; as guest at weddings, 226; practicing rituals for, 183; rethinking approaches to, 245–246; teaching about, 93–94; *See also* burial practices; mourning
death rites, 92
Deborah the prophet, 19, 63–64, 66, 122, 139, 161
defilement, 63
De'Ir Alla inscription, 18
deities, 23, 31, 66: communicating with, 101; dedication of places to, 80; Elohim, 43, 147; female, 3, 241; female experience of, 42; Hebrew, 31; *khnt* (queen of the city), 18; mourning for, 176; Near Eastern legends about, 109; priestesses of shrine of, 66; witches' mention of, 93; worship of, 160; *See also* God; goddesses (in general); God/dess
demonic power, 96

destinations, 201
Deuteronomic code, 65
Deuteronomy, 20, 64
directions, honoring, 88
divination, 101, 102: condemnation of, 92; daily practices of, 101; practice of, 102–104; tarot, 100–101; tools for, 62, 103; use of mirrors for, 79
the Divine: altar as home for, 237; being a conduit for, 249; connecting to, 23; diversity of being to, 43; embodiments of, 30, 34; encountering, 247–248; human connection to, 18, 25, 37, 114, 127, 206; images of, 3, 42, 45; to kabbalists, 25; Maiden as face of, 110; male aspects of, 31; manifestations of, 235–236; messages from, 79; as midwife, 150; offerings to, 60; in patriarchal stories, 109; portals to, 145, 191; pronouns for, 31; Rachel's imagining of, 54; relationship with, 139; sacred marriage to, 214; as weaver, 54; weavers as central image of, 43, 53
divine commandments *(mitzvot)*, 26–27, 39, 125, 180, 210
Divine feminine cult, 135
the Divine feminine/Divine She, 25, 27, 29, 32, 37, 68–69, 137, 168. *See also* Shekhinah (Divine Maiden)
Divine/human connection, 18, 25, 28, 37, 114, 127
divine inspiration, 64
Divine Maiden. *See* Shekhinah (Divine Maiden)
divine marriage, 25
the Divine masculine, 141
Divine Mother, 1, 124–125, 241, 257
Divine Presence, 1, 38, 39, 67, 77–78, 109, 209
divine spheres, 124
Divine union, 41, 211
divine world, 67
divorce, 24
Djerba, La Ghriba shrine, 194
doors/doorways: in ceremonies/rituals, 113–114; conversations with God at, 79; sacred functions of, 86; *See also* gatekeepers
doulas, 153. *See also* midwife-priestesses
dream alignment, 157
dream basket community, 71

dream circle practices, 74
Dream Court, 74
dream incubation technique, 73–74
Dream Priestess *(Ba'alat Chalom)*, 73
dreams/dreamwork: dream journals, 73; group (community) dreaming, 74; healing and medicine, 75; interpreting dreams, 25–26, 73, 74; paying attention to visions in, 69; practice of dreamwork, 73–75; sacred sleep, 73; symbols in, 70–71
drummer women/girls, 105–106
duels, 96
Dumuzi, 207
dwellings, holy, 49
The Dybbuk (film), 224–225
dynasties, 149
earth: connections of God/dess to, 43; as mother, 34; representations of, 37
earth-goddess, 33, 47–48
ecstatic movement, 69
Eden, 37
education, 93–94, 108, 166
Egypt/Egyptian culture: Egyptian gods as gatekeepers, 79; enslaved women in, 147–148; exiles from, 243; Jewish community in, 23–25, 140; life-sign of (ankh), 78; love poetry, 207; Pharaoh's command to kill male Hebrews, 148–149; priestesses in, 17; slaves, 24
Elat Chayyim Center for Jewish Spirituality, 29, 203. *See also* Isabella Freedman Jewish Retreat Center
elemental altars, 88
Elephantine (Yeb) fortress, 23–24
Eli, sons of, 79–80
Elijah, 68
Elisheva, 142, 147
Elohim, 43, 147
Elul, 9
emancipated women, 24
Emden, Jacob, 27
enclosed spaces, 37–38
Encounter, 168
Endor, Witch of, 19, 93
Enki, 49
Enoch, 52–53, 95
Enuma Elish epic, 61–62
Epic of Gilgamesh, 19, 20, 163
Ereshkigal, Queen, 136
erotic healing, 213

Esau, 191, 220
Esther, Queen, 66, 133, 136–137, 163, 194
Esther, Sarah, 127
eternal light, 125–126
ethics/ethical traditions, 7, 152, 197, 234
Ethiopian Jews, 188–190
eulogies, 180
European culture/traditions: baby-naming ceremonies, 52–53; Jewish culture before Holocaust, 225; Jewish women, 193
evil eye, 99
exiles: Absalom's, 162; after destruction of the Temple, 38; from Egypt, 243; Esther's, 136–137; First Exile of the Judeans, 21; Israelite exile in Babylonia, 21–22; Jews from Spain, 68; Miriam's, 63; mourning of children's, 177; Nechushta's, 136; poetry about, 194; return from, 106, 150; return of Jewish mystics after Second Exile, 41; Shekhinah's, 97
Eydl, 69
Ezekiel, 136, 175–176
Ezrahi, Dawn, 29, 211
Ezrahi, Ohad, 29, 211
fables, 220–221
fabric art, 53. *See also* weaver-priestesses; weavers
fairy tales, 169
fasts/fasting, Esther's, 137
Feiga, 69
female deities, 23, 31
feminine depictions of God, 42
feminine face of God, 25, 193
feminine Goddess practice, 237
feminism, 27, 43, 240
fertility, 127, 152, 222
food offerings, 19, 22–23
the Fool, 225–226
fool-priestesses: biblical period, 219–220; embracing change, 229–230; future of, 248–249; incarnations of, 226–228; making of a Fool shrine, 219; Middle Ages and beyond, 223–226; spirit journey, 228–229; Talmudic period, 220–223
Fool shrine, 219
Francesca Sarah, 25–26
Frank, Eva, 110–111, 141
Frank, Jacob, 27, 110, 141
Frank, Ray, 28, 84
Frank, Sarah, 141

Frankists, 110–111, 141, 211
Freedman, Paula, 153
Frymer-Kensky, Tikvah, 127
funerals, 178–180, 245–246
gatekeepers, 79
gates of cities, 160
Germany/German culture, 28, 151
Gershuny, Sarah Bracha, 84
Gilgamesh, Epic of, 19, 20, 163
girls/young women, 105–106, 110, 114
God: communications with Moses, 122; depictions of needs of, 208; divine image of, 31; feminine face of, 25, 193; gender categories of, 43–44; images of, 3, 43, 45; in Jewish liturgy, 42; messages from, 62, 79; midwife work by, 149–150; names of, 120; new ways to see, 242; *See also* YHWH/Yahweh
Goddess: beliefs of sages and mystics, 39–41; of biblical period, 32–39; connection between world and, 43, 44; contemporary, 41–44; conversations with, 197–198; elimination from Israelite worship of, 37; historical overview, 31–32; love of, 214–215; relationship with, 248; in Song of Songs, 208; speaking about the, 241–242; and the Temple, 37–39; as Weaver of divine intelligence, 54
goddess/earth connection, 43
goddesses (in general): ancient roles of, 31–32; biblical images of, 31; dressing of Sumerian, 21; figures of, 49; Great Goddess (India), 78; Hebrew (*See* Goddess); responsibility for blessing, 34; worship of, 22, 111; *See also specific goddess by name*
God/dess: beliefs about God as female, 5–6; connections of, 43; embodiment of, 214–215; embracing, 216–217; expressions of love of, 85; forms/images of, 30, 120; as one being, 39; as world, 38
Goddess-image, 38
goddess-related objects, 38
Goddess religion, 36, 99
godmother role, 126
gods: Egyptian, 79; Greek, 108–109; Sumerian, 21; *See also specific god by name*
Gold, Shefa, 242–243
Goldberg, Jeanette Miriam, 28
Gottlieb, Lynn, 55
Gratitude element of prayer, 59

graves, pilgrimages to, 193–194
Great Goddess (India), 78
Greece (ancient): gods/goddesses, 108–109; Greek titles for Jewish women, 82; priestesses, 17, 189; roles of girls in, 105–106; stories, 107; task assignment, 51–52; weaving-priestesses of Athens, 21
Grenn, Deborah, 29
grief: expressions of, 179; keepers of, 174; as Mourning Woman, 180–181; resources for expressing, 185; ritual, 174–176; *See also* mourning
guardians, ritual, 133, 143
Hagar, 120–121
Haman, 136–137
Hamutal, 135
Handwerger, Nancy, 167, 226
Hannah, 66, 123, 191
harvest celebrations, 19, 107–108, 209
Hasmonean dynasty, 137–138
Hatam Sofer, 166–167
Hathor, 78
healers: female, 166; midwives as, 151–152; Shekhinah as, 178; Turkish Jewish women, 99
healing: erotic/sexual, 213, 216–217; kabbalist beliefs, 209; medicine dreams, 75; the motherline, 253–257; Motherline Healing ritual, 130–131; rituals for, 112–114; safe spaces for, 240
heaven, 34, 41, 81, 95
Hebrew Goddess. *See* Goddess
Hebrew language, 61, 64, 83
Hebrew priestesses *(kohenet/kohanot)*, 18, 22, 23, 29; becoming, 251–252; choices for serving, 233; daughters of, 28–29; history of, 17; modern, 29; roles of, 243–244 *See also* fool-priestesses; lover-priestesses; maiden-priestesses; midwife-priestesses; mother-priestesses; mourning-woman-priestesses; priestesses (in general); prophetess-priestesses; queen-priestesses; seeker-priestesses; shrinekeeper-priestesses; wise-woman-priestesses; witch-priestesses
Hebron, 193
Hecate, 160
Helene the Queen of Adiabene, 123
heretical sects, 27

hidden information, 61
High Holidays, candlemaking for, 125
high priests/priestesses, 18
Hilkiah, 64
Hinduism, 128
history, weaving of, 52–53
Hittite priestesses, 17
Hodel, 69
holidays: candlemaking rituals, 125; Chanukah, 9, 110; funeral practices on, 178; High Holiday season, 26, 125; of mourning, 183; Purim, 226, 228; Shavuot, 54–55, 188–189, 210; Sukkot, 192–193, 236–237; Yom Kippur, 108, 109, 187, 225
Holocaust, 225
Holofernes, 139–140
Holy Day altars, 89
holy sites, pilgrimages to, 194
Holy Temple. *See* Temple (Holy Temple in Jerusalem)
home, as shrine, 83
home table, 82, 83
honorifics. *See* titles and honorifics
Hosea, 20, 34
hospitals, 152
household spirits *(terafim)*, 81, 220
houses (shrines, dynasties), 149, 160
Huldah, 64–65, 66, 67
human connection to the Divine, 18, 25, 37, 114, 127, 206
humor. *See* fool-priestesses
Hurwitz, Sara, 84
Hyrcanus II, 138
Ilsen, Eve, 74
impurity, ritual, 63
Inanna, 8, 32, 109, 175, 205, 207
initiation practices, 111, 170–172
inspiration, divine, 64
Insun, 19
integration practices, 144, 201, 217, 249
intentionality, 87, 103
intercessors, queen as, 136–137
interpreting dreams. *See* dreams/dreamwork
intimate priestessing, 247–248
Iranian Jewish women, pilgrimages to Esther's tomb, 194
Irigaray, Luce, 234
Isaac, 190, 191, 220

Isabella Freedman Jewish Retreat Center, 12. *See also* Elat Chayyim Center for Jewish Spirituality
Isaiah, 150, 204
Ishtar, 136–137
Israel (ancient): cultures of, 17; Ethiopian Jews in, 189–190; folk rituals, 203, 230; gender multiplicity, 31; kings of Judah, 120, 122, 135; monastic communities, 188; "mother in Israel," 120, 122; mystical communities, 68; oracles, 64; pilgrimages to, 196; priests of, 62; queen mothers of, 242; return after exile to, 22, 150; roles of girls, 105–106; sacred mourners, 179; sacred trees, 237; shrines, 36, 64, 191; wise women in, 161; young girls of, 105; *See also* Jerusalem
Israel (modern), 142, 180, 194
Israelite cult, 49: *am kohanim*, 29; attachment to goddesses in, 34; elimination of Goddess from, 36; evolution of, 21–22; priests, 18; role of wise women, 162–163; roles of Levites in, 19; tribal society, 191
Israelite tribes, 19, 63, 106, 204
Isserles, Moses, 126–127
Jacob, 164, 191, 220
Jaffe, Sharon, 167, 226–227
Jajara, Israel, 69
Jedwab, Shoshana, 9, 168, 227–228
Jehosheba, 18–19
Jephthah's daughter, 174–175
Jeremiah, 176
Jeroboam, 191–192
Jerusalem: conquering of, 138–139; destruction of, 107, 173–174, 176; non-monotheistic practices of, 121; pilgrimages to, 192, 194; *See also* Temple (Holy Temple in Jerusalem)
Jerusalem Talmud, 50, 52–53, 151
jesters, 223–226
Jewish *See also* Judaism: clergy, 82; female monastics (Therapeutrides), 24, 188–189; liturgy, 59; monks, 190; mystics. *See* kabbalists; temples. *See* Temple (Holy Temple in Jerusalem); temples/synagogues
Jewitches, 99
Jezebel, 135
Jonah, wife of, 192
Jonas, Regina, 84
Jonathan, 174

INDEX

Joseph, 164–165
Josephus, 37
Joshua, 79
Josiah, King, 20, 64, 174
Josianic reform era, 48
journals/journal writing: after divination, 104; dream journal, 73; during initiation, 171; spirit journeys, 57; journeys, 200, 201, 247. *See also* pilgrims/pilgrimages
Judah, 20, 204
Judah of Worms, Eleazar ben, 83
Judaism: Conservative movement, 28–29; conversion to, 29; divorce by women, 24; origins of, 246–247; Orthodox, 29, 180; Reconstructionist movement, 29; Reform movement, 29, 84; Renewal movement, 29–30; *See also* Jewish — *entries*
Judean royal court, 133–134
Judeans, 21
Judges, 19
Judith, 138–140
justice-seeking aspects of prophetess role, 71
Juvenal, 66
Kabalove, 211
kabbalah: depictions of Shekhinah, 40–41; images of divine feminine, 32; lover-priestess in, 203; women's study of, 27, 166–167
kabbalists: of 12th century Spain, 25; beliefs of, 209–210, 234; beliefs of embodied divinity, 39; female faces of the Divine, 31; Frankist, 211; healing through sexual intimacy, 209; identification of Esther with Shekhinah, 137; as magicians, 97; radical, 27; reclamation of old myths, 39; Shekhinah to, 141–142; study of Torah by, 210–211; women's functions, 25–26, 97; *See also* mystics/mysticism
kaddish, 179–180, 182, 183, 185
Kallos, Stephanie, 230
keepers of knowledge, 163–166
kindlers, mother-priestesses as, 124–126
kingmaking, 133–134
kings of Judah, 134–135
Klein, Margie, 128, 195–198
knowledge, keepers of, 163–166
kohenet/kohanim. *See* Hebrew priestesses *(kohenet/kohanot)*

Kol Nidre, 225
Koppelman, Rachel, 54
Kurdish Jews, 110, 166–167
Laban, 220
labyrinths, 71, 187, 197–198, 199
ladder to heaven, 41
Lady Wisdom (Chochmah), 35–36, 37, 38, 109, 124, 160. *See also* wise-woman-priestesses
lamentation, 174, 178–180
Landsman, Yocheved, 70–71, 168
language(s): Arabic, 62; of common experiences, 94; feminized, 44; of Goddess, 43–44; Goddess-language, 33, 241–242; God-language, 241; Hebrew, 61, 64, 83; "priestess" (use of), 44–45; pronouns for the Divine, 31; of royalty, 208; tricksters/fools/foolish, 219; use of word "priestess," 44–45; words for holy woman in Bible, 20; words for priests and priestesses in Bible, 20; Yiddish, 126
laws: interpreters of, 66; for midwives, 150–151; Shulchan Arukh, 41;
leadership, 24–25, 28–30, 29, 30
Lemba tribe, 111
Leontopolis, Temple at, 24
Lesser, Carly (Ketzirah), 53–54, 85, 101
letting go, 116
levirate marriage rules, 20, 205
Levites, 19, 22, 62, 85
Lewis, Justin, 176
Lilith, 97, 152
lineages, creating, 244–245
literacy, ability to read Hebrew, 83
looms. *See* weaver-priestesses
Lover archetype, 45
lover-priestesses: biblical period, 204–206; erotic/sexual healing, 216–217; future of, 247–248; incarnations of, 211–215; sacred marriage, 209–211; Second Temple period and Talmud, 208–209; Song of Songs, 206–208; spirit journey, 215; Tu b'Av ritual, 203
Luria, Isaac, 68, 69
Maacah (or Michayah), 135
Ma'at, 79
Maccabean period, 24, 137–138
Madrone, Juna, 100–101
magic: charms for protection, 97; condemnation of, 92;

magic (*continued*)
  cures for the sick (Turkish), 99;
  permitted and forbidden, 95–96
Mahalat, Igrat bat, 97
the Maiden, 27, 108–110
Maiden archetype, 45
Maiden of Ludomir (Hannah Rachel Webermacher), 28, 193–194
maiden-priestesses: becoming new (blood wisdom), 115–117; biblical period, 105–107; future of, 239–240; incarnations of, 112–114; in Jewish ritual, 110–111; philosophers and mystics on, 108–110; rabbinic period, 107–108; spirit journey, 114–115
Maimonides, 25, 178–179
male divinity, 40
male witches, 92
male women, 189
Malkhut, 25
Maron, Miriam, 29
marriage, 248: divine, 25; forced, 106; God/Goddess as one being, 39; levirate marriage rules, 20, 205; in Mishnaic period, 22; Moses', 62; sacred, 209–211, 213–214;
martyrs, Jewish women leaders, 83
Mary (mother of Jesus), 21, 51, 133, 176
Matan, Annie, 85, 195–197
material world, 37–38
Matriarch archetype, 45
matriarchs, 33–34, 45
Matronita, 140–141
McLaren, Karla, 170
Meade, Michael, 170
medicinal cures, 99
medicine dreams, 75
Medieval period, mystics of, 25–28
meditative practices, 26
Meir, Rabbi, 223
Melmed, Sheva, 70, 142
menarche/menstruation, 115–117
menorahs, 37, 120
mentors/guides, for initiation, 172
messages from God, 62, 79
messiahs, 27, 110
Meyers, Carol, 92
Micah, 63
Michaelson, Jay, 9
Michal, 81

midrash/midrashim, 147, 150, 151, 163; Midrash Tadshe 2, 37; Midrash Tanhuma, 124; references to women in, 209; Serach, 163–166; Shekhinah's suffering, 177; *See also* Bible; Talmud; Torah
midwife-priestesses: biblical period, 147–150; future of, 243–244; as healers and ritualists, 151–152; incarnations of, 153–155; rabbinic period, 150–151; spirit journey, 155–156; support of transformation, 156–157; in Talmudic period, 163; *See also* childbirth; pregnancy/pregnant women
midwifery, 152, 244
ministering women, 78, 79
miracle workers, 28
Mirapae, Tiana, 100, 153–154, 238–239
Miriam, 19, 62–63, 66, 79, 151
Mirror of the Abyss, 78
mirror-priestesses, of biblical period, 78–80
Mishnah (Jewish law code): criticism of, 240; marriage, 22; midwives, 150–151; Moses receiving the Torah in, 245; mourning women, 178–180; naming of priests and women weavers, 50; payment of Temple workers, 49; those banned from the Temple, 246;
mitzvot (divine commandments), 26–27, 39, 125, 180, 210
modern era: Jewish feminism, 43; midwife-priestesses, 153–155; model for spiritual leadership, 30; mother-priestesses, 126–127; mourning-woman-priestesses, 178–180; priestesses, 28–30; prophetess-priestesses, 69; weaver-priestesses, 52–53; wise-woman-priestesses, 166–167
Moishe Kavod House, 195
monastic orders, women's, 24, 188–190
monks, Jewish, 190
monotheism, 21, 31, 64
moon, as symbol of renewal, 115–116
Mordechai, 137
Morocco, 152
Moses, 62, 66, 122, 136, 151, 165, 244
Mother archetype, 45, 128
mother/daughter joining, 109–110
Mother Goddess, 121–122
MotherLine healing ritual, 130–131, 253–257
mother-priestesses, 83: biblical period, 120–122; future of, 241–242;

mother-priestesses (*continued*)
incarnations of, 127–129; as kindler of souls, 124–126; modern era, 126–127; mother as Nazirite, 122–123; motherhood, 119–120; spirit journey, 129
mothers/motherhood, 33–34, 119–120, 122, 126
mourning: reciting the kaddish, 179–180, 182, 183, 185; re-envisioning rituals of, 246; ritual practices, 112–113, 173–174; sacred mourners, 179; as transformation, 182–185; *See also* death
Mourning Woman, 180–181
mourning-woman-priestesses: biblical period, 174–176; future of, 245–246; incarnations, 180–181; mourning destruction of the Temple, 173–174; mythic mourning in post-Temple period, 176–178; spirit journey, 181–182; in Talmud, Middle Ages, and modern era, 178–180
Moving Traditions, 240
murder, 148–149, 162–163
music, 145
mystics/mysticism: beliefs about Hebrew Goddess, 39–41; beliefs of embodied divinity, 39; Chasidic origins in, 28; female faces of the Divine, 31; identification of Esther with Shekhinah, 137; on the Maiden, 108–110; Medieval period, 25–28; mystical communities, 68; mystical weeping, 74; prayers influenced by, 26; prophetess-priestesses, 68–70; radical, 27; Sabbath Queen, 140–141; sacred marriage, 209–211; sexual union, 210; Temple as world and God/dess, 38; witches in, 97; *See also* kabbalists
myths/mythology: daily prayer, 59; *Descent of Inanna*, 175; earth-goddess as weaver, 47–48; fairy tales, 169; Jewish, 140; kabbalist, 39; "mother" as term of respect, 122; mourning women at funerals, 178–180; mythic mourning, 176–178; Near Eastern, 32–33, 79; Sabbath as queen in, 140; sacred feminine in Middle Ages, 39–41; Talmudic, 209
Nachman, Rabbi, 10, 66, 221–223
Nachmanides, 78, 97, 209
names of God/goddesses, 23–24, 120, 207
naming ceremonies/rituals, 50, 52–53, 155

Naomi, 204–206
Nasi, Dona Gracia, 193–194
Nathan (prophet), 134
nazirites, women as, 122–123
Near East (ancient): ancient Hebrew priestesses of, 17, 19; archetypes of, 21; culture of ancient, 32; legends of deities, 109; myths of, 32–33, 79; rituals associated with, 31; wise women in texts of, 163; women musicians in temples of, 106
Nechushta, 135–136
Neti, 79
New Testament prophetesses, 65–66
Ninmah, 49
Ninsun, 163
non-monotheistic practices, purging from Jerusalem of, 21
North African Jewish rituals, 110
North American customs, bat mitzvah ceremony, 111
nuns, 190
Onan, 20
One-Heart, LaKota, 74
Onias, 24
oracles, 17, 27, 64, 65, 66
oracular speeches, 68
Orthodox Jews, 29, 180
Our Lady of Czestochowa, 110
palm tree, Deborah's, 63
parochet embroidery, 52–53
Pautz, Nathan Tamar, 214–215
Peninah, 191
Peretz, 149
Persephone, 107
Persian religion, 136
personal prayer, 58
personal priestess paths, 14–16
Petition element of prayer, 59
Pharaoh, 147–148, 243
Philo, 108, 188–189
Phoenicia, 18
pilgrims/pilgrimages, 63, 107: becoming spiritual pilgrims, 246–247; in biblical period, 190–194; to Jerusalem, 133; Jewish female monastics, 188; manifesting, 200; mourning as, 183; practice of pilgrimage, 199–201; reasons for, 187–188; resources for, 202; Shekhinah as pilgrim, 194; to Western Wall, 195–196;

pilgrims/pilgrimages (*continued*)
  wife of Jeroboam's, 191–192;
  See also seeker-priestesses
pillar figurines, 120
poetry, 85–86: about exile, 194; about sacred sexuality, 211–213; biblical, 107; by Jewish women, 53; "Lecha Dodi," 141; as liturgy, 4–5; Song of Songs, 206–208; Sumerian and Egyptian, 207
Praise element of prayer, 59
prayer(s): ancient forms of, 30; as form of intercourse with Shekhinah, 41; gathering places for, 82; Gratitude element of, 59; for midwives, 152; offerings in, 60; Petition element of, 59; Praise element of, 59; before sleep, 73; for transformation of one's dream, 74; weaving a personal, 57–60; women's ritual/sacred, 26–27; *yichudim*, 210; Yiddish, 126
pregnancy/pregnant women, 97: connection between self and other, 234; doulas, 153; Eastern European customs, 126; fetal development, 124; Nazirite status during, 122–123; Rebecca's pilgrimage, 190–191; rituals for umbilical cord and placenta, 127–128; *See also* childbirth; lover-priestesses; midwife-priestesses
Priestess archetype, 45
priestesses (in general): of Asherah, 20–21; biblical period, 18–19; contemporary, 28–30; in Jewish mysticism, 24–25; as lineage, 245; as microcosm of Goddess, 44; path of, 249; paths of, 44–45, 89; personal priestess paths, 14–16; roles of, 111; self-described, 29–30; titles and honorifics, 17, 19, 20, 23, 53; tools of, 84, 89–90; traditions of, 29;
  See also fool-priestesses; lover-priestesses; maiden-priestesses; midwife-priestesses; mother-priestesses; mourning-woman-priestesses; prophetess-priestesses; queen-priestesses; seeker-priestesses; shrinekeeper-priestesses; wise-woman-priestesses; witch-priestesses
priestesshood, loss of, 222
priestly clothing, 65
priestly cults, 219
priestly rituals, 234–235
priests/priesthood: Aaronide, 23; anointment for, 63; biblical period, 18;
priests/priesthood (*continued*)
  devaluation of, 82; *kohanot* in Talmudic tradition, 22; power of, 24; spiritual connections with the dead, 19
prophecy, 19, 66, 78
prophetess-priestesses: antinomian prophetesses, 27; biblical period, 61–65; connection between priestly cult and, 66; future of, 235–236; incarnations of, 70–71; justice-seeking aspects of role of, 71; Miriam, 19; in modern times, 69; mystic, 68–70; role of, 61; Roman period and Talmud, 65–67; spirit journey, 72
prophets, Sabbatean, 69
prostitutes/prostitution, 20, 81, 204
Protoevangelium of James, 51
Puah, 147–149, 151, 243
Purim, 226, 228
purity, 22, 63, 211
queen mothers, 133–136, 135–136, 136–137, 242
Queen of Heaven, 34, 81
queen-priestesses: biblical queen mothers, 133–136; Book of Esther, 136–137; future of, 242–243; incarnations of, 142–143; Judith, 138–140; Maccabean period, 137–138; practice of shadow integration, 144–145; ritual guardians of, 133; Sabbath Queen, 140–141; spirit journey, 143–144rabbinic period
  maiden-priestesses, 107–108
  midwife-priestesses, 150–151
  Shekhinah in, 176–177
rabbis/rabbinate: duels between rabbis and witches, 96; first woman rabbi, 84; women, 25, 29
Rachel, 81, 176: midwives to, 149; as trickster, 220; weeping/mourning by, 177–178
rape, 106, 107
Raphael, Rayzel, 29
Rashi, 98
realia, 81
Rebekah, 64, 190–191, 220
reborn souls, 113
Reconstructionist Jews, 29, 84
reflection, during initiation, 171
Reform movement, 29, 84
Reimers, Paula, 5–6
religious culture, 92
religious titles, women's, 25

remembering, 164–165, 182
Renewal movement, 29–30
resources: blood wisdom, 117; creating personal prayers, 60; dream alignment, 157; dreamwork, 75; expressing grief, 185; healing the motherline, 131; initiation, 172; MotherLine ritual materials, 253–257; pilgrimages, 202; practice of breaking, 231; sacred spaces, 90; sexual healing, 217; shadow integration, 145; witch-priestesses, 104
revelation, modes of, 235–236
revenge, 139
Richards, Erev, 143
Richenza of Nurenburg, 83
Richo, David, 145
righteousness, 66
rites: coming of age, 111; of passage, 111, 170–172; sovereignty, 214
ritual guardians, 133, 143
ritualists, midwives as, 151–152
ritual practices: banning of goddess-related, 34; baths, 91, 98; cakes for the Queen of Heaven, 81; candle lighting, 83; confirmation, 111; contemporary Jewish, 30; creation of ritual objects, 154; dances, 106–107; death rites, 92; doorways in, 85; dream-related, 74; dressing/undressing of Torah, 39; entering the world of the dead, 79; example, 251–252; fertility and death, 38; folk, 203, 238; for grief, 174–176; healing, 240; for healing and transformation, 112–114; inclusion of men in, 239–240; initiation, 170; items used in, 31; for lepers and priests, 63; the Maiden in Jewish, 110–111; making ancestor cords, 238–239; midwifery, 154–155; for midwives and newborns, 152; for month of Elul, 9–10; motherhood, childbirth, fertility, 127; Motherline Healing, 130–131; mourning, 112–113, 173–174, 174–176, 179; naming ceremonies, 50, 52–53; new moon, 126; offering-stands, 34; origin of women's knowledge of, 95; personal, 100–101; power of, 85; priestesses in, 17; priestly, 234–235; purity of *kohenet*, 22; related to Torah, 110, 140; remembering ancestors, 99; roles of girls in ancient Greece and Israel, 105–106; Sabbatean, 26, 27; sacred sexuality, 204;

ritual practices (*continued*)
seeking to become mothers, 119–120; sex by priests, 79–80; sexual practices, 211; Shabbat candles, 124–125; *sloshim*, 182; spiritual events, 243–244; Spring rituals, 136; Temple in Elephantine, 24; titles on tombstones, 23; treatment of bodily fluids, 38; wearing of garments, 108; weddings, 210; weeping, 176; wise-woman-priestesses, 167; in witchcraft, 97; of women pilgrims, 193; *yahrzeit*, 182; Yom Kippur Avodah service, 77–78; *See also* celebrations/ceremonies
ritual roles, 24, 168
Rome (ancient): Jewish priestesses, 23; prophetesses of, 65–67; task assignment, 51–52; tombstones in, 23
Rothman, Ashirah-Marni, 29
royalty: anointing of kings, 248; biblical, 133–134; Esther, 137; *gevirah* (king's mother), 21, 27, 134–135; Judean, 21; language in Song of Songs of, 208
Ruth, 204–206
Sabbath (Shabbat): laws for midwives, 150–151; rituals, 26, 27, 116; sexual union on, 210; significance of candles in, 124–125; Teezaza Sambat (Commandments of the Sabbath), 109
Sabbath as Maiden, 108
Sabbath Queen, 140–141
the sacred, cultivating, 216
Sacred Circles conference, 246
sacred curtain of the Ark, 53, 126
sacred drummers/dancers, 21
sacred feminine in Middle Ages, 39–41
sacred fools, 220–223, 222, 223–224, 227–228
sacred functions of doors/doorways, 86
sacred marriage, 39, 209–211, 213–214
sacred places, 83, 160, 237
sacred sexuality, 204, 209, 211–213, 243
sacred spaces, 37–38, 38–39, 52–53: altar-craft, 87–90; altars as, 236–237; biblical references to, 80–81; caves, 9–11; defining, 103; girls' and boys' rituals as, 240; for Jews of Middle Ages, 82; keepers of, 85–86; mindsets for thinking of, 85; resources for, 90; roles of participants in, 242–243; *See also* shrines
sacred texts, 235–236, 240

sacred trees, 63, 64, 237
sacrifices: food, 19, 22–23; Jephthah's daughter, 174–175; prayer as replacement for, 82; ritual, 23, 234–235; safe spaces, 239–240
Salome Alexandra, 137–138
Samaritans, 165
Sambathe (or Sabbe), 66
Samson, 123, 220
Samuel, 62, 93–94, 191
Sanford, Mei Mei Miriyam, 101, 133
Sarah, 66, 120–121, 190
Saul, 93–94
Schachar, D'vorah Klilah bat, 213
Schacter-Shalomi, Rabbi Zalman (Reb Zalman), 243–244
scholars. *See* education
Schurtman, Jess, 154, 181
Schuster, Terri Alumah, 113
seasonal altars, 89
Second Temple period, 21–23: culture of women weavers, 47; destruction of, 38; lover-priestesses, 208–209; practitioners of magic and witchcraft in, 95; women mourning in, 176; women's service in the Temple, 81–82
seeker-priestesses: biblical period, 190–194; future of, 246–247; incarnations of, 195–198; Jewish women monastics, 188–190; labyrinths, 185–188; in Middle Ages and beyond, 193–194; practice of pilgrimage, 199–201; spirit journey, 198–199; *See also* pilgrims/pilgrimages
Sefer Hasidim, 98
Sephardic Jews, 99, 110, 126
Serach bat Asher, 163–166
sexual abuse, 112–113
sexual identity, 8–9
sexuality: divine union, 39–40; Friday night union, 211; intimate priestessing, 247–248; of king as metaphor, 205; power of, 96; ritual sex, 79–80; sacred, 20–21, 204, 209, 211–213, 243; same-sex experiences, 211; symbols of sexual union, 78; in Talmud and Bible, 208–209; use of force of, 203; *See also* lover-priestesses
Shachar, Dvorah Klilah bat, 208
shadow integration, 144–146
shamanism, 93, 99
shamans/shamanesses, 29, 91, 100, 211. *See also* witches/witchcraft

Shaphan, 64
Shavuot, 54–55, 188–189, 210
Shekhinah (Divine Maiden): as bride, 38–39, 210–211; channeling the presence of, 211; customs about/for, 39; as face of God, 25; heart-connection to, 30; identification of Esther with, 137; invoking, 239, 251; in kabbalistic literature, 141–142; kabbalist imaginings of, 42, 44; as lamenter and healer, 178; as Mourning Woman, 181; peace without, 29; personal visions of, 41; as pilgrim, 194; poets' sentiments about, 41–42; prayers to, 59, 60; rediscovering, 4, 12; representations of, 110–111; role as mourning woman, 176–177; sacred union with, 40; as seeker, 193; suffering and hope of, 177; union of God and, 209–210
Shelah, 20
Shifrah, 147–149, 151, 243
Shiloh, 79–80, 80–82, 106, 191
shiva, 182
Shiva, 78
shrinekeeper-priestesses: biblical period, 80–82; future of, 236–237; within the home, 81; incarnations of, 84–86; Middle Ages and beyond, 82–84; mirror-priestesses of biblical period, 78–80; spirit journey of, 86–87; study of Torah by, 82; Yom Kippur Avodah service, 77–78
shrine rituals, 234–235
shrines, 36, 37, 68: archeological evidence of, 81; biblical references to, 80–81; Djerba, La Ghriba, 194; "houses," 149; making, 219; Shiloh, 79–80, 191; tending of, 82; of Thyatira, 66; to Wisdom, 160–161
shtetls, 83
Shulchan Arukh, 41
Sibylline Oracle, 66
sibyls, 66
Sigd, 190
signs, reading/interpreting, 91, 103–104, 234
Sisera, 64
slaves, Egyptian, 24, 147–148
Smyrna, rabbinic judges of, 27
Solomon, King, 67, 81, 134–135
Solomon's Temple. *See* Temple (Holy Temple in Jerusalem)
Somekh, Touba, 194
Song of Songs, 206–208

songs, 85–86
Sorceress archetype, 45
souls: giving birth to, 124; invitations to, 91; mother-priestesses as kindler of, 124–126; reborn, 113
Spanish Jews, 25
Spirit Mother, 176
spirits. *See* the dead/spirits
Spring rituals, 136
stages of life, 167–168, 170–171
Steinsaltz, Adin, 239
Stier, Suzanne, 197–198
Sukkot, 192–193, 236–237
Sumer/Sumerian culture: creation epic, 49; female monastics, 188–190; love poetry, 207; priestly gatekeepers, 79; roles of priestesses in ancient, 17, 20, 21, 25
supernatural contemplation, 69
symbols/symbolism, 120: ankh, 78; doors, 79, 85; in dreams, 70–71; feathers, 91; of God, 41; lamps, 84; mirrors, 78–79; moon, 115–116; number seven, 38; renewal, 136; seeds as, 206; Shabbat candles, 124–125; trees, 84; trees as, 120; umbilical cord, 127–128
synagogues. *See* temples/synagogues
Tabernacles, 18, 37, 47–48
Talmud: authors of, 25; blessing of new moon, 116; borrowing of clothing, 203; dance rituals in, 108; Dream Courts, 74; dream interpretation, 73; female prophets in, 67; feminine God-images in, 45; grape-harvest festival, 107–108; *kohenet* as priests, 22; lighting of Shabbat candles, 124–125; lover-priestesses, 208–209; mourning-woman-priestesses, 178–180; nazirites, 123; pilgrimages by women, 192; prophetesses of, 65–67; rabbis' conversations with Elijah or Abraham, 55; regard of women, 22–23; ritual gifts to *kohanot*, 23; Sabbath as queen in, 140; sacred fools, 220; seven prophetesses of, 65–66; stories of sages, 208–209; story of Rabbi Nachman and Ulla, 221–223; table as altar, 82, 83; wise women, 166, 245; witch-priestesses, 95–97; women at crossroads story, 160; *See also* Babylonian Talmud; Jerusalem Talmud
Tamar, 20–21, 204
Tamet, 24
Tammuz, 175
Tarot, 141
teachers, 159, 167–168
tekhine literature, 26, 27, 53, 179
Temple (Holy Temple in Jerusalem), 18, 21; Asherah tree in, 34; destruction of, 24, 38; Hebrew Goddess and, 37–39; *metofefet* (sacred drummer/dancer) in processions, 21; new temple as metaphor, 13–14; people who many not be in the, 246; removal of Asherah-objects, 48; roles of objects in, 37
Temple consciousness, 236–237
Temple cult, 22, 23–24
temples/synagogues: Egyptian Jewish, 23–25; Elephantine (Yeb), 23–24, 140; female heads of, 24; as gathering place, 82; Leontopolis, 24
Temple weavers. *See* weaver-priestesses; weavers
Tent of Meeting, 79–80
terafim (household spirits), 81, 220
Teubal, Savina, 167
Therapeutrides (Jewish female monastics), 24, 188–189
Tiamat, 33–34
Tisha B'Av, 173
Tishman, Gail (Maayana), 168
titles and honorifics: of female cantors, 83; Greek titles for Jewish women, 82; "mother" in Jewish culture, 122; of priestesses, 17, 19, 20, 23, 53; on tombstones, 23; wise woman/sage, 150; women's religious, 25
Tkhine Imrei Shifre, 125
tombstone inscriptions, 23, 24
Torah: allegorical meanings in, 188; connecting to sacred texts, 235–236; as connection to ancestors, 236; criticism of, 240; dressing and undressing of, 39; explanation of magic and witchcraft using, 95; genealogies in, 164; Jeremiah view of, 161; male/female scholars of, 210; Moses's receiving of, 245; rituals related to, 110, 140; study of, 82, 166–168, 210–211; as woman, 39; women-only services, 29; *See also* Ark (Holy Ark); Bible; midrash/midrashim
Tovim, Sarah bas, 125–126
traditional religious practice, 248–249
trances, 19, 69, 78

transformation, 112–113: initiation rituals, 170–172; mourning as, 182–185; practice of, 156–157; through erotic exploration, 216
transgendered God concept, 43
tree-goddess-figures, 34
Tree of Life, 36, 37, 127, 133, 160
tribes of Israel, 19, 63, 106, 204
tribes/tribalism, 38, 111, 147, 171, 236, 244
tricksters, 219–220
truth, 67, 71, 247
Tu b'Av story, 203
Tu b'Shevat, 203
Tzadok, Samson ben, 126
Udel (or Eydl or Hodel), 69
Uganda, Abayudaya Jews of, 29
Ulla, 221–222
underworld, 79
Urania of Germany, 25
Vashti, Queen, 133
Vegosen, Ariel, 211–213
virgins, 50–51
visions, 68–69
Vital, Hayyim, 68
vows, 45, 120, 122, 123, 174–175, 191
Wachtel, Amy, 227
wailing women, 174
wardrobe, priestly, 65
warrior-queen-priestess, 139
water, as instrument of Miriam's role as priestess, 63
weaver-priestesses: biblical references to, 47–49; creating personal prayer, 57–60; future of, 233–235; incarnations of, 53–55; Middle Ages and modern era, 52–53; as monastics, 188; power of, 55; Second Temple and post-temple period, 49–52; in Second Temple period, 81–82; spirit journey, 57–58
weavers: meaning of being, 53–54; role in community, 55; sacred, 23, 53; Temple weavers, 234; unmarried girls as, 50
web of life, 233–235
weddings: Ashkenazi, 225; customs in Middle Ages, 99; divine, 210; foolery at, 224; inviting souls of deceased parents, 91
weeping, 74, 176, 177, 178
Weinberg, Rabbi Ezra, 236–237

Weintraub, Melissa, 167–168
Weissler, Chava, 125, 238–239
Werbermacher, Hannah Rachel (Maiden of Ludomir), 28, 193–194
Western Wall, pilgrimages to, 195–196
whoredom, 81
Wicca, 99
widow witches, 98
Wisdom *(Chochmah)*, 35–38, 124
Wise Woman, 167–168
wise-woman-priestesses, 21, 150, 152: biblical period, 159–163; future of, 244–245; importance of teachers, 167–168; incarnations, 167–169; initiation practice, 170–172; Middle Ages and modern era, 166–167; Talmudic era, 163–166
witches/witchcraft, 19, 92, 96, 98–99, 236
Witch of Endor, 19, 93
witch-priestesses: in Book of Enoch, 95; future of, 238–239; in Middle Ages, 98–99; in mystical texts, 97; resources, 104; spirit journey, 102; in Talmud, 95–97
The Women's Wheel of Life (Davis and Leonard), 45
Wouk, Judith Maeryam, 155
Yalta, 221–223
Yemenite Jews, 126, 167
Yentl, 69–70
YHWH/Yahweh: female variations of name, 23–24; identification with cult of Asherah of, 34; male and female depictions of, 31; messages from, 62
Yiddish prayers, 26, 126
Yiddish theater, 226
Yoav, 161
Yocheved, 151
Yohani bat Retavi, 98
Yom Kippur, 108, 109, 187, 225
Yose the Galilean, Rabbi, 223
young women/girls, 105–106, 110, 114
Zelophehad's daughters, 163
Zeus, 109
Zevi, Shabbatai, 27, 41, 69
Zimri, 204
Zion-Lawi, Efraim, 190
Zipporah, 18, 244
Zohar. *See* kabbalah; kabbalists

Acknowledgments (Jill Hammer)

My warm thanks go to the staff of the Isabella Freedman Jewish Retreat Center, and the Elat Chayyim Center for Jewish Spirituality, for housing and supporting the Kohenet Institute: David Weisberg, Adam Segulah Sher, Rabbi Yaakov Reef, Margot Seidle, Shamu Sadeh, Chavi Stark, Gavriel Micha, Paul Heckler, Sarah Shamirah Chandler, Tara Tayyabkhan, Joanna Katz, Mia Cohen, Adam Berman, Ellen Carton, Tamuz Shiran, Lee Moore, Kvod Wieder, Ari Weller, Jesse Freedman, and many others. You have all helped make our dream come true. I also thank from the bottom of my heart Reb Zalman Schachter-Shalomi, founder of the Jewish Renewal movement, for his blessing of the Kohenet community.

I thank Taya Shere for her dedication to the Kohenet Institute, for her friendship, and for the wonderfully productive partnership she and I have shared over the last five years. Thank you to Shir Yaakov Feit for his amazing web and design support, his ideas, his levitical musicianship, and his raising up of this work.

Much gratitude goes to Jay Michaelson for introducing me to Taya, and for continuing to be a supporter, advisor, editor, and fellow seeker all these years. And, deep thanks to publisher Larry Yudelson for believing in this book.

My deep gratitude goes to the Kohenet students and graduates for their commitment to Hebrew priestessing, and for their willingness to write reflections and be interviewed in order to contribute to this volume. I thank those who have served as Kohenet faculty for the innovative teachings they have brought to our sessions: Maggie Anton, priestess Dawn Cherie Ezrahi, Rabbi and Kohenet Sarah Bracha Gershuny, Rabbi Lynn Gottlieb, Dr. Deborah Grenn, Rabbi Riqi Kosovske, Rabbi Leah Novick, Dr. Alicia Ostriker, Rabbi Rayzel Raphael, Rabbi David Seidenberg, Soferet Julie Seltzer, Rabbi Kaya Stern-Kaufman, Rabbi Melissa Weintraub, and others. I thank our devorot/assistant teachers: Kohenet Elsa Asher, Kohenet Sarah Shamirah Chandler, Lily-Rakia Chandler, Kohenet Sharon Jaffe, Kohenet Dvorah Klilah, Kohenet Yocheved Landsman, Kohenet Carly Ketzirah Lesser, Kohenet Annie Matan, Kohenet Sheva Melmed, Kohenet Nina Pick, Yael Schonzeit, Kohenet Alumah Schuster, Kohenet Ri J. Turner, and Kohenet Ariel Vegosen as well as our ritual guardian Erev Richards and her students Ellie Barbarash, Judith Hollander, and Mei Mei Sanford, and our initiation priestesses/kohanot Judi Dash, Judith Hollander, Tiana Mirapae, and Leah Chava Reiner. Thanks are due also to the staff and students of the Academy for Jewish Religion for their support of my ritual work and their willingness to be a "ceremonial laboratory."

Thank you from the bottom of my heart to Dr. Alicia Ostriker, my long-time teacher and mentor, for her generosity in commenting on drafts of this book. Deep thanks to my dear friends Dr. Elizabeth Denlinger and Jennifer Stern for reading and commenting on drafts of this book. I am grateful to Rabbi Julia Watts Belser for the insights she contributed on the Song of Songs and the Hebrew Goddess, and to Dr. Joy Ladin for her consistent reminder of the importance of the history and theology in this book. Thanks are due to the staff at the Library of the Jewish Theological Seminary for making the wealth of Jewish tradition available to me and to so many others. My appreciation also goes to the women of the Asherah listserve for broadening my understanding of Jewish Goddess talk. I thank Rabbi David Ingber, Rabbi Jessica Kate Meyer, Basya Schechter, Rabbi Dianne Cohler-Esses, Miriam Rubin, Laura Gold, Shir Yaakov Feit, Larry Schwartz, and all the wonderful people of Romemu for making my synagogue community a place where the divine feminine is welcomed and celebrated and where the teachings of this book can flourish. I am grateful beyond words for all the authors, researchers and scholars whose work allowed me to discover the lives of the priestesses.

I want to express my profound gratitude to my spouse Shoshana Jedwab for her vibrant presence at Kohenet retreats and her love and support of this work. She has aided me, advised me, and contributed to this work in every way possible, and she has also drummed us all into ecstatic trance over and over again! Thank you to my parents Leonard and Erna Hammer for their presence in my life (and for saving versions of the book on their hard drive so I could sleep at night). I also, with great love, thank my beloved daughter Raya Leela, to whom this book is dedicated. Her boldness, creativity, laughter, and affection make my life bright. Most of all, I give thanks to the Immah Ilaah—the cosmic Mother, may Her name be a blessing—for the gifts beyond count that She has given me.

Acknowledgments (Taya Shere)

Kissing the ground for you who have made this book possible: Jill, *Oreget Tehomot*, for exquisitely weaving the depths, and for collaborating, visioning and womanifesting magnificence; Shoshana BatShemesh, *Neviah uKesilah*, for balancing the Triple Goddess and for serious shamanic seeing and sustenance; Kohanot past, present, and future for trusting, yearning, and transforming, and for showing up; Yosefa R'faela HaKohenet z"l, *Sacred Listener, Clear Responder*, for playing in full-color and inspiring me not to hide; Savina Teubal z"l for fueling the fire of Kohenet in your transition; Jay for linking me and Jill; Reb Zalman for your blessing and Halleluyahs; EvaClear for being the first; Sunshine Muse and Indigo Bacal for spectacular sisterhood—Sunshine for leaping with me and Indigo for spiraling with me; Sarah, healing-priestess, for being my familiar; Poppa for your love; The Ancestors for blessing me up; The Elements for guiding my way; RenePeace, mother-priestess, for living and loving such that I revel in your song, *We Are Our Mothers Reborn*; Adé for being the heart of my journey; Sacred She for all I know and am and be.

Literary and Artistic Acknowledgments:

The artwork on the cover of this book was created by Lucy Pierce and is titled "She Drums the Moon."

Versions of Chapter 3, "Weaver-Priestesses," and Chapter 12, "Mourning-Women-Priestesses" have appeared in the anthology *Stepping into Ourselves: An Anthology of Writings on Priestesses*, ed. Candace Kent and Anne Key (Goddess-Ink, 2014), under the titles "Mourning-Woman-Priestess" and "Temple Weaving: Jewish Weaver-Priestesses and the Creation of the Cosmos."

A version of Chapter 4, "Prophetess-Priestesses" has appeared in the journal *Kerem*, Summer 2014, under the title "The Prophetess as Priestess: Women, Revelation, and the Sacred."

A version of the section in Chapter 7, "The Maiden" titled "She Who Becomes New: The Practice of Blood Wisdom" has appeared in Jay Michaelson's book *God in Your Body: Kabbalah, Mindfulness, and Embodied Spiritual Practice* (Jewish Lights, 2006) and in *One Love Magazine*.

Portions of Chapter 14, "Lover-Priestesses" are adapted from: Jill Hammer, "Ruth and Naomi: The Return of the Seed," in *G'vanim: The Journal of the Academy for Jewish Religion*, vol. 7 no. 1 (2011), p. 9-20.

Selections from Naomi Ruth Lowinsky's *The Motherline: Every Woman's Journey to Find Her Female Roots* (Fisher King Press, 2009) have been used with permission from the author.

About the authors

Rabbi Jill Hammer, Ph.D., is the Director of Spiritual Education at the Academy for Jewish Religion, and the co-founder of the Kohenet Hebrew Priestess Institute, a program in Jewish women's spiritual leadership. She is a ritualist, scholar, poet, storyteller, and lover of the earth, and has been called "a Jewish bard." She is also the author of *Sisters at Sinai: New Tales of Biblical Women, The Jewish Book of Days: A Companion for All Seasons, The Omer Calendar of Biblical Women, The Garden of Time,* and (with Taya Shere) *Siddur haKohanot: A Hebrew Priestess Prayerbook.* She lives in Manhattan with her wife and daughter.

Taya Shere, co-founder of the Kohenet Hebrew Priestess Institute, plays passionately in the realms of transformative ritual, primal movement and embodied vocalization. Her chant albums *Wild Earth Shebrew, Halleluyah All Night, Torah Tantrika,* and *This Bliss* have been heralded as "cutting-edge mystic medicine music." She is Spiritual Leader Emeritus of a Jewish congregation in the Washington D.C. area and now leads spiritual community, teaches ,and makes home, music and other magic in Oakland, California.

Printed in May 2022
by Rotomail Italia S.p.A., Vignate (MI) - Italy